The Story of the Tr
The Woul

Palgrave Macmillan Classics of Children's Literature

This series brings back into print some of the most important works in children's literature first published before 1939. Each volume, edited by a leading scholar, includes a substantial introduction, a note on the text, suggestions for further reading, and comprehensive annotation. While these full critical editions are an invaluable resource for students and scholars, the series is also designed to appeal to the general reader. *Classics of Children's Literature* presents wonderful stories that deserve a place in any adult's or child's library.

Series Editors:
M. O. Grenby, University of Newcastle, UK
Lynne Vallone, Rutgers University, USA

Maria Edgeworth, *Selected Tales for Children and Young People*
Edited by Susan Manly

E. Nesbit, *The Story of the Treasure Seekers* and *The Wouldbegoods*
Edited by Claudia Nelson

Little Goody Two-Shoes and Other Stories: Originally Published by John Newbery
Edited by M. O. Grenby

Hesba Stretton, *Jessica's First Prayer* and Brenda, *Froggy's Little Brother*
Edited by Elizabeth Theil

The Story of the Treasure Seekers and The Wouldbegoods

E. Nesbit

Edited with an Introduction by

Claudia Nelson

Professor of English, Texas A & M University, USA

First published 2013 by
PALGRAVE MACMILLAN

Palgrave Macmillan in the UK is an imprint of Macmillan Publishers Limited,
registered in England, company number 785998, of Houndmills, Basingstoke,
Hampshire RG21 6XS.

Palgrave Macmillan in the US is a division of St Martin's Press LLC,
175 Fifth Avenue, New York, NY 10010.

Palgrave Macmillan is the global academic imprint of the above companies
and has companies and representatives throughout the world.

Palgrave® and Macmillan® are registered trademarks in the United States,
the United Kingdom, Europe and other countries

ISBN: 978–0–230–36084–6 paperback

This book is printed on paper suitable for recycling and made from fully
managed and sustained forest sources. Logging, pulping and manufacturing
processes are expected to conform to the environmental regulations of the
country of origin.

A catalogue record for this book is available from the British Library.

A catalog record for this book is available from the Library of Congress.

This edition is dedicated to Mary Isabel,
Gabrielle, and Alex Nelson.

– C.N.

Contents

Acknowledgments		ix
Introduction		x
Note on the Texts		xviii
Further Reading		xxii

The Story of the Treasure Seekers   1

1.	The Council of Ways and Means	2
2.	Digging for Treasure	7
3.	Being Detectives	13
4.	Good Hunting	22
5.	The Poet and the Editor	28
6.	Noël's Princess	33
7.	Being Bandits	40
8.	Being Editors	47
9.	The G.B.	59
10.	Lord Tottenham	68
11.	Castilian Amoroso	75
12.	The Nobleness of Oswald	86
13.	The Robber and the Burglar	97
14.	The Divining Rod	111
15.	'Lo, the Poor Indian!'	118
16.	The End of the Treasure-Seeking	125

The Wouldbegoods   135

1.	The Jungle	136
2.	The Wouldbegoods	147
3.	Bill's Tombstone	162
4.	The Tower of Mystery	174
5.	The Water-Works	189
6.	The Circus	204

7.	Being Beavers; or, The Young Explorers (Arctic or Otherwise)	219
8.	The High-born Babe	234
9.	Hunting the Fox	246
10.	The Sale of Antiquities	261
11.	The Benevolent Bar	276
12.	The Canterbury Pilgrims	288
13.	The Dragon's Teeth; or, Army-seed	303
14.	Albert's Uncle's Grandmother; or, the Long-lost	319
	Notes	333

Acknowledgments

'Being editors,' as the Bastables discover, is a group endeavour. Lynne Vallone and Matthew Grenby persuaded me into the enjoyable task of focusing closely on Nesbit's texts, and at Palgrave, Macmillan Jenna Steventon and her assistant Felicity Noble patiently answered questions. My undergraduate research assistants Elizabeth Berry, Molly McGee, and Mary Ross performed heroic feats in connection with scrutinizing the serialized versions of the tales and formatting the manuscript; without their intelligent help, this edition would have been considerably delayed. At Texas A&M University, the Department of English and the Cornerstone Faculty Fellowship provided by the College of Liberal Arts funded the undergraduate research opportunities permitting me to work with these students. I am grateful for all this assistance.

My deepest appreciation, of course, must go to the memory of Edith Nesbit, whose stories and words these are. She's the author; I'm just the editor.

Introduction

When Edith Nesbit (1858–1924) began producing the Bastable stories, she was an experienced but undistinguished author. She had published many volumes of verse, novels, short-story collections, adaptations from Shakespeare, historical works for the young, and collaborative projects. Her output ranged from *The Prophet's Mantle* (1885), a novel written with her first husband, Hubert Bland (1855–1914), and expressing their support of socialism, marriage reform, and other aspects of the radical thought of the day, to potboilers such as *A Book of Dogs: Being a Discourse on Dogs, with Many Tales and Wonders Gathered by E. Nesbit* (1898). Bland, an erstwhile bank clerk turned brush manufacturer, had failed in the latter business in 1880 when, in an experience that Nesbit subsequently assigned to the Bastable children's father in *The Story of the Treasure Seekers*, he contracted smallpox and his partner decamped with whatever funds remained to their struggling enterprise. Since his intellectual interests were primarily political and policy-oriented, he moved on to journalism and pamphleteering; with Nesbit, he was one of the original members of the Fabian Society, a socialist group that also included in its numbers George Bernard Shaw and H. G. Wells, and he later helped to found the London School of Economics. While he was still recovering from his illness, however, Nesbit, then still a new wife and mother, took up the challenge of supporting the family, making steady if not particularly lucrative sales to various periodicals and book publishers.

At first glance, Nesbit might seem an unlikely children's author to emerge in the late Victorian years. From the eighteenth century onward, women writers had been associated with books for the young largely because such writing was viewed as an extension of child rearing, a way for (presumably) virtuous preceptresses to transmit moral messages in a form that children would find digestible. Although by the late nineteenth century many children's authors had preceded Nesbit in abandoning the emphasis on overtly Christian training that had once driven the juvenile marketplace, a more general emphasis on good moral tone remained the norm in books for the middle class. But while Nesbit was not averse to pointing morals in her tales, which often urge such values as courage, honesty, and consideration for others, some critics read her children's fiction as engaging in 'protest against the reinforcement of intellectual and social subjection of women in patriarchal culture,'[1] while others argue that the Bastable stories' major contribution was not to socialize child readers but rather to impersonate a child sensibility for the delight of young and old alike. As Erika Rothwell observes, the tales, 'though told from a child's point of view, address both child and adult readers and focus attention upon the common, but conflicting, experiences of adult and child.'[2]

Nesbit's emphasis on the importance of the child's experience is understandable in one whose early life was punctuated with dramatic changes. The youngest of four surviving children of Sarah and John Collis Nesbit (from an earlier marriage, Sarah Nesbit also had a daughter, Saretta Green, who was fifteen years Edith's senior), Edith spent some years of her childhood in France, where her mother had gone in search of a healthier climate for Edith's tubercular sister Mary. Edith lost her father to a sudden illness when she was three; ten years later, Mary died. Edith herself was sent as a boarder to a lengthy series of schools and private homes in England, France, and Germany, often feeling the pangs of disruption and homesickness.

Perhaps her unsettled early life contributed not only to Nesbit's frequent depictions of family separation and bereavement in her children's fiction but also to her evident desire to form a new family of her own as soon as possible. Her approach to family in her personal life, however, would have struck many of her middle-class contemporaries as inappropriate in someone who aspired to influence the young. Back in England and engaged at eighteen to another teenager, bank clerk Stuart Smith, Nesbit met his colleague Hubert Bland in 1877, broke her engagement, and married Bland in 1880, when she was seven months pregnant with their first

---

[1] Amelia A. Rutledge, 'E. Nesbit and the Woman Question,' in *Victorian Women Writers and the Woman Question*, ed. by Nicola Diane Thompson (New York: Cambridge University Press, 1999), pp. 223–40 (p. 227).

[2] Erika Rothwell, '"You Catch It If You Try to Do Otherwise": The Limitations of E. Nesbit's Cross-Written Vision of the Child,' *Children's Literature*, 25 (1997), 60–70 (p. 60).

child, Paul. Throughout their unorthodox marriage, which ended
thirty-four years later with Bland's death, husband and wife prac-
ticed infidelity both sexual and intellectual as they cycled through
assorted relationships and creeds, Nesbit at various times adopting
socialism, Catholicism, dress reform, public cigarette smoking (at
the time a shocking habit in a middle-class woman), and the belief
that Shakespeare's plays were written by Francis Bacon. The names
of three of the Bastable boys memorialize men who may have
been Nesbit's lovers, a tribute that would have raised eyebrows had
her public been aware of it. Nor would the Victorian bourgeoisie
necessarily have endorsed Nesbit's decision to help her unmarried
and pregnant friend Alice Hoatson by employing her as compan-
ion-housekeeper and passing off Hoatson's daughter, Rosamund,
as Nesbit's. This pattern was repeated when Hoatson produced a
second baby, John – even though by that time Nesbit had realized
that the father of both children was her own husband. Hoatson
continued to live with the family until Bland's death, the children's parentage kept secret from them and from all but close family friends until they were young adults.[3]

Even before her marriage, Nesbit had begun to sell her poems and
stories, and despite her turbulent home life, her growing knowledge of the literary marketplace and ability to use her precarious
finances and considerable good looks to play on the sympathies of
editors enabled her to publish many early works that do not rise
to the level of what she was to produce during her prime. The late
nineteenth century was a booming time for literary periodicals, all
hungry for material, and Nesbit could well have remained a hack
writer while still earning enough to contribute a useful sum to
the household budget. Instead, beginning tentatively in 1894 and
escalating from 1897, Nesbit 'discovered her voice and style,' as Jan
Susina puts it,[4] when she published as magazine instalments, first

---

[3] This complicated family dynamic has been well described by various
Nesbit critics; see particularly Julia Briggs's biography *A Woman of Passion:
The Life of E. Nesbit 1858–1924* (New York: New Amsterdam, 1987).

[4] Jan Susina, 'Textual Building Blocks: Charles Dickens and E. Nesbit's
Literary Borrowings in *Five Children and It*,' in *E. Nesbit's Psammead
Trilogy: A Children's Classic at 100*, ed. by Raymond E. Jones (Lanham,
MD: Children's Literature Association and Scarecrow Press, 2006), 151–68
(p. 153).

in *Nister's Holiday Annual* and the Christmas supplement to the *Illustrated London News* but subsequently and more extensively in *Pall Mall* and *Windsor*, the series of stories that, when collected and reordered, became her 1899 breakthrough book, *The Story of the Treasure Seekers.*[5] It was followed by two sequels, *The Wouldbegoods* (1901) and *The New Treasure Seekers* (1904), both of which also traced the adventures of the Bastable children.

After *The Wouldbegoods*, which was divided between *Pall Mall* and the *Illustrated London News*, Nesbit's children's works were usually serialized in a single magazine, the *Strand* (also the original home of Arthur Conan Doyle's Sherlock Holmes stories), before being published as books in Britain. That the Bastable tales appeared in an assortment of venues reflects her comparative lack of stature as a writer in the late 1890s; she could not know how well the stories would take with the public and how many she should therefore expect to produce and sell, especially to a single editor. In addition, the periodicals that published the instalments varied, most but not all being general-interest titles primarily aimed not at children but at adults, a blurring of audience that aids in the analysis of the stories' narrative strategy. It is also worth noting that the order in which the tales appeared in periodicals differs from the order in which they appeared when they were subsequently published in volume form. Because they were first published as free-standing works, the tales, considered as a novel rather than as a series of short stories, do not follow a conventional dramatic arc by moving from exposition through climax to denouement. Yet that the order of the chapters may seem somewhat random, insofar as most of the episodes do not build upon one another to any significant extent, is for many readers part of the charm.

Nesbit's biographer Julia Briggs ascribes the genesis of *The Treasure Seekers* and *The Wouldbegoods* to several factors, among them the 1894 death of Nesbit's brother Alfred and Nesbit's partnership, literary and probably sexual, with a younger writer, Oswald Barron. Barron, dedicatee of the first Bastable book, encouraged Nesbit to think and talk about her childhood and to mine it for

---

[5] See 'A Note on the Texts', pp. xviii–xx of the present volume, for a description of where each chapter originally appeared.

material. This exercise bore fruit when she published in the *Girl's Own Paper* (October 1896–September 1897) a set of reminiscences entitled 'My School-Days,' a memoir that Susina describes as 'pivotal for the transformation of Nesbit's children's writing,'[6] but her recollections of her early days also informed her fiction. Episodes in both *The Treasure Seekers* and *The Wouldbegoods*, including the burial of Albert-next-door, the exploration of the haunted tower, and the children's expedition to find 'the source of the Nile,' rework events in Nesbit's childhood, while she also heavily rewrote a sequence originally published, as 'The Play Times,' in *Nister's Holiday Annual* in 1894, 1895, and 1896, to fit it into the Bastable framework.[7] According to Nesbit's friend Edgar Jepson, some of the events of *The Treasure Seekers* are also based on the exploits of the Bland children, who 'were, to an extent, the children of the House of Bastable.' Thus, for instance, the instalment called 'The Nobleness of Oswald' incorporates Nesbit's rewriting of events that took place in 1895, when, Jepson recounts, eleven-year-old Rosamund and ten-year-old Fabian 'made posies of flowers from their garden, took off their shoes and stockings, and in their shabbiest clothes sold the posies to native residents on their way to catch the business trains to London. For a while the two children lived happily in an affluence beyond all dreams.'[8]

The Bastables' amusing doings establish a formula that Nesbit would repeatedly draw upon in her later writings, in which children's well-meant actions or high-spirited searches for entertainment go comically wrong but are eventually rewarded by a reunited family – a perennial Nesbit fantasy perhaps inspired by her father's death and her frequent separation from her mother. Yet the stories' success results most proximately from the vividness with which Nesbit establishes the voice of their narrator, Oswald Bastable. While Oswald is by no means either the first child narrator in Victorian children's fiction or the first of its protagonists to illustrate the realization that, as Angela Sorby puts it, 'children

[6] Jan Susina, p. 153.

[7] 'The Play Times,' which purports to be three numbers of a newspaper produced by a group of siblings, became the basis for the *Treasure Seekers* chapter 'Being Editors.' See 'A Note on the Texts,' p. xix in this volume.

[8] Edgar Jepson, *Memories of an Edwardian and Neo-Georgian* (London: Richards, 1937), p. 25; see also Julia Briggs, p. 180.

were not just undeveloped adults,'[9] he is arguably the most successful in terms of his transformative effect upon his creator's subsequent career.

In breathing life into Oswald, Nesbit draws not only upon lived experience and upon predecessor texts such as Charles Dickens's 1868 serial *A Holiday Romance*[10] but also upon her shrewd understanding of the furnishings of a bright child's mind. As a group, Oswald, his siblings, and their friends Daisy (Nesbit's own childhood nickname) and Denny have read extensively, much of this material imperfectly retained and all of it filtered through their individual sensibilities: Denny's vision of Charlotte Yonge's popular domestic novel *The Daisy Chain* (1856) is very different from Daisy's, for example. Among many other texts, the Bastables are familiar with tags from eighteenth-century poetry and Shakespeare plays, pieces of history perhaps encountered in the schools that they attended before the wreck of the family finances, news events such as battles and shipwrecks, advertising slogans, mass-market fiction about highwaymen or counterfeiters, hymns and music-hall songs, didactic tales, and the works of Nesbit's slightly younger contemporary and frequent inspiration Rudyard Kipling.

This reading in turn gives direction to the children's own creative energies, from Noël's versifying, to pieces of home entertainment such as the ill-starred attempt to re-enact *The Jungle Book*, to Oswald's self-consciously literary turns of phrase. Their schemes come from their reading, as do their assumptions about adult motivations or likely responses, their ways of transforming events into narratives, and the optimism that arises from their assurance that a happy ending is inevitable. For Marah Gubar, the effect of the insistence upon outside texts 'is to break down the divide between adult writer and child reader by suggesting that both parties can improvise on other people's stories to produce their own narratives.'[11] Moreover, just as in *The Wouldbegoods* Oswald

---

[9] Angela Sorby, 'Golden Age,' in *Keywords for Children's Literature*, ed. by Philip Nel and Lissa Paul (New York: New York University Press, 2011), 96–9 (p. 97).

[10] For a discussion of this connection, see Jan Susina, p. 157.

[11] Marah Gubar, *Artful Dodgers: Reconceiving the Golden Age of Children's Literature* (New York: Oxford University Press, 2009), p. 132.

praises Kenneth Grahame's *The Golden Age* (1895), a book about childhood aimed at an adult readership, as 'A1 except where it gets mixed up with grown-up nonsense' (p. 188), both adults and children can read the Bastable stories with pleasure, recognizing them as common ground.

Even so, Rothwell observes, Nesbit recognizes and exploits a division here: just as the children do not respond identically to texts that they all read or adventures that they all share, readers of different ages will understand and appreciate the children's voices and actions differently. Since much of the humour comes at the children's expense, Rothwell continues, child readers may be less ready than adults to recognize and be amused by childish misuses of language, mishandlings of social intercourse with adults, or naïve failures to perceive adult actions such as Albert's uncle's planting of a modest 'treasure' in the Bastables' back-garden excavations. For Rothwell, the tales often emphasize 'the disjunction between adult and child worlds: children do not understand adults to adults' satisfaction, and adults do not see children as they see themselves. Thus, adults and children seem to occupy separate spheres that are firmly segregated from each other.'[12]

Yet 'seem' is the operative word here. Just as the tales' audience encompasses both child and adult readers, within the tales these spheres repeatedly intersect, particularly through the sharing of story. Albert's uncle, a novelist, recognizes and appreciates the children's tendency to approach problems within the framework of popular fiction; some of the Bastables' experiences, as Oswald notes, testify to the verisimilitude of plots by adult authors whose works they enjoy, such as Dickens and Kipling; and if adults do not always appreciate the Bastables' outlook, energy, and manoeuvrings, nevertheless they often prove willing, with whatever initial reluctance, to participate in bringing about the happy ending that the children have plotted. Moreover, Isabelle Guillaume points out, if the child's understanding is presented as limited, the adult's vision is simultaneously critiqued as prosaic: Nesbit 'offers a negative vision of the adult world whose corollary is the representation of childhood as an autonomous space' sacred to imagination and creativity, and the Bastable children's very fail-

---

[12] Erika Rothwell, pp. 61–2.

ures 'sanction the divide between the two worlds.' Thus, according to Guillaume, Oswald's errors in judgment empower both segments of Nesbit's audience, in that they 'leave the field open to the reflections of the reader' and allow a childish reading and an adult reading to compete.[13]

The crossover between child and adult readership noted by critics such as Rothwell, Gubar, Guillaume, Mavis Reimer, and others is something that Nesbit continued in further instalments of this family saga. Not only did she incorporate into her adult novel *The Red House* (1902) interaction between the adult narrator and the Bastables, she subsequently retold the same episode from Oswald's point of view in *The New Treasure Seekers*. For Reimer, the point of this interweaving is to enable Nesbit to explore the 'mechanism by which her culture produced the structural relation of child and adult,'[14] a sophisticated question that also preoccupied such canonical authors as Dickens and Henry James. For the reader – and it is the adult reader, not the child, who is more likely to become familiar with both the Bastables and *The Red House* – Nesbit's playful move enables a journey both into childhood and back out of it as an appreciative observer, a vantage point that Nesbit adopted as her own throughout her career as successful children's writer. In taking this stance, Nesbit contributed to an important literary and cultural trend of the nineteenth and early twentieth centuries, an era obsessed with gaining a better understanding of childhood. Simultaneously, in creating with energy, detail, and humour the Bastables' collective sensibility, Nesbit produced a children's classic that continues to speak to readers today.

---

[13] Isabelle Guillaume, 'Les paradoxes de la representation chez Edith Nesbit,' in *Devenir adulte et rester enfant? Relire les productions pour la jeunesse*, ed. by Isabelle Cani, Nelly Chabrol-Gagne, and Catherine d'Humières (Clermont-Ferrand: Presses Université Blaise Pascal, 2008), pp. 163–76 (pp. 163, 170, 172; my translation).

[14] Mavis Reimer, 'Treasure Seekers and Invaders: E. Nesbit's Cross-Writing of the Bastables,' *Children's Literature*, 25 (1997), 50–9 (p. 58).

Note on the Texts

As the above introduction observes, the Bastable stories first appeared between 1894 and 1899 for *The Story of the Treasure Seekers* and between 1900 and 1901 for *The Wouldbegoods*. They were published in an assortment of periodicals – *Nister's Holiday Annual*, the *Illustrated London News* (*ILN*) and its Christmas supplement, *Pall Mall*, *Windsor* – sometimes as singletons but more often in a series of instalments, detailed in the list at the end of this Note.

In preparing this edition, I have used as the source text for *The Story of the Treasure Seekers* the first British edition, published by T. Fisher Unwin Ltd in 1899, and as the source text for *The Wouldbegoods* the first American edition, published by Harper & Brothers in 1901, whose approach to punctuation more closely resembles that found in the periodical instalments. Readers may thus derive a sense of the range of flavours presented to Nesbit's original readers.

The occasional typographical errors to be found in the 1899 and 1901 editions have been silently corrected, and although I have provided a generous sampling in the notes in order to indicate the kinds of changes that the texts underwent as they moved away from their original venues, minor discrepancies between volume and periodical versions are not always chronicled. With regard to *The Wouldbegoods*, for instance, my notes do not observe that the *Pall Mall* version sometimes uses contractions instead of spelling out words. Speaking generally, the Oswald of *Pall Mall* is a less polished writer than that of the Harper & Brothers version, sometimes producing repetitive sentences such as 'And we all felt this so much that we felt in our chests just as if we had swallowed a hard-boiled egg whole. At least, this is what Oswald felt,' and preferring more juvenile diction; thus *Pall Mall* has 'we hadn't really meant to be naughty' where Harper & Brothers has 'we had not really meant to do anything wrong.' Similarly, *ILN* uses 'Dickie' for 'Dicky' and 'minute-book' for 'Golden Deed book' throughout. As the notes make clear, *ILN* also omits references to instalments published elsewhere.

The most dramatic difference between the periodical instalments and the one-volume versions of the chapters has to do with the order in which they appeared. The lists below, organized chronologically from earliest appearance to latest, indicate the reorderings and, in some cases, the extensive rewritings that the tales underwent.

The Story of the Treasure Seekers

Chapter 8, 'Being Editors,' based, with revision too considerable to be reflected in the notes to the present edition, on a three-part serial that appeared as 'The Play Times' in *Nister's Holiday Annual* in 1894, 1895, and 1896.

Chapters 1, 2, and 7, 'The Council of Ways and Means,' 'Digging for Treasure,' and 'Being Bandits,' based, again too extensively for this edition to record, on 'The Treasure Seekers,' published under the pen name Ethel Mortimer in *Father Christmas*, a Christmas supplement to the *Illustrated London News* (*ILN*), in December 1897. Nesbit considered that the *Father Christmas* version had been 'miserably mutilated.'[1]

Chapters 4 and 5, 'Good Hunting' and 'The Editor,' published in a single instalment as 'Good Hunting' in *Pall Mall* for April 1898.

Chapter 10, 'Lord Tottenham,' published in *Pall Mall* for May 1898.

Chapter 6, 'Noël's Princess,' published in *Pall Mall* for June 1898.

Chapter 14, 'The Divining-Rod,' published in *Pall Mall* for July 1898.

Chapters 15 and 16, 'Lo, the Poor Indian!' and 'The End of the Treasure-Seeking,' published in a single instalment as 'Lo, the Poor Indian!' in *Pall Mall* for August 1898.

Chapter 9, 'The G.B.,' published in *Windsor Magazine* for September 1898.

----

[1] Quoted in Julia Briggs, p. 427.

Chapter 3, 'Being Detectives,' published in *Pall Mall* for May 1899.

Chapter 11, 'Castilian Amoroso,' published in *Pall Mall* for August 1899.

Chapter 13, 'The Robber and the Burglar,' published in *Pall Mall* for September 1899.

Chapter 12, 'The Nobleness of Oswald,' published in *Windsor* for October 1899.

The Wouldbegoods

Chapter 3, 'Bill's Tombstone,' published as 'The Soldier's Mother: Being a Passage from the Life of Master Oswald Bastable' in *Pall Mall* for July 1900.

Chapter 1, 'The Jungle,' with the subtitle 'Being a Passage from the Life of Master Oswald Bastable,' published in *Pall Mall* for August 1900.

Chapter 2, 'The Wouldbegoods,' published as 'The Perils of the Deep' in *ILN* for 18 August 1900.

Chapter 5, 'The Waterworks,' with the subtitle 'Passages in the Life of Master Oswald Bastable,' published in *Pall Mall* for October 1900.

Chapter 6, 'The Circus,' published in *Pall Mall* for November 1900.

Chapter 4, 'The Tower of Mystery,' published in *ILN* for 17 November 1900.

Chapter 7, 'Being Beavers,' published in *ILN* for 22 December 1900.

Chapter 9, 'Hunting the Fox,' published in *ILN* for 19 January 1901.

Chapter 8, 'The High-Born Babe,' published in *ILN* for 23 February 1901.

Chapter 10, 'The Sale of Antiquities,' published in *ILN* for 23 March 1901.

Chapter 11, 'The Benevolent Bar,' published in *ILN* for 20 April 1901.

Chapter 12, 'The Canterbury Pilgrims,' published in *ILN* for 18 May 1901.

Chapter 13, 'The Dragon's Teeth,' published in *ILN* for 29 June 1901.

Chapter 14, 'Albert's Uncle's Grandmother,' published in *ILN* for 20 July 1901.

Further Reading

Briggs, Julia. *A Woman of Passion: The Life of E. Nesbit 1858–1924*. New York: New Amsterdam, 1987.

Gubar, Marah. *Artful Dodgers: Reconceiving the Golden Age of Children's Literature*. New York: Oxford University Press, 2009.

Jones, Raymond, ed. *E. Nesbit's Psammead Trilogy: A Children's Classic at 100*. Children's Literature Association Centennial Series. Lanham, MD: Children's Literature Association and Scarecrow Press, 2006.

Maltz, Diana. 'The Newer New Life: A. S. Byatt, E. Nesbit and Socialist Subculture.' *Journal of Victorian Culture* 17.1 (2012): 79–84.

Miller, Kathleen A. 'The Mysteries of the In-Between: Re-reading Disability in E. Nesbit's Late Victorian Gothic Fiction.' *Journal of Literary and Cultural Disability Studies* 6.2 (2012): 143–57.

Moore, Doris Langley. *E. Nesbit: A Biography*, rev. ed. Philadelphia, PA: Chilton, 1966.

Nelson, Claudia. 'E. Nesbit.' *British Children's Writers, 1880–1914*. Ed. Laura M. Zaidman. Dictionary of Literary Biography v. 141. Detroit, MI: Gale, 1994. 199–216.

Reimer, Mavis. 'Treasure Seekers and Invaders: E. Nesbit's Cross-Writing of the Bastables.' *Children's Literature* 25 (1997): 50–9.

Rothwell, Erika. ' "You Catch It If You Try to Do Otherwise": The Limitations of E. Nesbit's Cross-Written Vision of the Child.' *Children's Literature* 25 (1997): 60–70.

Rutledge, Amelia A. 'E. Nesbit and the Woman Question.' *Victorian Women Writers and the Woman Question*. Ed. Nicola Diane Thompson. New York: Cambridge University Press, 1999. 223–40.

Smith, Michelle. 'E. Nesbit's Psammead Trilogy: Reconfiguring Time, Nation, and Gender.' *English Literature in Transition, 1880–1920* 52.3 (2009): 298–311.

Susina, Jan. 'Textual Building Blocks: Charles Dickens and E. Nesbit's Literary Borrowings in *Five Children and It*.' *E. Nesbit's Psammead Trilogy: A Children's Classic at 100*. Ed. Raymond E. Jones. Children's Literature Association Centennial Series. Lanham, MD: Children's Literature Association and Scarecrow Press, 2006. 151–68.

THE STORY OF THE TREASURE SEEKERS

Being the adventures of the Bastable children in search of a fortune

by E. Nesbit

To
OSWALD BARRON
Without whom this book could never have been written
The Treasure Seekers is dedicated in
memory of childhoods identical
but for the accidents of
time and space[1]

SOME chapters of this story have appeared in the *Pall Mall Magazine*, and in the *Windsor Magazine*, and some portions were printed by the *Illustrated London News* and in *Nister's Holiday Annual*. To the Editors of these journals my thanks are due. – E. NESBIT

Chapter 1
The Council of Ways and Means

This is the story of the different ways we looked for treasure, and I think when you have read it you will see that we were not lazy about the looking.

There are some things I must tell before I begin to tell about the treasure-seeking, because I have read books myself, and I know how beastly it is when a story begins, '"Alas!" said Hildegarde with a deep sigh, we must look our last on this ancestral home' – and then some one else says something – and you don't know for pages and pages where the home is, or who Hildegarde is, or anything about it. Our ancestral home is in the Lewisham Road.[1] It is semi-detached and has a garden, not a large one. We are the Bastables. There are six of us besides Father. Our Mother is dead, and if you think we don't care because I don't tell you much about her you only show that you do not understand people at all. Dora is the eldest. Then Oswald – and then Dicky. Oswald won the Latin prize at his preparatory school – and Dicky is good at sums. Alice and Noël are twins: they are ten, and Horace Octavius is my youngest brother. It is one of us that tells this story – but I shall not tell you which: only at the very end perhaps I will. While the story is going on you may be trying to guess, only I bet you don't.

It was Oswald who first thought of looking for treasure. Oswald often thinks of very interesting things. And directly he thought of it he did not keep it to himself, as some boys would have done, but he told the others, and said –

'I'll tell you what, we must go and seek for treasure: it is always what you do to restore the fallen fortunes of your House.'

Dora said it was all very well. She often says that. She was trying to mend a large hole in one of Noël's stockings. He tore it on a nail when we were playing shipwrecked mariners on top of the chicken-house the day H.O. fell off and cut his chin: he has the scar still. Dora is the only one of us who ever tries to mend anything. Alice tries to make things sometimes. Once she knitted a red scarf for Noël because his chest is delicate, but it was

2

much wider at one end than the other, and he wouldn't wear it. So we used it as a pennon, and it did very well, because most of our things are black or grey since Mother died; and scarlet was a nice change. Father does not like you to ask for new things. That was one way we had of knowing that the fortunes of the ancient House of Bastable were really fallen. Another way was that there was no more pocket-money – except a penny now and then to the little ones, and people did not come to dinner any more, like they used to, with pretty dresses, driving up in cabs – and the carpets got holes in them – and when the legs came off things they were not sent to be mended, and we gave up having the gardener except for the front garden, and not that very often. And the silver in the big oak plate-chest that is lined with green baize all went away to the shop to have the dents and scratches taken out of it, and it never came back. We think Father hadn't enough money to pay the silver man for taking out the dents and scratches. The new spoons and forks were yellowy-white, and not so heavy as the old ones, and they never shone after the first day or two.

Father was very ill after Mother died; and while he was ill his business-partner went to Spain – and there was never much money afterwards. I don't know why. Then the servants left and there was only one, a General.[2] A great deal of your comfort and happiness depends on having a good General. The last but one was nice: she used to make jolly good currant puddings for us, and let us have the dish on the floor and pretend it was a wild boar we were killing with our forks. But the General we have now nearly always makes sago puddings, and they are the watery kind, and you cannot pretend anything with them, not even islands, like you do with porridge.

Then we left off going to school, and Father said we should go to a good school as soon as he could manage it. He said a holiday would do us all good. We thought he was right, but we wished he had told us he couldn't afford it. For of course we knew.

Then a great many people used to come to the door with envelopes with no stamps on them, and sometimes they got very angry, and said they were calling for the last time before putting it in other hands. I asked Eliza what that meant, and she kindly explained to me, and I was so sorry for Father.

And once a long, blue paper came; a policeman brought it, and we were so frightened. But Father said it was all right, only when he went up to kiss the girls after they were in bed they said he had been crying, though I'm sure that's not true. Because only cowards and snivellers cry, and my Father is the bravest man in the world.

So you see it was time we looked for treasure and Oswald said so, and Dora said it was all very well. But the others agreed with Oswald. So we held a council. Dora was in the chair – the big dining-room chair, that we let the fireworks off from, the Fifth of November when we had the measles and couldn't do it in the garden.[3] The hole has never been mended, so now we have that chair in the nursery, and I think it was cheap at the blowing-up we boys got when the hole was burnt.

'We must do something,' said Alice, 'because the exchequer is empty.' She rattled the money-box as she spoke, and it really did rattle because we always keep the bad sixpence in it for luck.

'Yes – but what shall we do?' said Dicky. 'It's so jolly easy to say let's do *something.*' Dicky always wants everything settled exactly. Father calls him the Definite Article.

'Let's read all the books again. We shall get lots of ideas out of them.' It was Noël who suggested this, but we made him shut up, because we knew well enough he only wanted to get back to his old books. Noël is a poet. He sold some of his poetry once – and it was printed, but that does not come in this part of the story.

Then Dicky said, 'Look here. We'll be quite quiet for ten minutes by the clock – and each think of some way to find treasure. And when we've thought we'll try all the ways one after the other, beginning with the eldest.'

'I shan't be able to think in ten minutes, make it half an hour,' said H.O. His real name is Horace Octavius, but we call him H.O. because of the advertisement, and it's not so very long ago he was afraid to pass the hoarding where it says 'Eat H.O.' in big letters.[4] He says it was when he was a little boy, but I remember last Christmas but one, he woke in the middle of the night crying and howling, and they said it was the pudding. But he told me afterwards he had been dreaming that they really *had* come to eat H.O., and it couldn't have been the pudding, when you come to think of it, because it was so very plain.

Well, we made it half an hour – and we all sat quiet, and thought and thought. And I made up my mind before two minutes were over, and I saw the others had, all but Dora, who is always an awful time over everything. I got pins and needles in my leg from sitting still so long, and when it was seven minutes H.O. cried out –

'Oh, it must be more than half an hour!'

H.O. is eight years old, but he cannot tell the clock yet. Oswald could tell the clock when he was six.

We all stretched ourselves and began to speak at once, but Dora put up her hands to her ears and said –

'One at a time, please. We aren't playing Babel.'[5] (It is a very good game. Did you ever play it?)

So Dora made us all sit in a row on the floor, in ages, and then she pointed at us with the finger that had the brass thimble on. Her silver one got lost when the last General but two went away. We think she must have forgotten it was Dora's and put it in her box by mistake. She was a very forgetful girl. She used to forget what she had spent money on, so that the change was never quite right.

Oswald spoke first. 'I think we might stop people on Blackheath – with crape masks and horse-pistols – and say "Your money or your life! Resistance is useless, we are armed to the teeth" – like Dick Turpin and Claude Duval.[6] It wouldn't matter about not having horses, because coaches have gone out too.'

Dora screwed up her nose the way she always does when she is going to talk like the good elder sister in books, and said, 'That would be very wrong: it's like pickpocketing or taking pennies out of Father's great-coat when it's hanging in the hall.'

I must say I don't think she need have said that, especially before the little ones – for it was when I was only four.

But Oswald was not going to let her see he cared, so he said –

'Oh, very well. I can think of lots of other ways. We could rescue an old gentleman from deadly Highwaymen.'

'There aren't any,' said Dora.

'Oh, well, it's all the same – from deadly peril, then. There's plenty of that. Then he would turn out to be the Prince of Wales, and he would say, "My noble, my cherished preserver! Here is a million pounds a year. Rise up, Sir Oswald Bastable." '

But the others did not seem to think so, and it was Alice's turn to say.

She said, 'I think we might try the divining-rod. I'm sure I could do it. I've often read about it. You hold a stick in your hands, and when you come to where there is gold underneath the stick kicks about. So you know. And you dig.'

'Oh,' said Dora suddenly, 'I have an idea. But I'll say last. I hope the divining-rod isn't wrong. I believe it's wrong in the Bible.'

'So is eating pork and ducks,' said Dicky. 'You can't go by that.'

'Anyhow, we'll try the other ways first,' said Dora. 'Now, H.O.'

'Let's be Bandits,' said H.O. 'I dare say it's wrong but it would be fun pretending.'

'I'm sure it's wrong,' said Dora.

And Dicky said she thought everything wrong. She said she didn't, and Dicky was very disagreeable. So Oswald had to make peace, and he said –

'Dora needn't play if she doesn't want to. Nobody asked her. And, Dicky, don't be an idiot: do dry up and let's hear what Noël's idea is.'

Dora and Dicky did not look pleased, but I kicked Noël under the table to make him hurry up, and then he said he didn't think he wanted to play any more. That's the worst of it. The others are so jolly ready to quarrel. I told Noël to be a man and not a snivelling pig, and at last he said he had not made up his mind whether he would print his poetry in a book and sell it, or find a princess and marry her.

'Whichever it is,' he added, 'none of you shall want for anything, though Oswald did kick me, and say I was a snivelling pig.'

'I didn't,' said Oswald, 'I told you not to be.' And Alice explained to him that that was quite the opposite of what he thought. So he agreed to drop it.

Then Dicky spoke.

'You must all of you have noticed the advertisements in the papers, telling you that ladies and gentlemen can easily earn two pounds a week in their spare time, and to send two shillings for sample and instructions, carefully packed free from observation. Now that we don't go to school all our time is spare time. So I should think we could easily earn twenty pounds a week each. That would do us very well. We'll try some of the other things first, and directly we have any money we'll send for the sample and instructions. And I have another idea, but I must think about it before I say.'

We all said, 'Out with it – what's the other idea?'

But Dicky said, 'No.' That is Dicky all over. He never will show you anything he's making till it's quite finished, and the same with his inmost thoughts. But he is pleased if you seem to want to know, so Oswald said –

'Keep your silly old secret, then. Now, Dora, drive ahead. We've all said except you.'

Then Dora jumped up and dropped the stocking and the thimble (it rolled away, and we did not find it for days), and said –

'Let's try my way *now*. Besides, I'm the eldest, so it's only fair. Let's dig for treasure. Not any tiresome divining-rod – but just plain digging. People who dig for treasure always find it. And then we shall be rich and we needn't try your ways at all. Some of them are rather difficult: and I'm certain some of them are wrong – and we must always remember that wrong things – '

But we told her to shut up and come on, and she did.

I couldn't help wondering as we went down to the garden, why Father had never thought of digging there for treasure instead of going to his beastly office every day.

∗　∗　∗

Chapter 2
Digging for Treasure

I am afraid the last chapter was rather dull. It is always dull in books when people talk and talk, and don't do anything, but I was obliged to put it in, or else you wouldn't have understood all the rest. The best part of books is when things are happening. That is the best part of real things too. This is why I shall not tell you in this story about all the days when nothing happened. You will not catch me saying, 'thus the sad days passed slowly by' – or 'the years rolled on their weary course' – or 'time went on' – because it is silly; of course time goes on – whether you say so or not. So I shall just tell you the nice, interesting parts – and in between you will understand that we had our meals and got up and went to bed, and dull things like that. It would be sickening to write all that down, though of course it happens. I said so to Albert-next-door's uncle, who writes books, and he said, 'Quite right, that's what we call selection, a necessity of true art.' And he is very clever indeed. So you see.

I have often thought that if the people who write books for children knew a little more it would be better. I shall not tell you anything about us except what I should like to know about if I was reading the story and you were writing it. Albert's uncle says I ought to have put this in the preface, but I never read prefaces, and it is not much good writing things just for people to skip. I wonder other authors have never thought of this.

Well, when we had agreed to dig for treasure we all went down into the cellar and lighted the gas. Oswald would have liked to dig there, but it is stone flags. We looked among the old boxes and broken chairs and fenders and empty bottles and things, and at last we found the spades we had to dig in the sand with when we went to the seaside three years ago. They are not silly, babyish, wooden spades, that split if you look at them, but good iron, with a blue mark across the top of the iron part, and yellow wooden handles. We wasted a little time getting them dusted, because the girls wouldn't dig with spades that had cobwebs on them. Girls would never do for African explorers or anything like that, they are too beastly particular.

It was no use doing the thing by halves. We marked out a sort of square in the mouldy part of the garden, about three yards across, and began to dig. But we found nothing except worms and stones – and the ground was very hard.

So we thought we'd try another part of the garden, and we found a place in the big round flower bed, where the ground was much softer. We thought we'd make a smaller hole to begin with, and it was much better. We dug and dug and dug, and it was jolly hard work! We got very hot digging, but we found nothing.

Presently Albert-next-door looked over the wall. We do not like him very much, but we let him play with us sometimes, because his father is dead, and you must not be unkind to orphans, even if their mothers are alive. Albert is always very tidy. He wears frilly collars and velvet knickerbockers. I can't think how he can bear to.

So we said, 'Hullo!'

And he said, 'What are you up to?'

'We're digging for treasure,' said Alice; 'an ancient parchment revealed to us the place of concealment. Come over and help us. When we have dug deep enough we shall find a great pot of red clay, full of gold and precious jewels.'

Albert-next-door only sniggered and said, 'What silly non-sense!' He cannot play properly at all. It is very strange, because he has a very nice uncle. You see, Albert-next-door doesn't care for reading, and he has not read nearly so many books as we have, so he is very foolish and ignorant, but it cannot be helped, and you just have to put up with it when you want him to do anything. Besides, it is wrong to be angry with people for not being so clever as you are yourself. It is not always their faults.

So Oswald said, 'Come and dig! Then you shall share the treas-ure when we've found it.'

But he said, 'I shan't – I don't like digging – and I'm just going in to my tea.'

'Come along and dig, there's a good boy,' Alice said. 'You can use my spade. It's much the best – '

So he came along and dug, and when once he was over the wall we kept him at it, and we worked as well, of course, and the hole got deep. Pincher worked too – he is our dog and he is very good at digging. He digs for rats in the dustbin sometimes, and gets very dirty. But we love our dog, even when his face wants washing.

'I expect we shall have to make a tunnel,' Oswald said, 'to reach the rich treasure.' So he jumped into the hole and began to dig at one side. After that we took it in turns to dig at the tunnel, and Pincher was most useful in scraping the earth out of the tunnel – he does it with his back feet when you say 'Rats!' and he digs with his front ones, and burrows with his nose as well.

At last the tunnel was nearly a yard long, and big enough to creep along to find the treasure, if only it had been a bit longer. Now it was Albert's turn to go in and dig, but he funked it.

'Take your turn like a man,' said Oswald – nobody can say that Oswald doesn't take his turn like a man. But Albert wouldn't. So we had to make him, because it was only fair.

'It's quite easy,' Alice said. 'You just crawl in and dig with your hands. Then when you come out we can scrape out what you've done, with the spades. Come – be a man. You won't notice it being dark in the tunnel if you shut your eyes tight. We've all been in except Dora – and she doesn't like worms.'

'I don't like worms neither.' Albert-next-door said this; but we remembered how he had picked a fat red and black worm up in his fingers and thrown it at Dora only the day before.

So we put him in.

But he would not go in head first, the proper way, and dig with his hands as we had done, and though Oswald was angry at the time, for he hates snivellers, yet afterwards he owned that perhaps it was just as well. You should never be afraid to own that perhaps you were mistaken – but it is cowardly to do it unless you are quite sure you are in the wrong.

'Let me go in feet first,' said Albert-next-door. 'I'll dig with my boots – I will truly, honour bright.'

So we let him get in feet first – and he did it very slowly and at last he was in, and only his head sticking out into the hole; and all the rest of him in the tunnel.

'Now dig with your boots,' said Oswald; 'and, Alice, do catch hold of Pincher, he'll be digging again in another minute, and perhaps it would be uncomfortable for Albert if Pincher threw the mould into his eyes.'

You should always try to think of these little things. Thinking of other people's comfort makes them like you. Alice held Pincher, and we all shouted, 'Kick! dig with your feet, for all you're worth!'

So Albert-next-door began to dig with his feet, and we stood on the ground over him, waiting – and all in a minute the ground gave way, and we tumbled together in a heap: and when we got up there was a little shallow hollow where we had been standing, and Albert-next-door was underneath, stuck quite fast, because the roof of the tunnel had tumbled in on him. He is a horribly unlucky boy to have anything to do with.

It was dreadful the way he cried and screamed, though he had to own it didn't hurt, only it was rather heavy and he couldn't move his legs. We would have dug him out all right enough, in time, but he screamed so we were afraid the police would come, so Dicky climbed over the wall, to tell the cook there to tell Albert-next-door's uncle he had been buried by mistake, and to come and help dig him out.

Dicky was a long time gone. We wondered what had become of him, and all the while the screaming went on and on, for we had taken the loose earth off Albert's face so that he could scream quite easily and comfortably.

Presently Dicky came back and Albert-next-door's uncle came with him. He has very long legs, and his hair is light and his face is brown. He has been to sea, but now he writes books. I like him.

He told his nephew to stow it, so Albert did, and then he asked him if he was hurt – and Albert had to say he wasn't, for though he is a coward, and very unlucky, he is not a liar like some boys are.

'This promises to be a protracted if agreeable task,' said Albert-next-door's uncle, rubbing his hands and looking at the hole with Albert's head in it. 'I will get another spade,' so he fetched the big spade out of the next-door garden tool-shed, and began to dig his nephew out.

'Mind you keep very still,' he said, 'or I might chunk a bit out of you with the spade.' Then after a while he said –

'I confess that I am not absolutely insensible to the dramatic interest of the situation. My curiosity is excited. I own that I should like to know how my nephew happened to be buried. But don't tell me if you'd rather not. I suppose no force was used?'

'Only moral force,' said Alice. They used to talk a lot about moral force at the High School where she went, and in case you don't know what it means I'll tell you that it is making people do what they don't want to, just by slanging them, or laughing at them, or promising them things if they're good.

'Only moral force, eh?' said Albert-next-door's uncle. 'Well?'

'Well,' Dora said, 'I'm very sorry it happened to Albert – I'd rather it had been one of us. It would have been my turn to go into the tunnel, only I don't like worms, so they let me off. You see we were digging for treasure.'

'Yes,' said Alice, 'and I think we were just coming to the underground passage that leads to the secret hoard, when the tunnel fell in on Albert. He *is* so unlucky,' and she sighed.

Then Albert-next-door began to scream again, and his uncle wiped his face – his own face, not Albert's – with his silk handkerchief, and then he put it in his trousers pocket. It seems a strange place to put a handkerchief, but he had his coat and waistcoat off and I suppose he wanted the handkerchief handy. Digging is warm work.

He told Albert-next-door to drop it, or he wouldn't proceed further in the matter, so Albert stopped screaming, and presently his uncle finished digging him out. Albert did look so funny, with his hair all dusty and his velvet suit covered with mould and his face muddy with earth and crying.

We all said how sorry we were, but he wouldn't say a word back to us. He was most awfully sick to think he'd been the one buried, when it might just as well have been one of us. I felt myself that it was hard lines.

'So you were digging for treasure,' said Albert-next-door's uncle, wiping his face again with his handkerchief. 'Well, I fear that your chances of success are small. I have made a careful study of the whole subject. What I don't know about buried treasure is not worth knowing. And I never knew more than one coin buried in any one garden – and that is generally – Hullo – what's that?'

He pointed to something shining in the hole he had just dragged Albert out of. Oswald picked it up. It was a half-crown. We looked at each other, speechless with surprise and delight, like in books.

'Well, that's lucky, at all events,' said Albert-next-door's uncle.

'Let's see, that's fivepence each for you.'

'It's fourpence – something; I can't do fractions,' said Dicky; 'there are seven of us, you see.'

'Oh, you count Albert as one of yourselves on this occasion, eh?'

'Of course,' said Alice; 'and I say, he was buried after all. Why shouldn't we let him have the odd somethings, and we'll have fourpence each.'

We all agreed to do this, and told Albert-next-door we would bring his share as soon as we could get the half-crown changed. He cheered up a little at that, and his uncle wiped his face again – he did look hot – and began to put on his coat and waistcoat.

When he had done it he stooped and picked up something. He held it up, and you will hardly believe it, but it is quite true – it was another half-crown!

'To think that there should be two!' he said; 'in all my experience of buried treasure I never heard of such a thing!'

I wish Albert-next-door's uncle would come treasure-seeking with us regularly; he must have very sharp eyes: for Dora says she was looking just the minute before at the very place where the second half-crown was picked up from, and *she* never saw it.

* * *

Chapter 3
Being Detectives

The next thing that happened to us was very interesting. It was as real as the half-crowns – not just pretending. I shall try to write it as like a real book as I can.[1] Of course we have read Mr Sherlock Holmes, as well as the yellow-covered books with pictures outside that are so badly printed; and you get them for fourpence halfpenny at the bookstall when the corners of them are beginning to curl up and get dirty, with people looking to see how the story ends when they are waiting for trains. I think this is most unfair to the boy at the bookstall. The books are written by a gentleman named Gaboriau, and Albert's uncle says they are the worst translations in the world – and written in vile English. Of course they're not like Kipling, but they're jolly good stories. And we had just been reading a book by Dick Diddlington – that's not his right name, but I know all about libel actions, so I shall not say what his name is really, because his books are rot. Only they put it into our heads to do what I am going to narrate.[2]

It was in September, and we were not to go to the seaside because it is so expensive, even if you go to Sheerness, where it is all tin cans and old boots and no sand at all. But every one else went, even the people next door – not Albert's side, but the other. Their servant told Eliza they were all going to Scarborough, and next day sure enough all the blinds were down and the shutters up, and the milk was not left any more. There is a big horse-chestnut tree between their garden and ours, very useful for getting conkers out of and for making stuff to rub on your chilblains. This prevented our seeing whether the blinds were down at the back as well, but Dicky climbed to the top of the tree and looked, and they were.

It was jolly hot weather, and very stuffy indoors – we used to play a good deal in the garden. We made a tent out of the kitchen clothes-horse and some blankets off our beds, and though it was quite as hot in the tent as in the house it was a very different sort of hotness. Albert's uncle called it the Turkish Bath. It is not nice to be kept from the seaside, but we know that we have much to be thankful for. We might be poor little children living in a crowded alley where even at summer noon hardly a ray of sunlight penetrates; clothed in rags and with bare feet – though I do not mind holes in my clothes myself, and bare feet would not be at all bad in this sort of weather.[3] Indeed we do, sometimes, when we are playing at things which require it. It was shipwrecked mariners that day, I remember, and we were all in the blanket tent. We had just finished eating the things we had saved, at the peril of our lives, from the fast-sinking vessel. They were rather nice things. Two pennyworth of cocoa-nut candy – it was got in Greenwich, where it is four ounces a penny – three apples, some macaroni – the straight sort that is so useful to suck things through – some raw rice, and a large piece of cold suet pudding that Alice nicked from the larder when she went to get the rice and macaroni. And when we had finished some one said –

'I should like to be a detective.'

I wish to be quite fair, but I cannot remember exactly who said it. Oswald thinks he said it, and Dora says it was Dicky, but Oswald is too much of a man to quarrel about a little thing like that.[4]

'I should like to be a detective,' said – perhaps it was Dicky, but I think not – 'and find out strange and hidden crimes.'

'You would have to be much cleverer than you are,' said H.O.

'Not so very,' Alice said, 'because when you've read the books you know what the things mean: the red hair on the handle of the knife, or the grains of white powder on the velvet collar of the villain's overcoat. I believe we could do it.'

'I shouldn't like to have anything to do with murders,' said Dora; 'somehow it doesn't seem safe – '

'And it always ends in the poor murderer being hanged,' said Alice.

We explained to her why murderers have to be hanged, but she only said, 'I don't care. I'm sure no one would ever do murdering *twice*. Think of the blood and things, and what you would see when you woke up in the night![5] I shouldn't mind being a detective to lie in wait for a gang of coiners, now, and spring upon them unawares, and secure them – single-handed, you know, or with only my faithful bloodhound.'

She stroked Pincher's ears, but he had gone to sleep because he knew well enough that all suet pudding was finished. He is a very sensible dog.

'You always get hold of the wrong end of the stick,' Oswald said. 'You can't choose what crimes you'll be a detective about. You just have to get a suspicious circumstance, and then you look for a clue and follow it up. Whether it turns out a murder or a missing will is just a fluke.'

'That's one way,' Dicky said. 'Another is to get a paper and find two advertisements or bits of news that fit. Like this: "Young Lady Missing," and then it tells about all the clothes she had on, and the gold locket she wore, and the colour of her hair, and all that; and then in another piece of the paper you see, "Gold locket found," and then it all comes out.'

We sent H.O. for the paper at once, but we could not make any of the things fit in. The two best were about how some burglars broke into a place in Holloway where they made preserved tongues and invalid delicacies, and carried off a lot of them. And on another page there was, 'Mysterious deaths in Holloway.' Oswald thought there was something in it, and so did Albert's uncle when we asked him, but the others thought not, so Oswald agreed to drop it. Besides, Holloway is a long way off. All the time we were talking about the paper Alice seemed to be thinking about something else, and when we had done she said –

'I believe we might be detectives ourselves, but I should not like to get anybody into trouble.'

'Not murderers or robbers?' Dicky asked.

'It wouldn't be murderers,' she said; 'but I *have* noticed something strange. Only I feel a little frightened. Let's ask Albert's uncle first.'

Alice is a jolly sight too fond of asking grown-up people things. And we all said it was Tommy-rot, and she was to tell us.

'Well, promise you won't do anything without me,' Alice said, and we promised. Then she said –

'This is a dark secret, and any one who thinks it is better not to be involved in a career of crime-discovery had better go away ere yet it be too late.'

So Dora said she had had enough of tents, and she was going to look at the shops. H.O. went with her because he had twopence to spend. They thought it was only a game of Alice's but Oswald knew by the way she spoke. He can nearly always tell. And when people are not telling the truth Oswald generally knows by the way they look with their eyes. Oswald is not proud of being able to do this. He knows it is through no merit of his own that he is much cleverer than some people.

When they had gone, the rest of us got closer together and said – 'Now then.'

'Well,' Alice said, 'you know the house next door? The people have gone to Scarborough. And the house is shut up. But last night *I saw a light in the windows.*'

We asked her how and when, because her room is in the front, and she couldn't possibly have seen. And then she said –

'I'll tell you if you boys will promise not ever to go fishing again without me.'

So we had to promise. Then she said –

'It was last night. I had forgotten to feed my rabbits and I woke up and remembered it. And I was afraid I should find them dead in the morning, like Oswald did.'

'It wasn't my fault,' Oswald said; 'there was something the matter with the beasts. I fed them right enough.'

Alice said she didn't mean that, and she went on –

'I came down into the garden, and I saw a light in the house, and dark figures moving about. I thought perhaps it was burglars, but Father hadn't come home, and Eliza had gone to bed, so I couldn't do anything. Only I thought perhaps I would tell the rest of you.'

'Why didn't you tell us this morning?' Noël asked. And Alice explained that she did not want to get any one into trouble, even burglars. 'But we might watch to-night,' she said, 'and see if we see the light again.'[6]

'They might have been burglars,' Noël said. He was sucking the last bit of his macaroni. 'You know the people next door are very grand. They won't know us – and they go out in a real private carriage sometimes. And they have an "At Home" day, and people come in cabs. I daresay they have piles of plate and jewellery and rich brocades, and furs of price and things like that. Let us keep watch to-night.'

'It's no use watching to-night,' Dicky said; 'if it's only burglars they won't come again. But there are other things besides burglars that are discovered in empty houses where lights are seen moving.'

'You mean coiners,' said Oswald at once. 'I wonder what the reward is for setting the police on their track?'

Dicky thought it ought to be something fat, because coiners are always a desperate gang; and the machinery they make the coins with is so heavy and handy for knocking down detectives.

Then it was tea-time, and we went in; and Dora and H.O. had clubbed their money together and bought a melon; quite a big one, and only a little bit squashy at one end. It was very good, and then we washed the seeds and made things with them and with pins and cotton. And nobody said any more about watching the house next door.

Only when we went to bed Dicky took off his coat and waist-coat, but he stopped at his braces, and said –

'What about the coiners?'

Oswald had taken off his collar and tie, and he was just going to say the same, so he said, 'Of course I meant to watch, only my collar's rather tight, so I thought I'd take it off first.'

Dicky said he did not think the girls ought to be in it, because there might be danger, but Oswald reminded him that they had promised Alice, and that a promise is a sacred thing, even when you'd much rather not. So Oswald got Alice alone under pretence of showing her a caterpillar – Dora does not like them, and she screamed and ran away when Oswald offered to show it her. Then Oswald explained, and Alice agreed to come and watch if she could. This made us later than we ought to have been, because Alice had to wait till Dora was quiet and then creep out very slowly, for fear of the boards creaking. The girls sleep with their room-door open for fear of burglars. Alice had kept on her clothes under her nightgown when Dora wasn't looking, and presently we got down, creeping past Father's study, and out at the glass door that leads on to the veranda and the iron steps into the garden. And we went down very quietly, and got into the chestnut-tree; and then I felt that we had only been playing what Albert's uncle calls our favourite instrument – I mean the Fool. For the house next door was as dark as dark. Then suddenly we heard a sound – it came from the gate at the end of the garden. All the gardens have gates; they lead into a kind of lane that runs behind them. It is a sort of back way, very convenient when you don't want to say exactly where you are going. We heard the gate at the end of the next garden click, and Dicky nudged Alice so that she would have fallen out of the tree if it had not been for Oswald's extraordinary presence of mind. Oswald squeezed Alice's arm tight, and we all looked; and the others were rather frightened because really we had not exactly expected anything to happen except perhaps a light. But now a muffled figure, shrouded in a dark cloak, came swiftly up the path of the next door garden. And we could see that under its cloak the figure carried a mysterious burden. The figure was dressed to look like a woman in a sailor hat.

We held our breath as it passed under the tree where we were, and then it tapped very gently on the back door and was let in, and then a light appeared in the window of the downstairs back breakfast-room. But the shutters were up.

Dicky said, 'My eye!' and wouldn't the others be sick to think they hadn't been in this! But Alice didn't half like it – and as she is a girl I do not blame her. Indeed, I thought myself at first that perhaps it would be better to retire for the present, and return later with a strongly armed force.

'It's not burglars,' Alice whispered; 'the mysterious stranger was bringing things in, not taking them out. They must be coiners – and oh, Oswald! – don't let's! The things they coin with must hurt very much. Do let's go to bed!'

But Dicky said he was going to see; if there was a reward for finding out things like this he would like to have the reward.

'They locked the back door,' he whispered, 'I heard it go. And I could look in quite well through the holes in the shutters and be back over the wall long before they'd got the door open, even if they started to do it at once.'

There were holes at the top of the shutters the shape of hearts, and the yellow light came out through them as well as through the chinks of the shutters.

Oswald said if Dicky went he should, because he was the eldest; and Alice said, 'If any one goes it ought to be me, because I thought of it.'

So Oswald said, 'Well, go then'; and she said, 'Not for anything!' And she begged us not to, and we talked about it in the tree till we were all quite hoarse with whispering.

At last we decided on a plan of action.

Alice was to stay in the tree, and scream 'Murder!' if anything happened. Dicky and I were to get down into the next garden and take it in turns to peep.

So we got down as quietly as we could, but the tree made much more noise than it does in the day, and several times we paused, fearing that all was discovered. But nothing happened.

There was a pile of red flower-pots under the window and one very large one was on the window-ledge. It seemed as if it was the hand of Destiny had placed it there, and the geranium in it was dead, and there was nothing to stop your standing on it – so Oswald did. He went first because he is the eldest, and though Dicky tried to stop him because he thought of it first it could not be, on account of not being able to say anything.

So Oswald stood on the flower-pot and tried to look through one of the holes. He did not really expect to see the coiners at their fell work, though he had pretended to when we were talking in the tree. But if he had seen them pouring the base molten metal into tin moulds the shape of half-crowns he would not have been half so astonished as he was at the spectacle now revealed.

At first he could see little, because the hole had unfortunately been made a little too high, so that the eye of the detective could only see the Prodigal Son in a shiny frame on the opposite wall. But Oswald held on to the window-frame and stood on tiptoe and then he *saw*.

There was no furnace, and no base metal, no bearded men in leathern aprons with tongs and things, but just a table with a table-cloth on it for supper, and a tin of salmon and a lettuce and some bottled beer. And there on a chair was the cloak and the hat of the mysterious stranger, and the two people sitting at the table were the two youngest grown-up daughters of the lady next door, and one of them was saying –

'So I got the salmon three-halfpence cheaper, and the lettuces are only six a penny in the Broadway, just fancy! We must save as much as ever we can on our housekeeping money if we want to go away decent next year.'

And the other said, 'I wish we could *all* go *every* year, or else – Really, I almost wish – '

And all the time Oswald was looking Dicky was pulling at his jacket to make him get down and let Dicky have a squint. And just as she said 'I almost,' Dicky pulled too hard and Oswald felt himself toppling on the giddy verge of the big flower-pots. Putting forth all his strength our hero strove to recover his equi-what's-its-name, but it was now lost beyond recall.[7]

'You've done it this time!' he said, then he fell heavily among the flower-pots piled below. He heard them crash and rattle and crack, and then his head struck against an iron pillar used for holding up the next-door veranda. His eyes closed and he knew no more.

Now you will perhaps expect that at this moment Alice would have cried 'Murder!' If you think so you little know what girls are. Directly she was left alone in that tree she made a bolt to tell Albert's uncle all about it and bring him to our rescue in case the coiner's gang was a very desperate one. And just when I fell, Albert's uncle was getting over the wall. Alice never screamed at all when Oswald fell, but Dicky thinks he heard Albert's uncle say, 'Confound those kids!' which would not have been kind or polite, so I hope he did not say it.

The people next door did not come out to see what the row was. Albert's uncle did not wait for them to come out. He picked up Oswald and carried the insensible body of the gallant young detective to the wall, laid it on the top, and then climbed over and bore his lifeless burden into our house and put it on the sofa in Father's study. Father was out, so we needn't have *crept* so when we were getting into the garden. Then Oswald was restored to consciousness, and his head tied up, and sent to bed, and next day there was a lump on his young brow as big as a turkey's egg, and very uncomfortable.

Albert's uncle came in next day and talked to each of us separately. To Oswald he said many unpleasant things about its being ungentlemanly to spy on ladies, and about minding your own business; and when I began to tell him what I had heard he told me to shut up, and altogether he made me more uncomfortable than the bump did.

Oswald did not say anything to any one, but next day, as the shadows of eve were falling, he crept away, and wrote on a piece of paper, 'I want to speak to you,' and shoved it through the hole like a heart in the top of the next-door shutters.

And the youngest young lady put an eye to the heart-shaped hole, and then opened the shutter and said 'Well?' very crossly.

Then Oswald said –

'I am very sorry, and I beg your pardon. We wanted to be detectives, and we thought a gang of coiners infested your house, so we looked through your window last night. I saw the lettuce, and I heard what you said about the salmon being three-halfpence cheaper, and I know it is very dishonourable to pry into other people's secrets, especially ladies', and I never will again if you will forgive me this once.'

Then the lady frowned and then she laughed, and then she said –

'So it was *you* tumbling into the flower-pots last night? We thought it was burglars. It frightened us horribly. Why, what a bump on your poor head!'

And then she talked to me a bit, and presently she said she and her sister had not wished people to know they were at home, because – and then she stopped short and grew very red, and I said, 'I thought you were all at Scarborough; your servant told Eliza so. Why didn't you want people to know you were at home?'

The lady got redder still, and then she laughed and said –

'Never mind the reason why. I hope your head doesn't hurt much. Thank you for your nice, manly little speech. *You've* nothing to be ashamed of, at any rate.' Then she kissed me, and I did not mind. And then she said, 'Run away now, dear. I'm going

to – I'm going to pull up the blinds and open the shutters, and I
want to do it *at once*, before it gets dark, so that every one can see
we're at home, and not at Scarborough.'

* * *

Chapter 4
Good Hunting

When we had got that four shillings by digging for treasure we
ought, by rights, to have tried Dicky's idea of answering the
advertisement about ladies and gentlemen and spare time and
two pounds a week, but there were several things we rather
wanted.[1]

Dora wanted a new pair of scissors, and she said she was going
to get them with her eightpence. But Alice said –

'You ought to get her those, Oswald, because you know you broke
the points off hers getting the marble out of the brass thimble.'

It was quite true, though I had almost forgotten it, but then it
was H.O. who jammed the marble into the thimble first of all.[2]
So I said –

'It's H.O.'s fault as much as mine, anyhow. Why shouldn't he
pay?'

Oswald didn't so much mind paying for the beastly scissors, but
he hates injustice of every kind.[3]

'He's such a little kid,' said Dicky, and of course H.O. said he
wasn't a little kid, and it very nearly came to being a row between
them. But Oswald knows when to be generous; so he said –

'Look here! I'll pay sixpence of the scissors, and H.O. shall pay
the rest, to teach him to be careful.'

H.O. agreed: he is not at all a mean kid, but I found out afterwards that Alice paid his share out of her own money.[4]

Then we wanted some new paints, and Noël wanted a pencil
and a halfpenny account-book to write poetry with, and it does
seem hard never to have any apples. So, somehow or other nearly

all the money got spent, and we agreed that we must let the advertisement run loose a little longer.[5]

'I only hope,' Alice said, 'that they won't have got all the ladies and gentlemen they want before we have got the money to write for the sample and instructions.'

And I was a little afraid myself, because it seemed such a splendid chance; but we looked in the paper every day, and the advertisement was always there, so we thought it was all right.

Then we had the detective try-on – and it proved no go; and then, when all the money was gone, except a halfpenny of mine and twopence of Noël's and threepence of Dicky's and a few pennies that the girls had left, we held another council.[6]

Dora was sewing the buttons on H.O.'s Sunday things. He got himself a knife with his money, and he cut every single one of his best buttons off.[7] You've no idea how many buttons there are on a suit. Dora counted them. There are twenty-four, counting the little ones on the sleeves that don't undo.

Alice was trying to teach Pincher to beg; but he has too much sense when he knows you've got nothing in your hands, and the rest of us were roasting potatoes under the fire. We had made a fire on purpose, though it was rather warm. They are very good if you cut away the burnt parts – but you ought to wash them first, or you are a dirty boy.

'Well, what can we do?' said Dicky. 'You are so fond of saying "Let's do something!" and never saying what.'[8]

'We can't try the advertisement yet. Shall we try rescuing some one?' said Oswald. It was his own idea, but he didn't insist on doing it, though he is next to the eldest, for he knows it is bad manners to make people do what you want, when they would rather not.

'What was Noël's plan?' Alice asked.

'A Princess or a poetry book,' said Noël sleepily. He was lying on his back on the sofa, kicking his legs. 'Only I shall look for the Princess all by myself. But I'll let you see her when we're married.'[9]

'Have you got enough poetry to make a book?' Dicky asked that, and it was rather sensible of him, because when Noël came to look there were only seven of his poems that any of us could understand. There was the 'Wreck of the Malabar,' and the poem he wrote when Eliza took us to hear the Reviving Preacher, and everybody cried, and Father said it must have been the Preacher's Eloquence.[10] So Noël wrote:

> 'O Eloquence and what art thou?
> Ay, what art thou? because we cried
> And everybody cried inside;
> When they came out their eyes were red –
> And it was your doing, Father said.'

But Noël told Alice he got the first line and a half from a book a boy at school was going to write when he had time. Besides this there were the 'Lines on a Dead Black Beetle that was poisoned': –

> 'O Beetle! how I weep to see
> Thee lying on thy poor back!
> It is so very sad indeed.
> You were so shiny and black.
> I wish you were alive again
> But Eliza says wishing it is nonsense and a shame.'

It was very good beetle poison, and there were hundreds of them lying dead – but Noël only wrote a piece of poetry for one of them. He said he hadn't time to do them all, and the worst of it was he didn't know which one he'd written it to – so Alice couldn't bury the beetle and put the lines on its grave, though she wanted to very much.

Well, it was quite plain that there wasn't enough poetry for a book.

'We might wait a year or two,' said Noël. 'I shall be sure to make some more sometime. I thought of a piece about a fly this morning that knew condensed milk was sticky.'

'But we want the money *now*,' said Dicky, 'and you can go on writing just the same. It will come in sometime or other.'

'There's poetry in newspapers,' said Alice. 'Down, Pincher! you'll never be a clever dog, so it's no good trying.'

'Do they pay for it?' Dicky thought of that; he often thinks of things that are really important, even if they are a little dull.

'I don't know. But I shouldn't think any one would let them print their poetry without. I wouldn't I know.' That was Dora; but Noël said he wouldn't mind if he didn't get paid, so long as he saw his poetry printed and his name at the end.

'We might try, anyway,' said Oswald. He is always willing to give other people's ideas a fair trial.

So we copied out 'The Wreck of the Malabar' and the other six poems on drawing-paper – Dora did it, she writes best – and Oswald drew a picture of the Malabar going down with all hands. It was a full-rigged schooner, and all the ropes and sails were correct; because my cousin is in the Navy, and he showed me.

We thought a long time whether we'd write a letter and send it by post with the poetry – and Dora thought it would be best. But Noël said he couldn't bear not to know at once if the paper would print the poetry, So we decided to take it.

I went with Noël, because I am the eldest of the boys, and he is not old enough to go to London by himself. Dicky said poetry was rot – and he was glad he hadn't got to make a fool of himself: that was because there was not enough money for him to go with us. H.O. couldn't come either, but he came to the station to see us off, and waved his cap and called out 'Good hunting!' as the train started.

There was a lady in spectacles in the corner. She was writing with a pencil on the edges of long strips of paper that had print all down them.

When the train started she asked –

'What was that he said?'

So Oswald answered – 'It was "Good hunting" – it's out of the Jungle Book!'[11]

'That's very pleasant to hear,' the lady said; 'I am very pleased to meet people who know their Jungle Book. And where are you off to – the Zoological Gardens to look for Bagheera?'

We were pleased, too, to meet some one who knew the Jungle Book.

So Oswald said –

'We are going to restore the fallen fortunes of the House of Bastable – and we have all thought of different ways – and we're going to try them all. Noël's way is poetry. I suppose great poets get paid?'

The lady laughed – she was awfully jolly – and said she was a sort of poet, too, and the long strips of paper were the proofs of her new book of stories.[12] Because before a book is made into a real book with pages and a cover, they sometimes print it all on strips of paper, and the writer makes marks on it with a pencil to show the printers what idiots they are not to understand what a writer means to have printed.

We told her all about digging for treasure, and what we meant to do. Then she asked to see Noël's poetry – and he said he didn't like – so she said, 'Look here – if you'll show me yours I'll show you some of mine.' So he agreed.

The jolly lady read Noël's poetry, and she said she liked it very much. And she thought a great deal of the picture of the Malabar. And then she said, 'I write serious poetry like yours myself, too, but I have a piece here that I think you will like because it's about a boy.' She gave it to us – and so I can copy it down, and I will, for it shows that some grown-up ladies are not so silly as others. I like it better than Noël's poetry, though I told him I did not, because he looked as if he was going to cry. This was very wrong, for you should always speak the truth, however unhappy it makes people. And I generally do. But I did not want him crying in the railway carriage. The lady's piece of poetry:

> 'Oh when I wake up in my bed
> And see the sun all fat and red,
> I'm glad to have another day
> For all my different kinds of play.
>
> There are so many things to do –
> The things that make a man of you,
> If grown-ups did not get so vexed
> And wonder what you will do next.
>
> I often wonder whether they
> Ever made up our kinds of play –
> If they were always good as gold
> And only did what they were told.
>
> They like you best to play with tops
> And toys in boxes, bought in shops;

They do not even know the names
Of really interesting games.

They will not let you play with fire
Or trip your sister up with wire,
They grudge the tea-tray for a drum,
Or booby-traps when callers come.

They don't like fishing, and it's true
You sometimes soak a suit or two:
They look on fireworks, though they're dry,
With quite a disapproving eye.

They do not understand the way
To get the most out of your day:
They do not know how hunger feels
Nor what you need between your meals.

And when you're sent to bed at night,
They're happy, but they're not polite.
For through the door you hear them say:
'*He's* done *his* mischief for the day!''

She told us a lot of other pieces but I cannot remember them, and she talked to us all the way up, and when we got nearly to Cannon Street she said – [13]

'I've got two new shillings here! Do you think they would help to smooth the path to Fame?'

Noël said, 'Thank you,' and was going to take the shillings. But Oswald, who always remembers what he is told, said –

'Thank you very much, but Father told us we ought never to take anything from strangers.'

'That's a nasty one,' said the lady – she didn't talk a bit like a real lady, but more like a jolly sort of grown-up boy in a dress and hat – 'a very nasty one! But don't you think as Noël and I are both poets I might be considered a sort of relation? You've heard of brother poets, haven't you? Don't you think Noël and I are aunt and nephew poets, or some relationship of that kind?'

I didn't know what to say, and she went on –

'It's awfully straight of you to stick to what your Father tells you, but look here, you take the shillings, and here's my card. When you get home tell your Father all about it, and if he says No, you can just bring the shillings back to me.'

So we took the shillings, and she shook hands with us and said, 'Goodbye, and good hunting!'

We did tell Father about it, and he said it was all right, and when he looked at the card he told us we were highly honoured, for the lady wrote better poetry than any other lady alive now. We had never heard of her, and she seemed much too jolly for a poet. Good old Kipling! We owe him those two shillings, as well as the Jungle Books!

* * *

Chapter 5
The Poet and the Editor

It was not bad sport – being in London entirely on our own hook. We asked the way to Fleet Street, where Father says all the newspaper offices are. They said straight on down Ludgate Hill – but it turned out to be quite another way. At least *we* didn't go straight on.

We got to St Paul's. Noël *would* go in, and we saw where Gordon was buried – at least the monument. It is very flat, considering what a man he was.[1]

When we came out we walked a long way, and when we asked a policeman he said we'd better go back through Smithfield. So we did. They don't burn people any more there now, so it was rather dull, besides being a long way, and Noël got very tired.[2] He's a peaky little chap; it comes of being a poet, I think. We had a bun or two at different shops – out of the shillings – and it was quite late in the afternoon when we got to Fleet Street. The gas was lighted and the electric lights. There is a jolly Bovril sign that comes off and on in different coloured lamps.[3] We went to the

Daily Recorder office, and asked to see the Editor. It is a big office, very bright, with brass and mahogany and electric lights.

They told us the Editor wasn't there, but at another office. So we went down a dirty street, to a very dull-looking place. There was a man there inside, in a glass case, as if he was a museum, and he told us to write down our names and our business. So Oswald wrote –

OSWALD BASTABLE
NOËL BASTABLE
Business very private indeed.

Then we waited on the stone stairs; it was very draughty. And the man in the glass case looked at us as if we were the museum instead of him. We waited a long time, and then a boy came down and said –

'The Editor can't see you. Will you please write your business?' And he laughed. I wanted to punch his head.[4]

But Noël said, 'Yes, I'll write it if you'll give me a pen and ink, and a sheet of paper and an envelope.'

The boy said he'd better write by post. But Noël is a bit pig-headed; it's his worst fault. So he said –

'No, I'll write it *now*.' So I backed him up by saying –

'Look at the price penny stamps are since the coal strike!'[5]

So the boy grinned, and the man in the glass case gave us pen and paper, and Noël wrote. Oswald writes better than he does; but Noël would do it; and it took a very long time, and then it was inky.[6]

'DEAR MR EDITOR, – I want you to print my poetry and pay for it, and I am a friend of Mrs Leslie's; she is a poet too.

'Your affectionate friend,
'NOËL BASTABLE.'

He licked the envelope a good deal, so that that boy shouldn't read it going upstairs; and he wrote 'Very private' outside, and gave the letter to the boy. I thought it wasn't any good; but in a minute the grinning boy came back, and he was quite respectful, and said –

'The Editor says, please will you step up?'

We stepped up. There were a lot of stairs and passages, and a queer sort of humming, hammering sound and a very funny smell. The boy was now very polite, and said it was the ink we smelt, and the noise was the printing machines.

After going through a lot of cold passages we came to a door; the boy opened it, and let us go in. There was a large room, with a big, soft, blue-and-red carpet, and a roaring fire, though it was only October; and a large table with drawers, and littered with papers, just like the one in Father's study. A gentleman was sitting at one side of the table; he had a light moustache and light eyes, and he looked very young to be an editor – not nearly so old as Father. He looked very tired and sleepy as if he had got up very early in the morning; but he was kind, and we liked him. Oswald thought he looked clever. Oswald is considered a judge of faces.[7]

'Well,' said he, 'so you are Mrs Leslie's friends?'

'I think so,' said Noël; 'at least she gave us each a shilling, and she wished us "good hunting!"'

'Good hunting, eh? Well, what about this poetry of yours? Which is the poet?'

I can't think how he could have asked! Oswald is said to be a very manly-looking boy for his age. However, I thought it would look duffing to be offended, so I said –

'This is my brother Noël. He is the poet.'

Noël had turned quite pale. He is disgustingly like a girl in some ways. The Editor told us to sit down, and he took the poems from Noël, and began to read them. Noël got paler and paler; I really thought he was going to faint, like he did when I held his hand under the cold-water tap, after I had accidentally cut him with my chisel. When the Editor had read the first poem – it was the one about the beetle – he got up and stood with his back to us. It was not manners; but Noël thinks he did it 'to conceal his emotion,' as they do in books.

He read all the poems, and then he said –

'I like your poetry very much, young man. I'll give you – let me see; how much shall I give you for it?'

'As much as ever you can,' said Noël. 'You see I want a good deal of money to restore the fallen fortunes of the house of Bastable.'

The gentleman put on some eye-glasses and looked hard at us. Then he sat down.[8]

'That's a good idea,' said he. 'Tell me how you came to think of it. And, I say, have you had any tea? They've just sent out for mine.'

He rang a tingly bell, and the boy brought in a tray with a tea-pot and a thick cup and saucer and things, and he had to fetch another tray for us, when he was told to; and we had tea with the Editor of the *Daily Recorder*. I suppose it was a very proud moment for Noël, though I did not think of that till afterwards. The Editor asked us a lot of questions, and we told him a good deal, though of course I did not tell a stranger all our reasons for thinking that the family fortunes wanted restoring. We stayed about half an hour, and when we were going away he said again –

'I shall print all your poems, my poet; and now what do you think they're worth?'

'I don't know,' Noël said. 'You see I didn't write them to sell.'

'Why did you write them then?' he asked.

Noël said he didn't know; he supposed because he wanted to.

'Art for Art's sake, eh?' said the Editor, and he seemed quite delighted, as though Noël had said something clever.

'Well, would a guinea meet your views?' he asked.

I have read of people being at a loss for words, and dumb with emotion, and I've read of people being turned to stone with aston-ishment, or joy, or something, but I never knew how silly it looked till I saw Noël standing staring at the Editor with his mouth open. He went red and he went white, and then he got crimson, as if you were rubbing more and more crimson lake on a palette. But he didn't say a word, so Oswald had to say –

'I should jolly well think so.'

So the Editor gave Noël a sovereign and a shilling, and he shook hands with us both, but he thumped Noël on the back and said –

'Buck up, old man! It's your first guinea, but it won't be your last. Now go along home, and in about ten years you can bring me some more poetry. Not before – see? I'm just taking this poetry of yours because I like it very much; but we don't put poetry in this paper at all. I shall have to put it in another paper I know of.'

'What *do* you put in your paper?' I asked, for Father always takes the *Daily Chronicle*, and I didn't know what the *Recorder* was like. We chose it because it has such a glorious office, and a clock out-side lighted up.[9]

'Oh, news,' said he, 'and dull articles, and things about Celebrities. If you know any Celebrities, now?'

Noël asked him what Celebrities were.

'Oh, the Queen and the Princes, and people with titles, and people who write, or sing, or act – or do something clever or wicked.'

'I don't know anybody wicked,' said Oswald, wishing he had known Dick Turpin, or Claude Duval, so as to be able to tell the Editor things about them. 'But I know some one with a title – Lord Tottenham.'

'The mad old Protectionist, eh?[10] How did you come to know him?'

'We don't know him to speak to. But he goes over the Heath every day at three, and he strides along like a giant – with a black cloak like Lord Tennyson's flying behind him, and he talks to himself like one o'clock.'[11]

'What does he say?' The Editor had sat down again, and he was fiddling with a blue pencil.

'We only heard him once, close enough to understand, and then he said, "The curse of the country, sir – ruin and desolation!" And then he went striding along again, hitting at the furze-bushes as if they were the heads of his enemies.'

'Excellent descriptive touch,' said the Editor. 'Well, go on.'

'That's all I know about him, except that he stops in the middle of the Heath every day, and he looks all round to see if there's any one about, and if there isn't, he takes his collar off.'

The Editor interrupted – which is considered rude – and said –

'You're not romancing?'

'I beg your pardon?' said Oswald.

'Drawing the long bow, I mean,' said the Editor.

Oswald drew himself up, and said he wasn't a liar.

The Editor only laughed, and said romancing and lying were not at all the same; only it was important to know what you were playing at. So Oswald accepted his apology, and went on.

'We were hiding among the furze-bushes one day, and we saw him do it. He took off his collar, and he put on a clean one, and he threw the other among the furze-bushes. We picked it up afterwards, and it was a beastly paper one!'[12]

'Thank you,' said the Editor, and he got up and put his hand in his pocket. 'That's well worth five shillings, and there they are. Would you like to see round the printing offices before you go home?'

I pocketed my five bob, and thanked him, and I said we should like it very much. He called another gentleman and said something we couldn't hear. Then he said goodbye again; and all this time Noël hadn't said a word. But now he said, 'I've made a poem about you. It is called "Lines to a Noble Editor." Shall I write it down?'

The Editor gave him the blue pencil, and he sat down at the Editor's table and wrote. It was this, he told me afterwards as well as he could remember –

> 'May Life's choicest blessings be your lot
> I think you ought to be very blest
> For you are going to print my poems –
> And you may have this one as well as the rest.'

'Thank you,' said the Editor. 'I don't think I ever had a poem addressed to me before. I shall treasure it, I assure you.'

Then the other gentleman said something about Mecænas, and we went off to see the printing office with at least one pound seven in our pockets.[13]

It *was* good hunting, and no mistake!

But he never put Noël's poetry in the *Daily Recorder*. It was quite a long time afterwards we saw a sort of story thing in a magazine, on the station bookstall, and that kind, sleepy-looking Editor had written it, I suppose. It was not at all amusing. It said a lot about Noël and me, describing us all wrong, and saying how we had tea with the Editor; and all Noël's poems were in the story thing. I think myself the Editor seemed to make game of them, but Noël was quite pleased to see them printed – so that's all right.[14] It wasn't my poetry anyhow, I am glad to say.

* * *

Chapter 6
Noël's Princess

She happened quite accidentally. We were not looking for a Princess at all just then; but Noël had said he was going to find a Princess all by himself; and marry her – and he really did. Which was rather odd, because when people say things are going to befall, very often they don't. It was different, of course, with the prophets of old.

We did not get any treasure by it, except twelve chocolate drops; but we might have done, and it was an adventure, anyhow.[1]

Greenwich Park is a jolly good place to play in, especially the parts that aren't near Greenwich. The parts near the Heath are first-rate. I often wish the Park was nearer our house; but I suppose a Park is a difficult thing to move.[2]

Sometimes we get Eliza to put lunch in a basket, and we go up to the Park. She likes that – it saves cooking dinner for us; and sometimes she says of her own accord, 'I've made some pasties for you, and you might as well go into the Park as not. It's a lovely day.'

She always tells us to rinse out the cup at the drinking-fountain, and the girls do; but I always put my head under the tap and drink. Then you are an intrepid hunter at a mountain stream – and besides, you're sure it's clean. Dicky does the same, and so does H.O.[3] But Noël always drinks out of the cup. He says it is a golden goblet wrought by enchanted gnomes.

The day the Princess happened was a fine, hot day, last October, and we were quite tired with the walk up to the Park.

We always go in by the little gate at the top of Croom's Hill.[4] It is the postern gate that things always happen at in stories. It was dusty walking, but when we got in the Park it was ripping, so we rested a bit, and lay on our backs, and looked up at the trees, and wished we could play monkeys. I have done it before now, but the Park-keeper makes a row if he catches you.

When we'd rested a little, Alice said –

'It was a long way to the enchanted wood, but it is very nice now we are there. I wonder what we shall find in it?'

'We shall find deer,' said Dicky, 'if we go to look; but they go on the other side of the Park because of the people with buns.'

Saying buns made us think of lunch, so we had it; and when we had done we scratched a hole under a tree and buried the papers, because we know it spoils pretty places to leave beastly, greasy papers lying about. I remember Mother teaching me and Dora that, when we were quite little. I wish everybody's parents would teach them this useful lesson, and the same about orange-peel.

When we'd eaten everything there was, Alice whispered –

'I see the white witch bear yonder among the trees! Let's track it and slay it in its lair.'

'I am the bear,' said Noël; so he crept away, and we followed him among the trees. Often the witch bear was out of sight, and then you didn't know where it would jump out from; but sometimes we saw it, and just followed.

'When we catch it there'll be a great fight,' said Oswald; 'and I shall be Count Folko of Mont Faucon.'[5]

'I'll be Gabrielle,' said Dora. She is the only one of us who likes doing girl's parts.

'I'll be Sintram,' said Alice; 'and H.O. can be the Little Master.'

'What about Dicky?'

'Oh, I can be the Pilgrim with the bones.'

'Hist!' whispered Alice. 'See his white fairy fur gleaming amid yonder covert!'

And I saw a bit of white too. It was Noël's collar, and it had come undone at the back.

We hunted the bear in and out of the trees, and then we lost him altogether; and suddenly we found the wall of the Park – in a place where I'm sure there wasn't a wall before. Noël wasn't anywhere about, and there was a door in the wall. And it was open; so we went through.

'The bear has hidden himself in these mountain fastnesses,' Oswald said. 'I will draw my good sword and after him.'

So I drew the umbrella, which Dora always will bring in case it rains, because Noël gets a cold on the chest at the least thing – and we went on.

The other side of the wall it was a stable yard, all cobble-stones. There was nobody about – but we could hear a man rubbing down a horse and hissing in the stable; so we crept very quietly past, and Alice whispered –

''Tis the lair of the Monster Serpent; I hear his deadly hiss! Beware! Courage and despatch!'

We went over the stones on tiptoe, and we found another wall with another door in it on the other side. We went through that too, on tiptoe. It really was an adventure. And there we were in a shrubbery, and we saw something white through the trees. Dora said it was the white bear. That is so like Dora. She always begins to take part in a play just when the rest of us are getting tired of it. I don't mean this unkindly, because I am very fond of Dora. I cannot forget how kind she was when I had bronchitis; and ingratitude is a dreadful vice.[6] But it is quite true.

'It is not a bear,' said Oswald; and we all went on, still on tiptoe, round a twisty path and on to a lawn, and there was Noël. His collar had come undone, as I said, and he had an inky mark on his face that he made just before we left the house, and he wouldn't let Dora wash it off, and one of his boot-laces was coming down. He was standing looking at a little girl; she was the funniest little girl you ever saw.

She was like a china doll – the sixpenny kind; she had a white face, and long yellow hair, done up very tight in two pigtails; her forehead was very big and lumpy, and her cheeks came high up, like little shelves under her eyes. Her eyes were small and blue. She had on a funny black frock, with curly braid on it, and button boots that went almost up to her knees. Her legs were very thin.[7] She was sitting in a hammock chair nursing a blue kitten – not a sky-blue one, of course, but the colour of a new slate pencil. As we came up we heard her say to Noël –

'Who are you?'

Noël had forgotten about the bear, and he was taking his favourite part, so he said –

'I'm Prince Camaralzaman.'[8]

The funny little girl looked pleased –

'I thought at first you were a common boy,' she said. Then she saw the rest of us and said –

'Are you all Princesses and Princes too?'

Of course we said 'Yes,' and she said –

'I am a Princess also.' She said it very well too, exactly as if it were true. We were very glad, because it is so seldom you meet any children who can begin to play right off without having everything explained to them. And even then they will say they are going to 'pretend to be' a lion, or a witch, or a king. Now this little girl just said 'I *am* a Princess.' Then she looked at Oswald and said, 'I fancy I've seen you at Baden.'

Of course Oswald said, 'Very likely.'

The little girl had a funny voice, and all her words were quite plain, each word by itself; she didn't talk at all like we do.

H.O. asked her what the cat's name was, and she said 'Katinka.' Then Dicky said –

'Let's get away from the windows; if you play near windows some one inside generally knocks at them and says "Don't."'

The Princess put down the cat very carefully and said –

'I am forbidden to walk off the grass.'

'That's a pity,' said Dora.[9]

'But I will if you like,' said the Princess.

'You mustn't do things you are forbidden to do,' Dora said; but Dicky showed us that there was some more grass beyond the shrubs with only a gravel path between. So I lifted the Princess over the gravel, so that she should be able to say she hadn't walked off the grass. When we got to the other grass we all sat down, and the Princess asked us if we liked 'dragées' (I know that's how you spell it, for I asked Albert-next-door's uncle).[10]

We said we thought not, but she pulled a real silver box out of her pocket and showed us; they were just flat, round chocolates. We had two each. Then we asked her her name, and she began, and when she began she went on, and on, and on, till I thought she was never going to stop. H.O. said she had fifty names, but Dicky is very good at figures, and he says there were only eighteen. The first were Pauline, Alexandra, Alice, and Mary was one, and Victoria, for we all heard that, and it ended up with Hildegarde Cunigonde something or other, Princess of something else.[11]

When she'd done, H.O. said, 'That's jolly good! Say it again!' and she did, but even then we couldn't remember it. We told her our names, but she thought they were too short, so when it was Noël's turn he said he was Prince Noël Camaralzaman Ivan Constantine Charlemagne James John Edward Biggs Maximilian Bastable Prince of Lewisham, but when she asked him to say it again of course he could only get the first two names right, because he'd made it up as he went on.[12]

So the Princess said, 'You are quite old enough to know your own name.' She was very grave and serious.

She told us that she was the fifth cousin of Queen Victoria. We asked who the other cousins were, but she did not seem to understand. She went on and said she was seven times removed. She couldn't tell us what that meant either, but Oswald thinks it means that the Queen's cousins are so fond of her that they will keep coming bothering, so the Queen's servants have orders to remove them. This little girl must have been very fond of the Queen to try so often to see her, and to have been seven times removed. We could see that it is considered something to be proud of; but we thought it was hard on the Queen that her cousins wouldn't let her alone.

Presently the little girl asked us where our maids and governesses were.

We told her we hadn't any just now. And she said –

'How pleasant! And did you come here alone?'

'Yes,' said Dora; 'we came across the Heath.'

'You are very fortunate,' said the little girl. She sat very upright on the grass, with her fat little hands in her lap. 'I should like to go on the Heath. There are donkeys there, with white saddle covers. I should like to ride them, but my governess will not permit.'

'I'm glad we haven't a governess,' H.O. said. 'We ride the donkeys whenever we have any pennies, and once I gave the man another penny to make it gallop.'

'You are indeed fortunate!' said the Princess again, and when she looked sad the shelves on her cheeks showed more than ever. You could have laid a sixpence on them quite safely if you had had one.

'Never mind,' said Noël; 'I've got a lot of money. Come out and have a ride now.'[13] But the little girl shook her head and said she was afraid it would not be correct.

Dora said she was quite right; then all of a sudden came one of those uncomfortable times when nobody can think of anything to say, so we sat and looked at each other. But at last Alice said we ought to be going.[14]

'Do not go yet,' the little girl said. 'At what time did they order your carriage?'

'Our carriage is a fairy one, drawn by griffins, and it comes when we wish for it,' said Noël.

The little girl looked at him very queerly, and said, 'That is out of a picture-book.'

Then Noël said he thought it was about time he was married if we were to be home in time for tea. The little girl was rather stupid over it, but she did what we told her, and we married them with

Dora's pocket-handkerchief for a veil, and the ring off the back of one of the buttons on H.O.'s blouse just went on her little finger.

Then we showed her how to play cross-touch, and puss in the corner, and tag. It was funny, she didn't know any games but battledore and shuttlecock and les graces.[15] But she really began to laugh at last and not to look quite so like a doll.

She was Puss and was running after Dicky when suddenly she stopped short and looked as if she was going to cry. And we looked too, and there were two prim ladies with little mouths and tight hair. One of them said in quite an awful voice, 'Pauline, who are these children?' and her voice was gruff; with very curly R's.[16]

The little girl said we were Princes and Princesses – which was silly, to a grown-up person that is not a great friend of yours.

The gruff lady gave a short, horrid laugh, like a husky bark, and said –

'Princes, indeed! They're only common children!'

Dora turned very red and began to speak, but the little girl cried out 'Common children! Oh, I am so glad! When I am grown up I'll always play with common children.'

And she ran at us, and began to kiss us one by one, beginning with Alice; she had got to H.O. when the horrid lady said –

'Your Highness – go indoors at once!'

The little girl answered, 'I won't!' Then the prim lady said –

'Wilson, carry her Highness indoors.'

And the little girl was carried away screaming, and kicking with her little thin legs and her buttoned boots, and between her screams she shrieked: 'Common children! I am glad, glad, glad! Common children! Common children!'

The nasty lady then remarked –

'Go at once, or I will send for the police!'

So we went. H.O. made a face at her and so did Alice, but Oswald took off his cap and said he was sorry if she was annoyed about anything; for Oswald has always been taught to be polite to ladies, however nasty. Dicky took his off, too, when he saw me do it; he says he did it first, but that is a mistake. If I were really a common boy I should say it was a lie.

Then we all came away, and when we got outside Dora said, 'So she was really a Princess. Fancy a Princess living *there*!'

'Even Princesses have to live somewhere,' said Dicky.

'And I thought it was play. And it was real. I wish I'd known! I should have liked to ask her lots of things,' said Alice.

H.O. said he would have liked to ask her what she had for dinner and whether she had a crown.

I felt, myself, we had lost a chance of finding out a great deal about kings and queens. I might have known such a stupid-looking little girl would never have been able to pretend, as well as that.

So we all went home across the Heath, and made dripping toast for tea.

When we were eating it Noël said, 'I wish I could give *her* some! It is very good.'

He sighed as he said it, and his mouth was very full, so we knew he was thinking of his Princess. He says now that she was as beautiful as the day, but we remember her quite well, and she was nothing of the kind.

* * *

Chapter 7
Being Bandits

Noël was quite tiresome for ever so long after we found the Princess. He would keep on wanting to go to the Park when the rest of us didn't, and though we went several times to please him, we never found that door open again, and all of us except him knew from the first that it would be no go.

So now we thought it was time to do something to rouse him from the stupor of despair, which is always done to heroes when anything baffling has occurred. Besides, we were getting very short of money again – the fortunes of your house cannot be restored (not so that they will last, that is), even by the one pound eight we got when we had the 'good hunting.' We spent a good deal of that on presents for Father's birthday. We got him a paper-weight, like a glass bun, with a picture of Lewisham Church at the bottom; and a blotting-pad, and a box of preserved fruits, and an ivory penholder with a view of Greenwich Park in the little hole where you look through at the top. He was most awfully pleased and surprised, and when he heard how Noël and Oswald had earned the money to buy the things he was more surprised still. Nearly all the rest of our money went to get fireworks for the Fifth of November. We got six Catherine wheels and four rockets; two hand-lights, one red and one green; a sixpenny maroon; two Roman-candles – they cost a shilling; some Italian streamers, a fairy fountain, and a tourbillon that cost eighteenpence and was very nearly worth it.

But I think crackers and squibs are a mistake. It's true you get a lot of them for the money, and they are not bad fun for the first two or three dozen, but you get jolly sick of them before you've let off your sixpenn'orth. And the only amusing way is not allowed: it is putting them in the fire.

It always seems a long time till the evening when you have got fireworks in the house, and I think as it was a rather foggy day we should have decided to let them off directly after breakfast, only Father had said he would help us to let them off at eight o'clock after he had had his dinner, and you ought never to disappoint your Father if you can help it.

You see we had three good reasons for trying H.O.'s idea of restoring the fallen fortunes of our house by becoming bandits on the Fifth of November. We had a fourth reason as well, and that was the best reason of the lot. You remember Dora thought it would be wrong to be bandits. And the Fifth of November came while Dora was away at Stroud staying with her godmother. Stroud is in Gloucestershire. We were determined to do it while she was out of the way, because we did not think it wrong, and besides we meant to do it anyhow.

We held a Council, of course, and laid our plans very carefully. We let H.O. be Captain, because it was his idea. Oswald was Lieutenant. Oswald was quite fair, because he let H.O. call himself Captain; but Oswald is the eldest next to Dora, after all.

Our plan was this. We were all to go up on to the Heath. Our house is in the Lewisham Road, but it's quite close to the Heath if you cut up the short way opposite the confectioner's, past the nursery gardens and the cottage hospital, and turn to the left again and afterwards to the right. You come out then at the top of the hill, where the big guns are with the iron fence round them, and where the bands play on Thursday evenings in the summer.[1]

We were to lurk in ambush there, and waylay an unwary traveller. We were to call upon him to surrender his arms, and then bring him home and put him in the deepest dungeon below the castle moat; then we were to load him with chains and send to his friends for ransom.

You may think we had no chains, but you are wrong, because we used to keep two other dogs once, besides Pincher, before the fall of the fortunes of the ancient House of Bastable. And they were quite big dogs.

It was latish in the afternoon before we started. We thought we could lurk better if it was nearly dark. It was rather foggy, and we waited a good while beside the railings, but all the belated travellers were either grown up or else they were Board School children.[2] We weren't going to get into a row with grown-up people – especially strangers – and no true bandit would ever stoop to ask a ransom from the relations of the poor and needy. So we thought it better to wait.

As I said, it was Guy Fawkes Day, and if it had not been we should never have been able to be bandits at all, for the unwary traveller we did catch had been forbidden to go out because he had a cold in his head. But he would run out to follow a guy, without even putting on a coat or a comforter, and it was a very damp, foggy afternoon and nearly dark, so you see it was his own fault entirely, and served him jolly well right.

We saw him coming over the Heath just as we were deciding to go home to tea. He had followed that guy right across to the village (we call Blackheath the village; I don't know why), and he was coming back dragging his feet and sniffing.[3]

'Hist, an unwary traveller approaches!' whispered Oswald.

'Muffle your horses' heads and see to the priming of your pistols,' muttered Alice. She always will play boys' parts, and she makes Ellis cut her hair short on purpose. Ellis is a very obliging hairdresser.

'Steal softly upon him,' said Noël; 'for lo! 'tis dusk, and no human eyes can mark our deeds.'

So we ran out and surrounded the unwary traveller. It turned out to be Albert-next-door, and he was very frightened indeed until he saw who we were.

'Surrender!' hissed Oswald, in a desperate-sounding voice, as he caught the arm of the Unwary. And Albert-next-door said, 'All right! I'm surrendering as hard as I can. You needn't pull my arm off.'

We explained to him that resistance was useless, and I think he saw that from the first. We held him tight by both arms, and we marched him home down the hill in a hollow square of five.

He wanted to tell us about the guy, but we made him see that it was not proper for prisoners to talk to the guard, especially about guys that the prisoner had been told not to go after because of his cold.

When we got to where we live he said, 'All right, I don't want to tell you. You'll wish I had afterwards. You never saw such a guy.'

'I can see *you*!' said H.O. It was very rude, and Oswald told him so at once, because it is his duty as an elder brother. But H.O. is very young and does not know better yet, and besides it wasn't bad for H.O.

Albert-next-door said, 'You haven't any manners, and I want to go in to my tea. Let go of me!'

But Alice told him, quite kindly, that he was not going in to his tea, but coming with us.

'I'm not,' said Albert-next-door; 'I'm going home. Leave go! I've got a bad cold. You're making it worse.' Then he tried to cough, which was very silly, because we'd seen him in the morning, and he'd told us where the cold was that he wasn't to go out with. When he had tried to cough, he said, 'Leave go of me! You see my cold's getting worse.'

'You should have thought of that before,' said Dicky; 'you're coming in with us.'

'Don't be a silly,' said Noël; 'you know we told you at the very beginning that resistance was useless. There is no disgrace in yielding. We are five to your one.'

By this time Eliza had opened the door, and we thought it best to take him in without any more parlaying. To parley with a prisoner is not done by bandits.

Directly we got him safe into the nursery, H.O. began to jump about and say, 'Now you're a prisoner really and truly!'

And Albert-next-door began to cry. He always does. I wonder he didn't begin long before – but Alice fetched him one of the dried fruits we gave Father for his birthday. It was a green walnut. I have noticed the walnuts and the plums always get left till the last in the box; the apricots go first, and then the figs and pears; and the cherries, if there are any.

So he ate it and shut up. Then we explained his position to him, so that there should be no mistake, and he couldn't say afterwards that he had not understood.

'There will be no violence,' said Oswald – he was now Captain of the Bandits, because we all know H.O. likes to be Chaplain when we play prisoners – 'no violence. But you will be confined in a dark, subterranean dungeon where toads and snakes crawl, and but little of the light of day filters through the heavily mullioned windows. You will be loaded with chains. Now don't begin again, Baby, there's nothing to cry about; straw will be your pallet; beside you the gaoler will set a ewer – a ewer is only a jug, stupid; it won't eat you – a ewer with water; and a mouldering crust will be your food.'

But Albert-next-door never enters into the spirit of a thing. He mumbled something about tea-time.

Now Oswald, though stern, is always just, and besides we were all rather hungry, and tea was ready. So we had it at once, Albert-next-door and all – and we gave him what was left of the four-pound jar of apricot jam we got with the money Noël got for his poetry. And we saved our crusts for the prisoner.

Albert-next-door was very tiresome. Nobody could have had a nicer prison than he had. We fenced him into a corner with the old wire nursery fender and all the chairs, instead of putting him in the coal-cellar as we had first intended. And when he said the dog-chains were cold the girls were kind enough to warm his fetters thoroughly at the fire before we put them on him.

We got the straw cases of some bottles of wine someone sent Father one Christmas – it is some years ago, but the cases are quite good. We unpacked them very carefully and pulled them to pieces and scattered the straw about. It made a lovely straw pallet, and took ever so long to make – but Albert-next-door has yet to learn what gratitude really is. We got the bread trencher for the wooden platter where the prisoner's crusts were put –

they were not mouldy, but we could not wait till they got so, and for the ewer we got the toilet jug out of the spare-room where nobody ever sleeps. And even then Albert-next-door couldn't be happy like the rest of us. He howled and cried and tried to get out, and he knocked the ewer over and stamped on the mouldering crusts. Luckily there was no water in the ewer because we had forgotten it, only dust and spiders. So we tied him up with the clothes line from the back kitchen, and we had to hurry up, which was a pity for him. We might have had him rescued by a devoted page if he hadn't been so tiresome. In fact Noël was actually dressing up for the page when Albert-next-door kicked over the prison ewer.

We got a sheet of paper out of an old exercise-book, and we made H.O. prick his own thumb, because he is our little brother and it is our duty to teach him to be brave. We none of us mind pricking ourselves; we've done it heaps of times. H.O. didn't like it, but he agreed to do it, and I helped him a little because he was so slow, and when he saw the red bead of blood getting fatter and bigger as I squeezed his thumb he was very pleased, just as I had told him he would be.

This is what we wrote with H.O.'s blood, only the blood gave out when we got to 'Restored,' and we had to write the rest with crimson lake, which is not the same colour, though I always use it, myself, for painting wounds.

While Oswald was writing it he heard Alice whispering to the prisoner that it would soon be over, and it was only play. The prisoner left off howling, so I pretended not to hear what she said. A Bandit Captain has to overlook things sometimes. This was the letter –

'Albert Morrison is held a prisoner by Bandits. On payment of three thousand pounds he will be restored to his sorrowing relatives, and all will be forgotten and forgiven.'

I was not sure about the last part, but Dicky was certain he had seen it in the paper, so I suppose it must have been all right.

We let H.O. take the letter; it was only fair, as it was his blood it was written with, and told him to leave it next door for Mrs Morrison.

H.O. came back quite quickly, and Albert-next-door's uncle came with him.

'What is all this, Albert?' he cried. 'Alas, alas, my nephew! Do I find you the prisoner of a desperate band of brigands?'

'Bandits,' said H. O; 'you know it says bandits.'

'I beg your pardon, gentlemen,' said Albert-next-door's uncle, 'bandits it is, of course. This, Albert, is the direct result of the pursuit of the guy on an occasion when your doting mother had expressly warned you to forgo the pleasures of the chase.'

Albert said it wasn't his fault, and he hadn't wanted to play.

'So ho!' said his uncle, 'impenitent too! Where's the dungeon?'

We explained the dungeon, and showed him the straw pallet and the ewer and the mouldering crusts and other things.

'Very pretty and complete,' he said. 'Albert, you are more highly privileged than ever I was. No one ever made me a nice dungeon when I was your age. I think I had better leave you where you are.'

Albert began to cry again and said he was sorry, and he would be a good boy.

'And on this old familiar basis you expect me to ransom you, do you? Honestly, my nephew, I doubt whether you are worth it. Besides, the sum mentioned in this document strikes me as excessive: Albert really is *not* worth three thousand pounds. Also by a strange and unfortunate chance I haven't the money about me. Couldn't you take less?'

We said perhaps we could.

'Say eightpence,' suggested Albert-next-door's uncle, 'which is all the small change I happen to have on my person.'

'Thank you very much,' said Alice as he held it out; 'but are you sure you can spare it? Because really it was only play.'

'Quite sure. Now, Albert, the game is over. You had better run home to your mother and tell her how much you've enjoyed yourself.'

When Albert-next-door had gone his uncle sat in the Guy Fawkes armchair and took Alice on his knee, and we sat round the fire waiting till it would be time to let off our fireworks. We roasted the chestnuts he sent Dicky out for, and he told us stories till it was nearly seven. His stories are first-rate – he does all the parts in different voices. At last he said –

'Look here, young uns. I like to see you play and enjoy yourselves, and I don't think it hurts Albert to enjoy himself too.'

'I don't think he did much,' said H.O. But I knew what Albert-next-door's uncle meant because I am much older than H.O. He went on –

'But what about Albert's Mother? Didn't you think how anxious she would be at his not coming home? As it happens I saw him come in with you, so we knew it was all right. But if I hadn't, eh?'

He only talks like that when he is very serious, or even angry. Other times he talks like people in books – to us, I mean.

We none of us said anything. But I was thinking. Then Alice spoke.

Girls seem not to mind saying things that we don't say. She put her arms round Albert-next-door's uncle's neck and said –

'We're very, very sorry. We didn't think about his Mother. You see we try very hard not to think about other people's Mothers because – '

Just then we heard Father's key in the door and Albert-next-door's uncle kissed Alice and put her down, and we all went down to meet Father. As we went I thought I heard Albert-next-door's uncle say something that sounded like 'Poor little beggars!'

He couldn't have meant us, when we'd been having such a jolly time, and chestnuts, and fireworks to look forward to after dinner and everything!

∗ ∗ ∗

Chapter 8
Being Editors

It was Albert's uncle who thought of our trying a newspaper. He said he thought we should not find the bandit business a paying industry, as a permanency, and that journalism might be.

We had sold Noël's poetry and that piece of information about Lord Tottenham to the good editor, so we thought it would not be a bad idea to have a newspaper of our own. We saw plainly that editors must be very rich and powerful, because of the grand office and the man in the glass case, like a museum, and the soft carpets and big writing-table. Besides our having seen a whole handful of money that the editor pulled out quite carelessly from his trousers pocket when he gave me my five bob.

Dora wanted to be editor and so did Oswald, but he gave way to her because she is a girl, and afterwards he knew that it is true what it says in the copy-books about Virtue being its own Reward.[1] Because you've no idea what a bother it is. Everybody wanted to put in everything just as they liked, no matter how much room there was on the page. It was simply awful! Dora put up with it as long as she could and then she said if she wasn't let alone she wouldn't go on being editor; they could be the paper's editors themselves, so there.

Then Oswald said, like a good brother: 'I will help you if you like, Dora,' and she said, 'You're more trouble than all the rest of them! Come and be editor and see how you like it. I give it up to you.' But she didn't, and we did it together. We let Albert-next-door be sub-editor, because he had hurt his foot with a nail in his boot that gathered.

When it was done Albert-next-door's uncle had it copied for us in typewriting, and we sent copies to all our friends, and then of course there was no one left that we could ask to buy it. We did not think of that until too late. We called the paper the *Lewisham Recorder*; Lewisham because we live there, and Recorder in memory of the good editor. I could write a better paper on my head, but an editor is not allowed to write all the paper. It is very hard, but he is not. You just have to fill up with what you can get from other writers. If I ever have time I will write a paper all by myself. It won't be patchy. We had no time to make it an illustrated paper, but I drew the ship going down with all hands for the first copy. But the typewriter can't draw ships, so it was left out in the other copies. The time the first paper took to write out no one would believe! This was the Newspaper: –

The Lewisham Recorder.
EDITORS: DORA AND OSWALD BASTABLE.

———

EDITORIAL NOTE.

Every paper is written for some reason. Ours is because we want to sell it and get money. If what we have written brings happiness to any sad heart we shall not have laboured in vain. But we want the money too. Many papers are content with the sad heart and the happiness, but we are not like that, and it is best not to be deceitful. – EDITORS.

———

There will be two serial stories; One by Dicky and one by all of us. In a serial story you only put in one chapter at a time. But we shall put all our serial story at once, if Dora has time to copy it. Dicky's will come later on.

———

SERIAL STORY.
BY US ALL
CHAPTER I. – *By Dora.*

The sun was setting behind a romantic-looking tower when two strangers might have been observed descending the crest of the hill. The eldest, a man in the prime of life; the other a handsome youth who reminded everybody of Quentin Durward.[2] They approached the Castle, in which the fair Lady Alicia awaited her deliverers. She leaned from the castellated window and waved her lily hand as they approached. They returned her signal, and retired to seek rest and refreshment at a neighbouring hostelry.

———

CHAPTER II. – *By Alice.*

The Princess was very uncomfortable in the tower, because her fairy godmother had told her all sorts of horrid things would happen if she didn't catch a mouse every day, and she had caught so many mice that now there were hardly any left to catch. So she sent her carrier pigeon to ask the noble strangers if they could send her a few mice – because she would be of age in a few days and then it wouldn't matter. So the fairy godmother————(I'm very sorry, but there's no room to make the chapters any longer. – ED.)

———

CHAPTER III. – *By the Sub-Editor.*

(I can't – I'd much rather not – I don't know how.)

———

CHAPTER IV. – *By Dicky.*

I must now retrace my steps and tell you something about our hero. You must know he had been to an awfully jolly school, where they had turkey and goose every day for dinner, and never any mutton, and as many helps of pudding as a fellow cared to send up his plate for – so of course they had all grown up very strong, and before he left school he challenged the Head to have it out man to man, and he gave it him, I tell you. That was the education that made him able to fight Red Indians, and to be the stranger who might have been observed in the first chapter.

———

CHAPTER V. – *By Noël.*

I think it's time something happened in this story. So then the dragon he came out, blowing fire out of his nose, and he said –

'Come on, you valiant man and true,
I'd like to have a set-to along of you!'

(That's bad English. – ED. I don't care; it's what the dragon said. Who told you dragons didn't talk bad English? – NOËL.)

So the hero, whose name was Noëloninuris, replied –

'My blade is sharp, my axe is keen,
You're not nearly as big as a good many dragons I've seen.'

(Don't put in so much poetry, Noël. It's not fair, because none of the others can do it. – ED.)

And then they went at it, and he beat the dragon, just as he did the Head in Dicky's part of the Story, and so he married the Princess, and they lived————(No they didn't – not till the last chapter. – ED.)

————

CHAPTER VI. – *By H.O.*

I think it's a very nice story – but what about the mice? I don't want to say any more. Dora can have what's left of my chapter.

————

CHAPTER VII. – *By the Editors.*

And so when the dragon was dead there were lots of mice, because he used to kill them for his tea but now they rapidly multiplied and ravaged the country, so the fair lady Alicia, sometimes called the Princess, had to say she would not marry any one unless they could rid the country of this plague of mice. Then the Prince, whose real name didn't begin with N, but was Osrawalddo, waved his magic sword, and the dragon stood before them, bowing gracefully. They made him promise to be good, and then they forgave him; and when the wedding breakfast came, all the bones were saved for him. And so they were married and lived happy ever after.

(What became of the other stranger? – NOËL. The dragon ate him because he asked too many questions. – EDITORS.)

This is the end of the story.

INSTRUCTIVE.

It only takes four hours and a quarter now to get from London to Manchester; but I should not think any one would if they could help it.

————

A dreadful warning. – A wicked boy told me a very instructive thing about ginger. They had opened one of the large jars, and he happened to take out quite a lot, and he made it all right by dropping marbles in, till there was as much ginger as before. But he told me that on the Sunday, when it was coming near the part where there is only juice generally, I had no idea what his feelings were. I don't see what he could have said when they asked him. I should be sorry to act like it.

———

SCIENTIFIC.

Experiments should always be made out of doors. And don't use benzoline. – DICKY.

(That was when he burnt his eyebrows off. – ED.)

———

The earth is 2,400 miles round, and 800 through – at least I think so, but perhaps it's the other way. – DICKY.

(You ought to have been sure before you began. – ED.)

———

SCIENTIFIC COLUMN.

In this so-called Nineteenth Century Science is but too little considered in the nurseries of the rich and proud. But we are not like that.

It is not generally known that if you put bits of camphor in luke-warm water it will move about. If you drop sweet oil in, the camphor will dart away and then stop moving. But don't drop any till you are tired of it, because the camphor won't any more afterwards. Much amusement and instruction is lost by not knowing things like this.

If you put a sixpence under a shilling in a wine-glass, and blow hard down the side of the glass, the sixpence will jump up and sit on the top of the shilling. At least I can't do it myself, but my cousin can. He is in the Navy.

———

ANSWERS TO CORRESPONDENTS.

Noël. – You are very poetical, but I am sorry to say it will not do.

Alice. – Nothing will ever make your hair curl, so it's no use. Some people say it's more important to tidy up as you go along. I don't mean you in particular, but every one.

H.O. – We never said you were tubby, but the Editor does not know any cure.

Noël. – If there is any of the paper over when this newspaper is finished, I will exchange it for your shut-up inkstand, or the knife that has the useful thing in it for taking stones out of horses' feet, but you can't have it without.

H.O. – There are many ways how your steam engine might stop working. You might ask Dicky. He knows one of them. I think it is the way yours stopped.

Noël. – If you think that by filling the garden with sand you can make crabs build their nests there you are not at all sensible.

You have altered your poem about the battle of Waterloo so often that we cannot read it except where the Duke waves his sword and says some thing we can't read either. Why did you write it on blotting-paper with purple chalk? – ED.

(Because YOU KNOW WHO sneaked my pencil. – NOËL.)

———

POETRY.

The Assyrian came down like a wolf on the fold,
And the way he came down was awful, I'm told;
But it's nothing to the way one of the Editors comes down on me,
If I crumble my bread-and-butter or spill my tea.[3]   – NOËL.

———

CURIOUS FACTS.

If you hold a guinea-pig up by his tail his eyes drop out.

You can't do half the things yourself that children in books do, making models or so on. I wonder why? – ALICE.

If you take a date's stone out and put in an almond and eat them together, it is prime. I found this out. – SUB-EDITOR.

If you put your wet hand into boiling lead it will not hurt you if you draw it out quickly enough. I have never tried this. – DORA.

––––––

THE PURRING CLASS.
(*Instructive Article.*)

If I ever keep a school everything shall be quite different. Nobody shall learn anything they don't want to. And sometimes instead of having masters and mistresses we will have cats, and we will dress up in cat skins and learn purring.

'Now, my dears,' the old cat will say, 'one, two, three all purr together,' and we shall purr like anything.

She won't teach us to mew, but we shall know how without teaching. Children do know some things without being taught. – ALICE.

––––––

POETRY.
(*Translated into French by Dora*)

Quand j'étais jeune et j'étais fou
J'achetai un violon pour dix-huit sous
Et tous les airs que je jouai
Était over the hills and far away.[4]

––––––

Another piece of it.

Mercie jolie vache qui fait
Bon lait pour mondéjeuner

Tous les matins tous les soirs
Mon pain je mange, ton lait je boire.[5]

———

RECREATIONS

It is a mistake to think that cats are playful. I often try to get a cat to play with me, and she never seems to care about the game, no matter how little it hurts. – H.O.

Making pots and pans with clay is fun, but do not tell the grown-ups. It is better to surprise them; and then you must say at once how easily it washes off – much easier than ink. – DICKY.

———

SAM REDFERN, OR THE BUSHRANGER'S BURIAL.[6]
By Dicky

'Well, Annie, I have bad news for you,' said Mr Ridgway, as he entered the comfortable dining-room of his cabin in the Bush. 'Sam Redfern the Bushranger is about this part of the Bush just now. I hope he will not attack us with his gang.'

'I hope not,' responded Annie, a gentle maiden of some sixteen summers.

Just then came a knock at the door of the hut, and a gruff voice asked them to open the door.

'It is Sam Redfern the Bushranger, father,' said the girl.

'The same,' responded the voice, and the next moment the hall door was smashed in, and Sam Redfern sprang in, followed by his gang.

———

CHAPTER II.

Annie's Father was at once overpowered, and Annie herself lay bound with cords on the drawing-room sofa. Sam Redfern set a guard round the lonely hut, and all human aid was despaired of. But you never know. Far away in the Bush a different scene was being enacted.

'Must be Injuns,' said a tall man to himself as he pushed his way through the brushwood. It was Jim Carlton, the celebrated detective. 'I know them,' he added; 'they are Apaches.' Just then ten Indians in full war-paint appeared. Carlton raised his rifle and fired, and slinging their scalps on his arm he hastened towards the humble log hut where resided his affianced bride, Annie Ridgway, sometimes known as the Flower of the Bush.

———

Chapter III.

The moon was low on the horizon, and Sam Redfern was seated at a drinking bout with some of his boon companions.

They had rifled the cellars of the hut, and the rich wines flowed like water in the golden goblets of Mr Ridgway.

But Annie had made friends with one of the gang, a noble, good-hearted man who had joined Sam Redfern by mistake, and she had told him to go and get the police as quickly as possible.

'Ha! ha!' cried Redfern, 'now I am enjoying myself!' He little knew that his doom was near upon him.

Just then Annie gave a piercing scream, and Sam Redfern got up, seizing his revolver.

'Who are you?' he cried, as a man entered.

'I am Jim Carlton, the celebrated detective,' said the new arrival.

Sam Redfern's revolver dropped from his nerveless fingers, but the next moment he had sprung upon the detective with the well-known activity of the mountain sheep, and Annie shrieked, for she had grown to love the rough Bushranger.

(To be continued at the end of the paper if there is room.)

———

Scholastic.

A new slate is horrid till it is washed in milk. I like the green spots on them to draw patterns round. I know a good way to make a slate-pencil squeak, but I won't put it in because I don't want to make it common.[7] – Sub-Editor.

Peppermint is a great help with arithmetic. The boy who was second in the Oxford Local always did it.[8] He gave me two. The examiner said to him, 'Are you eating peppermints?' And he said, 'No, Sir.' He told me afterwards it was quite true, because he was only sucking one. I'm glad I wasn't asked. I should never have thought of that, and I would have had to say 'Yes.' – OSWALD.

————

THE WRECK OF THE 'MALABAR'
By Noël

(Author of 'A Dream of Ancient Ancestors.') He isn't really – but he put it in to make it seem more real.

Hark! what is that noise of rolling
    Waves and thunder in the air?
'Tis the death-knell of the sailors
    And officers and passengers of the good ship *Malabar*.

It was a fair and lovely noon
    When the good ship put out of port
And people said 'ah little we think
    How soon she will be the elements' sport.'

She was indeed a lovely sight
    Upon the billows with sails spread.
But the captain folded his gloomy arms,
    Ah – if she had been a life-boat instead!

See the captain stern yet gloomy
    Flings his son upon a rock,
Hoping that there his darling boy
    May escape the wreck.

Alas in vain the loud winds roared
    And nobody was saved.
That was the wreck of the *Malabar,*
    Then let us toll for the brave. – NOËL.

————

Gardening Notes.

It is useless to plant cherry-stones in the hope of eating the fruit, because they don't!

Alice won't lend her gardening tools again, because the last time Noël left them out in the rain, and I don't like it. He said he didn't.

———

Seeds and Bulbs.

These are useful to play at shop with, until you are ready. Not at dinner-parties, for they will not grow unless uncooked. Potatoes are not grown with seed, but with chopped-up potatoes. Apple trees are grown from twigs, which is less wasteful.

Oak trees come from acorns. Every one knows this. When Noël says he could grow one from a peach stone wrapped up in oak leaves, he shows that he knows nothing about gardening but marigolds, and when I passed by his garden I thought they seemed just like weeds now the flowers have been picked.

A boy once dared me to eat a bulb.

Dogs are very industrious and fond of gardening. Pincher is always planting bones, but they never grow up. There couldn't be a bone tree. I think this is what makes him bark so unhappily at night. He has never tried planting dog-biscuit, but he is fonder of bones, and perhaps he wants to be quite sure about them first.

———

Sam Redfern, or the Bushranger's Burial.
By Dicky.
Chapter IV. and Last.

This would have been a jolly good story if they had let me finish it at the beginning of the paper as I wanted to. But now I have forgotten how I meant it to end, and I have lost my book about Red Indians, and all my *Boys of England* have been sneaked. The girls say 'Good riddance!' so I expect they did it.

They want me just to put in which Annie married, but I shan't, so they will never know.

———

We have now put everything we can think of into the paper. It takes a lot of thinking about. I don't know how grown-ups manage to write all they do. It must make their heads ache, especially lesson books.

Albert-next-door only wrote one chapter of the serial story, but he could have done some more if he had wanted to. He could not write out any of the things because he cannot spell. He says he can, but it takes him such a long time he might just as well not be able. There are one or two things more. I am sick of it, but Dora says she will write them in.

Legal answer wanted. – A quantity of excellent string is offered if you know whether there really is a law passed about not buying gunpowder under thirteen. – DICKY.

The price of this paper is one shilling each, and sixpence extra for the picture of the *Malabar* going down with all hands. If we sell one hundred copies we will write another paper.

* * *

And so we would have done, but we never did. Albert-next-door's uncle gave us two shillings, that was all. You can't restore fallen fortunes with two shillings!

* * *

Chapter 9
The G.B.

Being editors is not the best way to wealth. We all feel this now, and highwaymen are not respected any more like they used to be.

I am sure we had tried our best to restore our fallen fortunes. We felt their fall very much, because we knew the Bastables had been rich once. Dora and Oswald can remember when Father was always bringing nice things home from London, and there used to be turkeys and geese and wine and cigars come by the carrier at Christmas-time, and boxes of candied fruit and French plums in ornamental boxes with silk and velvet and gilding on them. They were called prunes, but the prunes you buy at the grocer's are quite different. But now there is seldom anything nice brought from London, and the turkey and the prune people have forgotten Father's address.

'How *can* we restore those beastly fallen fortunes?' said Oswald. 'We've tried digging and writing and princesses and being editors.'

'And being bandits,' said H.O.

'When did you try that?' asked Dora quickly. 'You know I told you it was wrong.'

'It wasn't wrong the way we did it,' said Alice, quicker still, before Oswald could say, 'Who asked you to tell us anything about it?' which would have been rude, and he is glad he didn't. 'We only caught Albert-next-door.'

'Oh, Albert-next-door!' said Dora contemptuously, and I felt more comfortable; for even after I didn't say, 'Who asked you, and cetera,' I was afraid Dora was going to come the good elder sister over us. She does that a jolly sight too often.

Dicky looked up from the paper he was reading and said, 'This sounds likely,' and he read out –

'£100 secures partnership in lucrative business for sale of useful patent. £10 weekly. No personal attendance necessary. Jobbins, 300, Old Street Road.'[1]

'I wish *we* could secure that partnership,' said Oswald. He is twelve, and a very thoughtful boy for his age.

Alice looked up from her painting. She was trying to paint a fairy queen's frock with green bice, and it wouldn't rub.[2] There is something funny about green bice. It never will rub off; no matter how expensive your paint-box is – and even boiling water is very little use.

She said, 'Bother the bice! And, Oswald, it's no use thinking about that. Where are we to get a hundred pounds?'

'Ten pounds a week is five pounds to us,' Oswald went on – he had done the sum in his head while Alice was talking – 'because partnership means halves. It would be A1.'

Noël sat sucking his pencil – he had been writing poetry as usual. I saw the first two lines –

> 'I wonder why Green Bice
> Is never very nice.'

Suddenly he said, 'I wish a fairy would come down the chimney and drop a jewel on the table – a jewel worth just a hundred pounds.'

'She might as well give you the hundred pounds while she was about it,' said Dora.

'Or while she was about it she might as well give us five pounds a week,' said Alice.

'Or fifty,' said I.

'Or five hundred,' said Dicky.

I saw H.O. open his mouth, and I knew he was going to say, 'Or five thousand,' so I said –[3]

'Well, she won't give us fivepence, but if you'd only do as I am always saying, and rescue a wealthy old gentleman from deadly peril he would give us a pot of money, and we could have the partnership and five pounds a week. Five pounds a week would buy a great many things.'

Then Dicky said, 'Why shouldn't we borrow it?'

So we said, 'Who from?' and then he read this out of the paper –

MONEY PRIVATELY WITHOUT FEES.
THE BOND STREET BANK.
Manager, Z. Rosenbaum.

Advances cash from £20 to £10,000 on ladies' or gentlemen's note of hand alone, without security. No fees. No inquiries. Absolute privacy guaranteed.

'What does it all mean?' asked H.O.

'It means that there is a kind gentleman who has a lot of money, and he doesn't know enough poor people to help, so he puts it in the paper that he will help them, by lending them his money – that's it, isn't it, Dicky?'

Dora explained this and Dicky said, 'Yes.' And H.O. said he was a Generous Benefactor, like in Miss Edgeworth.[4] Then Noël wanted to know what a note of hand was, and Dicky knew that, because he had read it in a book, and it was just a letter saying you will pay the money when you can, and signed with your name.

'No inquiries!' said Alice. 'Oh – Dicky – do you think he would?'

'Yes, I think so,' said Dicky. 'I wonder Father doesn't go to this kind gentleman. I've seen his name before on a circular in Father's study.'

'Perhaps he has,' said Dora.

But the rest of us were sure he hadn't, because, of course, if he had, there would have been more money to buy nice things. Just then Pincher jumped up and knocked over the painting-water. He is a very careless dog. I wonder why painting-water is always such an ugly colour? Dora ran for a duster to wipe it up, and H.O. dropped drops of the water on his hands and said he had got the plague. So we played at the plague for a bit, and I was an Arab physician with a bath-towel turban, and cured the plague with magic acid-drops. After that it was time for dinner, and after dinner we talked it all over and settled that we would go and see the Generous Benefactor the very next day.[5] But we thought perhaps the G.B. – it is short for Generous Benefactor – would not like it if there were so many of us. I have often noticed that it is the worst of our being six – people think six a great many, when it's children. That sentence looks wrong somehow. I mean they don't mind six pairs of boots, or six pounds of apples, or six oranges, especially in equations, but they seem to think you ought not to have five brothers and sisters. Of course Dicky was to go, because it was his idea. Dora had to go to Blackheath to see an old lady, a friend of Father's, so she couldn't go. Alice said *she* ought to go, because it said, 'Ladies *and* gentlemen,' and perhaps the G.B. wouldn't let us have the money unless there were both kinds of us.

H.O. said Alice wasn't a lady; and she said *he* wasn't going, anyway. Then he called her a disagreeable cat, and she began to cry.

But Oswald always tries to make up quarrels, so he said –

'You're little sillies, both of you!'

And Dora said, 'Don't cry, Alice; he only meant you weren't a grown-up lady.'

Then H.O. said, 'What else did you think I meant, Disagreeable?'

So Dicky said, 'Don't be disagreeable yourself, H.O. Let her alone and say you're sorry, or I'll jolly well make you!'

So H.O. said he was sorry. Then Alice kissed him and said she was sorry too; and after that H.O. gave her a hug, and said, 'Now I'm *really and truly* sorry,' so it was all right.

Noël went the last time any of us went to London, so he was out of it, and Dora said she would take him to Blackheath if we'd take H.O. So as there'd been a little disagreeableness we thought it was better to take him, and we did. At first we thought we'd tear our oldest things a bit more, and put some patches of different colours on them, to show the G.B. how much we wanted money. But Dora said that would be a sort of cheating, pretending we were poorer than we are. And Dora is right sometimes, though she is our elder sister.[6] Then we thought we'd better wear our best things, so that the G.B. might see we weren't so very poor that he couldn't trust us to pay his money back when we had it. But Dora said that would be wrong too. So it came to our being quite honest, as Dora said, and going just as we were, without even washing our faces and hands; but when I looked at H.O. in the train I wished we had not been quite so particularly honest.

Every one who reads this knows what it is like to go in the train, so I shall not tell about it – though it was rather fun, especially the part where the guard came for the tickets at Waterloo, and H.O. was under the seat and pretended to be a dog without a ticket. We went to Charing Cross, and we just went round to Whitehall to see the soldiers and then by St James's for the same reason – and when we'd looked in the shops a bit we got to Brook Street, Bond Street.[7] It was a brass plate on a door next to a shop – a very grand place, where they sold bonnets and hats – all very bright and smart, and no tickets on them to tell you the price. We rang a bell and a boy opened the door and we asked for Mr Rosenbaum. The boy was not polite; he did not ask us in. So then Dicky gave him his visiting card; it was one of Father's really, but the name is the same, Mr Richard Bastable, and we others wrote our names underneath. I happened to have a piece of pink chalk in my pocket and we wrote them with that.

Then the boy shut the door in our faces and we waited on the step. But presently he came down and asked our business. So Dicky said –

'Money advanced, young shaver! and don't be all day about it!'

And then he made us wait again, till I was quite stiff in my legs, but Alice liked it because of looking at the hats and bonnets, and at last the door opened, and the boy said –

'Mr Rosenbaum will see you,' so we wiped our feet on the mat, which said so, and we went up stairs with soft carpets and into a room. It was a beautiful room. I wished then we had put on our best things, or at least washed a little. But it was too late now.

The room had velvet curtains and a soft, soft carpet, and it was full of the most splendid things. Black and gold cabinets, and china, and statues, and pictures. There was a picture of a cabbage and a pheasant and a dead hare that was just like life, and I would have given worlds to have it for my own. The fur was so natural I should never have been tired of looking at it; but Alice liked the one of the girl with the broken jug best. Then besides the pictures there were clocks and candlesticks and vases, and gilt looking-glasses, and boxes of cigars and scent and things littered all over the chairs and tables. It was a wonderful place, and in the middle of all the splendour was a little old gentleman with a very long black coat and a very long white beard and a hooky nose – like a falcon. And he put on a pair of gold spectacles and looked at us as if he knew exactly how much our clothes were worth. And then, while we elder ones were thinking how to begin, for we had all said 'Good morning' as we came in, of course, H.O. began before we could stop him. He said:

'Are you the G.B.?'

'The *what*?' said the little old gentleman.

'The G.B.,' said H.O., and I winked at him to shut up, but he didn't see me, and the G.B. did. He waved his hand at *me* to shut up, so I had to, and H.O. went on –

'It stands for Generous Benefactor.'

The old gentleman frowned. Then he said, 'Your Father sent you here, I suppose?'

'No he didn't,' said Dicky. 'Why did you think so?'

The old gentleman held out the card, and I explained that we took that because Father's name happens to be the same as Dicky's.

'Doesn't he know you've come?'

'No,' said Alice, 'we shan't tell him till we've got the partnership, because his own business worries him a good deal and we don't want to bother him with ours till it's settled, and then we shall give him half our share.'

The old gentleman took off his spectacles and rumpled his hair with his hands, then he said, 'Then what *did* you come for?'

'We saw your advertisement,' Dicky said, 'and we want a hundred pounds on our note of hand, and my sister came so that there should be both kinds of us; and we want it to buy a partnership with in the lucrative business for sale of useful patent. No personal attendance necessary.'

'I don't think I quite follow you,' said the G.B. 'But one thing I should like settled before entering more fully into the matter: why did you call me Generous Benefactor?'

'Well, you see,' said Alice, smiling at him to show she wasn't frightened, though I know really she was, awfully, 'we thought it was so *very* kind of you to try to find out the poor people who want money and to help them and lend them your money.'

'Hum!' said the G.B. 'Sit down.'

He cleared the clocks and vases and candlesticks off some of the chairs, and we sat down. The chairs were velvety, with gilt legs. It was like a king's palace.

'Now,' he said, 'you ought to be at school, instead of thinking about money. Why aren't you?'

We told him that we should go to school again when Father could manage it, but meantime we wanted to do something to restore the fallen fortunes of the House of Bastable. And we said we thought the lucrative patent would be a very good thing. He asked a lot of questions, and we told him everything we didn't think Father would mind our telling, and at last he said –

'You wish to borrow money. When will you repay it?'

'As soon as we've got it, of course,' Dicky said.

Then the G.B. said to Oswald, 'You seem the eldest,' but I explained to him that it was Dicky's idea, so my being eldest didn't matter. Then he said to Dicky –

'You are a minor, I presume?'

Dicky said he wasn't yet, but he had thought of being a mining engineer some day, and going to Klondike.[8]

'Minor, not miner,' said the G.B. 'I mean you're not of age?'

'I shall be in ten years, though,' said Dicky.

'Then you might repudiate the loan,' said the G.B., and Dicky said 'What?' Of course he ought to have said 'I beg your pardon. I didn't quite catch what you said' – that is what Oswald would have said. It is more polite than 'What.'

'Repudiate the loan,' the G.B. repeated. 'I mean you might say you would not pay me back the money, and the law could not compel you to do so.'

'Oh, well, if you think we're such sneaks,' said Dicky, and he got up off his chair. But the G.B. said, 'Sit down, sit down; I was only joking.'

Then he talked some more, and at last he said –

'I don't advise you to enter into that partnership. It's a swindle. Many advertisements are. And I have not a hundred pounds by me to-day to lend you. But I will lend you a pound, and you can spend it as you like. And when you are twenty-one you shall pay me back.'

'I shall pay you back long before that,' said Dicky. 'Thanks, awfully! And what about the note of hand?'

'Oh,' said the G.B., 'I'll trust to your honour. Between gentlemen, you know – and ladies' – he made a beautiful bow to Alice – 'a word is as good as a bond.'

Then he took out a sovereign, and held it in his hand while he talked to us. He gave us a lot of good advice about not going into business too young, and about doing our lessons – just swatting a bit, on our own hook, so as not to be put in a low form when we went back to school. And all the time he was stroking the sovereign and looking at it as if he thought it very beautiful. And so it was, for it was a new one. Then at last he held it out to Dicky, and when Dicky put out his hand for it the G.B. suddenly put the sovereign back in his pocket.[9]

'No,' he said, 'I won't give you the sovereign. I'll give you fifteen shillings, and this nice bottle of scent. It's worth far more than the five shillings I'm charging you for it. And, when you can, you shall pay me back the pound, and sixty per cent. interest – sixty per cent., sixty per cent. – '

'What's that?' said H.O.

The G.B. said he'd tell us that when we paid back the sovereign, but sixty per cent. was nothing to be afraid of. He gave Dicky the money. And the boy was made to call a cab, and the G.B. put us in and shook hands with us all, and asked Alice to give him a kiss, so she did, and H.O. would do it too, though his face was dirtier than ever. The G.B. paid the cabman and told him what station to go to, and so we went home.

That evening Father had a letter by the seven-o'clock post. And when he had read it he came up into the nursery. He did not look quite so unhappy as usual, but he looked grave.

'You've been to Mr Rosenbaum's,' he said.

So we told him all about it. It took a long time, and Father sat in the armchair. It was jolly.[10] He doesn't often come and talk to us now. He has to spend all his time thinking about his business. And when we'd told him all about it he said –

'You haven't done any harm this time, children; rather good than harm, indeed. Mr Rosenbaum has written me a very kind letter.'

'Is he a friend of yours, Father?' Oswald asked.

'He is an acquaintance,' said my father, frowning a little, 'we have done some business together. And this letter – ' he stopped and then said: 'No; you didn't do any harm to-day; but I want you for the future not to do anything so serious as to try to buy a partnership without consulting me, that's all. I don't want to interfere with your plays and pleasures; but you will consult me about business matters, won't you?'

Of course we said we should be delighted, but then Alice, who was sitting on his knee, said, 'We didn't like to bother you.'

Father said, 'I haven't much time to be with you, for my business takes most of my time. It is an anxious business – but I can't bear to think of your being left all alone like this.'

He looked so sad we all said we liked being alone. And then he looked sadder than ever.

Then Alice said, 'We don't mean that exactly, Father. It is rather lonely sometimes, since Mother died.'[11]

Then we were all quiet a little while. Father stayed with us till we went to bed, and when he said good night he looked quite cheerful. So we told him so, and he said –

'Well, the fact is, that letter took a weight off my mind.' I can't think what he meant – but I am sure the G.B. would be pleased if he could know he had taken a weight off somebody's mind. He is that sort of man, I think.[12]

We gave the scent to Dora. It is not quite such good scent as we thought it would be, but we had fifteen shillings – and they were all good, so is the G.B.

And until those fifteen shillings were spent we felt almost as jolly as though our fortunes had been properly restored. You do not notice your general fortune so much, as long as you have money in your pocket. This is why so many children with regular pocket-money have never felt it their duty to seek for treasure. So, perhaps, our not having pocket-money was a blessing in disguise. But the disguise was quite impenetrable, like the villains' in the books; and it seemed still more so when the fifteen shillings were all spent. Then at last the others agreed to let Oswald try his way of seeking for treasure, but they were not at all keen about it, and many a boy less firm than Oswald would have chucked the whole thing. But Oswald knew that a hero must rely on himself alone. So he stuck to it, and presently the others saw their duty, and backed him up.

*   *   *

Chapter 10
Lord Tottenham

Oswald is a boy of firm and unswerving character, and he had never wavered from his first idea. He felt quite certain that the books were right, and that the best way to restore fallen fortunes was to rescue an old gentleman in distress.[1] Then he brings you up as his own son: but if you preferred to go on being your own father's son I expect the old gentleman would make it up to you some other way. In the books the least thing does it – you put up the railway carriage window – or you pick up his purse when he drops it – or you say a hymn when he suddenly asks you to, and then your fortune is made.

The others, as I said, were very slack about it, and did not seem to care much about trying the rescue.[2] They said there wasn't any deadly peril, and we should have to make one before we could rescue the old gentleman from it, but Oswald didn't see that that mattered. However, he thought he would try some of the easier ways first, by himself.

So he waited about the station, pulling up railway carriage windows for old gentlemen who looked likely – but nothing happened, and at last the porters said he was a nuisance. So that was no go. No one ever asked him to say a hymn, though he had learned a nice short one, beginning 'New every morning' – and when an old gentleman did drop a two-shilling piece just by Ellis's the hairdresser's, and Oswald picked it up, and was just thinking what he should say when he returned it, the old gentleman caught him by the collar and called him a young thief.[3] It would have been very unpleasant for Oswald if he hadn't happened to be a very brave boy, and knew the policeman on that beat very well indeed. So the policeman backed him up, and the old gentleman said he was sorry, and offered Oswald sixpence. Oswald refused it with polite disdain, and nothing more happened at all.

When Oswald had tried by himself and it had not come off, he said to the others, 'We're wasting our time, not trying to rescue the old gentleman in deadly peril. Come – buck up![4] Do let's do something!'

It was dinner-time, and Pincher was going round getting the bits off the plates. There were plenty because it was cold-mutton day. And Alice said –

'It's only fair to try Oswald's way – he has tried all the things the others thought of. Why couldn't we rescue Lord Tottenham?'

Lord Tottenham is the old gentleman who walks over the Heath every day in a paper collar at three o'clock – and when he gets half way, if there is no one about, he changes his collar and throws the dirty one into the furze-bushes.

Dicky said, 'Lord Tottenham's all right – but where's the deadly peril?'

And we couldn't think of any. There are no highwaymen on Blackheath now, I am sorry to say. And though Oswald said half of us could be highwaymen and the other half rescue party, Dora kept on saying it would be wrong to be a highwayman – and so we had to give that up.

Then Alice said, 'What about Pincher?'

And we all saw at once that it could be done.

Pincher is very well bred, and he does know one or two things, though we never could teach him to beg.[5] But if you tell him to hold on – he will do it, even if you only say 'Seize him!' in a whisper.

So we arranged it all. Dora said she wouldn't play; she said she thought it was wrong, and she knew it was silly – so we left her out, and she went and sat in the dining-room with a goody-book, so as to be able to say she didn't have anything to do with it, if we got into a row over it.[6]

Alice and H.O. were to hide in the furze-bushes just by where Lord Tottenham changes his collar, and they were to whisper, 'Seize him!' to Pincher; and then when Pincher had seized Lord Tottenham we were to go and rescue him from his deadly peril. And he would say, 'How can I reward you, my noble young pre-servers?' and it would be all right.

So we went up to the Heath. We were afraid of being late. Oswald told the others what Procrastination was – so they got to the furze-bushes a little after two o'clock, and it was rather cold. Alice and H.O. and Pincher hid, but Pincher did not like it any more than they did, and as we three walked up and down we • heard him whining. And Alice kept saying, 'I *am* so cold! Isn't he coming yet?' And H.O. wanted to come out and jump about to warm himself. But we told him he must learn to be a Spartan boy, and that he ought to be very thankful he hadn't got a beastly fox eating his inside all the time.[7] H.O. is our little brother, and we are not going to let it be our fault if he grows up a milksop. Besides, it was not really cold. It was his knees – he wears socks. So they stayed where they were. And at last, when even the other three who were walking about were beginning to feel rather chilly, we saw Lord Tottenham's big black cloak coming along, flapping in the wind like a great bird. So we said to Alice –

'Hist! he approaches. You'll know when to set Pincher on by hearing Lord Tottenham talking to himself – he always does while he is taking off his collar.'

Then we three walked slowly away whistling to show we were not thinking of anything. Our lips were rather cold, but we man-aged to do it.

Lord Tottenham came striding along, talking to himself. People call him the mad Protectionist.[8] I don't know what it means – but I don't think people ought to call a Lord such names.

As he passed us he said, 'Ruin of the country, sir! Fatal error, fatal error!' And then we looked back and saw he was getting quite near where Pincher was, and Alice and H.O. We walked on – so that he shouldn't think we were looking – and in a minute we heard Pincher's bark, and then nothing for a bit; and then we looked round, and sure enough good old Pincher had got Lord Tottenham by the trouser leg and was holding on like billy-oh, so we started to run.

Lord Tottenham had got his collar half off – it was sticking out sideways under his ear – and he was shouting, 'Help, help, murder!' exactly as if some one had explained to him beforehand what he was to do. Pincher was growling and snarling and holding on. When we got to him I stopped and said –

'Dicky, we must rescue this good old man.'

Lord Tottenham roared in his fury, 'Good old man be – ' something or othered. 'Call the dog off!'

So Oswald said, 'It is a dangerous task – but who would hesitate to do an act of true bravery?'

And all the while Pincher was worrying and snarling, and Lord Tottenham shouting to us to get the dog away. He was dancing about in the road with Pincher hanging on like grim death; and his collar flapping about, where it was undone.

Then Noël said, 'Haste, ere yet it be too late.' So I said to Lord Tottenham –

'Stand still, aged sir, and I will endeavour to alleviate your distress.'

He stood still, and I stooped down and caught hold of Pincher and whispered, 'Drop it, sir; drop it!'

So then Pincher dropped it, and Lord Tottenham fastened his collar again – he never does change it if there's any one looking – and he said –

'I'm much obliged, I'm sure. Nasty vicious brute! Here's something to drink my health.'

But Dicky explained that we are teetotallers, and do not drink people's healths.[9] So Lord Tottenham said, 'Well, I'm much obliged any way. And now I come to look at you – of course, you're not young ruffians, but gentlemen's sons, eh? Still, you won't be above taking a tip from an old boy – I wasn't when I was your age,' and he pulled out half a sovereign.

It was very silly; but now we'd done it I felt it would be beastly mean to take the old boy's chink after putting him in such a funk. He didn't say anything about bringing us up as his own sons – so I didn't know what to do. I let Pincher go, and was just going to say he was very welcome, and we'd rather not have the money, which seemed the best way out of it, when that beastly dog spoiled the whole show. Directly I let him go he began to jump about at us and bark for joy, and try to lick our faces. He was so proud of what he'd done. Lord Tottenham opened his eyes and he just said, 'The dog seems to know you.'

And then Oswald saw it was all up, and he said, 'Good morning,' and tried to get away. But Lord Tottenham said –

'Not so fast!' And he caught Noël by the collar. Noël gave a howl, and Alice ran out from the bushes. Noël is her favourite. I'm sure I don't know why. Lord Tottenham looked at her, and he said –

'So there are more of you!' And then H.O. came out.

'Do you complete the party?' Lord Tottenham asked him. And H.O. said there were only five of us this time.

Lord Tottenham turned sharp off and began to walk away, holding Noël by the collar. We caught up with him, and asked him where he was going, and he said, 'To the Police Station.' So then I said quite politely, 'Well, don't take Noël; he's not strong, and he easily gets upset. Besides, it wasn't his doing. If you want to take any one take me – it was my idea entirely.'

Dicky behaved very well. He said, 'If you take Oswald I'll go too, but don't take Noël; he's such a delicate little chap.'

Lord Tottenham stopped, and he said, 'You should have thought of that before.' Noël was howling all the time, and his face was very white, and Alice said –

'Oh, do let Noël go, dear, good, kind Lord Tottenham; he'll faint if you don't, I know he will, he does sometimes. Oh, I wish we'd never done it! Dora said it was wrong.'

'Dora displayed considerable common sense,' said Lord Tottenham, and he let Noël go. And Alice put her arm round Noël and tried to cheer him up, but he was all trembly, and as white as paper.[10]

Then Lord Tottenham said –

'Will you give me your word of honour not to try to escape?'

So we said we would.

'Then follow me,' he said, and led the way to a bench. We all followed, and Pincher too, with his tail between his legs – he knew something was wrong. Then Lord Tottenham sat down, and he made Oswald and Dicky and H.O. stand in front of him, but he let Alice and Noël sit down. And he said –

'You set your dog on me, and you tried to make me believe you were saving me from it. And you would have taken my half-sovereign. Such conduct is most – No – you shall tell me what it is, sir, and speak the truth.'

So I had to say it was most ungentlemanly, but I said I hadn't been going to take the half-sovereign.

'Then what did you do it for?' he asked. 'The truth, mind.'

So I said, 'I see now it was very silly, and Dora said it was wrong, but it didn't seem so till we did it. We wanted to restore the fallen fortunes of our house, and in the books if you rescue an old gentleman from deadly peril, he brings you up as his own son – or if you prefer to be your father's son, he starts you in business, so that you end in wealthy affluence; and there wasn't any deadly peril, so we made Pincher into one – and so – ' I was so ashamed I couldn't go on, for it did seem an awfully mean thing.[11] Lord Tottenham said –

'A very nice way to make your fortune – by deceit and trickery. I have a horror of dogs. If I'd been a weak man the shock might have killed me. What do you think of yourselves, eh?'

We were all crying except Oswald, and the others say he was; and Lord Tottenham went on –

'Well, well, I see you're sorry. Let this be a lesson to you; and we'll say no more about it. I'm an old man now, but I was young once.'

Then Alice slid along the bench close to him, and put her hand on his arm: her fingers were pink through the holes in her woolly gloves, and said, 'I think you're very good to forgive us, and we are really very, very sorry. But we wanted to be like the children in the books – only we never have the chances they have. Everything they do turns out all right. But we *are* sorry, very, very. And I know Oswald wasn't going to take the half-sovereign. Directly you said that about a tip from an old boy I began to feel bad inside, and I whispered to H.O. that I wished we hadn't.'[12]

Then Lord Tottenham stood up, and he looked like the Death of Nelson, for he is clean shaved and it is a good face, and he said – [13]

'Always remember never to do a dishonourable thing, for money or for anything else in the world.'

And we promised we would remember. Then he took off his hat, and we took off ours, and he went away, and we went home. I never felt so cheap in all my life! Dora said, 'I told you so,' but we didn't mind even that so much, though it was indeed hard to bear. It was what Lord Tottenham had said about ungentlemanly. We didn't go on to the Heath for a week after that; but at last we all went, and we waited for him by the bench. When he came along Alice said, 'Please, Lord Tottenham, we have not been on the Heath for a week, to be a punishment because you let us off. And we have brought you a present each if you will take them to show you are willing to make it up.'

He sat down on the bench, and we gave him our presents. Oswald gave him a sixpenny compass – he bought it with my own money on purpose to give him. Oswald always buys useful presents. The needle would not move after I'd had it a day or two, but Lord Tottenham used to be an admiral, so he will be able to make that go all right. Alice had made him a shaving-case, with a rose worked on it. And H.O. gave him his knife – the same one he once cut all the buttons off his best suit with. Dicky gave him his prize, *Naval Heroes*, because it was the best thing he had, and Noël gave him a piece of poetry he had made himself –

> When sin and shame bow down the brow
> Then people feel just like we do now.
> We are so sorry with grief and pain
> We never will be so ungentlemanly again.

Lord Tottenham seemed very pleased. He thanked us, and talked to us for a bit, and when he said good-bye he said –

'All's fair weather now, mates,' and shook hands.

And whenever we meet him he nods to us, and if the girls are with us he takes off his hat, so he can't really be going on thinking us ungentlemanly now.[14]

*   *   *

Chapter 11
Castilian Amoroso

One day when we suddenly found that we had half a crown we decided that we really ought to try Dicky's way of restoring our fallen fortunes while yet the deed was in our power. Because it might easily have happened to us never to have half a crown again. So we decided to dally no longer with being journalists and bandits and things like them, but to send for sample and instructions how to earn two pounds a week each in our spare time.[1] We had seen the advertisement in the paper, and we had always wanted to do it, but we had never had the money before, somehow. The advertisement says: 'Any lady or gentleman can easily earn two pounds a week in their spare time. Sample and instructions, two shillings. Packed free from observation.' A good deal of the half-crown was Dora's. It came from her god-mother; but she said she would not mind letting Dicky have it if he would pay her back before Christmas, and if we were sure it was right to try to make our fortune that way. Of course that was quite easy, because out of two pounds a week in your spare time you can easily pay all your debts, and have almost as much left as you began with; and as to the right we told her to dry up.

Dicky had always thought that this was really the best way to restore our fallen fortunes, and we were glad that now he had a chance of trying because of course we wanted the two pounds a week each, and besides, we were rather tired of Dicky's always saying when our ways didn't turn out well, 'Why don't you try the sample and instructions about our spare time?'

When we found out about our half-crown we got the paper. Noël was playing admirals in it, but he had made the cocked hat without tearing the paper, and we found the advertisement, and it said just the same as ever. So we got a two-shilling postal order and a stamp, and what was left of the money it was agreed we would spend in ginger-beer to drink success to trade.

We got some nice paper out of Father's study, and Dicky wrote the letter, and we put in the money and put on the stamp, and made H.O. post it. Then we drank the ginger-beer, and then we waited for the sample and instructions. It seemed a long time coming, and the postman got quite tired of us running out and stopping him in the street to ask if it had come.

But on the third morning it came. It was quite a large parcel, and it was packed, as the advertisement said it would be, 'free from observation.' That means it was in a box; and inside the box was some stiff browny cardboard, crinkled like the galvanized iron on the tops of chicken-houses, and inside that was a lot of paper, some of it printed and some scrappy, and in the very middle of it all a bottle, not very large, and black, and sealed on the top of the cork with yellow sealing-wax.

We looked at it as it lay on the nursery table, and while all the others grabbed at the papers to see what the printing said, Oswald went to look for the corkscrew, so as to see what was inside the bottle. He found the corkscrew in the dresser drawer – it always gets there, though it is supposed to be in the sideboard drawer in the dining-room – and when he got back the others had read most of the printed papers.

'I don't think it's much good, and I don't think it's quite nice to sell wine,' Dora said, 'and besides, it's not easy to suddenly begin to sell things when you aren't used to it.'

'I don't know,' said Alice; 'I believe I could.'

They all looked rather down in the mouth, though, and Oswald asked how you were to make your two pounds a week.

'Why, you've got to get people to taste that stuff in the bottle. It's sherry – Castilian Amoroso its name is – and then you get them to buy it, and then you write to the people and tell them the other people want the wine, and then for every dozen you sell you get two shillings from the wine people, so if you sell twenty dozen a week you get your two pounds. I don't think we shall sell as much as that,' said Dicky.

'We might not the first week,' Alice said, 'but when people found out how nice it was, they would want more and more. And if we only got ten shillings a week it would be something to begin with, wouldn't it?'

Oswald said he should jolly well think it would, and then Dicky took the cork out with the corkscrew. The cork broke a good deal, and some of the bits went into the bottle. Dora got the medicine glass that has the teaspoons and tablespoons marked on it, and we agreed to have a teaspoonful each, to see what it was like.

'No one must have more than that,' Dora said, 'however nice it is.' Dora behaved rather as if it were her bottle. I suppose it was, because she had lent the money for it.

Then she measured out the teaspoonful, and she had first go, because of being the eldest. We asked at once what it was like, but Dora could not speak just then.

Then she said, 'It's like the tonic Noël had in the spring; but perhaps sherry ought to be like that.'

Then it was Oswald's turn. He thought it was very burny; but he said nothing. He wanted to see first what the others would say.

Dicky said his was simply beastly, and Alice said Noël could taste next if he liked.

Noël said it was the golden wine of the gods, but he had to put his handkerchief up to his mouth all the same, and I saw the face he made.

Then H.O. had his, and he spat it out in the fire, which was very rude and nasty, and we told him so.

Then it was Alice's turn. She said, 'Only half a teaspoonful for me, Dora. We mustn't use it all up.' And she tasted it and said nothing.

Then Dicky said: 'Look here, I chuck this. I'm not going to hawk round such beastly stuff. Any one who likes can have the bottle. Quis?'

And Alice got out 'Ego' before the rest of us.[2] Then she said, 'I know what's the matter with it. It wants sugar.'

And at once we all saw that that was all there was the matter with the stuff. So we got two lumps of sugar and crushed it on the floor with one of the big wooden bricks till it was powdery, and mixed it with some of the wine up to the tablespoon mark, and it was quite different, and not nearly so nasty.

'You see it's all right when you get used to it,' Dicky said. I think he was sorry he had said 'Quis?' in such a hurry.

'Of course,' Alice said, 'it's rather dusty. We must crush the sugar carefully in clean paper before we put it in the bottle.'

Dora said she was afraid it would be cheating to make one bottle nicer than what people would get when they ordered a dozen bottles, but Alice said Dora always made a fuss about everything, and really it would be quite honest.

'You see,' she said, 'I shall just tell them, quite truthfully, what we have done to it, and when their dozens come they can do it for themselves.'

So then we crushed eight more lumps, very cleanly and carefully between newspapers, and shook it up well in the bottle, and corked it up with a screw of paper, brown and not news, for fear of the poisonous printing ink getting wet and dripping down into the wine and killing people.[3] We made Pincher have a taste, and he sneezed for ever so long, and after that he used to go under the sofa whenever we showed him the bottle.

Then we asked Alice who she would try and sell it to. She said: 'I shall ask everybody who comes to the house. And while we are doing that, we can be thinking of outside people to take it to. We must be careful: there's not much more than half of it left, even counting the sugar.'

We did not wish to tell Eliza – I don't know why. And she opened the door very quickly that day, so that the Taxes and a man who came to our house by mistake for next door got away before Alice had a chance to try them with the Castilian Amoroso. But about five Eliza slipped out for half an hour to see a friend who was making her a hat for Sunday, and while she was gone there was a knock.

Alice went, and we looked over the banisters.

When she opened the door, she said at once, 'Will you walk in, please?'

The person at the door said, 'I called to see your Pa, miss. Is he at home?'

Alice said again, 'Will you walk in, please?'

Then the person – it sounded like a man – said, 'He is in, then?' But Alice only kept on saying, 'Will you walk in, please?' so at last the man did, rubbing his boots very loudly on the mat. Then Alice shut the front door, and we saw that it was the butcher, with an envelope in his hand. He was not dressed in blue, like when he is cutting up the sheep and things in the shop, and he wore knickerbockers. Alice says he came on a bicycle. She led the way into the dining-room, where the Castilian Amoroso bottle and the medicine glass were standing on the table all ready.

The others stayed on the stairs, but Oswald crept down and looked through the door-crack.

'Please sit down,' said Alice quite calmly, though she told me afterwards I had no idea how silly she felt. And the butcher sat down. Then Alice stood quite still and said nothing, but she fiddled with the medicine glass and put the screw of brown paper straight in the Castilian bottle.

'Will you tell your Pa I'd like a word with him?' the butcher said, when he got tired of saying nothing.

'He'll be in very soon, I think,' Alice said.

And then she stood still again and said nothing. It was beginning to look very idiotic of her, and H.O. laughed. I went back and cuffed him for it quite quietly, and I don't think the butcher heard. But Alice did, and it roused her from her stupor. She spoke suddenly, very fast indeed – so fast that I knew she had made up what she was going to say before. She had got most of it out of the circular.

She said, 'I want to call your attention to a sample of sherry wine I have here. It is called Castilian something or other, and at the price it is unequalled for flavour and bouquet.'

The butcher said, 'Well – I never!'

And Alice went on, 'Would you like to taste it?'

'Thank you very much, I'm sure, miss,' said the butcher.

Alice poured some out.

The butcher tasted a very little. He licked his lips, and we thought he was going to say how good it was. But he did not. He put down the medicine glass with nearly all the stuff left in it (we put it back in the bottle afterwards to save waste) and said, 'Excuse me, miss, but isn't it a little sweet? – for sherry I mean?'

'The *real* isn't,' said Alice. 'If you order a dozen it will come quite different to that – we like it best with sugar. I wish you *would* order some.'

The butcher asked why.

Alice did not speak for a minute, and then she said –

'I don't mind telling *you*: you are in business yourself, aren't you? We are trying to get people to buy it, because we shall have two shillings for every dozen we can make any one buy. It's called a purr something.'

'A percentage. Yes, I see,' said the butcher, looking at the hole in the carpet.

'You see there are reasons,' Alice went on, 'why we want to make our fortunes as quickly as we can.'

'Quite so,' said the butcher, and he looked at the place where the paper is coming off the wall.

'And this seems a good way,' Alice went on. 'We paid two shillings for the sample and instructions, and it says you can make two pounds a week easily in your leisure time.'

'I'm sure I hope you may, miss,' said the butcher.

And Alice said again would he buy some?

'Sherry is my favourite wine,' he said.

Alice asked him to have some more to drink.

'No, thank you, miss,' he said; 'it's my favourite wine, but it doesn't agree with me; not the least bit. But I've an uncle drinks it. Suppose I ordered him half a dozen for a Christmas present? Well, miss, here's the shilling commission, anyway,' and he pulled out a handful of money and gave her the shilling.

'But I thought the wine people paid that,' Alice said.

But the butcher said not on half-dozens they didn't. Then he said he didn't think he'd wait any longer for Father – but would Alice ask Father to write him?

Alice offered him the sherry again, but he said something about 'Not for worlds!' – and then she let him out and came back to us with the shilling, and said, 'How's that?'

And we said 'A1.'

And all the evening we talked of our fortune that we had begun to make.

Nobody came next day, but the day after a lady came to ask for money to build an orphanage for the children of dead sailors. And we saw her. I went in with Alice. And when we had explained to her that we had only a shilling and we wanted it for something else, Alice suddenly said, 'Would you like some wine?'

And the lady said, 'Thank you very much,' but she looked surprised. She was not a young lady, and she had a mantle with beads, and the beads had come off in places – leaving a browny braid showing, and she had printed papers about the dead sailors in a sealskin bag, and the seal had come off in places, leaving the skin bare.

We gave her a tablespoonful of the wine in a proper wine-glass out of the sideboard, because she was a lady. And when she had tasted it she got up in a very great hurry, and shook out her dress and snapped her bag shut, and said, 'You naughty, wicked children! What do you mean by playing a trick like this? You ought to be ashamed of yourselves! I shall write to your Mamma about it. You dreadful little girl! – you might have poisoned me. But your Mamma...'

Then Alice said, 'I'm very sorry; the butcher liked it, only he said it was sweet. And please don't write to Mother. It makes Father so unhappy when letters come for her!' – and Alice was very near crying.

'What do you mean, you silly child?' said the lady, looking quite bright and interested. 'Why doesn't your Father like your Mother to have letters – eh?'

And Alice said, '*Oh*, you...!' and began to cry, and bolted out of the room.

Then I said, 'Our Mother is dead, and will you please go away now?'

The lady looked at me a minute, and then she looked quite different, and she said, 'I'm very sorry. I didn't know. Never mind about the wine. I daresay your little sister meant it kindly.' And she looked round the room just like the butcher had done. Then she said again, 'I didn't know – I'm very sorry...'

So I said, 'Don't mention it,' and shook hands with her, and let her out. Of course we couldn't have asked her to buy the wine after what she'd said. But I think she was not a bad sort of person. I do like a person to say they're sorry when they ought to be – especially a grown-up. They do it so seldom. I suppose that's why we think so much of it.

But Alice and I didn't feel jolly for ever so long afterwards. And when I went back into the dining-room I saw how different it was from when Mother was here, and we are different, and Father is different, and nothing is like it was. I am glad I am not made to think about it every day.

I went and found Alice, and told her what the lady had said, and when she had finished crying we put away the bottle and said we would not try to sell any more to people who came. And we did not tell the others – we only said the lady did not buy any – but we went up on the Heath, and some soldiers went by and there was a Punch-and-Judy show, and when we came back we were better.[4]

The bottle got quite dusty where we had put it, and perhaps the dust of ages would have laid thick and heavy on it, only a clergyman called when we were all out. He was not our own clergyman – Mr Bristow is our own clergyman, and we all love him, and we would not try to sell sherry to people we like, and make two pounds a week out of them in our spare time. It was another clergyman, just a stray one; and he asked Eliza if the dear children would not like to come to his little Sunday school. We always spend Sunday afternoons with Father. But as he had left the name of his vicarage with Eliza, and asked her to tell us to come, we thought we would go and call on him, just to explain about Sunday afternoons, and we thought we might as well take the sherry with us.

'I won't go unless you all go too,' Alice said, 'and I won't do the talking.'

Dora said she thought we had much better not go; but we said 'Rot!' and it ended in her coming with us, and I am glad she did.

Oswald said he would do the talking if the others liked, and he learned up what to say from the printed papers.

We went to the Vicarage early on Saturday afternoon, and rang at the bell. It is a new red house with no trees in the garden, only very yellow mould and gravel. It was all very neat and dry. Just before we rang the bell we heard some one inside call 'Jane! Jane!' and we thought we would not be Jane for anything. It was the sound of the voice that called that made us sorry for her.

The door was opened by a very neat servant in black, with a white apron; we saw her tying the strings as she came along the hall, through the different-coloured glass in the door. Her face was red, and I think she was Jane.

We asked if we could see Mr Mallow.

The servant said Mr Mallow was very busy with his sermon just then, but she would see.

But Oswald said, 'It's all right. He asked us to come.'

So she let us all in and shut the front door, and showed us into a very tidy room with a bookcase full of a lot of books covered in black cotton with white labels, and some dull pictures, and a harmonium. And Mr Mallow was writing at a desk with drawers, copying something out of a book. He was stout and short, and wore spectacles.

He covered his writing up when we went in – I didn't know why. He looked rather cross, and we heard Jane or somebody being scolded outside by the voice. I hope it wasn't for letting us in, but I have had doubts.

'Well,' said the clergyman, 'what is all this about?'

'You asked us to call,' Dora said, 'about your little Sunday school. We are the Bastables of Lewisham Road.'

'Oh – ah, yes,' he said; 'and shall I expect you all to-morrow?' He took up his pen and fiddled with it, and he did not ask us to sit down. But some of us did.

'We always spend Sunday afternoon with Father,' said Dora; 'but we wished to thank you for being so kind as to ask us.'

'And we wished to ask you something else!' said Oswald; and he made a sign to Alice to get the sherry ready in the glass. She did – behind Oswald's back while he was speaking.

'My time is limited,' said Mr Mallow, looking at his watch; 'but still – ' Then he muttered something about the fold, and went on: 'Tell me what is troubling you, my little man, and I will try to give you any help in my power. What is it you want?'

Then Oswald quickly took the glass from Alice, and held it out to him, and said, 'I want your opinion on that.'

'On *that*,' he said. 'What is it?'

'It is a shipment,' Oswald said; 'but it's quite enough for you to taste.' Alice had filled the glass half-full; I suppose she was too excited to measure properly.

'A shipment?' said the clergyman, taking the glass in his hand.

'Yes,' Oswald went on; 'an exceptional opportunity. Full-bodied and nutty.'

'It really does taste rather like one kind of Brazil-nut.' Alice put her oar in as usual.

The Vicar looked from Alice to Oswald, and back again, and Oswald went on with what he had learned from the printing. The clergyman held the glass at half-arm's-length, stiffly, as if he had caught cold.

'It is of a quality never before offered at the price. Old Delicate Amoro – what's its name – '

'Amorolio,' said H.O.

'Amoroso,' said Oswald. 'H.O., you just shut up – Castilian Amoroso – it's a true after-dinner wine, stimulating and yet...'

'*Wine*?' said Mr Mallow, holding the glass further off. 'Do you *know*,' he went on, making his voice very thick and strong (I expect he does it like that in church), 'have you never been *taught* that it is the drinking of *wine* and *spirits* – yes, and *beer*, which makes half the homes in England full of *wretched* little children, and *degraded, miserable* parents?'[5]

'Not if you put sugar in it,' said Alice firmly; 'eight lumps and shake the bottle. We have each had more than a teaspoonful of it, and we were not ill at all. It was something else that upset H.O. Most likely all those acorns he got out of the Park.'

The clergyman seemed to be speechless with conflicting emotions, and just then the door opened and a lady came in. She had a white cap with lace, and an ugly violet flower in it, and she was tall, and looked very strong, though thin. And I do believe she had been listening at the door.

'But why,' the Vicar was saying, 'why did you bring this dreadful fluid, this curse of our country, to *me* to taste?'

'Because we thought you might buy some,' said Dora, who never sees when a game is up.[6] 'In books the parson loves his bottle of old port; and new sherry is just as good – with sugar – for people who like sherry. And if you would order a dozen of the wine, then we should get two shillings.'

The lady said (and it *was* the voice), 'Good gracious! Nasty, sordid little things! Haven't they any one to teach them better?'

And Dora got up and said, 'No, we are not those things you say; but we are sorry we came here to be called names. We want to make our fortune just as much as Mr Mallow does – only no one would listen to us if we preached, so it's no use our copying out sermons like him.'

And I think that was smart of Dora, even if it was rather rude.

Then I said perhaps we had better go, and the lady said, 'I should think so!' But when we were going to wrap up the bottle and glass the clergyman said, 'No; you can leave that,' and we were so upset we did, though it wasn't his after all.

We walked home very fast and not saying much, and the girls went up to their rooms. When I went to tell them tea was ready, and there was a teacake, Dora was crying like anything and Alice hugging her. I am afraid there is a great deal of crying in this chapter, but I can't help it. Girls will sometimes; I suppose it is their nature, and we ought to be sorry for their affliction.

'It's no good,' Dora was saying, 'you all hate me, and you think I'm a prig and a busybody, but I do try to do right – oh, I do! Oswald, go away; don't come here making fun of me!'

So I said, 'I'm not making fun, Sissy; don't cry, old girl.'

Mother taught me to call her Sissy when we were very little and before the others came, but I don't often somehow, now we are old.[7] I patted her on the back, and she put her head against my sleeve, holding on to Alice all the time, and she went on. She was in that laughy-cryey state when people say things they wouldn't say at other times.

'Oh dear, oh dear – I do try, I do. And when Mother died she said, "Dora, take care of the others, and teach them to be good, and keep them out of trouble and make them happy." She said, "Take care of them for me, Dora dear." And I have tried, and all of you hate me for it; and to-day I let you do this, though I knew all the time it was silly.'

I hope you will not think I was a muff but I kissed Dora for some time. Because girls like it. And I will never say again that she comes the good elder sister too much. And I have put all this in though I do hate telling about it, because I own I have been hard on Dora, but I never will be again. She is a good old sort; of course we never knew before about what Mother told her, or we wouldn't have ragged her as we did. We did not tell the little ones, but I got Alice to speak to Dicky, and we three can sit on the others if requisite.[8]

This made us forget all about the sherry; but about eight o'clock there was a knock, and Eliza went, and we saw it was poor Jane, if her name was Jane, from the Vicarage. She handed in a brown-paper parcel and a letter. And three minutes later Father called us into his study.

On the table was the brown-paper parcel, open, with our bottle and glass on it, and Father had a letter in his hand. He pointed to the bottle and sighed, and said, 'What have you been doing now?' The letter in his hand was covered with little black writing, all over the four large pages.

So Dicky spoke up, and he told Father the whole thing, as far as he knew it, for Alice and I had not told about the dead sailors' lady.

And when he had done, Alice said, 'Has Mr Mallow written to you to say he will buy a dozen of the sherry after all? It is really not half bad with sugar in it.'

Father said no, he didn't think clergymen could afford such expensive wine; and he said *he* would like to taste it. So we gave him what there was left, for we had decided coming home that we would give up trying for the two pounds a week in our spare time.

Father tasted it, and then he acted just as H.O. had done when he had his teaspoonful, but of course we did not say anything. Then he laughed till I thought he would never stop. I think it was the sherry, because I am sure I have read somewhere about 'wine that maketh glad the heart of man.'[9] He had only a very little, which shows that it was a good after-dinner wine, stimulating, and yet...I forget the rest.

But when he had done laughing he said, 'It's all right, kids. Only don't do it again. The wine trade is overcrowded; and besides, I thought you promised to consult me before going into business?'

'Before buying one I thought you meant,' said Dicky. 'This was only on commission.' And Father laughed again. I am glad we got the Castilian Amoroso, because it did really cheer Father up, and you cannot always do that, however hard you try, even if you make jokes, or give him a comic paper.[10]

* * *

Chapter 12
The Nobleness of Oswald

The part about his nobleness only comes at the end, but you would not understand it unless you knew how it began. It began, like nearly everything about that time, with treasure seeking.[1]

Of course as soon as we had promised to consult my Father about business matters we all gave up wanting to go into business. I don't know how it is, but having to consult about a thing with grown-up people, even the bravest and the best, seems to make the thing not worth doing afterwards.

We don't mind Albert's uncle chipping in sometimes when the thing's going on, but we are glad he never asked us to promise to consult him about anything. Yet Oswald saw that my Father was quite right; and I daresay if we had had that hundred pounds we should have spent it on the share in that lucrative business for the sale of useful patent, and then found out afterwards that we should have done better to spend the money in some other way. My Father says so, and he ought to know. We had several ideas about that time, but having so little chink always stood in the way. This was the case with H.O.'s idea of setting up a cocoanut-shy on this side of the Heath, where there are none generally. We had no sticks or wooden balls, and the greengrocer said he could not book so many as twelve dozen cocoanuts without Mr Bastable's written order. And as we did not wish to consult my Father it was decided to drop it.[2] And when Alice dressed up Pincher in some of the dolls' clothes and we made up our minds to take him round with an organ as soon as we had taught him to dance, we were stopped at once by Dicky's remembering how he had once heard that an organ cost seven hundred pounds. Of course this was the big church kind, but even the ones on three legs can't be got for one-and-sevenpence, which was all we had when we first thought of it. So we gave that up too.

It was a wet day, I remember, and mutton hash for dinner – very tough with pale gravy with lumps in it. I think the others would have left a good deal on the sides of their plates, although they know better, only Oswald said it was a savoury stew made of the red deer that Edward shot. So then we were the Children of the New Forest, and the mutton tasted much better.[3] No one in the New Forest minds venison being tough and the gravy pale.

Then after dinner we let the girls have a dolls' tea-party, on condition they didn't expect us boys to wash up; and it was when we were drinking the last of the liquorice water out of the little cups that Dicky said – [4]

'This reminds me.'

So we said, 'What of?'

Dicky answered us at once, though his mouth was full of bread with liquorice stuck in it to look like cake. You should not speak with your mouth full, even to your own relations, and you shouldn't wipe your mouth on the back of your hand, but on your handkerchief, if you have one. Dicky did not do this. He said –

'Why, you remember when we first began about treasure seeking, I said I had thought of something, only I could not tell you because I hadn't finished thinking about it.'

We said 'Yes.'

'Well, this liquorice water – '

'Tea,' said Alice softly.

'Well, tea then – made me think.' He was going on to say what it made him think, but Noël interrupted and cried out, 'I say; let's finish off this old tea-party and have a council of war.'

So we got out the flags and the wooden sword and the drum, and Oswald beat it while the girls washed up, till Eliza came up to say she had the jumping toothache, and the noise went through her like a knife. So of course Oswald left off at once. When you are polite to Oswald he never refuses to grant your requests.

When we were all dressed up we sat down round the camp fire, and Dicky began again.[5]

'Every one in the world wants money. Some people get it. The people who get it are the ones who see things. I have seen one thing.'

Dicky stopped and smoked the pipe of peace. It is the pipe we did bubbles with in the summer, and somehow it has not got broken yet. We put tea-leaves in it for the pipe of peace, but the girls are not allowed to have any. It is not right to let girls smoke. They get to think too much of themselves if you let them do everything the same as men.[6]

Oswald said, 'Out with it.'

'I see that glass bottles only cost a penny. H.O., if you dare to snigger I'll send you round selling old bottles, and you shan't have any sweets except out of the money you get for them. And the same with you, Noël.'

'Noël wasn't sniggering,' said Alice in a hurry; 'it is only his taking so much interest in what you were saying makes him look like that. Be quiet, H.O., and don't you make faces, either.[7] Do go on, Dicky dear.'

So Dicky went on.

'There must be hundreds of millions of bottles of medicines sold every year. Because all the different medicines say, "Thousands of cures daily," and if you only take that as two thousand, which it must be, at least, it mounts up. And the people who sell them must make a great deal of money by them because they are nearly always two and ninepence the bottle, and three and six for one nearly double the size. Now the bottles, as I was saying, don't cost anything like that.'

'It's the medicine costs the money,' said Dora; 'look how expensive jujubes are at the chemist's, and peppermints too.'

'That's only because they're nice,' Dicky explained; 'nasty things are not so dear. Look what a lot of brimstone you get for a penny, and the same with alum. We would not put the nice kinds of chemist's things in our medicine.'

Then he went on to tell us that when we had invented our medicine we would write and tell the editor about it, and he would put it in the paper, and then people would send their two and ninepence and three and six for the bottle nearly double the size, and then when the medicine had cured them they would write to the paper and their letters would be printed, saying how they had been suffering for years, and never thought to get about again, but thanks to the blessing of our ointment –

Dora interrupted and said, 'Not ointment – it's so messy.' And Alice thought so too. And Dicky said he did not mean it, he was quite decided to let it be in bottles. So now it was all settled, and we did not see at the time that this would be a sort of going into business, but afterwards when Albert's uncle showed us we saw it, and we were sorry.[8] We only had to invent the medicine. You might think that was easy, because of the number of them you see every day in the paper, but it is much harder than you think. First we had to decide what sort of illness we should like to cure, and a 'heated discussion ensued,' like in Parliament.[9]

Dora wanted it to be something to make the complexion of dazzling fairness, but we remembered how her face came all red and rough when she used the Rosabella soap that was advertised to make the darkest complexion fair as the lily, and she agreed that perhaps it was better not.[10] Noël wanted to make the medicine first and then find out what it would cure, but Dicky thought not, because there are so many more medicines than there are things the matter with us, so it would be easier to choose the disease first.

Oswald would have liked wounds. I still think it was a good idea, but Dicky said, 'Who has wounds, especially now there aren't any wars? We shouldn't sell a bottle a day!' So Oswald gave in because he knows what manners are, and it was Dicky's idea. H.O. wanted a cure for the uncomfortable feeling that they give you powders for, but we explained to him that grown-up people do not have this feeling, however much they eat, and he agreed. Dicky said he did not care a straw what the loathsome disease was, as long as we hurried up and settled on something. Then Alice said –

'It ought to be something very common, and only one thing. Not the pains in the back and all the hundreds of things the people have in somebody's syrup. What's the commonest thing of all?'

And at once we said, 'Colds.'

So that was settled.

Then we wrote a label to go on the bottle. When it was written it would not go on the vinegar bottle that we had got, but we knew it would go small when it was printed. It was like this:

BASTABLE'S

CERTAIN CURE FOR COLDS.

Coughs, Asthma, Shortness of Breath, and all
infections of the Chest.
One dose gives immediate relief.
It will cure your cold in one bottle.
Especially the larger size at 3s. 6d.
Order at once of the Makers.
To prevent disappointment.
Makers:
D., O., R., A., N., and H.O. BASTABLE,
150, Lewisham Road, S.E.
(*A halfpenny for all bottles returned.*)

Of course the next thing was for one of us to catch a cold and try what cured it; we all wanted to be the one, but it was Dicky's idea, and he said he was not going to be done out of it, so we let him. It was only fair. He left off his undershirt that very day, and next morning he stood in a draught in his nightgown for quite a long time. And we damped his day-shirt with the nail-brush before he put it on. But all was vain. They always tell you that these things will give you cold, but we found it was not so.

So then we all went over to the Park, and Dicky went right into the water with his boots on, and stood there as long as he could bear it, for it was rather cold, and we stood and cheered him on. He walked home in his wet clothes, which they say is a sure thing, but it was no go, though his boots were quite spoiled. And three days after Noël began to cough and sneeze.

So then Dicky said it was not fair.

'I can't help it,' Noël said. 'You should have caught it yourself, then it wouldn't have come to me.'

And Alice said she had known all along Noël oughtn't to have stood about on the bank cheering in the cold.

Noël had to go to bed, and then we began to make the medicines; we were sorry he was out of it, but he had the fun of taking the things.

We made a great many medicines. Alice made herb tea. She got sage and thyme and savory and marjoram and boiled them all up together with salt and water, but she *would* put parsley in too. Oswald is sure parsley is not a herb. It is only put on the cold meat and you are not supposed to eat it. It kills parrots to eat parsley, I believe.[11] I expect it was the parsley that disagreed so with Noël. The medicine did not seem to do the cough any good.

Oswald got a pennyworth of alum, because it is so cheap, and some turpentine which every one knows is good for colds, and a little sugar and an aniseed ball. These were mixed in a bottle with water, but Eliza threw it away and said it was nasty rubbish, and I hadn't any money to get more things with.

Dora made him some gruel, and he said it did his chest good; but of course that was no use, because you cannot put gruel in bottles and say it is medicine. It would not be honest, and besides nobody would believe you.

Dick mixed up lemon-juice and sugar and a little of the juice of the red flannel that Noël's throat was done up in. It comes out beautifully in hot water. Noël took this and he liked it. Noël's own idea was liquorice-water, and we let him have it, but it is too plain and black to sell in bottles at the proper price.

Noël liked H.O.'s medicine the best, which was silly of him, because it was only peppermints melted in hot water, and a little cobalt to make it look blue. It was all right, because H.O.'s paint-box is the French kind, with Couleurs non Vénéneuses on it.[12] This means you may suck your brushes if you want to, or even your paints if you are a very little boy.

It was rather jolly while Noël had that cold. He had a fire in his bedroom which opens out of Dicky's and Oswald's, and the girls used to read aloud to Noël all day; they will not read aloud to you when you are well. Father was away at Liverpool on business, and Albert's uncle was at Hastings. We were rather glad of this, because we wished to give all the medicines a fair trial, and grown-ups are but too fond of interfering. As if we should have given him anything poisonous!

His cold went on – it was bad in his head, but it was not one of the kind when he has to have poultices and can't sit up in bed. But when it had been in his head nearly a week, Oswald happened to tumble over Alice on the stairs. When we got up she was crying.

'Don't cry silly!' said Oswald; 'you know I didn't hurt you.' I was very sorry if I had hurt her, but you ought not to sit on the stairs in the dark and let other people tumble over you. You ought to remember how beastly it is for them if they do hurt you.

'Oh, it's not that, Oswald,' Alice said. 'Don't be a pig! I am so miserable. Do be kind to me.'

So Oswald thumped her on the back and told her to shut up.[13]

'It's about Noël,' she said. 'I'm sure he's very ill; and playing about with medicines is all very well, but I know he's ill, and Eliza won't send for the doctor: she says it's only a cold. And I know the doctor's bills are awful. I heard Father telling Aunt Emily so in the summer. But he *is* ill, and perhaps he'll die or something.'

Then she began to cry again. Oswald thumped her again, because he knows how a good brother ought to behave, and said, 'Cheer up.' If we had been in a book Oswald would have embraced his little sister tenderly, and mingled his tears with hers.

Then Oswald said, 'Why not write to Father?' And she cried more and said, 'I've lost the paper with the address. H.O. had it to draw on the back of, and I can't find it now; I've looked everywhere. I'll tell you what I'm going to do. No I won't. But I'm going out. Don't tell the others. And I say, Oswald, do pretend I'm in if Eliza asks. Promise.'

'Tell me what you're going to do,' I said. But she said 'No'; and there was a good reason why not. So I said I wouldn't promise if it came to that. Of course I meant to all right. But it did seem mean of her not to tell me.[14]

So Alice went out by the side door while Eliza was setting tea, and she was a long time gone; she was not in to tea. When Eliza asked Oswald where she was he said he did not know, but perhaps she was tidying her corner drawer. Girls often do this, and it takes a long time. Noël coughed a good bit after tea, and asked for Alice. Oswald told him she was doing something and it was a secret. Oswald did not tell any lies even to save his sister. When Alice came back she was very quiet, but she whispered to Oswald that it was all right. When it was rather late Eliza said she was going out to post a letter. This always takes her an hour, because she *will* go to the post-office across the Heath instead of the pillar-box, because once a boy dropped fusees in our pillar-box and burnt the letters. It was not any of us; Eliza told us about it. And when there was a knock at the door a long time after we thought it was Eliza come back, and that she had forgotten the back-door key. We made H.O. go down to open the door, because it is his place to run about: his legs are younger than ours. And we heard boots on the stairs besides H.O.'s, and we listened spellbound till the door opened, and it was Albert's uncle. He looked very tired.[15]

'I am glad you've come,' Oswald said. 'Alice began to think Noël – '

Alice stopped me, and her face was very red, her nose was shiny too, with having cried so much before tea.

She said, 'I only said I thought Noël ought to have the doctor. Don't you think he ought?' She got hold of Albert's uncle and held on to him.

'Let's have a look at you, young man,' said Albert's uncle, and he sat down on the edge of the bed. It is a rather shaky bed, the bar that keeps it steady underneath got broken when we were playing burglars last winter. It was our crowbar. He began to feel Noël's pulse, and went on talking.

'It was revealed to the Arab physician as he made merry in his tents on the wild plains of Hastings that the Presence had a cold in its head. So he immediately seated himself on the magic carpet, and bade it bear him hither, only pausing in the flight to purchase a few sweetmeats in the bazaar.'

He pulled out a jolly lot of chocolate and some butterscotch, and grapes for Noël. When we had all said thank you, he went on.

'The physician's are the words of wisdom: it's high time this kid was asleep. I have spoken. Ye have my leave to depart.'[16]

So we bunked, and Dora and Albert's uncle made Noël comfortable for the night.

Then they came to the nursery which we had gone down to, and he sat down in the Guy Fawkes chair and said, 'Now then.'

Alice said, 'You may tell them what I did. I daresay they'll all be in a wax, but I don't care.'

'I think you were very wise,' said Albert's uncle, pulling her close to him to sit on his knee. 'I am very glad you telegraphed.'

So then Oswald understood what Alice's secret was. She had gone out and sent a telegram to Albert's uncle at Hastings. But Oswald thought she might have told him. Afterwards she told me what she had put in the telegram. It was, 'Come home. We have given Noël a cold, and I think we are killing him.' With the address it came to tenpence halfpenny.

Then Albert's uncle began to ask questions, and it all came out, how Dicky had tried to catch the cold, but the cold had gone to Noël instead, and about the medicines and all.[17] Albert's uncle looked very serious.

'Look here,' he said, 'You're old enough not to play the fool like this. Health is the best thing you've got; you ought to know better than to risk it. You might have killed your little brother with your precious medicines. You've had a lucky escape, certainly. But poor Noël!'

'Oh, do you think he's going to die?' Alice asked that, and she was crying again.

'No, no,' said Albert's uncle; 'but look here. Do you see how silly you've been? And I thought you promised your Father – ' And then he gave us a long talking-to. He can make you feel most awfully small. At last he stopped, and we said we were very sorry, and he said, 'You know I promised to take you all to the pantomime?'

So we said, 'Yes,' and knew but too well that now he wasn't going to. Then he went on –

'Well, I will take you if you like, or I will take Noël to the sea for a week to cure his cold. Which is it to be?'

Of course he knew we should say, 'Take Noël' and we did; but Dicky told me afterwards he thought it was hard on H.O.

Albert's uncle stayed till Eliza came in, and then he said good night in a way that showed us that all was forgiven and forgotten.

And we went to bed. It must have been the middle of the night when Oswald woke up suddenly, and there was Alice with her teeth chattering, shaking him to wake him.

'Oh, Oswald!' she said, 'I am so unhappy. Suppose I should die in the night!'

Oswald told her to go to bed and not gas. But she said, 'I must tell you; I wish I'd told Albert's uncle. I'm a thief, and if I die to-night I know where thieves go to.'

So Oswald saw it was no good and he sat up in bed and said –

'Go ahead.'

So Alice stood shivering and said –

'I hadn't enough money for the telegram, so I took the bad six-pence out of the exchequer. And I paid for it with that and the fivepence I had. And I wouldn't tell you, because if you'd stopped me doing it I couldn't have borne it; and if you'd helped me you'd have been a thief too. Oh, what shall I do?'

Oswald thought a minute, and then he said –

'You'd better have told me. But I think it will be all right if we pay it back. Go to bed. Cross with you? No, stupid! Only another time you'd better not keep secrets.' So she kissed Oswald, and he let her, and she went back to bed. The next day Albert's uncle took Noël away, before Oswald had time to persuade Alice that we ought to tell him about the sixpence. Alice was very unhappy, but not so much as in the night: you can be very miserable in the night if you have done anything wrong and you happen to be awake. I know this for a fact.

None of us had any money except Eliza, and she wouldn't give us any unless we said what for; and of course we could not do that because of the honour of the family. And Oswald was anxious to get the sixpence to give to the telegraph people because he feared that the badness of that sixpence might have been found out, and that the police might come for Alice at any moment. I don't think I ever had such an unhappy day. Of course we could have written to Albert's uncle, but it would have taken a long time, and every moment of delay added to Alice's danger. We thought and thought, but we couldn't think of any way to get that sixpence. It seems a small sum, but you see Alice's liberty depended on it.[18] It was quite late in the afternoon when I met Mrs Leslie on the Parade. She had a brown fur coat and a lot of yellow flowers in her hands. She stopped to speak to me, and asked me how the Poet was. I told her he had a cold, and I wondered whether she would lend me sixpence if I asked her, but I could not make up my mind how to begin to say it. It is a hard thing to say – much harder than you would think.[19] She talked to me for a bit, and then she suddenly got into a cab, and said –

'I'd no idea it was so late,' and told the man where to go. And just as she started she shoved the yellow flowers through the window and said, 'For the sick poet, with my love,' and was driven off.

Gentle reader, I will not conceal from you what Oswald did. He knew all about not disgracing the family, and he did not like doing what I am going to say: and they were really Noël's flowers, only he could not have sent them to Hastings, and Oswald knew he would say 'Yes' if Oswald asked him. Oswald sacrificed his family pride because of his little sister's danger. I do not say he was a noble boy – I just tell you what he did, and you can decide for yourself about the nobleness.[20]

He put on his oldest clothes – they're much older than any you would think he had if you saw him when he was tidy – and he took those yellow chrysanthemums and he walked with them to Greenwich Station and waited for the trains bringing people from London. He sold those flowers in penny bunches and got ten-pence. Then he went to the telegraph office at Lewisham, and said to the lady there:

'A little girl gave you a bad sixpence yesterday. Here are six good pennies.'

The lady said she had not noticed it, and never mind, but Oswald knew that 'Honesty is the best Policy,' and he refused to take back the pennies. So at last she said she should put them in the plate on Sunday. She is a very nice lady. I like the way she does her hair.

Then Oswald went home to Alice and told her, and she hugged him, and said he was a dear, good, kind boy, and he said 'Oh, it's all right.'

We bought peppermint bullseyes with the fourpence I had over, and the others wanted to know where we got the money, but we would not tell.

Only afterwards when Noël came home we told him, because they were his flowers, and he said it was quite right. He made some poetry about it. I only remember one bit of it.

> The noble youth of high degree
> Consents to play a menial part,
> All for his sister Alice's sake,
> Who was so dear to his faithful heart.

But Oswald himself has never bragged about it.

We got no treasure out of this, unless you count the peppermint bullseyes.

* * *

Chapter 13
The Robber and the Burglar

A day or two after Noël came back from Hastings there was snow; it was jolly.[1] And we cleared it off the path. A man to do it is sixpence at least, and you should always save when you can. A penny saved is a penny earned. And then we thought it would be nice to clear it off the top of the portico, where it lies so thick, and the edges as if they had been cut with a knife. And just as we had got out of the landing-window on to the portico, the Water Rates came up the path with his book that he tears the thing out of that says how much you have got to pay, and the little ink-bottle hung on to his buttonhole in case you should pay him.[2] Father says the Water Rates is a sensible man, and knows it is always well to be prepared for whatever happens, however unlikely. Alice said afterwards that she rather liked the Water Rates, really, and Noël said he had a face like a good vizier, or the man who rewards the honest boy for restoring the purse, but we did not think about these things at the time, and as the Water Rates came up the steps, we shovelled down a great square slab of snow like an avalanche – and it fell right on his head. Two of us thought of it at the same moment, so it was quite a large avalanche. And when the Water Rates had shaken himself he rang the bell. It was Saturday, and Father was at home. We know now that it is very wrong and ungentlemanly to shovel snow off porticoes on to the Water Rates, or any other person, and we hope he did not catch a cold, and we are very sorry. We apologized to the Water Rates when Father told us to. We were all sent to bed for it.

We all deserved the punishment, because the others would have shoveled down snow just as we did if they'd thought of it – only they are not so quick at thinking of things as we are. And even quite wrong things sometimes lead to adventures; as every one knows who has ever read about pirates or highwaymen.

Eliza hates us to be sent to bed early, because it means her having to bring meals up, and it means lighting the fire in Noël's room ever so much earlier than usual. He had to have a fire because he still had a bit of a cold. But this particular day we got Eliza into a good temper by giving her a horrid brooch with pretending amethysts in it, that an aunt once gave to Alice, so Eliza brought up an extra scuttle of coals, and when the greengrocer came with the potatoes (he is always late on Saturdays) she got some chestnuts from him. So that when we heard Father go out after his dinner, there was a jolly fire in Noël's room, and we were able to go in and be Red Indians in blankets most comfortably. Eliza had gone out; she says she gets things cheaper on Saturday nights. She has a great friend, who sells fish at a shop, and he is very generous, and lets her have herrings for less than half the natural price.[3]

So we were all alone in the house; Pincher was out with Eliza, and we talked about robbers. And Dora thought it would be a dreadful trade, but Dicky said –

'I think it would be very interesting. And you would only rob rich people, and be very generous to the poor and needy, like Claude Duval.'

Dora said, 'It is wrong to be a robber.'

'Yes,' said Alice, 'you would never know a happy hour. Think of trying to sleep with the stolen jewels under your bed, and remembering all the quantities of policemen and detectives that there are in the world!'

'There are ways of being robbers that are not wrong,' said Noël; 'if you can rob a robber it is a right act.'

'But you can't,' said Dora; 'he is too clever, and besides, it's wrong anyway.'

'Yes you can, and it isn't; and murdering him with boiling oil is a right act, too, so there!' said Noël. 'What about Ali Baba?[4] Now then!' And we felt it was a score for Noël.

'What would you do if there *was* a robber?' said Alice.

H.O. said he would kill him with boiling oil; but Alice explained that she meant a real robber – now – this minute – in the house.

Oswald and Dicky did not say; but Noël said he thought it would only be fair to ask the robber quite politely and quietly to go away, and then if he didn't you could deal with him.

Now what I am going to tell you is a very strange and wonderful thing, and I hope you will be able to believe it. I should not, if a boy told me, unless I knew him to be a man of honour, and perhaps not then unless he gave his sacred word. But it is true, all the same, and it only shows that the days of romance and daring deeds are not yet at an end.

Alice was just asking Noël *how* he would deal with the robber who wouldn't go if he was asked politely and quietly, when we heard a noise downstairs – quite a plain noise, not the kind of noise you fancy you hear.[5] It was like somebody moving a chair. We held our breath and listened and then came another noise, like some one poking a fire. Now, you remember there was no one *to* poke a fire or move a chair downstairs, because Eliza and Father were both out. They could not have come in without our hearing them, because the front door is as hard to shut as the back one, and whichever you go in by you have to give a slam that you can hear all down the street.

H.O. and Alice and Dora caught hold of each other's blankets and looked at Dicky and Oswald, and every one was quite pale. And Noël whispered –

'It's ghosts, I know it is' – and then we listened again, but there was no more noise. Presently Dora said in a whisper –

'Whatever shall we do? Oh, whatever shall we do – what *shall* we do?' And she kept on saying it till we had to tell her to shut up.

O reader, have you ever been playing Red Indians in blankets round a bedroom fire in a house where you thought there was no one but you – and then suddenly heard a noise like a chair, and a fire being poked, downstairs? Unless you have you will not be able to imagine at all what it feels like. It was not like in books; our hair did not stand on end at all, and we never said 'Hist!' once, but our feet got very cold, though we were in blankets by the fire, and the insides of Oswald's hands got warm and wet, and his nose was cold like a dog's, and his ears were burning hot.

The girls said afterwards that they shivered with terror, and their teeth chattered, but we did not see or hear this at the time.[6]

'Shall we open the window and call police?' said Dora; and then Oswald suddenly thought of something, and he breathed more freely and he said –

'I *know* it's not ghosts, and I don't believe it's robbers. I expect it's a stray cat got in when the coals came this morning, and she's been hiding in the cellar, and now she's moving about. Let's go down and see.'

The girls wouldn't, of course; but I could see that they breathed more freely too. But Dicky said, 'All right; I will if you will.'

H.O. said, 'Do you think it's *really* a cat?' So we said he had better stay with the girls. And of course after that we had to let him and Alice both come. Dora said if we took Noël down with his cold, she would scream 'Fire!' and 'Murder!' and she didn't mind if the whole street heard.

So Noël agreed to be getting his clothes on, and the rest of us said we would go down and look for the cat.

Now Oswald *said* that about the cat, and it made it easier to go down, but in his inside he did not feel at all sure that it might not be robbers after all. Of course, we had often talked about robbers before, but it is very different when you sit in a room and listen and listen and listen; and Oswald felt somehow that it would be easier to go down and see what it was, than to wait, and listen, and wait, and wait, and listen, and wait, and then perhaps to hear *it*, whatever it was, come creeping slowly up the stairs as softly as *it* could with *its* boots off, and the stairs creaking, towards the room where we were with the door open in case of Eliza coming back suddenly, and all dark on the landings.[7] And then it would have been just as bad, and it would have lasted longer, and you would have known you were a coward besides. Dicky says he felt all these same things. Many people would say we were young heroes to go down as we did; so I have tried to explain, because no young hero wishes to have more credit than he deserves.

The landing gas was turned down low – just a blue bead – and we four went out very softly, wrapped in our blankets, and we stood on the top of the stairs a good long time before we began to go down. And we listened and listened till our ears buzzed.

And Oswald whispered to Dicky, and Dicky went into our room and fetched the large toy pistol that is a foot long, and that has the trigger broken, and I took it because I am the eldest; and I don't think either of us thought it was the cat now. But Alice and H.O. did. Dicky got the poker out of Noël's room, and told Dora it was to settle the cat with when we caught her.

Then Oswald whispered, 'Let's play at burglars; Dicky and I are armed to the teeth, we will go first. You keep a flight behind us, and be a reinforcement if we are attacked. Or you can retreat and defend the women and children in the fortress, if you'd rather.'

But they said they would be a reinforcement.

Oswald's teeth chattered a little when he spoke. It was not with anything else except cold.

So Dicky and Oswald crept down, and when we got to the bottom of the stairs, we saw Father's study door just ajar, and the crack of light. And Oswald was so pleased to see the light, knowing that burglars prefer the dark, or at any rate the dark lantern, that he felt really sure it *was* the cat after all, and then he thought it would be fun to make the others upstairs think it was really a robber. So he cocked the pistol – you can cock it, but it doesn't go off – and he said, 'Come on, Dick!' and he rushed at the study door and burst into the room, crying, 'Surrender! you are discovered! Surrender, or I fire! Throw up your hands!'

And, as he finished saying it, he saw before him, standing on the study hearthrug, a Real Robber. There was no mistake about it. Oswald was sure it was a robber, because it had a screwdriver in its hands, and was standing near the cupboard door that H.O. broke the lock off; and there were gimlets and screws and things on the floor. There is nothing in that cupboard but old ledgers and magazines and the tool chest, but of course, a robber could not know that beforehand.

When Oswald saw that there really was a robber, and that he was so heavily armed with the screwdriver, he did not feel comfortable. But he kept the pistol pointed at the robber, and – you will hardly believe it, but it is true – the robber threw down the screwdriver clattering on the other tools, and he *did* throw up his hands, and said –

'I surrender; don't shoot me! How many of you are there?'

So Dicky said, 'You are outnumbered. Are you armed?'

And the robber said, 'No, not in the least.'

And Oswald said, still pointing the pistol, and feeling very strong and brave and as if he was in a book, 'Turn out your pockets.'

The robber did: and while he turned them out, we looked at him. He was of the middle height, and clad in a black frock-coat and grey trousers. His boots were a little gone at the sides, and his shirt-cuffs were a bit frayed, but otherwise he was of gentlemanly demeanour. He had a thin, wrinkled face, with big, light eyes that sparkled, and then looked soft very queerly, and a short beard. In his youth it must have been of a fair golden colour, but now it was tinged with grey. Oswald was sorry for him, especially when he saw that one of his pockets had a large hole in it, and that he had nothing in his pockets but letters and string and three boxes of matches, and a pipe and a handkerchief and a thin tobacco pouch and two pennies.[8] We made him put all the things on the table, and then he said –

'Well, you've caught me; what are you going to do with me? Police?'

Alice and H.O. had come down to be reinforcements, when they heard a shout, and when Alice saw that it was a Real Robber, and that he had surrendered, she clapped her hands and said, 'Bravo, boys!' and so did H.O. And now she said, 'If he gives his word of honour not to escape, I shouldn't call the police: it seems a pity. Wait till Father comes home.'

The robber agreed to this, and gave his word of honour, and asked if he might put on a pipe, and we said 'Yes,' and he sat in Father's armchair and warmed his boots, which steamed, and I sent H.O. and Alice to put on some clothes and tell the others, and bring down Dicky's and my knickerbockers, and the rest of the chestnuts.

And they all came, and we sat round the fire, and it was jolly. The robber was very friendly, and talked to us a great deal.

'I wasn't always in this low way of business,' he said, when Noël said something about the things he had turned out of his pockets.[9] 'It's a great come-down to a man like me. But, if I must be caught, it's something to be caught by brave young heroes like you. My stars! How you did bolt into the room, – "Surrender, and up with your hands!" You might have been born and bred to the thief-catching.'

Oswald is sorry if it was mean, but he could not own up just then that he did not think there was any one in the study when he did that brave if rash act. He has told since.

'And what made you think there was any one in the house?' the robber asked, when he had thrown his head back, and laughed for quite half a minute. So we told him. And he applauded our valour, and Alice and H.O. explained that they would have said 'Surrender,' too, only they were reinforcements. The robber ate some of the chestnuts – and we sat and wondered when Father would come home, and what he would say to us for our intrepid conduct. And the robber told us of all the things he had done before he began to break into houses. Dicky picked up the tools from the floor, and suddenly he said –

'Why, this is Father's screwdriver and his gimlets, and all! Well, I do call it jolly cheek to pick a man's locks with his own tools!'

'True, true,' said the robber. 'It is cheek, of the jolliest! But you see I've come down in the world. I was a highway robber once, but horses are so expensive to hire – five shillings an hour, you know – and I couldn't afford to keep them. The highwayman business isn't what it was.'

'What about a bike?' said H.O.

But the robber thought cycles were low – and besides you couldn't go across country with them when occasion arose, as you could with a trusty steed. And he talked of highwaymen as if he knew just how we liked hearing it.

Then he told us how he had been a pirate captain – and how he had sailed over waves mountains high, and gained rich prizes – and how he *did* begin to think that here he had found a profession to his mind.

'I don't say there are no ups and downs in it,' he said, 'especially in stormy weather. But what a trade! And a sword at your side, and the Jolly Roger flying at the peak, and a prize in sight. And all the black mouths of your guns pointed at the laden trader – and the wind in your favour, and your trusty crew ready to live and die for you! Oh – but it's a grand life!'

I did feel so sorry for him. He used such nice words, and he had a gentleman's voice.

'I'm sure you weren't brought up to be a pirate,' said Dora. She had dressed even to her collar – and made Noël do it too – but the rest of us were in blankets with just a few odd things put on anyhow underneath.

The robber frowned and sighed.

'No,' he said, 'I was brought up to the law. I was at Balliol, bless your hearts, and that's true anyway.'[10] He sighed again, and looked hard at the fire.

'That was my Father's college,' H.O. was beginning, but Dicky said – 'Why did you leave off being a pirate?'

'A pirate?' he said, as if he had not been thinking of such things. 'Oh, yes; why I gave it up because – because I could not get over the dreadful sea-sickness.'

'Nelson was sea-sick,' said Oswald.

'Ah,' said the robber; 'but I hadn't his luck or his pluck, or something. He stuck to it and won Trafalgar, didn't he? "Kiss me, Hardy" – and all that, eh? *I* couldn't stick to it – I had to resign. And nobody kissed *me*.'[11]

I saw by his understanding about Nelson that he was really a man who had been to a good school as well as to Balliol.

Then we asked him, 'And what did you do then?'

And Alice asked if he was ever a coiner, and we told him how we had thought we'd caught the desperate gang next door, and he was very much interested and said he was glad he had never taken to coining.

'Besides, the coins are so ugly nowadays,' he said, 'no one could really find any pleasure in making them. And it's a hole-and-corner business at the best, isn't it? – and it must be a very thirsty one – with the hot metal and furnaces and things.'

And again he looked at the fire.

Oswald forgot for a minute that the interesting stranger was a robber, and asked him if he wouldn't have a drink. Oswald has heard Father do this to his friends, so he knows it is the right thing. The robber said he didn't mind if he did. And that is right, too.

And Dora went and got a bottle of Father's ale – the Light Sparkling Family – and a glass, and we gave it to the robber.[12] Dora said she would be responsible.

Then when he had had a drink he told us about bandits, but he said it was so bad in wet weather. Bandits' caves were hardly ever properly weathertight. And bush-ranging was the same.

'As a matter of fact,' he said, 'I was bush-ranging this afternoon, among the furze-bushes on the Heath, but I had no luck. I stopped the Lord Mayor in his gilt coach, with all his footmen in plush and gold lace, smart as cockatoos. But it was no go. The Lord Mayor hadn't a stiver in his pockets. One of the footmen had six new pennies: the Lord Mayor always pays his servants' wages in new pennies. I spent fourpence of that in bread and cheese, that on the table's the tuppence. Ah, it's a poor trade!' And then he filled his pipe again.

We had turned out the gas, so that Father should have a jolly good surprise when he did come home, and we sat and talked as pleasant as could be. I never liked a new man better than I liked that robber. And I felt so sorry for him. He told us he had been a war-correspondent and an editor, in happier days, as well as a horse-stealer and a colonel of dragoons.[13]

And quite suddenly, just as we were telling him about Lord Tottenham and our being highwaymen ourselves, he put up his hand and said 'Shish!' and we were quiet and listened.

There was a scrape, scrape, scraping noise; it came from downstairs.

'They're filing something,' whispered the robber, 'here – shut up, give me that pistol, and the poker. There is a burglar now, and no mistake.'

'It's only a toy one and it won't go off,' I said, 'but you can cock it.'

Then we heard a snap. 'There goes the window bar,' said the robber softly. 'Jove! what an adventure! You kids stay here, I'll tackle it.'

But Dicky and I said we should come. So he let us go as far as the bottom of the kitchen stairs, and we took the tongs and shovel with us. There was a light in the kitchen; a very little light. It is curious we never thought, any of us, that this might be a plant of our robber's to get away. We never thought of doubting his word of honour. And we were right.

That noble robber dashed the kitchen door open, and rushed in with the big toy pistol in one hand and the poker in the other, shouting out just like Oswald had done –

'Surrender! You are discovered! Surrender, or I'll fire! Throw up your hands!' And Dicky and I rattled the tongs and shovel so that he might know there were more of us, all bristling with weapons.

And we heard a husky voice in the kitchen saying –

'All right, governor! Stow that scent sprinkler. I'll give in. Blowed if I ain't pretty well sick of the job, anyway.'

Then we went in. Our robber was standing in the grandest manner with his legs very wide apart, and the pistol pointing at the cowering burglar. The burglar was a large man who did not mean to have a beard, I think, but he had got some of one, and a red comforter, and a fur cap, and his face was red and his voice was thick. How different from our own robber! The burglar had a dark lantern, and he was standing by the plate-basket. When we had lit the gas we all thought he was very like what a burglar ought to be.

He did not look as if he could ever have been a pirate or a highwayman, or anything really dashing or noble, and he scowled and shuffled his feet and said: 'Well, go on: why don't yer fetch the pleece?'

'Upon my word, I don't know,' said our robber, rubbing his chin. 'Oswald, why don't we fetch the police?'

It is not every robber that I would stand Christian names from, I can tell you but just then I didn't think of that. I just said – 'Do you mean I'm to fetch one?'

Our robber looked at the burglar and said nothing.

Then the burglar began to speak very fast, and to look different ways with his hard, shiny little eyes.

'Lookee 'ere, governor,' he said, 'I was stony broke, so help me, I was. And blessed if I've nicked a haporth of your little lot. You know yourself there ain't much to tempt a bloke,' he shook the plate-basket as if he was angry with it, and the yellowy spoons and forks rattled. 'I was just a-looking through this 'ere Bank-ollerday show, when you come.[14] Let me off, sir. Come now, I've got kids of my own at home, strike me if I ain't – same as yours – I've got a nipper just about 'is size, and what'll come of them if I'm lagged? I ain't been in it long, sir, and I ain't 'andy at it.'

'No,' said our robber; 'you certainly are not.' Alice and the others had come down by now to see what was happening. Alice told me afterwards they thought it really was the cat this time.

'No, I ain't 'andy, as you say, sir, and if you let me off this once I'll chuck the whole blooming bizz; rake my civvy, I will. Don't be hard on a cove, mister; think of the missis and the kids. I've got one just the cut of little missy there bless 'er pretty 'eart.'

'Your family certainly fits your circumstances very nicely,' said our robber. Then Alice said –

'Oh, do let him go! If he's got a little girl like me, whatever will she do? Suppose it was Father!'

'I don't think he's got a little girl like you, my dear,' said our robber, 'and I think he'll be safer under lock and key.'

'You ask yer Father to let me go, miss,' said the burglar; 'e won't 'ave the 'art to refuse you.'

'If I do,' said Alice, 'will you promise never to come back?'

'Not me, miss,' the burglar said very earnestly, and he looked at the plate-basket again, as if that alone would be enough to keep him away, our robber said afterwards.[15]

'And will you be good and not rob any more?' said Alice.

'I'll turn over a noo leaf, miss, so help me.'

Then Alice said – 'Oh, do let him go! I'm sure he'll be good.'

But our robber said no, it wouldn't be right; we must wait till Father came home. Then H.O. said, very suddenly and plainly:

'I don't think it's at all fair, when you're a robber yourself.'

The minute he'd said it the burglar said, 'Kidded, by gum!' – and then our robber made a step towards him to catch hold of him, and before you had time to think 'Hullo!' the burglar knocked the pistol up with one hand and knocked our robber down with the other, and was off out of the window like a shot, though Oswald and Dicky did try to stop him by holding on to his legs.

And that burglar had the cheek to put his head in at the window and say, 'I'll give yer love to the kids and the missis' – and he was off like winking, and there were Alice and Dora trying to pick up our robber, and asking him whether he was hurt, and where. He wasn't hurt at all, except a lump at the back of his head. And he got up, and we dusted the kitchen floor off him. Eliza is a dirty girl.

Then he said, 'Let's put up the shutters. It never rains but it pours. Now you've had two burglars I daresay you'll have twenty.' So we put up the shutters, which Eliza has strict orders to do before she goes out, only she never does, and we went back to Father's study, and the robber said, 'What a night we are having!' and put his boots back in the fender to go on steaming, and then we all talked at once. It was the most wonderful adventure we ever had, though it wasn't treasure-seeking – at least not ours. I suppose it was the burglar's treasure-seeking, but he didn't get much – and our robber said he didn't believe a word about those kids that were so like Alice and me.

And then there was the click of the gate, and we said, 'Here's Father,' and the robber said, 'And now for the police.'

Then we all jumped up. We did like him so much, and it seemed so unfair that he should be sent to prison, and the horrid, lumping big burglar not.

And Alice said, 'Oh, *no* – run! Dicky will let you out at the back door. Oh, do go, go *now*.'

And we all said, 'Yes, *go*,' and pulled him towards the door, and gave him his hat and stick and the things out of his pockets.

But Father's latchkey was in the door, and it was too late.

Father came in quickly, purring with the cold, and began to say, 'It's all right, Foulkes, I've got – ' And then he stopped short and stared at us. Then he said, in the voice we all hate, 'Children, what is the meaning of all this?' And for a minute nobody spoke.

Then my Father said, 'Foulkes, I must really apologize for these very naughty – ' And then our robber rubbed his hands and laughed, and cried out:

'You're mistaken, my dear sir, I'm not Foulkes; I'm a robber, captured by these young people in the most gallant manner. "Hands up, surrender, or I fire," and all the rest of it. My word, Bastable, but you've got some kids worth having! I wish my Denny had their pluck.'

Then we began to understand, and it was like being knocked down, it was so sudden. And our robber told us he wasn't a robber after all. He was only an old college friend of my Father's, and he had come after dinner, when Father was just trying to mend the lock H.O. had broken, to ask Father to get him a letter to a doctor about his little boy Denny, who was ill. And Father had gone over the Heath to Vanbrugh Park to see some rich people he knows and get the letter.[16] And he had left Mr Foulkes to wait till he came back, because it was important to know at once whether Father could get the letter, and if he couldn't Mr Foulkes would have had to try some one else directly.

We were dumb with amazement.

Our robber told my Father about the other burglar, and said he was sorry he'd let him escape, but my Father said, 'Oh, it's all right: poor beggar; if he really had kids at home: you never can tell – forgive us our debts, don't you know; but tell me about the first business. It must have been moderately entertaining.'

Then our robber told my Father how I had rushed into the room with a pistol, crying out … but you know all about that. And he laid it on so thick and fat about plucky young-uns, and chips of old blocks, and things like that, that I felt I was purple with shame, even under the blanket. So I swallowed that thing that tries to prevent you speaking when you ought to, and I said, 'Look here, Father, I didn't really think there was any one in the study. We thought it was a cat at first, and then I thought there was no one there, and I was just larking. And when I said surrender and all that, it was just the game, don't you know?'

Then our robber said, 'Yes, old chap; but when you found there really *was* someone there, you dropped the pistol and bunked, didn't you, eh?'

And I said, 'No; I thought, "Hullo! here's a robber! Well, it's all up, I suppose, but I may as well hold on and see what happens."'

And I was glad I'd owned up, for Father slapped me on the back, and said I was a young brick, and our robber said I was no funk anyway, and though I got very hot under the blanket I liked it, and I explained that the others would have done the same if they had thought of it.

Then Father got up some more beer, and laughed about Dora's responsibility, and he got out a box of figs he had bought for us, only he hadn't given it to us because of the Water Rates, and Eliza came in and brought up the bread and cheese, and what there was left of the neck of mutton – cold wreck of mutton, Father called it – and we had a feast – like a picnic – all sitting anywhere, and eating with our fingers.[17] It was prime. We sat up till past twelve o'clock, and I never felt so pleased to think I was not born a girl. It was hard on the others; they would have done just the same if they'd thought of it. But it does make you feel jolly when your pater says you're a young brick!

When Mr Foulkes was going, he said to Alice, 'Good-bye, Hardy.'

And Alice understood, of course, and kissed him as hard as she could.

And she said, 'I wanted to, when you said no one kissed you when you left off being a pirate.' And he said, 'I know you did, my dear.' And Dora kissed him too, and said, 'I suppose none of these tales were true?'

And our robber just said, 'I tried to play the part properly, my dear.'

And he jolly well did play it, and no mistake. We have often seen him since, and his boy Denny, and his girl Daisy, but that comes in another story.[18]

And if any of you kids who read this ever had two such adventures in one night you can just write and tell me. That's all.

*   *   *

Chapter 14
The Divining Rod

You have no idea how uncomfortable the house was on the day when we sought for gold with the divining-rod.[1] It was like a spring-cleaning in the winter-time. All the carpets were up, because Father had told Eliza to make the place decent as there was a gentleman coming to dinner the next day. So she got in a charwoman, and they slopped water about, and left brooms and brushes on the stairs for people to tumble over. H.O. got a big bump on his head in that way, and when he said it was too bad, Eliza said he should keep in the nursery then, and not be where he'd no business. We bandaged his head with a towel, and then he stopped crying and played at being England's wounded hero dying in the cockpit, while every man was doing his duty, as the hero had told them to, and Alice was Hardy, and I was the doctor, and the others were the crew.[2] Playing at Hardy made us think of our own dear robber, and we wished he was there, and wondered if we should ever see him any more.

We were rather astonished at Father's having anyone to dinner, because now he never seems to think of anything but business. Before Mother died people often came to dinner, and Father's business did not take up so much of his time and was not the bother it is now.[3] And we used to see who could go furthest down in our nightgowns and get nice things to eat, without being seen, out of the dishes as they came out of the dining-room. Eliza can't cook very nice things. She told Father she was a good plain cook, but he says it was a fancy portrait. We stayed in the nursery till the charwoman came in and told us to be off – she was going to make one job of it, and have our carpet up as well as all the others, now the man was here to beat them. It came up, and it was very dusty – and under it we found my threepenny-bit that I lost ages ago, which shows what Eliza is.[4] H.O. had got tired of being the wounded hero, and Dicky was so tired of doing nothing that Dora said she knew he'd begin to tease Noël in a minute; then of course Dicky said he wasn't going to tease anybody – he was going out to the Heath. He said he'd heard that nagging women drove a man from his home, and now he found it was quite true. Oswald always tries to be a peacemaker, so he told Dicky to shut up and not make an ass of himself. And Alice said, 'Well, Dora began – ' And Dora tossed her chin up and said it wasn't any business of Oswald's any way, and no one asked Alice's opinion.[5] So we all felt very uncomfortable till Noël said, 'Don't let's quarrel about nothing. You know let dogs delight – and I made up another piece while you were talking – [6]

> 'Quarrelling is an evil thing,
> It fills with gall life's cup;
> For when once you begin
> It takes such a long time to make it up.'

We all laughed then and stopped jawing at each other. Noël is very funny with his poetry. But that piece happened to come out quite true. You begin to quarrel and then you can't stop; often, long before the others are ready to cry and make it up, I see how silly it is, and I want to laugh; but it doesn't do to say so – for it only makes the others crosser than they were before.[7] I wonder why that is?

Alice said Noël ought to be poet laureate, and she actually went out in the cold and got some laurel leaves – the spotted kind – out of the garden, and Dora made a crown and we put it on him. He was quite pleased; but the leaves made a mess, and Eliza said, 'Don't.' I believe that's a word grown-ups use more than any other. Then suddenly Alice thought of that old idea of hers for finding treasure, and she said –

'Do let's try the divining-rod.'

So Oswald said, 'Fair priestess, we do greatly desire to find gold beneath our land, therefore we pray thee practise with the divining-rod, and tell us where we can find it.'

'Do ye desire to fashion of it helms and hauberks?' said Alice.

'Yes,' said Noël; 'and chains and ouches.'

'I bet you don't know what an "ouch" is,' said Dicky.

'Yes I do, so there!' said Noël. 'It's a carcanet. I looked it out in the dicker, now then!' We asked him what a carcanet was, but he wouldn't say.[8]

'And we want to make fair goblets of the gold,' said Oswald.

'Yes, to drink cocoanut milk out of,' said H.O.

'And we desire to build fair palaces of it,' said Dicky.

'And to buy things,' said Dora; 'a great many things. New Sunday frocks and hats and kid gloves and – '

She would have gone on for ever so long only we reminded her that we hadn't found the gold yet.

By this Alice had put on the nursery table-cloth, which is green, and tied the old blue and yellow antimacassar over her head, and she said –

'If your intentions are correct, fear nothing and follow me.'[9]

And she went down into the hall. We all followed chanting 'Heroes.'[10] It is a gloomy thing the girls learnt at the High School, and we always use it when we want a priestly chant.

Alice stopped short by the hat-stand, and held up her hands as well as she could for the table-cloth, and said –

'Now, great altar of the golden idol, yield me the divining-rod that I may use it for the good of the suffering people.'

The umbrella-stand was the altar of the golden idol, and it yielded her the old school umbrella. She carried it between her palms.

'Now,' she said, 'I shall sing the magic chant. You mustn't say anything, but just follow wherever I go – like follow my leader, you know – and when there is gold underneath the magic rod will twist in the hand of the priestess like a live thing that seeks to be free. Then you will dig, and the golden treasure will be revealed.[11] H.O., if you make that clatter with your boots they'll come and tell us not to. Now come on all of you.'

So she went upstairs and down and into every room. We followed her on tiptoe, and Alice sang as she went. What she sang is not out of a book – Noël made it up while she was dressing up for the priestess.

> 'Ashen rod cold
> That here I hold,
> Teach me where to find the gold.'

When we came to where Eliza was, she said, 'Get along with you'; but Dora said it was only a game, and we wouldn't touch anything, and our boots were quite clean, and Eliza might as well let us. So she did.

It was all right for the priestess, but it was a little dull for the rest of us, because she wouldn't let us sing, too; so we said we'd had enough of it, and if she couldn't find the gold we'd leave off and play something else. The priestess said, 'All right, wait a minute,' and went on singing. Then we all followed her back into the nursery, where the carpet was up and the boards smelt of soft soap. Then she said, 'It moves, it moves! Once more the choral hymn!' So we sang 'Heroes' again, and in the middle the umbrella dropped from her hands.

'The magic rod has spoken,' said Alice; 'dig here, and that with courage and despatch.' We didn't quite see how to dig, but we all began to scratch on the floor with our hands, but the priestess said, 'Don't be so silly! It's the place where they come to do the gas. The board's loose. Dig an you value your lives, for ere sundown the dragon who guards this spoil will return in his fiery fury and make you his unresisting prey.'[12]

So we dug – that is, we got the loose board up. And Alice threw up her arms and cried –

'See the rich treasure – the gold in thick layers, with silver and diamonds stuck in it!'

'Like currants in cake,' said H.O.

'It's a lovely treasure,' said Dicky yawning. 'Let's come back and carry it away another day.'

But Alice was kneeling by the hole.

'Let me feast my eyes on the golden splendour,' she said, 'hidden these long centuries from the human eye. Behold how the magic rod has led us to treasures more – Oswald, don't push so! – more bright than ever monarch – I say, there *is* something down there, really. I saw it shine!'

We thought she was kidding, but when she began to try to get into the hole, which was much too small, we saw she meant it, so I said, 'Let's have a squint,' and I looked, but I couldn't see anything, even when I lay down on my stomach. The others lay down on their stomachs too and tried to see, all but Noël, who stood and looked at us and said we were the great serpents come down to drink at the magic pool. He wanted to be the knight and slay the great serpents with his good sword – he even drew the umbrella ready – but Alice said, 'All right, we will in a minute. But now – I'm sure I saw it; do get a match, Noël, there's a dear.'

'What did you see?' asked Noël, beginning to go for the matches very slowly.

'Something bright, away in the corner under the board against the beam.'

'Perhaps it was a rat's eye,' Noël said, 'or a snake's,' and we did not put our heads quite so close to the hole till he came back with the matches.

Then I struck a match, and Alice cried, 'There it is!'

And there it was, and it was a half-sovereign, partly dusty and partly bright. We think perhaps a mouse, disturbed by the carpets being taken up, may have brushed the dust of years from part of the half-sovereign with his tail. We can't imagine how it came there, only Dora thinks she remembers once when H.O. was very little Mother gave him some money to hold, and he dropped it, and it rolled all over the floor. So we think perhaps this was part of it. We were very glad. H.O. wanted to go out at once and buy a mask he had seen for fourpence. It had been a shilling mask, but now it was going very cheap because Guy Fawkes' Day was over, and it was a little cracked at the top.[13] But Dora said, 'I don't know that it's our money. Let's wait and ask Father.'

But H.O. did not care about waiting, and I felt for him. Dora is rather like grown-ups in that way; she does not seem to understand that when you want a thing you do want it, and that you don't wish to wait, even a minute.

So we went and asked Albert-next-door's uncle. He was pegging away at one of the rotten novels he has to write to make his living, but he said we weren't interrupting him at all.

'My hero's folly has involved him in a difficulty,' he said. 'It is his own fault. I will leave him to meditate on the incredible fatuity – the hare-brained recklessness – which have brought him to this pass. It will be a lesson to him. I, meantime, will give myself unreservedly to the pleasures of your conversation.'[14]

That's one thing I like Albert's uncle for. He always talks like a book, and yet you can always understand what he means. I think he is more like us, inside of his mind, than most grown-up people are. He can pretend beautifully. I never met anyone else so good at it, except our robber, and we began it, with him. But it was Albert's uncle who first taught us how to make people talk like books when you're playing things, and he made us learn to tell a story straight from the beginning, not starting in the middle like most people do.[15] So now Oswald remembered what he had been told, as he generally does, and began at the beginning, but when he came to where Alice said she was the priestess, Albert's uncle said –

'Let the priestess herself set forth the tale in fitting speech.'

So Alice said, 'O high priest of the great idol, the humblest of thy slaves took the school umbrella for a divining-rod, and sang the song of inver – what's-it's-name?'

'Invocation perhaps?' said Albert's uncle.

'Yes; and then I went about and about and the others got tired, so the divining-rod fell on a certain spot, and I said, "Dig", and we dug – it was where the loose board is for the gas men – and then there really and truly was a half-sovereign lying under the boards, and here it is.'

Albert's uncle took it and looked at it.

'The great high priest will bite it to see if it's good,' he said, and he did. 'I congratulate you,' he went on; 'you are indeed among those favoured by the Immortals. First you find half-crowns in the garden, and now this. The high priest advises you to tell your Father, and ask if you may keep it. My hero has become penitent, but impatient. I must pull him out of this scrape. Ye have my leave to depart.'[16]

Of course we know from Kipling that that means, 'You'd better bunk, and be sharp about it,' so we came away. I do like Albert's uncle. I shall be like that when I'm a man. He gave us our Jungle books, and he is awfully clever, though he does have to write grown-up tales.

We told Father about it that night. He was very kind. He said we might certainly have the half-sovereign, and he hoped we should enjoy ourselves with our treasure-trove.

Then he said, 'Your dear Mother's Indian Uncle is coming to dinner here to-morrow night. So will you not drag the furniture about overhead, please, more than you're absolutely obliged; and H.O. might wear slippers or something. I can always distinguish the note of H.O.'s boots.'

We said we would be very quiet, and Father went on –

'This Indian Uncle is not used to children, and he is coming to talk business with me. It is really important that he should be quiet. Do you think, Dora, that perhaps bed at six for H.O. and Noël – '

But H.O. said, 'Father, I really and truly won't make a noise. I'll stand on my head all the evening sooner than disturb the Indian Uncle with my boots.'

And Alice said Noël never made a row anyhow.[17]

So Father laughed and said, 'All right.' And he said we might do as we liked with the half-sovereign. 'Only for goodness' sake don't try to go in for business with it,' he said. 'It's always a mistake to go into business with an insufficient capital.'

We talked it over all that evening, and we decided that as we were not to go into business with our half-sovereign it was no use not spending it at once, and so we might as well have a right royal feast. The next day we went out and bought the things. We got figs, and almonds and raisins, and a real raw rabbit, and Eliza promised to cook it for us if we would wait till tomorrow, because of the Indian Uncle coming to dinner. She was very busy cooking nice things for him to eat. We got the rabbit because we are so tired of beef and mutton, and Father hasn't a bill at the poultry shop. And we got some flowers to go on the dinner-table for Father's party. And we got hardbake and raspberry noyau and peppermint rock and oranges and a cocoanut, with other nice things. We put it all in the top long drawer. It is H.O.'s play drawer, and we made him turn his things out and put them in Father's old portmanteau. H.O. is getting old enough now to learn to be unselfish, and besides, his drawer wanted tidying very badly. Then we all vowed by the honour of the ancient House of Bastable that we would not touch any of the feast till Dora gave the word next day. And we gave H.O. some of the hardbake, to make it easier for him to keep his vow. The next day was the most rememorable day in all our lives, but we didn't know that then. But that is another story. I think that is such a useful way to know when you can't think how to end up a chapter.[18] I learnt it from another writer named Kipling. I've mentioned him before, I believe, but he deserves it!

* * *

Chapter 15
'Lo, the Poor Indian!'

It was all very well for Father to ask us not to make a row because the Indian Uncle was coming to talk business, but my young brother's boots are not the only things that make a noise. We took his boots away and made him wear Dora's bath slippers, which are soft and woolly, and hardly any soles to them; and of course we wanted to see the Uncle, so we looked over the banisters when he came, and we were as quiet as mice – but when Eliza had let him in she went straight down to the kitchen and made the most awful row you ever heard, it sounded like the Day of Judgment, or all the saucepans and crockery in the house being kicked about the floor, but she told me afterwards it was only the tea-tray and one or two cups and saucers, that she had knocked over in her flurry. We heard the Uncle say, 'God bless my soul!' and then he went into Father's study and the door was shut – we didn't see him properly at all that time.[1]

I don't believe the dinner was very nice. Something got burned I'm sure – for we smelt it. It was an extra smell, besides the mutton. I know *that* got burned. Eliza wouldn't have any of us in the kitchen except Dora – till dinner was over. Then we got what was left of the dessert, and had it on the stairs – just round the corner where they can't see you from the hall, unless the first landing gas is lighted. Suddenly the study door opened and the Uncle came out and went and felt in his great-coat pocket. It was his cigar-case he wanted. We saw that afterwards. We got a much better view of him then.[2] He didn't look like an Indian but just like a kind of brown, big Englishman, and of course he didn't see us, but we heard him mutter to himself –

'Shocking bad dinner! Eh! – what?' When he went back to the study he didn't shut the door properly. That door has always been a little tiresome since the day we took the lock off to get out the pencil sharpener H.O. had shoved into the keyhole. We didn't listen – really and truly – but the Indian Uncle has a very big voice, and Father was not going to be beaten by a poor Indian in talking or anything else – so he spoke up too, like a man, and I heard him say it was a very good business, and only wanted a little capital – and he said it as if it was an imposition he had learned, and he hated having to say it.[3] The Uncle said, 'Pooh, pooh!' to that, and then he said he was afraid that what that same business wanted was not capital but management. Then I heard my Father say, 'It is not a pleasant subject: I am sorry I introduced it. Suppose we change it, sir. Let me fill your glass.' Then the poor Indian said something about vintage – and that a poor, broken-down man like he was couldn't be too careful. And then Father said, 'Well, whisky then,' and afterwards they talked about Native Races and Imperial something or other and it got very dull.[4]

So then Oswald remembered that you must not hear what people do not intend you to hear – even if you are not listening and he said, 'We ought not to stay here any longer. Perhaps they would not like us to hear – '

Alice said, 'Oh, do you think it could possibly matter?' and went and shut the study door softly but quite tight. So it was no use staying there any longer, and we went to the nursery.

Then Noël said, 'Now I understand. Of course my Father is making a banquet for the Indian, because he is a poor, broken-down man. We might have known that from "Lo, the poor Indian!" you know.'[5]

We all agreed with him, and we were glad to have the thing explained, because we had not understood before what Father wanted to have people to dinner for – and not let us come in.

'Poor people are very proud,' said Alice, 'and I expect Father thought the Indian would be ashamed, if all of us children knew how poor he was.'

Then Dora said, 'Poverty is no disgrace. We should honour honest Poverty.'

And we all agreed that that was so.

'I wish his dinner had not been so nasty,' Dora said, while Oswald put lumps of coal on the fire with his fingers, so as not to make a noise. He is a very thoughtful boy, and he did not wipe his fingers on his trouser leg as perhaps Noël or H.O. would have done, but he just rubbed them on Dora's handkerchief while she was talking. 'I am afraid the dinner was horrid.' Dora went on. 'The table looked very nice with the flowers we got.[6] I set it myself, and Eliza made me borrow the silver spoons and forks from Albert-next-door's Mother.'

'I hope the poor Indian is honest,' said Dicky gloomily, 'when you are a poor, broken-down man silver spoons must be a great temptation.'

Oswald told him not to talk such tommy-rot because the Indian was a relation, so of course he couldn't do anything dishonourable. And Dora said it was all right any way, because she had washed up the spoons and forks herself and counted them, and they were all there, and she had put them into their wash-leather bag, and taken them back to Albert-next-door's Mother.[7]

'And the brussels sprouts were all wet and swimmy,' she went on, 'and the potatoes looked grey – and there were bits of black in the gravy – and the mutton was bluey-red and soft in the middle. I saw it when it came out. The apple-pie looked very nice – but it wasn't quite done in the apply part. The other thing that was burnt – you must have smelt it, was the soup.'

'It is a pity,' said Oswald; 'I don't suppose he gets a good dinner every day.'

'No more do we,' said H.O., 'but we shall to-morrow.'

I thought of all the things we had bought with our half-sovereign – the rabbit and the sweets and the almonds and raisins and figs and the cocoanut: and I thought of the nasty mutton and things, and while I was thinking about it all Alice said –

'Let's ask the poor Indian to come to dinner with *us* to-morrow.' I should have said it myself if she had given me time.

We got the little ones to go to bed by promising to put a note on their dressing-table saying what had happened, so that they might know the first thing in the morning, or in the middle of the night if they happened to wake up, and then we elders arranged everything.[8]

I waited by the back door, and when the Uncle was beginning to go Dicky was to drop a marble down between the banisters for a signal, so that I could run round and meet the Uncle as he came out.

This seems like deceit, but if you are a thoughtful and considerate boy you will understand that we could not go down and say to the Uncle in the hall under Father's eye, 'Father has given you a beastly, nasty dinner, but if you will come to dinner with us to-morrow, we will show you our idea of good things to eat.' You will see, if you think it over, that this would not have been at all polite to Father.

So when the Uncle left, Father saw him to the door and let him out, and then went back to the study, looking very sad, Dora says.[9]

As the poor Indian came down our steps he saw me there at the gate. I did not mind his being poor, and I said, 'Good evening, Uncle,' just as politely as though he had been about to ascend into one of the gilded chariots of the rich and affluent, instead of having to walk to the station a quarter of a mile in the mud, unless he had the money for a tram fare.

'Good evening, Uncle.' I said it again, for he stood staring at me. I don't suppose he was used to politeness from boys – some boys are anything but – especially to the Aged Poor.

So I said, 'Good evening, Uncle,' yet once again. Then he said –

'Time you were in bed, young man. Eh! – what?'

Then I saw I must speak plainly with him, man to man. So I did. I said –

'You've been dining with my Father, and we couldn't help hearing you say the dinner was shocking. So we thought as you're an Indian, perhaps you're very poor' – I didn't like to tell him we had heard the dreadful truth from his own lips, so I went on, 'because of "Lo, the poor Indian" – you know – and you can't get a good dinner every day. And we are very sorry if you're poor; and won't you come and have dinner with us to-morrow – with us children, I mean? It's a very, very good dinner – rabbit, and hardbake, and cocoanut – and you needn't mind us knowing you're poor, because we know honourable poverty is no disgrace, and – ' I could have gone on much longer, but he interrupted me to say –

'Upon my word! And what's *your* name, eh?'

'Oswald Bastable,' I said; and I do hope you people who are reading this story have not guessed before that I was Oswald all the time.

'Oswald Bastable, eh? Bless my soul!' said the poor Indian. 'Yes, I'll dine with you, Mr Oswald Bastable, with all the pleasure in life. Very kind and cordial invitation, I'm sure. Good night, sir. At one o'clock, I presume?'

'Yes, at one,' I said. 'Good night, sir.'

Then I went in and told the others, and we wrote a paper and put it on the boys' dressing-table, and it said –

'The poor Indian is coming at one. He seemed very grateful to me for my kindness.'[10]

We did not tell Father that the Uncle was coming to dinner with us, for the polite reason that I have explained before. But we had to tell Eliza; so we said a friend was coming to dinner and we wanted everything very nice. I think she thought it was Albert-next-door, but she was in a good temper that day, and she agreed to cook the rabbit and to make a pudding with currants in it. And when one o'clock came the Indian Uncle came too.[11] I let him in and helped him off with his great-coat, which was all furry inside, and took him straight to the nursery. We were to have dinner there as usual, for we had decided from the first that he would enjoy himself more if he was not made a stranger of. We agreed to treat him as one of ourselves, because if we were too polite, he might think it was our pride because he was poor.

He shook hands with us all and asked our ages, and what schools we went to, and shook his head when we said we were having a holiday just now. I felt rather uncomfortable – I always do when they talk about schools – and I couldn't think of anything to say to show him we meant to treat him as one of ourselves. I did ask if he played cricket. He said he had not played lately. And then no one said anything till dinner came in. We had all washed our faces and hands and brushed our hair before he came in, and we all looked very nice, especially Oswald, who had had his hair cut that very morning. When Eliza had brought in the rabbit and gone out again, we looked at each other in silent despair, like in books. It seemed as if it were going to be just a dull dinner like the one the poor Indian had had the night before; only, of course, the things to eat would be nicer. Dicky kicked Oswald under the table to make him say something – and he had his new boots on, too! – but Oswald did not kick back; then the Uncle asked – [12]

'Do you carve, sir, or shall I?'

Suddenly Alice said –

'Would you like grown-up dinner, Uncle, or play-dinner?'

He did not hesitate a moment, but said, 'Play-dinner, by all means. Eh! – what?' and then we knew it was all right.

So we at once showed the Uncle how to be a dauntless hunter. The rabbit was the deer we had slain in the green forest with our trusty yew bows, and we toasted the joints of it, when the Uncle had carved it, on bits of firewood sharpened to a point. The Uncle's piece got a little burnt, but he said it was delicious, and he said game was always nicer when you had killed it yourself. When Eliza had taken away the rabbit bones and brought in the pudding, we waited till she had gone out and shut the door, and then we put the dish down on the floor and slew the pudding in the dish in the good old-fashioned way. It was a wild boar at bay, and very hard indeed to kill, even with forks. The Uncle was very fierce indeed with the pudding, and jumped and howled when he speared it, but when it came to his turn to be helped, he said, 'No, thank you; think of my liver. Eh! – what?'

But he had some almonds and raisins – when we had climbed to the top of the chest of drawers to pluck them from the boughs of the great trees; and he had a fig from the cargo that the rich merchants brought in their ship – the long drawer was the ship – and the rest of us had the sweets and the cocoanut. It was a very glorious and beautiful feast, and when it was over we said we hoped it was better than the dinner last night. And he said –

'I never enjoyed a dinner more.' He was too polite to say what he really thought about Father's dinner. And we saw that though he might be poor, he was a true gentleman.

He smoked a cigar while we finished up what there was left to eat, and told us about tiger shooting and about elephants. We asked him about wigwams, and wampum, and mocassins, and beavers, but he did not seem to know, or else he was shy about talking of the wonders of his native land.

We liked him very much indeed, and when he was going at last, Alice nudged me, and I said – 'There's one and threepence farthing left out of our half-sovereign. Will you take it, please, because we do like you very much indeed, and we don't want it, really; and we would rather you had it.' And I put the money into his hand.

'I'll take the threepenny-bit,' he said, turning the money over and looking at it, 'but I couldn't rob you of the rest. By the way, where did you get the money for this most royal spread – half a sovereign you said – eh, what?'

We told him all about the different ways we had looked for treasure, and when we had been telling some time he sat down, to listen better; and at last we told him how Alice had played at divining-rod, and how it really had found a half-sovereign.[13] Then he said he would like to see her do it again. But we explained that the rod would only show gold and silver, and that we were quite sure there was no more gold in the house, because we happened to have looked very carefully.

'Well, silver, then,' said he; 'let's hide the plate-basket, and little Alice shall make the divining-rod find it. Eh! – what?'

'There isn't any silver in the plate-basket now,' Dora said. 'Eliza asked me to borrow the silver spoons and forks for your dinner last night from Albert-next-door's Mother. Father never notices, but she thought it would be nicer for you. Our own silver went to have the dents taken out; and I don't think Father could afford to pay the man for doing it, for the silver hasn't come back.'

'Bless my soul!' said the Uncle again, looking at the hole in the big chair that we burnt when we had Guy Fawkes' Day indoors. 'And how much pocket-money do you get? Eh! – what?'

'We don't have any now,' said Alice; 'but indeed we don't want the other shilling. We'd much rather you had it, wouldn't we?'

And the rest of us said, 'Yes.' The Uncle wouldn't take it, but he asked a lot of questions, and at last he went away. And when he went he said –

'Well, youngsters, I've enjoyed myself very much. I shan't forget your kind hospitality. Perhaps the poor Indian may be in a position to ask you all to dinner some day.'

Oswald said if he ever could we should like to come very much, but he was not to trouble to get such a nice dinner as ours, because we could do very well with cold mutton and rice pudding. We do not like these things, but Oswald knows how to behave. Then the poor Indian went away.

We had not got any treasure by this party, but we had had a very good time, and I am sure the Uncle enjoyed himself.

We were so sorry he was gone that we could none of us eat much tea; but we did not mind, because we had pleased the poor Indian and enjoyed ourselves too. Besides, as Dora said, 'A contented mind is a continual feast,' so it did not matter about not wanting tea.[14]

Only H.O. did not seem to think a continual feast was a contented mind, and Eliza gave him a powder in what was left of the red-currant jelly Father had for the nasty dinner.

But the rest of us were quite well, and I think it must have been the cocoanut with H.O. We hoped nothing had disagreed with the Uncle, but we never knew.

*   *   *

Chapter 16
The End of the Treasure-Seeking

Now it is coming near the end of our treasure-seeking, and the end was so wonderful that now nothing is like it used to be. It is like as if our fortunes had been in an earthquake, and after those, you know, everything comes out wrong-way up.

The day after the Uncle speared the pudding with us opened in gloom and sadness. But you never know. It was destined to be a day when things happened. Yet no sign of this appeared in the early morning. Then all was misery and upsetness. None of us felt quite well; I don't know why: and Father had one of his awful colds, so Dora persuaded him not to go to London, but to stay cosy and warm in the study, and she made him some gruel. She makes it better than Eliza does; Eliza's gruel is all little lumps, and when you suck them it is dry oatmeal inside.

We kept as quiet as we could, and I made H.O. do some lessons, like the G.B. had advised us to. But it was very dull. There are some days when you seem to have got to the end of all the things that could ever possibly happen to you, and you feel you will spend all the rest of your life doing dull things just the same way. Days like this are generally wet days. But, as I said, you never know.

Then Dicky said if things went on like this he should run away to sea, and Alice said she thought it would be rather nice to go into a convent. H.O. was a little disagreeable because of the powder Eliza had given him, so he tried to read two books at once, one with each eye, just because Noël wanted one of the books, which was very selfish of him, so it only made his headache worse. H.O. is getting old enough to learn by experience that it is wrong to be selfish, and when he complained about his head Oswald told him whose fault it was, because I am older than he is, and it is my duty to show him where he is wrong. But he began to cry, and then Oswald had to cheer him up because of Father wanting to be quiet. So Oswald said –

'They'll eat H.O. if you don't look out!'

And Dora said Oswald was too bad.

Of course Oswald was not going to interfere again, so he went to look out of the window and see the trams go by, and by and by H.O. came and looked out too, and Oswald, who knows when to be generous and forgiving, gave him a piece of blue pencil and two nibs, as good as new, to keep.[1]

As they were looking out at the rain splashing on the stones in the street they saw a four-wheeled cab come lumbering up from the way the station is. Oswald called out –

'Here comes the coach of the Fairy Godmother. It'll stop here, you see if it doesn't!'

So they all came to the window to look. Oswald had only said that about stopping and he was stricken with wonder and amaze when the cab really did stop. It had boxes on the top and knobby parcels sticking out of the window, and it was something like going away to the seaside and something like the gentleman who takes things about in a carriage with the wooden shutters up, to sell to the drapers' shops. The cabman got down, and some one inside handed out ever so many parcels of different shapes and sizes, and the cabman stood holding them in his arms and grinning over them.[2]

Dora said, 'It is a pity some one doesn't tell him this isn't the house.' And then from inside the cab some one put out a foot feeling for the step, like a tortoise's foot coming out from under his shell when you are holding him off the ground, and then a leg came and more parcels, and then Noël cried –

'It's the poor Indian!'

And it was.

Eliza opened the door, and we were all leaning over the banisters. Father heard the noise of parcels and boxes in the hall, and he came out without remembering how bad his cold was. If you do that yourself when you have a cold they call you careless and naughty. Then we heard the poor Indian say to Father –

'I say, Dick, I dined with your kids yesterday – as I daresay they've told you. Jolliest little cubs I ever saw! Why didn't you let me see them the other night? The eldest is the image of poor Janey – and as to young Oswald, he's a man! If he's not a man, I'm a nigger![3] Eh! – what? And Dick, I say, I shouldn't wonder if I could find a friend to put a bit into that business of yours – eh?'

Then he and Father went into the study and the door was shut – and we went down and looked at the parcels. Some were done up in old, dirty newspapers, and tied with bits of rag, and some were in brown paper and string from the shops, and there were boxes.[4] We wondered if the Uncle had come to stay and this was his luggage, or whether it was to sell. Some of it smelt of spices, like merchandise – and one bundle Alice felt certain was a bale. We heard a hand on the knob of the study door after a bit, and Alice said –

'Fly!' and we all got away but H.O., and the Uncle caught him by the leg as he was trying to get upstairs after us.

'Peeping at the baggage, eh?' said the Uncle, and the rest of us came down because it would have been dishonourable to leave H.O. alone in a scrape, and we wanted to see what was in the parcels.

'I didn't touch,' said H.O. 'Are you coming to stay? I hope you are.'

'No harm done if you did touch,' said the good, kind, Indian man to all of us. 'For all these parcels are *for you*.'

I have several times told you about our being dumb with amazement and terror and joy, and things like that, but I never remember us being dumber than we were when he said this.

The Indian Uncle went on: 'I told an old friend of mine what a pleasant dinner I had with you, and about the threepenny bit, and the divining-rod, and all that, and he sent all these odds and ends as presents for you. Some of the things came from India.'

'Have you come from India, Uncle?' Noël asked; and when he said 'Yes' we were all very much surprised, for we never thought of his being that sort of Indian. We thought he was the Red kind, and of course his not being accounted for his ignorance of beavers and things.[5]

He got Eliza to help, and we took all the parcels into the nursery and he undid them and undid them and undid them, till the papers lay thick on the floor. Father came too and sat in the Guy Fawkes chair. I cannot begin to tell you all the things that kind friend of Uncle's had sent us. He must be a very agreeable person.

There were toys for the kids and model engines for Dick and me, and a lot of books, and Japanese china tea sets for the girls, red and white and gold – there were sweets by the pound and by the box – and long yards and yards of soft silk from India, to make frocks for the girls – and a real Indian sword for Oswald and a book of Japanese pictures for Noël, and some ivory chessmen for Dicky: the castles of the chessmen are elephant-and-castles. There is a railway station called that; I never knew what it meant before.[6] The brown paper and string parcels had boxes of games in them – and big cases of preserved fruits and things. And the shabby old newspaper parcels and the boxes had the Indian things in. I never saw so many beautiful things before. There were carved fans and silver bangles and strings of amber beads, and necklaces of uncut gems – turquoises and garnets, the Uncle said they were – and shawls and scarves of silk, and cabinets of brown and gold, and ivory boxes and silver trays, and brass things. The Uncle kept saying, 'This is for you, young man,' or 'Little Alice will like this fan,' or 'Miss Dora would look well in this green silk, I think. Eh! – what?'[7]

And Father looked on as if it was a dream, till the Uncle suddenly gave him an ivory paper-knife and a box of cigars, and said, 'My old friend sent you these, Dick; he's an old friend of yours too, he says.' And he winked at my Father, for H.O. and I saw him. And my Father winked back, though he has always told us not to.[8]

That was a wonderful day. It was a treasure, and no mistake! I never saw such heaps and heaps of presents, like things out of a fairy-tale – and even Eliza had a shawl.[9] Perhaps she deserved it, for she did cook the rabbit and the pudding; and Oswald says it is not her fault if her nose turns up and she does not brush her hair. I do not think Eliza likes brushing things. It is the same with the carpets. But Oswald tries to make allowances even for people who do not wash their ears.

The Indian Uncle came to see us often after that, and his friend always sent us something. Once he tipped us a sovereign each – the Uncle brought it; and once he sent us money to go to the Crystal Palace, and the Uncle took us; and another time to a circus; and when Christmas was near the Uncle said – [10]

'You remember when I dined with you, some time ago, you promised to dine with me some day, if I could ever afford to give a dinner-party. Well, I'm going to have one – a Christmas party. Not on Christmas Day, because every one goes home then – but on the day after. Cold mutton and rice pudding. You'll come? Eh! – what?'

We said we should be delighted, if Father had no objection, because that is the proper thing to say, and the poor Indian, I mean the Uncle, said, 'No, your Father won't object – he's coming too, bless your soul!'

We all got Christmas presents for the Uncle. The girls made him a handkerchief case and a comb bag, out of some of the pieces of silk he had given them. I got him a knife with three blades; H.O. got a siren whistle, a very strong one, and Dicky joined with me in the knife, and Noël would give the Indian ivory box that Uncle's friend had sent on the wonderful Fairy Cab day. He said it was the very nicest thing he had, and he was sure Uncle wouldn't mind his not having bought it with his own money.

I think Father's business must have got better – perhaps Uncle's friend put money in it and that did it good, like feeding the starving. Anyway we all had new suits, and the girls had the green silk from India made into frocks, and on Boxing Day we went in two cabs – Father and the girls in one, and us boys in the other.

We wondered very much where the Indian Uncle lived, because we had not been told. And we thought when the cab began to go up the hill towards the Heath that perhaps the Uncle lived in one of the poky little houses up at the top of Greenwich. But the cab went right over the Heath and in at some big gates, and through a shrubbery all white with frost like a fairy forest, because it was Christmas time. And at last we stopped before one of those jolly, big, ugly red houses with a lot of windows, that are so comfortable inside, and on the steps was the Indian Uncle, looking very big and grand, in a blue cloth coat and yellow sealskin waistcoat, with a bunch of seals hanging from it.

'I wonder whether he has taken a place as butler here?' said Dicky. 'A poor, broken-down man – '

Noël thought it was very likely, because he knew that in these big houses there were always thousands of stately butlers.

The Uncle came down the steps and opened the cab door himself, which I don't think butlers would expect to have to do. And he took us in. It was a lovely hall, with bear and tiger skins on the floor, and a big clock with the faces of the sun and moon dodging out when it was day or night, and Father Time with a scythe coming out at the hours, and the name on it was 'Flint. Ashford. 1776'; and there was a fox eating a stuffed duck in a glass case, and horns of stags and other animals over the doors.[11]

'We'll just come into my study first,' said the Uncle, 'and wish each other a Merry Christmas.' So then we knew he wasn't the butler, but it must be his own house, for only the master of the house has a study.

His study was not much like Father's. It had hardly any books, but swords and guns and newspapers and a great many boots, and boxes half unpacked, with more Indian things bulging out of them.

We gave him our presents and he was awfully pleased. Then he gave us his Christmas presents. You must be tired of hearing about presents, but I must remark that all the Uncle's presents were watches; there was a watch for each of us, with our names engraved inside, all silver except H.O.'s, and that was a Waterbury, 'To match his boots,' the Uncle said.[12] I don't know what he meant.

Then the Uncle looked at Father, and Father said, 'You tell them, sir.'

So the Uncle coughed and stood up and made a speech. He said –

'Ladies and gentlemen, we are met together to discuss an important subject which has for some weeks engrossed the attention of the honourable member opposite and myself.'

I said, 'Hear, hear,' and Alice whispered, 'What happened to the guinea-pig?' Of course you know the answer to that.[13]

The Uncle went on –

'I am going to live in this house, and as it's rather big for me, your Father has agreed that he and you shall come and live with me. And so, if you're agreeable, we're all going to live here together, and, please God, it'll be a happy home for us all. Eh! – what?'

He blew his nose and kissed us all round. As it was Christmas time I did not mind, though I am much too old for it on other dates. Then he said, 'Thank you all very much for your presents; but I've got a present here I value more than anything else I have.'[14]

I thought it was not quite polite of him to say so, till I saw that what he valued so much was a threepenny-bit on his watch-chain, and, of course, I saw it must be the one we had given him.

He said, 'You children gave me that when you thought I was the poor Indian, and I'll keep it as long as I live. And I've asked some friends to help us to be jolly, for this is our house-warming. Eh! – what?'

Then he shook Father by the hand, and they blew their noses; and then Father said, 'Your Uncle has been most kind – most – '

But Uncle interrupted by saying, 'Now, Dick, no nonsense!'

Then H.O. said, 'Then you're not poor at all?' as if he were very disappointed.

The Uncle replied, 'I have enough for my simple wants, thank you, H.O.; and your Father's business will provide him with enough for yours. Eh! – what?'

Then we all went down and looked at the fox thoroughly, and made the Uncle take the glass off so that we could see it all round and then the Uncle took us all over the house, which is the most comfortable one I have ever been in. There is a beautiful portrait of Mother in Father's sitting-room. The Uncle must be very rich indeed. This ending is like what happens in Dickens's books; but I think it was much jollier to happen like a book, and it shows what a nice man the Uncle is, the way he did it all.

Think how flat it would have been if the Uncle had said, when we first offered him the one and threepence farthing, 'Oh, I don't want your dirty one and threepence! I'm very rich indeed.' Instead of which he saved up the news of his wealth till Christmas, and then told us all in one glorious burst. Besides, I can't help it if it is like Dickens, because it happens this way. Real life is often something like books.

Presently, when we had seen the house, we were taken into the drawing-room, and there was Mrs Leslie, who gave us the shillings and wished us good hunting, and Lord Tottenham, and Albert-next-door's Uncle – and Albert-next-door, and his Mother (I'm not very fond of her), and best of all our own Robber and his two kids, and our Robber had a new suit on. The Uncle told us he had asked the people who had been kind to us, and Noël said, 'Where is my noble editor that I wrote the poetry to?'

The Uncle said he had not had the courage to ask a strange editor to dinner; but Lord Tottenham was an old friend of Uncle's, and he had introduced Uncle to Mrs Leslie, and that was how he had the pride and pleasure of welcoming her to our house-warming. And he made her a bow like you see on a Christmas card.

Then Alice asked, 'What about Mr Rosenbaum? He was kind; it would have been a pleasant surprise for him.'

But everybody laughed, and Uncle said –

'Your father has paid him the sovereign he lent you. I don't think he could have borne another pleasant surprise.'

And I said there was the butcher, and he was really kind; but they only laughed, and Father said you could not ask all your business friends to a private dinner.

Then it was dinner-time, and we thought of Uncle's talk about cold mutton and rice. But it was a beautiful dinner, and I never saw such a dessert! We had ours on plates to take away into another sitting-room, which was much jollier than sitting round the table with the grown-ups. But the Robber's kids stayed with their Father. They were very shy and frightened, and said hardly anything, but looked all about with very bright eyes. H.O. thought they were like white mice; but afterwards we got to know them very well, and in the end they were not so mousy. And there is a good deal of interesting stuff to tell about them; but I shall put all that in another book, for there is no room for it in this one. We played desert islands all the afternoon and drank Uncle's health in ginger wine. It was H.O. that upset his over Alice's green silk dress, and she never even rowed him. Brothers ought not to have favourites, and Oswald would never be so mean as to have a favourite sister, or, if he had, wild horses should not make him tell who it was.

And now we are to go on living in the big house on the Heath, and it is very jolly.

Mrs Leslie often comes to see us, and our own Robber and Albert-next-door's uncle. The Indian Uncle likes him because he has been in India too and is brown; but our Uncle does not like Albert-next-door. He says he is a muff. And I am to go to Rugby, and so are Noël and H.O., and perhaps to Balliol afterwards. Balliol is my Father's college. It has two separate coats of arms, which many other colleges are not allowed. Noël is going to be a poet and Dicky wants to go into Father's business. The Uncle is a real good old sort; and just think, we should never have found him if we hadn't made up our minds to be Treasure Seekers!

Noël made a poem about it –

'Lo! the poor Indian from lands afar,
Comes where the treasure seekers are;
We looked for treasure, but we find
The best treasure of all is the Uncle good and kind.'

I thought it was rather rot, but Alice would show it to the Uncle, and he liked it very much. He kissed Alice and he smacked Noël on the back, and he said, 'I don't think *I've* done so badly either, if you come to that, though I was never a regular professional treasure seeker. Eh! – what?

THE WOULDBEGOODS

Being the Further Adventures of the Treasure Seekers

by E. Nesbit

To
My Dear Son
Fabian Bland[1]

Chapter 1
The Jungle[1]

'Children are like jam: all very well in the proper place, but you can't stand them all over the shop – eh, what?'

These were the dreadful words of our Indian uncle. They made us feel very young and angry; and yet we could not be comforted by calling him names to ourselves, as you do when nasty grown-ups say nasty things, because he is not nasty, but quite the exact opposite when not irritated. And we could not think it ungentle-manly of him to say we were like jam, because, as Alice says, jam is very nice indeed – only not on furniture and improper places like that.[2] My father said, 'Perhaps they had better go to boarding-school.' And that was awful, because we know father disapproves of boarding-schools. And he looked at us and said, 'I am ashamed of them, sir!'

Your lot is indeed a dark and terrible one when your father is ashamed of you. And we all knew this, so that we felt in our chests just as if we had swallowed a hard-boiled egg whole. At least, this is what Oswald felt, and father said once that Oswald, as the eld-est, was the representative of the family, so, of course, the others felt the same.[3]

And then everybody said nothing for a short time. At last Father said:

'You may go – but remember – ' The words that followed I am not going to tell you. It is no use telling you what you know before – as they do in schools. And you must all have had such words said to you many times. We went away when it was over. The girls cried, and we boys got out books and began to read, so that nobody should think we cared. But we felt it deeply in our interior hearts, especially Oswald, who is the eldest and the representative of the family.

We felt it all the more because we had not really meant to do anything wrong. We only thought perhaps the grown-ups would not be quite pleased if they knew, and that is quite different. Besides, we meant to put all the things back in their proper places when we had done with them before any one found out about it. But I must not anticipate (that means telling the end of the story before the beginning. I tell you this because it is so sickening to have words you don't know in a story, and to be told to look it up in the dicker).[4]

We are the Bastables – Oswald, Dora, Dicky, Alice, Noël, and H.O. If you want to know why we call our youngest brother H.O. you can jolly well read *The Treasure Seekers* and find out. We were the Treasure Seekers, and we sought it high and low, and quite regularly, because we particularly wanted to find it. And at last we did not find it, but we were found by a good, kind Indian uncle, who helped father with his business, so that father was able to take us all to live in a jolly big red house on Blackheath, instead of in the Lewisham Road, where we lived when we were only poor but honest Treasure Seekers.[5] When we were poor but honest we always used to think that if only father had plenty of business, and we did not have to go short of pocket-money and wear shabby clothes (I don't mind this myself, but the girls do), we should be quite happy and very, very good.

And when we were taken to the beautiful big Blackheath house we thought now all would be well, because it was a house with vineries and pineries, and gas and water, and shrubberies and stabling, and replete with every modern convenience, like it says in Dyer & Hilton's list of Eligible House Property.[6] I read all about it, and I have copied the words quite right.

It is a beautiful house, all the furniture solid and strong, no casters off the chairs, and the tables not scratched, and the silver not dented; and lots of servants, and the most decent meals every day – and lots of pocket-money.[7]

But it is wonderful how soon you get used to things, even the things you want most. Our watches, for instance. We wanted them frightfully; but when I had mine a week or two, after the mainspring got broken and was repaired at Bennett's in the village, I hardly cared to look at the works at all, and it did not make me feel happy in my heart any more, though, of course, I should have been very unhappy if it had been taken away from me.[8] And the same with new clothes and nice dinners and having enough of everything. You soon get used to it all, and it does not make you extra happy, although, if you had it all taken away, you would be very dejected. (That is a good word, and one I have never used before.) You get used to everything, as I said, and then you want something more. Father says this is what people mean by the deceitfulness of riches; but Albert's uncle says it is the spirit of progress, and Mrs Leslie said some people called it 'divine discontent.' Oswald asked them all what they thought, one Sunday at dinner. Uncle said it was rot, and what we wanted was bread and water and a licking; but he meant it for a joke. This was in the Easter holidays.[9]

We went to live at Morden House at Christmas. After the holidays the girls went to the Blackheath High School, and we boys went to the Prop. (that means the Proprietary School).[10] And we had to swot rather during term; but about Easter we knew the deceitfulness of riches in the vac., when there was nothing much on, like pantomimes and things.[11] Then there was the summer term, and we swotted more than ever; and it was boiling hot, and masters' tempers got short and sharp, and the girls used to wish the exams. came in cold weather. I can't think why they don't. But I suppose schools don't think of sensible things like that. They teach botany at girls' schools.[12]

Then the midsummer holidays came, and we breathed again – but only for a few days. We began to feel as if we had forgotten something, and did not know what it was. We wanted something to happen – only we didn't exactly know what. So we were very pleased when father said:

'I've asked Mr Foulkes to send his children here for a week or two. You know – the kids who came at Christmas. You must be jolly to them, and see that they have a good time, don't you know.'

We remembered them right enough – they were little pinky, frightened things, like white mice, with very bright eyes. They had not been to our house since Christmas, because Denis, the boy, had been ill, and they had been with an aunt at Ramsgate.[13]

Alice and Dora would have liked to get the bedrooms ready for the honoured guests, but a really good housemaid is sometimes more ready to say 'Don't' than even a general. So the girls had to chuck it. Jane only let them put flowers in the pots on the visitors' mantelpieces, and then they had to ask the gardener which kind they might pick, because nothing worth gathering happened to be growing in our own gardens just then.

Their train got in at 12.27. We all went to meet them. Afterwards I thought that was a mistake, because their aunt was with them, and she wore black with beady things and a tight bonnet, and she said, when we took our hats off, 'Who are you?' quite crossly.[14]

We said, 'We are the Bastables; we've come to meet Daisy and Denny.'

The aunt is a very rude lady, and it made us sorry for Daisy and Denny when she said to them:

'*Are* these the children? Do you remember them?'

We weren't very tidy, perhaps, because we'd been playing brigands in the shrubbery; and we knew we should have to wash for dinner as soon as we got back, anyhow. But still –

Denny said he thought he remembered us. But Daisy said, 'Of course they are,' and then looked as if she was going to cry.

So then the aunt called a cab, and told the man where to drive, and put Daisy and Denny in, and then she said:

'You two little girls may go too, if you like, but you little boys must walk.'

So the cab went off, and we were left. The aunt turned to us to say a few last words. We knew it would have been about brushing your hair and wearing gloves, so Oswald said, 'Good-bye,' and turned haughtily away, before she could begin, and so did the others. No one but that kind of black, beady, tight lady would say 'little boys.' She is like Miss Murdstone in *David Copperfield*. I should like to tell her so; but she would not understand. I don't suppose she has ever read anything but *Markham's History* and *Mangnall's Questions* – improving books like that.[15]

When we got home we found all four of those who had ridden in the cab sitting in our sitting-room – we don't call it nursery now[16] – looking very thoroughly washed, and our girls were asking polite questions and the others were saying 'Yes' and 'No,' and 'I don't know.' We boys did not say anything. We stood at the window and looked out till the gong went for our dinner. We felt it was going to be awful – and it was. The new-comers would never have done for knight-errants, or to carry the cardinal's sealed message through the heart of France on a horse; they would never have thought of anything to say to throw the enemy off the scent when they got into a tight place.

They said, 'Yes, please,' and 'No, thank you'; and they ate very neatly, and always wiped their mouths before they drank, as well as after, and never spoke with them full.

And after dinner it got worse and worse.

We got out all our books, and they said, 'Thank you,' and didn't look at them properly. And we got out all our toys, and they said, 'thank you, it's very nice,' to everything. And it got less and less pleasant, and towards teatime it came to nobody saying anything except Noël and H.O. – and they talked to each other about cricket.

After tea father came in, and he played 'Letters' with them and the girls, and it was a little better; but while late dinner was going on – I shall never forget it. Oswald felt like the hero of a book – 'almost at the end of his resources.' I don't think I was ever glad of bedtime before, but that time I was.

When they had gone to bed (Daisy had to have all her strings and buttons undone for her, Dora told me, though she is nearly ten, and Denny said he couldn't sleep without the gas being left a little bit on) we held a council in the girls' room. We all sat on the bed – it is a mahogany four-poster with green curtains very good for tents, only the housekeeper doesn't allow it, and Oswald said:

'This is jolly nice, isn't it?'

'They'll be better to-morrow,' Alice said; 'They're only shy.'

Dicky said shy was all very well, but you needn't behave like a perfect idiot.

'They're frightened. You see, we're all strange to them,' Dora said.

'We're not wild beasts or Indians; we sha'n't eat them.[17] What have they got to be frightened of?' Dicky said this.

Noël told us he thought they were an enchanted prince and princess who'd been turned into white rabbits, and their bodies had got changed back, but not their insides.

But Oswald told him to dry up.

'It's no use making things up about them,' he said. 'The thing is: what are we going to *do*? We can't have our holidays spoiled by these snivelling kids.'

'No,' Alice said, 'but they can't possibly go on snivelling for ever. Perhaps they've got into the habit of it with that Murdstone aunt. She's enough to make anyone snivel.'

'All the same,' said Oswald, 'we jolly well aren't going to have another day like to-day. We must do something to rouse them from their snivelling leth – what's its name? – something sudden and – what is it? – decisive.'

'A booby trap,' said H.O., 'the first thing when they get up, and an apple-pie bed at night.'[18]

But Dora would not hear of it, and I own she was right.

'Suppose,' she said, 'we could get up a good play – like we did when we were Treasure Seekers.'

We said, 'Well, what?' But she did not say.

'It ought to be a good long thing – to last all day,' Dicky said; 'and if they like they can play, and if they don't – '

'If they don't, I'll read to them,' Alice said.

But we all said: 'No, you don't; if you begin that way you'll have to go on.'

And Dicky added: 'I wasn't going to say that at all. I was going to say if they didn't like it they could jolly well do the other thing.'[19]

We all agreed that we must think of something, but we none of us could, and at last the council broke up in confusion because Mrs Blake – she is the housekeeper – came up and turned off the gas.

But next morning when we were having breakfast, and the two strangers were sitting there so pink and clean, Oswald suddenly said:

'I know; we'll have a jungle in the garden.'

And the others agreed, and we talked about it till brek was over. The little strangers only said 'I don't know' whenever we said anything to them.

After brekker Oswald beckoned his brothers and sisters mysteriously apart and said:

'Do you agree to let me be captain to-day, because I thought of it?'

And they said they would.

Then he said: 'We'll play jungle-book, and I shall be Mowgli.[20] The rest of you can be what you like – Mowgli's father and mother, or any of the beasts.'

'I don't suppose they know the book,' said Noël. 'They don't look as if they read anything, except at lesson times.'

'Then they can go on being beasts all the time,' Oswald said. 'Any one can be a beast.'

So it was settled.

And now Oswald – Albert's uncle has sometimes said he is clever at arranging things – began to lay his plans for the jungle. The day was indeed well chosen. Our Indian uncle was away; father was away; Mrs Blake was going away, and the housemaid had an afternoon off. Oswald's first conscious act was to get rid of the white mice – I mean the little good visitors.[21] He explained to them that there would be a play in the afternoon, and they could be what they liked, and gave them the jungle-book to read the stories he told them to – all the ones about Mowgli. He led the strangers to a secluded spot among the sea-kale pots in the kitchen garden and left them. Then he went back to the others, and we had a jolly morning under the cedar talking about what we would do when Blakie was gone. She went just after our dinner.

When we asked Denny what he would like to be in the play, it turned out he had not read the stories Oswald told him at all, but only the 'White Seal' and 'Rikki Tikki.'[22]

We then agreed to make the jungle first and dress up for our parts afterwards. Oswald was a little uncomfortable about leaving the strangers alone all the morning, so he said Denny should be his aide-de-camp, and he was really quite useful. He is rather handy with his fingers, and things that he does up do not come untied. Daisy might have come too, but she wanted to go on reading, so we let her, which is the truest manners to a visitor.[23] Of course the shrubbery was to be the jungle, and the lawn under the cedar a forest glade, and then we began to collect the things. The cedar lawn is just nicely out of the way of the windows. It was a jolly hot day – the kind of day when the sunshine is white and the shadows are dark grey, not black like they are in the evening.

We all thought of different things. Of course first we dressed up pillows in the skins of beasts and set them about on the grass to look as natural as we could. And then we got Pincher, and rubbed him all over with powdered slate-pencil, to make him the right colour for Grey Brother. But he shook it all off, and it had taken an awful time to do. Then Alice said:

'Oh, I know!' and she ran off to father's dressing-room, and came back with the tube of *crème d'Amande pour la barbe et les mains*, and we squeezed it on Pincher and rubbed it in, and then the slate-pencil stuff stuck all right, and he rolled in the dust-bin of his own accord, which made him just the right colour.[24] He is a very clever dog, but soon after he went off and we did not find him till quite late in the afternoon. Denny helped with Pincher, and with the wild-beast skins, and when Pincher was finished he said:

'Please, may I make some paper birds to put in the trees? I know how.'

And of course we said 'Yes,' and he only had red ink and news-papers, and quickly he made quite a lot of large paper birds with red tails. They didn't look half bad on the edge of the shrubbery.

While he was doing this he suddenly said, or rather screamed, 'Oh!'

And we looked, and it was a creature with great horns and a fur rug – something like a bull and something like a minotaur[25] – and I don't wonder Denny was frightened. It was Alice, and it was first-class.

Up to now all was not yet lost beyond recall. It was the stuffed fox that did the mischief – and I am sorry to own it was Oswald who thought of it. He is not ashamed of having *thought* of it. That was rather clever of him. But he knows now that it is better not to take other people's foxes and things without asking, even if you live in the same house with them.

It was Oswald who undid the back of the glass case in the hall and got out the fox with the green and grey duck in its mouth, and when the others saw how awfully like life they looked on the lawn, they all rushed off to fetch the other stuffed things. Uncle has a tremendous lot of stuffed things. He shot most of them him-self – but not the fox, of course.[26] There was another fox's mask, too, and we hung that in a bush to look as if the fox was peeping out. And the stuffed birds we fastened on to the trees with string. The duck-bill – what's its name? – looked very well sitting on his tail with the otter snarling at him.[27] Then Dicky had an idea; and though not nearly so much was said about it afterwards as there was about the stuffed things, I think myself it was just as bad, though it was a good idea, too. He just got the hose and put the end over a branch of the cedar-tree. Then we got the steps they clean windows with, and let the hose rest on the top of the steps and run. It was to be a water-fall, but it ran between the steps and was only wet and messy; so we got Father's mackintosh and uncle's and covered the steps with them, so that the water ran down all right and was glorious, and it ran away in a stream across the grass where we had dug a little channel for it – and the otter and the duck-bill thing were as if in their native haunts. I hope all this is not very dull to read about. I know it was jolly good fun to do. Taking one thing with another, I don't know that we ever had a better time while it lasted.

We got all the rabbits out of the hutches and put pink paper tails on to them, and hunted them with horns, made out of the *Times*. They got away somehow, and before they were caught next day they had eaten a good many lettuces and other things. Oswald is very sorry for this. He rather likes the gardener.

Denny wanted to put paper tails on the guinea-pigs, and it was no use our telling him there was nothing to tie the paper on to. He thought we were kidding until we showed him, and then he said, 'Well, never mind,' and got the girls to give him bits of the blue stuff left over from their dressing-gowns.

'I'll make them sashes to tie round their little middles,' he said. And he did, and the bows stuck up on the tops of their backs. One of the guinea-pigs was never seen again, and the same with the tortoise when we had done his shell with vermilion paint. He crawled away and returned no more. Perhaps someone collected him and thought he was an expensive kind, unknown in these cold latitudes.

The lawn under the cedar was transformed into a dream of beauty, what with the stuffed creatures and the paper-tailed things and the waterfall. And Alice said:

'I wish the tigers did not look so flat.' For of course with pillows you can only pretend it is a sleeping tiger getting ready to make a spring out at you. It is difficult to prop up tiger-skins in a life-like manner when there are no bones inside them, only pillows and sofa-cushions.

'What about the beer-stands?' I said. And we got two out of the cellar. With bolsters and string we fastened insides to the tigers – and they were really fine. The legs of the beer-stands did for tigers' legs. It was indeed the finishing touch.

Then we boys put on just our bathing drawers and vests – so as to be able to play with the water-fall without hurting our clothes. I think this was thoughtful. The girls only tucked up their frocks and took their shoes and stockings off. H.O. painted his legs and his hands with Condy's fluid – to make him brown, so that he might be Mowgli, although Oswald was captain and had plainly said he was going to be Mowgli himself.[28] Of course the others weren't going to stand that. So Oswald said:

'Very well. Nobody asked you to brown yourself like that. But now you've done it, you've simply got to go and be a beaver, and live in the dam under the water-fall till it washes off.'

He said he didn't want to be beavers.[29] And Noël said:

'Don't make him. Let him be the bronze statue in the palace gardens that the fountain plays out of.'

So we let him have the hose and hold it up over his head. It made a lovely fountain, only he remained brown. So then Dicky and Oswald did ourselves brown too, and dried H.O. as well as we could with our handkerchiefs, because he was just beginning to snivel. The brown did not come off any of us for days.

Oswald was to be Mowgli, and we were just beginning to arrange the different parts. The rest of the hose that was on the ground was Kaa, the Rock Python, and Pincher was Grey Brother, only we couldn't find him. And while most of us were talking, Dicky and Noël got messing about with the beer-stand tigers.

And then a really sad event instantly occurred, which was not really our fault, and we did not mean to.

That Daisy girl had been mooning indoors all the afternoon with the jungle books, and now she came suddenly out, just as Dicky and Noël had got under the tigers and were shoving them along to fight each other. Of course, this is not in the Mowgli book at all: but they did look jolly like real tigers, and I am very far from wishing to blame the girl, though she little knew what would be the awful consequence of her rash act. But for her we might have got out of it all much better than we did.

What happened was truly horrid.

As soon as Daisy saw the tigers she stopped short, and uttering a shriek like a railway whistle, she fell flat on the ground.

'Fear not, gentle Indian maiden,' Oswald cried, thinking with surprise that perhaps after all she did know how to play,[30] 'I myself will protect thee.' And he sprang forward with the native bow and arrows out of uncle's study.

The gentle Indian maiden did not move.

'Come hither,' Dora said, 'let us take refuge in yonder covert while this good knight does battle for us.'

Dora might have remembered that we were savages, but she did not. And that is Dora all over.[31] And still the Daisy girl did not move.

Then we were truly frightened. Dora and Alice lifted her up, and her mouth was a horrid violet colour and her eyes half shut. She looked horrid. Not at all like fair fainting damsels, who are always of an interesting pallor. She was green, like a cheap oyster on a stall.[32]

We did what we could, a prey to alarm as we were. We rubbed her hands and let the hose play gently but perseveringly on her unconscious brow. The girls loosened her dress, though it was only the kind that comes down straight without a waist. And we were all doing what we could as hard as we could, when we heard the click of the front gate. There was no mistake about it.

'I hope whoever it is will go straight to the front door,' said Alice. But whoever it was did not. There were feet on the gravel, and there was the uncle's voice, saying, in his hearty manner:

'This way. This way. On such a day as this we shall find our young barbarians all at play somewhere about the grounds.'

And then, without further warning, the uncle, three other gentlemen, and two ladies burst upon the scene.

We had no clothes on to speak of – I mean us boys. We were all wet through. Daisy was in a faint or a fit, or dead, none of us then knew which. And all the stuffed animals were there staring the uncle in the face. Most of them had got a sprinkling, and the otter and the duck-bill brute were simply soaked. And three of us were dark brown. Concealment, as so often happens, was impossible.

The quick brain of Oswald saw, in a flash, exactly how it would strike the uncle, and his brave young blood ran cold in his veins. His heart stood still.

'What's all this – eh, what?' said the tones of the wronged uncle.

Oswald spoke up and said it was jungles we were playing, and he didn't know what was up with Daisy. He explained as well as anyone could, but words were now in vain.

The uncle had a Malacca cane in his hand, and we were but ill prepared to meet the sudden attack. Oswald and H.O. caught it worst. The other boys were under the tigers – and, of course, my uncle would not strike a girl. Denny was a visitor and so got off. But it was bread and water for us for the next three days, and our own rooms. I will not tell you how we sought to vary the monotonousness of imprisonment. Oswald thought of taming a mouse, but he could not find one. The reason of the wretched captives might have given way but for the gutter that you can crawl along from our room to the girls'. But I will not dwell on this because you might try it yourselves, and it really is dangerous. When my father came home we got the talking to, and we said we were sorry – and we really were – especially about Daisy, though she had behaved with muffishness, and then it was settled that we were to go into the country and stay till we had grown into better children.

Albert's uncle was writing a book in the country; we were to go to his house. We were glad of this – Daisy and Denny too.[33] This we bore nobly. We knew we had deserved it. We were all very sorry for everything, and we resolved that for the future we *would* be good.

I am not sure whether we kept this resolution or not. Oswald thinks now that perhaps we made a mistake in trying so very hard to be good all at once.[34] You should do everything by degrees.

P.S. – It turned out Daisy was not really dead at all. It was only fainting – so like a girl.

N.B. – Pincher was found on the drawing-room sofa.

Appendix. – I have not told you half the things we did for the jungle – for instance, about the elephants' tusks and the horsehair sofa-cushions and uncle's fishing-boots.

* * *

Chapter 2
The Wouldbegoods[1]

When we were sent down into the country to learn to be good we felt it was rather good business, because we knew our being sent there was really only to get us out of the way for a little while, and we knew right enough that it wasn't a punishment, though Mrs Blake said it was, because we had been punished thoroughly for taking the stuffed animals out and making a jungle on the lawn with them, and the garden hose.[2] And you cannot be punished twice for the same offence. This is the English law; at least I think so. And at any rate no one would punish you three times, and we had had the Malacca cane and the solitary confinement; and the uncle had kindly explained to us that all ill-feeling between him and us was wiped out entirely by the bread and water we had endured. And what with the bread and water and being prisoners, and not being able to tame any mice in our prisons, I quite feel that we had suffered it up thoroughly, and now we could start fair.[3]

I think myself that descriptions of places are generally dull, but I have sometimes thought that was because the authors do not tell you what you truly want to know. However, dull or not, here goes – because you won't understand anything unless I tell you what the place was like.

The Moat House was the one we went to stay at. There has been a house there since Saxon times. It is a manor, and a manor goes on having a house on it whatever happens. The Moat House was burned down once or twice in ancient centuries – I don't remember which – but they always built a new one, and Cromwell's soldiers smashed it about, but it was patched up again.[4] It is a very odd house: the front door opens straight into the dining-room, and there are red curtains and a black-and-white marble floor like a chess-board, and there is a secret staircase, only it is not secret now – only rather rickety. It is not very big, but there is a watery moat all round it with a brick bridge that leads to the front door.[5] Then, on the other side of the moat there is the farm, with barns and oast-houses and stables, or things like that. And the other way the garden lawn goes on till it comes to the church-yard. The church-yard is not divided from the garden at all except by a little grass bank. In the front of the house there is more garden, and the big fruit-garden is at the back.

The man the house belongs to likes new houses, so he built a big one with conservatories and a stable with a clock in a turret on the top, and he let the Moat House. And Albert's uncle took it, and my father was to come down sometimes from Saturday to Monday, and Albert's uncle was to live with us all the time, and he would be writing a book, and we were not to bother him, but he would give an eye to us.[6] I hope all this is plain. I have said it as short as I can.

We got down rather late, but there was still light enough to see the big bell hanging at the top of the house. The rope belonging to it went right down the house, through our bedroom to the dining-room. H.O. saw the rope and pulled it while he was washing his hands for supper, and Dicky and I let him, and the bell tolled solemnly. Father shouted to him not to, and we went down to supper. But presently there were many feet trampling on the gravel, and Father went out to see. When he came back he said:

'The whole village, or half of it, has come up to see why the bell rang. It's only rung for fire or burglars. Why can't you kids let things alone?'

Albert's uncle said:

'Bed follows supper as the fruit follows the flower. They'll do no more mischief to-night, sir. To-morrow I will point out a few of the things to be avoided in this bucolic retreat.'

So it was bed directly after supper, and that was why we did not see much that night.

But in the morning we were all up rather early, and we seemed to have awakened in a new world, rich in surprises beyond the dreams of anybody, as it says in the quotation.

We went everywhere we could in the time, but when it was breakfast-time we felt we had not seen half or a quarter. The room we had breakfast in was exactly like in a story – black oak panels and china in corner cupboards with glass doors. These doors were locked. There were green curtains, and honeycomb for breakfast. After brekker my father went back to town, and Albert's uncle went too, to see publishers. We saw them to the station, and father gave us a long list of what we weren't to do. It began with 'Don't pull ropes unless you're quite sure what will happen at the other end,' and it finished with 'For goodness' sake, try to keep out of mischief till I come down on Saturday.' There were lots of other things in between.

We all promised we would. And we saw them off, and waved till the train was quite out of sight. Then we started to walk home. Daisy was tired, so Oswald carried her home on his back. When we got home she said:

'I do like you, Oswald.'

She is not a bad little kid; and Oswald felt it was his duty to be nice to her because she was a visitor. Then we looked all over everything. It was a glorious place. You did not know where to begin.

We were all a little tired before we found the hay-loft, but we pulled ourselves together to make a fort with the trusses of hay – great square things – and we were having a jolly good time, all of us, when suddenly a trap-door opened and a head bobbed up with a straw in its mouth. We knew nothing about the country then, and the head really did scare us rather, though, of course, we found out directly that the feet belonging to it were standing on the bar of the loose-box underneath. The head said:

'Don't you let the governor catch you a-spoiling of that there hay, that's all.' And it spoke thickly because of the straw.

It is strange to think how ignorant you were in the past. We can hardly believe now that once we really did not know that it spoiled hay to mess about with it. Horses don't like to eat it after-wards. Always remember this.

When the head had explained a little more it went away, and we turned the handle of the chaff-cutting machine, and nobody got hurt, though the head *had* said we should cut our fingers off if we touched it.[7]

And then we sat down on the floor, which is dirty with the nice clean dirt that is more than half chopped hay, and those there was room for hung their legs down out of the top door, and we looked down at the farmyard, which is very sloshy when you get down into it, but most interesting.

Then Alice said:

'Now we're all here, and the boys are tired enough to sit still for a minute, I want to have a council.'

We said, 'What about?' And she said, 'I'll tell you. H.O., don't wriggle so; sit on my frock if the straws tickle your legs.'

You see he wears socks, and so he can never be quite as comfort-able as any one else.[8]

'Promise not to laugh,' Alice said, getting very red, and looking at Dora, who got red too.

We did, and then she said: 'Dora and I have talked this over, and Daisy too, and we have written it down because it is easier than saying it. Shall I read it? or will you, Dora?'

Dora said it didn't matter; Alice might. So Alice read it, and though she gabbled a bit we all heard it. I copied it afterwards. This is what she read:

'NEW SOCIETY FOR BEING GOOD IN

'I, Dora Bastable, and Alice Bastable, my sister, being of sound mind and body, when we were shut up with bread and water on that jungle day, we thought a great deal about our naughty sins, and we made our minds up to be good forever after. And we talked to Daisy about it, and she had an idea. So we want to start a society for being good in. It is Daisy's idea, but we think so too.'

'You know,' Dora interrupted, 'when people want to do good things they always make a society. There are thousands – there's the Missionary Society.'

'Yes,' Alice said, 'and the Society for the Prevention of something or other, and the Young Men's Mutual Improvement Society, and the S.P.G.'⁹

'What's S.P.G.?' Oswald asked.

'Society for the Propagation of the Jews, of course,' said Noël, who cannot always spell.

'No, it isn't; but do let me go on.'

Alice did go on.¹⁰

'We propose to get up a society, with a chairman and a treasurer and a secretary, and keep a journal-book saying what we've done. If that doesn't make us good it won't be my fault.

'The aim of the society is nobleness and goodness, and great and unselfish deeds. We wish not to be such a nuisance to grown-up people, and to perform prodigies of real goodness. We wish to spread our wings' – here Alice read very fast. She told me afterwards Daisy had helped her with that part, and she thought when she came to the wings they sounded rather silly – 'to spread our wings and rise above the kind of interesting things that you ought not to do, but to do kindnesses to all, however low and mean.'

Denny was listening carefully. Now he nodded three or four times.

> 'Little words of kindness' (he said),
> 'Little deeds of love,
> Make this earth an eagle
> Like the one above.'¹¹

This did not sound right, but we let it pass, because an eagle *does* have wings, and we wanted to hear the rest of what the girls had written. But there was no rest.

'That's all,' said Alice, and Daisy said:

'Don't you think it's a good idea?'

'That depends,' Oswald answered, 'who is president, and what you mean by being good.' Oswald did not care very much for the idea himself, because being good is not the sort of thing he thinks it is proper to talk about, especially before strangers. But the girls and Denny seemed to like it, so Oswald did not say exactly what he thought, especially as it was Daisy's idea. This was true politeness.

'I think it would be nice,' Noël said, 'if we made it a sort of play. Let's do the "Pilgrim's Progress." '

We talked about that for some time, but it did not come to anything, because we all wanted to be Mr Greatheart, except H.O., who wanted to be the lions, and you could not have lions in a Society for Goodness.[12]

Dicky said he did not wish to play if it meant reading books about children who die; he really felt just as Oswald did about it, he told me afterwards. But the girls were looking as if they were in Sunday school, and we did not wish to be unkind.

At last Oswald said, 'Well, let's draw up the rules of the society, and choose the president and settle the name.'

Dora said Oswald should be president, and he modestly consented. She was secretary, and Denny treasurer if we ever had any money.

Making the rules took us all the afternoon. They were these:

RULES

1. Every member is to be as good as possible.
2. There is to be no more jaw than necessary about being good. (Oswald and Dicky put that rule in.)
3. No day must pass without our doing some kind action to a suffering fellow-creature.
4. We are to meet every day, or as often as we like.
5. We are to do good to people we don't like as often as we can.
6. No one is to leave the Society without the consent of all the rest of us.

7. The Society is to be kept a profound secret from all the world except us.

8. The name of our Society is –

And when we got as far as that we all began to talk at once. Dora wanted it called the Society for Humane Improvement; Denny said the Society for Reformed Outcast Children; but Dicky said, 'No, we really were not so bad as all that.' Then H.O. said, 'Call it the Good Society.'

'Or the Society for Being Good In,' said Daisy.

'Or the Society of Goods,' said Noël.

'That's priggish,' said Oswald; 'besides, we don't know whether we shall be so very.'

'You see,' Alice explained, 'we only said if we *could* we would be good.'

'Well, then,' Dicky said, getting up and beginning to dust the chopped hay off himself, 'call it the Society of the Wouldbegoods and have done with it.'

Oswald thinks Dicky was getting sick of it and wanted to make himself a little disagreeable. If so, he was doomed to disappointment. For every one else clapped hands and called out, 'That's the very thing!' Then the girls went off to write out the rules, and took H.O. with them, and Noël went to write some poetry to put in the minute book. That's what you call the book that a society's secretary writes what it does in. Denny went with him to help. He knows a lot of poetry. I think he went to a lady's school where they taught nothing but that. He was rather shy of us, but he took to Noël. I can't think why. Dicky and Oswald walked round the garden and told each other what they thought of the new society.

'I'm not sure we oughtn't to have put our foot down at the beginning,' Dicky said. 'I don't see much in it, anyhow.'

'It pleases the girls,' Oswald said, for he is a kind brother.

'But we're not going to stand jaw, and "words in season," and "loving sisterly warnings." I tell you what it is, Oswald, we'll have to run this thing our way, or it'll be jolly beastly for everybody.'

Oswald saw this plainly.

'We must do something,' Dicky said; 'it's very hard, though. Still, there must be *some* interesting things that are not wrong.'

'I suppose so,' Oswald said, 'but being good is so much like being a muff, generally. Anyhow I'm not going to smooth the pillows of the sick, or read to the aged poor, or any rot out of *Ministering Children*.'[13]

'No more am I,' Dicky said. He was chewing a straw like the head had in its mouth,[14] 'but I suppose we must play the game fair. Let's begin by looking out for something useful to do – something like mending things or cleaning them, not just showing off.'

'The boys in books chop kindling wood and save their pennies to buy tea and tracts.'

'Little beasts!' said Dick. 'I say, let's talk about something else.' And Oswald was glad to, for he was beginning to feel jolly uncomfortable.

We were all rather quiet at tea, and afterwards Oswald played draughts with Daisy and the others yawned. I don't know when we've had such a gloomy evening. And everyone was horribly polite, and said 'Please' and 'Thank you,' far more than requisite.

Albert's uncle came home after tea. He was jolly, and told us stories, but he noticed us being a little dull, and asked what blight had fallen on our young lives. Oswald could have answered and said, 'It is the Society of the Wouldbegoods that is the blight,' but of course he didn't; and Albert's uncle said no more, but he went up and kissed the girls when they were in bed, and asked them if there was anything wrong. And they told him no, on their honour.

The next morning Oswald awoke early. The refreshing beams of the morning sun shone on his narrow, white bed and on the sleeping forms of his dear little brothers and Denny, who had got the pillow on top of his head and was snoring like a kettle when it sings. Oswald could not remember at first what was the matter with him, and then he remembered the Wouldbegoods, and wished he hadn't. He felt at first as if there was nothing you could do, and even hesitated to buzz a pillow at Denny's head. But he soon saw that this could not be. So he chucked his boot and caught Denny right in the waistcoat part, and thus the day began more brightly than he had expected.

Oswald had not done anything out of the way good the night before, except that when no one was looking he polished the brass candlestick in the girls' bedroom with one of his socks. And he might just as well have let it alone, for the servants cleaned it again with the other things in the morning, and he could never find the sock afterwards.[15] There were two servants. One of them had to be called Mrs Pettigrew instead of Jane and Eliza like others. She was cook and managed things.

After breakfast Albert's uncle said:

'I now seek the retirement of my study. At your peril violate my privacy before 1.30 sharp. Nothing short of bloodshed will warrant the intrusion, and nothing short of man – or rather boy – slaughter shall avenge it.'

So we knew he wanted to be quiet, and the girls decided that we ought to play out of doors so as not to disturb him; we should have played out of doors anyhow on a jolly fine day like that.

But as we were going out Dicky said to Oswald:

'I say, come along here a minute, will you?'

So Oswald came along, and Dicky took him into the other parlour and shut the door, and Oswald said:

'Well, spit it out: what is it?' He knows that is vulgar, and he would not have said it to anyone but his own brother.

Dicky said:

'It's a pretty fair nuisance. I told you how it would be.'

And Oswald was patient with him, and said:

'What is? Don't be all day about it.'

Dicky fidgeted about a bit, and then he said:

'Well, I did as I said. I looked about for something useful to do. And you know that dairy window that wouldn't open – only a little bit like that? Well, I mended the catch with wire and whipcord and it opened wide.'

'And I suppose they didn't want it mended,' said Oswald. He knows but too well that grown-up people sometimes like to keep things far different from what we would, and you catch it if you try to do otherwise.

'I shouldn't have minded *that*,' Dicky said, 'because I could easily have taken it all off again if they'd only said so. But the sillies went and propped up a milk-pan against the window. They never took the trouble to notice I had mended it. So the wretched thing pushed the window open all by itself directly they propped it up, and it's tumbled through into the moat, and they are most awfully waxy.[16] All the men are out in the fields, and they haven't any spare milk-pans. If I were a farmer, I must say I wouldn't stick at an extra milk-pan or two. Accidents must happen sometimes. I call it mean.'

Dicky spoke in savage tones. But Oswald was not so unhappy, first because it wasn't his fault, and next because he is a far-seeing boy.

'Never mind,' he said, kindly. 'Keep your tail up. We'll get the beastly milk-pan out all right. Come on.'

He rushed hastily to the garden and gave a low signifying whistle, which the others know well enough to mean something extra being up.

And when they were all gathered round him he spoke.

'Fellow-countrymen,' he said, 'we're going to have a rousing good time.'

'It's nothing naughty, is it,' Daisy asked, 'like the last time you had that was rousingly good?'[17]

Alice said 'Shish,' and Oswald pretended not to hear.

'A precious treasure,' he said, 'has inadvertently been laid low in the moat by one of us.'

'The rotten thing tumbled in by itself,' Dicky said.

Oswald waved his hand and said, 'Anyhow, it's there. It's our duty to restore it to its sorrowing owners. I say, look here – we're going to drag the moat.'

Everyone brightened up at this. It was our duty and it was interesting too. This is very uncommon.

So we went out to where the orchard is, at the other side of the moat. There were gooseberries and things on the bushes, but we did not take any till we had asked if we might.[18] Alice went and asked. Mrs Pettigrew said, 'Law! I suppose so; you'd eat 'em anyhow, leave or no leave.'

She little knows the honourable nature of the house of Bastable. But she has much to learn.

The orchard slopes gently down to the dark waters of the moat. We sat there in the sun and talked about dragging the moat, till Denny said, 'How *do* you drag moats?'

And we were speechless, because, though we had read many times about a moat being dragged for missing heirs and lost wills, we really had never thought about exactly how it was done.

'Grappling-irons are right, I believe,' Denny said, 'but I don't suppose they'd have any at the farm.'

And we asked, and found they had never even heard of them. I think myself he meant some other word, but he was quite positive.

So then we got a sheet off Oswald's bed, and we all took our shoes and stockings off, and we tried to see if the sheet would drag the bottom of the moat, which is shallow at that end. But it would keep floating on the top of the water, and when we tried sewing stones into one end of it, it stuck on something in the bottom, and when we got it up it was torn. We were very sorry, and the sheet was in an awful mess; but the girls said they were sure they could wash it in the basin in their room, and we thought as we had torn it any way, we might as well go on. That washing never came off.[19]

'No human being,' Noël said, 'knows half the treasures hidden in this dark tarn.'

And we decided we would drag a bit more at that end, and work gradually round to under the dairy window where the milk-pan was. We could not see that part very well, because of the bushes that grow between the cracks of the stones where the house goes down into the moat. And opposite the dairy window the barn goes straight down into the moat too. It is like pictures of Venice; but you cannot get opposite the dairy window anyhow.

We got the sheet down again when we had tied the torn parts together in a bunch with string, and Oswald was just saying:

'Now then, my hearties, pull together, pull with a will! One, two, three,' when suddenly Dora dropped her bit of the sheet with a piercing shriek and cried out:

'Oh! it's all wormy at the bottom. I felt them wriggle.' And she was out of the water almost before the words were out of her mouth. The other girls all scuttled out too, and they let the sheet go in such a hurry that we had no time to steady ourselves, and one of us went right in, and the rest got wet up to our waistbands. The one who went right in was only H.O.; but Dora made an awful fuss and said it was our fault. We told her what we thought, and it ended in the girls going in with H.O. to change his things. We had some more gooseberries while they were gone.[20] Dora was in an awful wax when she went away, but she is not of a sullen disposition though sometimes hasty, and when they all came back we saw it was all right, so we said:

'What shall we do now?'

Alice said, 'I don't think we need drag any more. It *is* wormy. I felt it when Dora did. And besides, the milk-pan is sticking a bit of itself out of the water. I saw it through the dairy window.'

'Couldn't we get it up with fish-hooks?' Noël said. But Alice explained that the dairy was now locked up and the key taken out.

So then Oswald said:

'Look here, we'll make a raft. We should have to do it some time, and we might as well do it now. I saw an old door in that corner stable that they don't use. You know. The one where they chop the wood.'

We got the door.

We had never made a raft, any of us, but the way to make rafts is better described in books, so we knew what to do.

We found some nice little tubs stuck up on the fence of the farm garden, and nobody seemed to want them for anything just then, so we took them. Denny had a box of tools some one had given him for his last birthday; they were rather rotten little things, but the gimlet worked all right, so we managed to make holes in the edges of the tubs and fasten them with string under the four corners of the old door.[21] This took us a long time. Albert's uncle asked us at dinner what we had been playing at, and we said it was a secret, and it was nothing wrong. You see we wished to atone for Dicky's mistake before anything more was said. The house has no windows in the side that faces the orchard.

The rays of the afternoon sun were beaming along the orchard grass when at last we launched the raft. She floated out beyond reach with the last shove of the launching. But Oswald waded out and towed her back; he is not afraid of worms. Yet if he had known of the other things that were in the bottom of that moat he would have kept his boots on. So would the others, especially Dora, as you will see.

At last the gallant craft rode upon the waves. We manned her, though not up to our full strength, because if more than four got on the water came up too near our knees, and we feared she might founder if over-manned.

Daisy and Denny did not want to go on the raft, white mice that they were, so that was all right.[22] And as H.O. had been wet through once he was not very keen. Alice promised Noël her best paint-brush if he'd give up and not go, because we knew well that the voyage was fraught with deep dangers,[23] though the exact danger that lay in wait for us under the dairy window we never even thought of.

So we four elder ones got on the raft very carefully; and even then, every time we moved the water swished up over the raft and hid our feet. But I must say it was a jolly decent raft.

Dicky was captain, because it was his adventure. We had hop-poles from the hop-garden beyond the orchard to punt with. We made the girls stand together in the middle and hold on to each other to keep steady. Then we christened our gallant vessel. We called it the *Richard*, after Dicky, and also after the splendid admiral who used to eat wine-glasses and died after the Battle of the *Revenge* in Tennyson's poetry.[24]

Then those on shore waved a fond adieu as well as they could with the dampness of their handkerchiefs, which we had had to use to dry our legs and feet when we put on our stockings for dinner, and slowly and stately the good ship moved away from shore, riding on the waves as though they were her native element.

We kept her going with the hop-poles, and we kept her steady in the same way, but we could not always keep her steady enough, and we could not always keep her in the wind's eye. That is to say, she went where we did not want, and once she bumped her corner against the barn wall, and all the crew had to sit down suddenly to avoid falling overboard into a watery grave. Of course then the waves swept her decks, and when we got up again we said that we should have to change completely before tea.

But we pressed on undaunted, and at last our saucy craft came into port under the dairy window, and there was the milk-pan, for whose sake we had endured such hardships and privations, standing up on its edge quite quietly.

The girls did not wait for orders from the captain, as they ought to have done; but they cried out, 'Oh, here it is!' and then both reached out to get it. Any one who has pursued a naval career will see that of course the raft capsized. For a moment it felt like standing on the roof of the house, and the next moment the ship stood up on end and shot the whole crew into the dark waters.

We boys can swim all right. Oswald has swum three times across the Ladywell Swimming Baths at the shallow end, and Dicky is nearly as good; but just then we did not think of this; though, of course, if the water had been deep we should have.[25]

As soon as Oswald could get the muddy water out of his eyes he opened them on a horrid scene.

Dicky was standing up to his shoulders in the inky waters; the raft had righted itself, and was drifting gently away towards the front of the house, where the bridge is, and Dora and Alice were rising from the deep, with their hair all plastered over their faces – like Venus in the Latin verses.[26]

There was a great noise of splashing. And besides that a feminine voice, looking out of the dairy window and screaming:

'Lord love the children!'

It was Mrs Pettigrew. She disappeared at once, and we were sorry we were in such a situation that she would be able to get at Albert's uncle before we could. Afterwards we were not so sorry.

Before a word could be spoken about our desperate position, Dora staggered a little in the water, and suddenly shrieked, 'Oh, my foot! oh, it's a shark! I know it is – or a crocodile!'

The others on the bank could hear her shrieking, but they could not see us properly; they did not know what was happening. Noël told me afterwards he never could care for that paint-brush.

Of course we knew it could not be a shark, but I thought of pike, which are large and very angry always, and I caught hold of Dora. She screamed without stopping.[27] I shoved her along to where there was a ledge of brickwork, and shoved her up, till she could sit on it, then she got her foot out of the water, still screaming.

It was indeed terrible. The thing she thought was a shark came up with her foot, and it was a horrid, jagged, old meat-tin, and she had put her foot right into it. Oswald got it off, and directly he did so blood began to pour from the wounds. The tin edges had cut it in several spots. It was very pale blood, because her foot was wet, of course.

She stopped screaming, and turned green, and I thought she was going to faint, like Daisy did on the jungle day.[28]

Oswald held her up as well as he could, but it really was one of the least agreeable moments in his life. For the raft was gone, and she couldn't have waded back anyway, and we didn't know how deep the moat might be in other places.

But Mrs Pettigrew had not been idle. She is not a bad sort really.

Just as Oswald was wondering whether he could swim after the raft and get it back, a boat's nose shot out from under a dark archway a little further up under the house. It was the boathouse, and Albert's uncle had got the punt and took us back in it. When we had regained the dark arch where the boat lives we had to go up the cellar stairs. Dora had to be carried.[29]

There was but little said to us that day. We were sent to bed – those who had not been on the raft the same as the others, for they owned up all right, and Albert's uncle is the soul of justice.[30]

Next day but one was Saturday. Father gave us a talking to – with other things.

The worst, though, was when Dora couldn't get her shoe on, so they sent for the doctor, and Dora had to lie down for ever so long. It was indeed poor luck.

When the doctor had gone Alice said to me:

'It *is* hard lines, but Dora's very jolly about it. Daisy's been telling her about how we should all go to her with our little joys and sorrows and things, and about the sweet influence from a sick bed that can be felt all over the house, like in *What Katy Did*, and Dora said she hoped she might prove a blessing to us all while she's laid up.[31]

Oswald said he hoped so, but he was not pleased. Because this sort of jaw was exactly the sort of thing he and Dicky didn't want to have happen.

The thing we got it hottest for was those little tubs off the garden railings. They turned out to be butter-tubs that had been put out there 'to sweeten.'

But as Denny said, 'After the mud in that moat not all the perfumes of somewhere or other could make them fit to use for butter again.'[32]

I own this was rather a bad business. Yet we did not do it to please ourselves, but because it was our duty. But that made no difference to our punishment when father came down. I have known this mistake occur before.

✱ ✱ ✱

Chapter 3
Bill's Tombstone[1]

There were soldiers riding down the road, on horses, two and two. That is the horses were two and two, and the men not. Because each man was riding one horse and leading another. To exercise them. They came from Chatham Barracks. We all drew up in a line outside the church-yard wall, and saluted as they went by, though we had not read *Toady Lion* then.[2] We have since. It is the only decent book I have ever read written by *Toady Lion's* author. The others are mere piffle. But many people like them.

In *Sir Toady Lion* the officer salutes the child.

There was only a lieutenant with those soldiers, and he did not salute me. He kissed his hand to the girls; and a lot of the soldiers behind kissed theirs too. We waved ours back.

Next day we made a Union Jack out of pocket-handkerchiefs and part of a red flannel petticoat of the White Mouse's, which she did not want just then, and some blue ribbon we got at the village shop.[3]

Then we watched for the soldiers, and after three days they went by again, by twos and twos as before. It was A1.

We waved our flag, and we shouted. We gave them three cheers. Oswald can shout loudest. So as soon as the first man was level with us (not the advance guard, but the first of the battery) – he shouted:

'Three cheers for the Queen and the British Army!'

And then we waved the flag, and bellowed. Oswald stood on the wall to bellow better, and Denny waved the flag because he was a visitor, and so politeness made us let him enjoy the fat of whatever there was going.[4]

The soldiers did not cheer that day; they only grinned and kissed their hands.

The next day we all got up as much like soldiers as we could. H.O. and Noël had tin swords, and we asked Albert's uncle to let us wear some of the real arms that are on the wall in the dining-room. And he said, 'Yes,' if we would clean them up afterwards.

But we jolly well cleaned them up first with Brooke's soap and brick dust and vinegar, and the knife polish (invented by the great and immortal Duke of Wellington in his spare time when he was not conquering Napoleon. Three cheers for our Iron Duke!), and with emery paper and wash leather and whitening.[5] Oswald wore a cavalry sabre in its sheath. Alice and the Mouse had pistols in their belts, large old flint-locks, with bits of red flannel behind the flints.[6] Denny had a naval cutlass, a very beautiful blade, and old enough to have been at Trafalgar. I hope it was. The others had French sword-bayonets that were used in the Franco-German war.[7] They are very bright, when you get them bright, but the sheaths are hard to polish. Each sword-bayonet has the name on the blade of the warrior who once wielded it. I wonder where they are now. Perhaps some of them died in the war. Poor chaps! But it is a very long time ago.

I should like to be a soldier. It is better than going to the best schools, and to Oxford afterwards, even if it is Balliol you go to. Oswald wanted to go to South Africa for a bugler, but father would not let him.[8] And it is true that Oswald does not yet know how to bugle, though he can play the infantry 'advance,' and the 'charge' and the 'halt' on a penny whistle. Alice taught them to him with the piano, out of the red book Father's cousin had when he was in the Fighting Fifth.[9] Oswald cannot play the 'retire,' and he would scorn to do so. But I suppose a bugler has to play what he is told, no matter how galling to the young boy's proud spirit.

The next day, being thoroughly armed, we put on everything red, white, and blue that we could think of – night-shirts are good for white, and you don't know what you can do with red socks and blue jerseys till you try – and we waited by the church-yard wall for the soldiers.[10] When the advance guard (or whatever you call it of artillery – it's that for infantry, I know) came by we got ready, and when the first man of the first battery was level with us Oswald played on his penny whistle the 'advance' and the 'charge' – and then shouted:

'Three cheers for the Queen and the British Army!'

This time they had the guns with them. And every man of the battery cheered too. It was glorious. It made you tremble all over. The girls said it made them want to cry – but no boy would own to this, even if it were true. It is babyish to cry. But it was glorious, and Oswald felt different to what he ever did before.

Then suddenly the officer in front said, 'Battery! Halt!'[11] and all the soldiers pulled their horses up, and the great guns stopped too. Then the officer said, 'Sit at ease,' and something else, and the sergeant repeated it, and some of the men got off their horses and lit their pipes, and some sat down on the grass edge of the road, holding their horses' bridles.

We could see all the arms and accoutrements as plain as plain.

Then the officer came up to us. We were all standing on the wall that day, except Dora, who had to sit, because her foot was bad, but we let her have the three-edged rapier to wear, and the blunderbuss to hold as well – it has a brass mouth and is like in Mr Caldecott's pictures.[12]

He was a beautiful man the officer. Like a Viking. Very tall and fair, with moustaches very long, and bright blue eyes.

He said:

'Good morning.'

So did we.

Then he said:

'You seem to be a military lot.'

We said we wished we were.

'And patriotic,' said he.

Alice said she should jolly well think so.

Then he said he had noticed us there for several days, and he had halted the battery because he thought we might like to look at the guns.

Alas! there are but too few grown-up people so far-seeing and thoughtful as this brave and distinguished officer.

We said, 'Oh, yes,' and then we got off the wall, and that good and noble man showed us the string that moves the detonator, and the breech-block (when you take it out and carry it away, the gun is in vain to the enemy, even if he takes it); and he let us look down the gun to see the rifling, all clean and shiny; and he showed us the ammunition boxes, but there was nothing in them. He also told us how the gun was unlimbered (this means separating the gun from the ammunition carriage), and how quick it could be done – but he did not make the men do this then, because they were resting. There were six guns. Each had painted on the carriage, in white letters, 15 Pr., which the captain told us meant fifteen-pounder.

'I should have thought the gun weighed more than fifteen pounds,' Dora said. 'It would if it was beef, but I suppose wood and gun are lighter.'[13]

And the officer explained to her very kindly and patiently that 15 Pr. meant the gun could throw a *shell* weighing fifteen pounds.

When we had told him how jolly it was to see the soldiers go by so often, he said:

'You won't see us many more times. We're ordered to the front; and we sail on Tuesday week; and the guns will be painted mud-colour, and the men will wear mud-colour too, and so shall I.'

The men looked very nice, though they were not wearing their busbies, but only Tommy caps, put on all sorts of ways.[14]

We were very sorry they were going, but Oswald, as well as others, looked with envy on those who would soon be allowed – being grown up, and no nonsense about your education – to go and fight for their Queen and country.

Then suddenly Alice whispered to Oswald, and he said:

'All right; but tell him yourself.'

So Alice said to the captain:

'Will you stop next time you pass?'

He said, 'I'm afraid I can't promise that.'

Alice said, 'You might; there's a particular reason.'

He said, 'What?' which was a natural remark; not rude, as it is with children.

Alice said:

'We want to give the soldiers a keepsake. I will write to ask my father. He is very well off just now. Look here – if we're not on the wall when you come by, don't stop; but if we are, *please*, PLEASE do!'

The officer pulled his moustache and looked as if he did not quite know; but at last he said 'Yes,' and we were very glad, though but Alice and Oswald knew the dark but pleasant scheme at present fermenting in their youthful nuts.

The captain talked a lot to us. At last Noël said:

'I think you are like Diarmid of the Golden Collar.[15] But I should like to see your sword out, and shining in the sun like burnished silver.'

The captain laughed and grasped the hilt of his good blade. But Oswald said, hurriedly:

'Don't. Not yet. We sha'n't ever have a chance like this. If you'd only show us the pursuing practice! Albert's uncle knows it; but he only does it on an arm-chair, because he hasn't a horse.'

And that brave and swagger captain did really do it. He rode his horse right into our gate when we opened it, and showed us all the cuts, thrusts, and guards. There are four of each kind. It was splendid. The morning sun shone on his flashing blade, and his good steed stood with all its legs far apart and stiff on the lawn. Then we opened the paddock gate, and he did it again, while the horse galloped as if upon the bloody battle-field among the fierce foes of his native land, and this was far more ripping still.

Then we thanked him very much, and he went away, taking his men with him. And the guns, of course.

Then we wrote to my father, and he said 'Yes,' as we knew he would, and next time the soldiers came by – but they had no guns this time, only the captive Arabs of the desert – we had the keep-sakes ready in a wheelbarrow, and we were on the church-yard wall.

And the bold captain called an immediate halt.

Then the girls had the splendid honour and pleasure of giving a pipe and four whole ounces of tobacco to each soldier.

Then we shook hands with the captain, and the sergeant, and the corporals, and the girls kissed the captain – I can't think why girls will kiss everybody – and we all cheered for the Queen.

It was grand. And I wish my father had been there to see how much you can do with £12 if you order the things from the Stores.[16]

We have never seen those brave soldiers again.

I have told you all this to show you how we got so keen about soldiers, and why we sought to aid and abet the poor widow at the white cottage in her desolation and oppressedness.

Her name was Simpkins, and her cottage was just beyond the church-yard, on the other side from our house. On the differ-ent military occasions which I have remarked upon this widow woman stood at her garden gate and looked on. And after the cheering she rubbed her eyes with her apron. Alice noticed this slight but signifying action.

We felt quite sure Mrs Simpkins liked soldiers, and so we felt friendly to her. But when we tried to talk to her she would not. She told us to go along with us, do, and not bother her. And Oswald, with his usual delicacy and good breeding, made the others do as she said.

But we were not to be thus repulsed with impunity. We made complete but cautious inquiries, and found out that the reason she cried when she saw soldiers was that she had only one son, a boy. He was twenty-two, and he had gone to the War last April. So that she thought of him when she saw the soldiers, and that was why she cried. Because when your son is at the wars you always think he is being killed. I don't know why. A great many of them are not. If I had a son at the wars I should never think he was dead till I heard he was, and perhaps not then, considering everything.

After we had found this out we held a council.

Dora said, 'We must do something for the soldier's widowed mother.'

We all agreed, but added 'What?'

Alice said, 'The gift of money might be deemed an insult by that proud, patriotic spirit. Besides, we haven't more than eighteenpence among us.'

We had put what we had to father's £12 to buy the baccy and pipes.

The Mouse then said, 'Couldn't we make her a flannel petticoat and leave it without a word upon her doorstep?'[17]

But everyone said, 'Flannel petticoats in this weather?' so that was no go.

Noël said he would write her a poem, but Oswald had a deep, inward feeling that Mrs Simpkins would not understand poetry. Many people do not.

H.O. said, 'Why not sing "Rule Britannia" under her window after she had gone to bed, like waits,' but no one else thought so.

Denny thought we might get up a subscription for her among the wealthy and affluent, but we said again that we knew money would be no balm to the haughty mother of a brave British soldier.

'What we want,' Alice said, 'is something that will be a good deal of trouble to us and some good to her.'

'A little help is worth a deal of poetry,' said Denny. I should not have said that myself. Noël did look sick.[18]

'What *does* she do that we can help in?' Dora asked. 'Besides, she won't let us help.'

H.O. said, 'She does nothing but work in the garden. At least if she does anything inside you can't see it, because she keeps the door shut.'

Then at once we saw. And we agreed to get up the very next day, ere yet the rosy dawn had flushed the east, and have a go at Mrs Simpkins's garden.

We got up. We really did. But too often when you mean to, over night, it seems so silly to do it when you come to waking in the dewy morn. We crept downstairs with our boots in our hands.[19] Denny is rather unlucky, though a most careful boy. It was he who dropped his boot, and it went blundering down the stairs, echoing like thunder-bolts, and waking up Albert's uncle. But when we explained to him that we were going to do some gardening he let us, and went back to bed.

Everything is very pretty and different in the early morning, before people are up. I have been told this is because the shadows go a different way from what they do in the awake part of the day. But I don't know. Noël says the fairies have just finished tidying up then. Anyhow it all feels quite otherwise.

We put on our boots in the porch, and we got our gardening tools and we went down to the white cottage. It is a nice cottage, with a thatched roof, like in the drawing-copies you get at girls' schools, and you do the thatch – if you can – with a B.B. pencil.[20] If you cannot, you just leave it. It looks just as well, somehow, when it is mounted and framed.

We looked at the garden. It was very neat. Only one patch was coming up thick with weeds. I could see groundsel and chickweed, and others that I did not know. We set to work with a will. We used all our tools – spades, forks, hoes, and rakes – and Dora worked with the trowel, sitting down, because her foot was hurt.[21] We cleared the weedy patch beautifully, scraping off all the nasty weeds and leaving the nice clean brown dirt. We worked as hard as ever we could. And we were happy, because it was unselfish toil, and no one thought then of putting it in the Book of Golden Deeds, where we had agreed to write down our virtuous actions and the good doings of each other, when we happen to notice them.[22]

We had just done, and we were looking at the beautiful production of our honest labour, when the cottage door burst open, and the soldier's widowed mother came out like a wild tornado, and her eyes looked like upas-trees – death to the beholder.[23]

'You wicked, meddlesome, nasty children!' she said, 'ain't you got enough of your own good ground to runch up and spoil but you must come into *my* little lot?'[24]

Some of us were deeply alarmed, but we stood firm.

'We have only been weeding your garden,' Dora said; 'We wanted to do something to help you.'

'Dratted little busybodies,' she said. It was indeed hard, but everyone in Kent says 'Dratted' when they are cross. 'It's my turnips,' she went on, 'you've hoed up, and my cabbages. My turnips that my boy sowed afore he went. There, get along with you do, afore I come at you with my broom-handle.'

She did come at us with her broom-handle as she spoke, and even the boldest turned and fled. Oswald was even the boldest.

'They looked like weeds right enough,' he said.

And Dicky said, 'It all comes of trying to do golden deeds.'

This was when we were out in the road.

As we went along, in a silence full of gloomy remorse, we met the postman. He said:

'Here's the letters for the Moat,' and passed on hastily. He was a bit late.

When we came to look through the letters, which were nearly all for Albert's uncle, we found there was a post-card that had got stuck in a magazine wrapper. Alice pulled it out. It was addressed to Mrs Simpkins.

We honourably only looked at the address, although it is allowed by the rules of honourableness to read post-cards that come to your house if you like, even if they are not for you.

After a heated discussion, Alice and Oswald said they were not afraid, whoever was, and they retraced their steps, Alice holding the post-card right way up, so that we should not look at the lettery part of it, but only the address.

With quickly beating heart, but outwardly unmoved, they walked up to the white cottage door.

It opened with a bang when we knocked.

'Well?' Mrs Simpkins said, and I think she said it what people in books call 'sourly.'

Oswald said, 'We are very, very sorry we spoiled your turnips, and we will ask my father to try and make it up to you some other way.'

She muttered something about not wanting to be beholden to anybody.

'We came back,' Oswald went on, with his always unruffled politeness, 'because the postman gave us a post-card in mistake with our letters, and it is addressed to you.'

'We haven't read it,' Alice said quickly. I think she needn't have said that. Of course we hadn't. But perhaps girls know better than we do what women are likely to think you capable of.

The soldier's mother took the post-card (she snatched it really, but 'took' is a kinder word, considering everything) and she looked at the address a long time. Then she turned it over and read what was on the back. Then she drew her breath in as far as it would go, and caught hold of the door-post. Her face got awful. It was like the wax face of a dead king I saw once at Madame Tussaud's.

Alice understood. She caught hold of the soldier's mother's hand and said:

'Oh, *no* – it's *not* your boy Bill!'

And the woman said nothing, but shoved the post-card into Alice's hand, and we both read it – and it *was* her boy Bill.

Alice gave her back the card. She had held on to the woman's hand all the time, and now she squeezed the hand, and held it against her face. But she could not say a word because she was crying so. The soldier's mother took the card again and she pushed Alice away, but it was not an unkind push, and she went in and shut the door; and as Alice and Oswald went down the road Oswald looked back, and one of the windows of the cottage had a white blind. Afterwards the other windows had too. There were no blinds really to the cottage. It was aprons and things she had pinned up.

Alice cried most of the morning, and so did the other girls.[25] We wanted to do something for the soldier's mother, but you can do nothing when people's sons are shot. It is the most dreadful thing to want to do something for people who are unhappy, and not to know what to do.

It was Noël who thought of what we *could* do at last.

He said, 'I suppose they don't put up tombstones to soldiers when they die in war. But there – I mean – '

Oswald said, 'Of course not.'

Noël said, 'I daresay you'll think it's silly, but I don't care. Don't you think she'd like it if we put one up to *him*? Not in the church-yard, of course, because we shouldn't be let, but in our garden, just where it joins on to the church-yard?'[26]

And we all thought it was a first-rate idea.

This is what we meant to put on the tombstone:

> 'Here lies
> BILL SIMPKINS
> Who died fighting for Queen
> and Country.
>
> 'A faithful son,
> A son so dear,
> A soldier brave
> Lies buried here.'

Then we remembered that poor, brave Bill was really buried far away in the Southern hemisphere, if at all.

So we altered it to –

> 'A soldier brave
> We weep for here.'

Then we looked out a nice flagstone in the stable-yard, and we got a cold-chisel out of the Dentist's tool-box, and began.[27]

But stone-cutting is difficult and dangerous work.

Oswald went at it a bit, but he chipped his thumb, and it bled so he had to chuck it. Then Dicky tried, and then Denny, but Dicky hammered his finger, and Denny took all day over every stroke, so that by tea-time we had only done the H, and about half the E – and the E awfully crooked. Oswald chipped his thumb over the H.[28]

We looked at it the next morning, and even the most sangui-nary of us saw that it was a hopeless task.

Then Denny said, 'Why not wood and paint?' and he showed us how. We got a board and two stumps from the carpenter's in the village, and we painted it all white, and when that was dry Denny did the words on it.[29]

It was something like this:

> 'IN MEMORY OF BILL SIMPKINS
> DEAD FOR QUEEN & COUNTRY
> HONOUR TO HIS NAME AND ALL
> OTHER BRAVE SOLDIERS.'

We could not get in what we meant to at first, so we had to give up the poetry.

We fixed it up when it was dry. We had to dig jolly deep to get the posts to stand up, but the gardener helped us.

Then the girls made wreaths of white flowers, roses and Canterbury bells, and lilies and pinks, and sweet-peas and daisies, and put them over the posts, like you see in the picture.[30] And I think if Bill Simpkins had known how sorry we were, he would have been glad. Oswald only hopes if *he* falls on the wild battle-field, which is his highest ambition, that somebody will be as sorry about him as he was about Bill, that's all!

When all was done, and what flowers there were over from the wreaths scattered under the tombstone between the posts, we wrote a letter to Mrs Simpkins, and said:

'DEAR MRS SIMPKINS, – We are very, very sorry about the turnips and things, and we beg your pardon humbly. We have put up a tombstone to your brave son.'

And we signed our names.

Alice took the letter.

The soldier's mother read it, and said something about our oughting to know better than to make fun of people's troubles with our tombstones and tomfoolery.

Alice told me she could not help crying.

She said,

'It's *not*! it's NOT! Dear, *dear* Mrs Simpkins, do come with me and see! You don't know how sorry we are about Bill. Do come and see. We can go through the church-yard, and the others have all gone in, so as to leave it quiet for you. Do come.'

And Mrs Simpkins did. And when she read what we had put up, and Alice told her the verse we had not had room for, she leaned against the wall by the grave – I mean the tombstone – and Alice hugged her, and they both cried bitterly. The poor soldier's mother was very, very pleased. And she forgave us about the turnips, and we were friends after that, but she always liked Alice the best. A great many people do, somehow.

After that we used to put fresh flowers every day on Bill's tombstone, and I do believe his mother *was* pleased, though she got us to move it away from the church-yard edge and put it in a corner of our garden under a laburnum, where people could not see it from the church. But you could from the road, though I think she thought you couldn't. She came every day to look at the new wreaths. When the white flowers gave out we put coloured, and she liked it just as well.

About a fortnight after the erecting of the tombstone the girls were putting fresh wreaths on it when a soldier in a red coat came down the road, and he stopped and looked at us. He walked with a stick, and he had a bundle in a blue cotton handkerchief, and one arm in a sling.

And he looked again, and he came nearer, and he leaned on the wall, so that he could read the black printing on the white paint.

And he grinned all over his face, and he said:

'Well, I *am* blessed!'

And he read it all out in a sort of half whisper, and when he came to the end, where it says, 'and all such brave soldiers,' he said:

'Well, I really *am*!' I suppose he meant he really was blessed.

Oswald thought it was like the soldier's cheek, so he said:

'I daresay you aren't so very blessed as you think. What's it to do with you, anyway, eh, Tommy?'

Of course Oswald knew from Kipling that an infantry soldier is called that.[31] The soldier said:

'Tommy yourself, young man. That's *me*!' and he pointed to the tombstone.

We stood rooted to the spot. Alice spoke first.

'Then you're Bill, and you're not dead,' she said. 'Oh, Bill, I am so glad! Do let *me* tell your mother.'

She started running, and so did we all. Bill had to go slowly because of his leg,[32] but I tell you he went as fast as ever he could.

We all hammered at the soldier's mother's door, and shouted:

'Come out! come out!' and when she opened the door we were going to speak, but she pushed us away, and went tearing down the garden path like winking. I never saw a grown-up woman run like it, because she saw Bill coming.

She met him at the gate, running right into him, and caught hold of him, and she cried much more than when she thought he was dead.

And we all shook his hand and said how glad we were.

The soldier's mother kept hold of him with both hands, and I couldn't help looking at her face. It was like wax that had been painted pink on both cheeks, and the eyes shining like candles. And when we had all said how glad we were, she said:

'Thank the dear Lord for His mercies,' and she took her boy Bill into the cottage and shut the door.

We went home and chopped up the tombstone with the wood-axe and had a blazing big bonfire, and cheered till we could hardly speak.

The postcard was a mistake; he was only missing. There was a pipe and a whole pound of tobacco left over from our keepsake to the other soldiers. We gave it to Bill. Father is going to have him for under-gardener when his wounds get well. He'll always be a bit lame, so he cannot fight any more.

I am very glad *some* soldiers' mothers get their boys home again.

But if they have to die, it is a glorious death; and I hope mine will be that.

And three cheers for the Queen, and the mothers who let their boys go, and the mothers' sons who fight and die for Old England. Hip, hip, hurrah!

* * *

Chapter 4
The Tower of Mystery

It was very rough on Dora having her foot bad, but we took it in turns to stay in with her, and she was very decent about it. Daisy was most with her. I do not dislike Daisy, but I wish she had been taught how to play. Because Dora is rather like that naturally, and sometimes I have thought that Daisy makes her worse.

I talked to Albert's uncle about it one day, when the others had gone to church, and I did not go because of ear-ache, and he said it came from reading the wrong sort of books partly – she has read *Ministering Children*, and *Anna Ross, or The Orphan of Waterloo*, and *Ready Work for Willing Hands*, and *Elsie, or Like a Little Candle*, and even a horrid little blue book about the something or other of Little Sins.[1] After this conversation Oswald took care she had plenty of the right sort of books to read, and he was surprised and pleased when she got up early one morning to finish *Monte Cristo*.[2] Oswald felt that he was really being useful to a suffering fellow-creature when he gave Daisy books that were not all about being good.

A few days after Dora was laid up Alice called a council of the Wouldbegoods, and Oswald and Dicky attended with darkly clouded brows. Alice had the minute-book, which was an exercise-book that had not much written in it. She had begun at the other end. I hate doing that myself, because there is so little room at the top compared with right way up.

Dora and a sofa had been carried out on to the lawn, and we were on the grass. It was very hot and dry. We had sherbet. Alice read:

' "Society of the Wouldbegoods.

' "We have not done much. Dicky mended a window, and we got the milk-pan out of the moat that dropped through where he mended it. Dora, Oswald, Dicky and me got upset in the moat. This was not goodness. Dora's foot was hurt. We hope to do better next time." '

Then came Noël's poem:

> ' "We are the Wouldbegoods Society,
> We are not good yet, but we mean to try.
> And if we try, and if we don't succeed,
> It must mean we are very bad indeed." '

This sounded so much righter than Noël's poetry generally does, that Oswald said so, and Noël explained that Denny had helped him.

'He seems to know the right length for lines of poetry. I suppose it comes of learning so much at school,' Noël said.

Then Oswald proposed that anybody should be allowed to write in the book if they found out anything good that any one else had done, but not things that were public acts; and nobody was to write about themselves, or anything other people told them, only what they found out.

After a brief jaw the others agreed, and Oswald felt, not for the first time in his young life, that he would have made a good diplomatic hero to carry despatches and outwit the other side. For now he had put it out of the minute-book's power to be the kind of thing readers of *Ministering Children* would have wished.

'And if any one tells other people any good thing he's done he is to go to Coventry for the rest of the day.'[3] And Denny remarked, 'We shall do good by stealth and blush to find it shame.'[4]

After that nothing was written in the book for some time. I looked about, and so did the others, but I never caught any one in the act of doing anything extra; though several of the others have told me since of things they did at this time, and really wondered nobody had noticed.

I think I said before, that when you tell a story you cannot tell everything. It would be silly to do it. Because ordinary kinds of play are dull to read about; and the only other thing is meals, and to dwell on what you eat is greedy and not like a hero at all. A hero is always contented with a venison pasty and a horn of sack. All the same, the meals *were* very interesting; with things you do not get at home – Lent pies with custard and currants in them, sausage rolls and flede cakes, and raisin cakes and apple turnovers, and honeycomb and syllabubs, besides as much new milk as you cared about, and cream now and then, and cheese always on the table for tea. Father told Mrs Pettigrew to get what meals she liked, and she got these strange but attractive foods.

In a story about Wouldbegoods it is not proper to tell of times when only some of us were naughty, so I will pass lightly over the time when Noël got up the kitchen chimney and brought three bricks and an old starling's nest and about a ton of soot down with him when he fell. They never use the big chimney in the summer, but cook in the wash-house. Nor do I wish to dwell on what H.O. did when he went into the dairy. I do not know what his motive was. But Mrs Pettigrew said *she* knew; and she locked him in, and said if it was cream he wanted he should have enough, and she wouldn't let him out till tea-time. The cat had also got into the dairy for some reason of her own, and when H.O. was tired of whatever he went in for he poured all the milk into the churn and tried to teach the cat to swim in it. He must have been desperate. The cat did not even try to learn, and H.O. had the scars on his hands for weeks. I do not wish to tell tales of H.O., for he is very young, and whatever he does he always catches it for; but I will just allude to our being told not to eat the greengages in the garden. And we did not. And whatever H.O. did was Noël's fault – for Noël told H.O. that greengages would grow again all right if you did not bite as far as the stone, just as wounds are not mortal except when you are pierced through the heart. So the two of them bit bites out of every greengage they could reach. And of course the pieces did not grow again.

Oswald did not do things like these, but then he is older than his brothers. The only thing he did just about then was making a booby-trap for Mrs Pettigrew when she had locked H.O. up in the dairy, and unfortunately it was the day she was going out in her best things, and part of the trap was a can of water. Oswald was not willingly vicious; it was but a light and thoughtless act which he had every reason to be sorry for afterwards. And he is sorry even without those reasons, because he knows it is ungentlemanly to play tricks on women.

I remember mother telling Dora and me when we were little that you ought to be very kind and polite to servants, because they have to work very hard, and do not have so many good times as we do. I used to think about mother more at the Moat House than I did at Blackheath, especially in the garden. She was very fond of flowers, and she used to tell us about the big garden where she used to live; and, I remember, Dora and I helped her to plant seeds. But it is no use wishing. She would have liked that garden, though.

The girls and the white mice did not do anything boldly wicked – though of course they used to borrow Mrs Pettigrew's needles, which made her very nasty. Needles that are borrowed might just as well be stolen. But I say no more.

I have only told you these things to show the kind of events which occurred on the days I don't tell you about. On the whole, we had an excellent time.

It was on the day we had the pillow-fight that we went for the long walk. Not the Pilgrimage – that is another story. We did not mean to have a pillow-fight. It is not usual to have them after breakfast, but Oswald had come up to get his knife out of the pocket of his Etons, to cut some wire we were making rabbit snares of. It is a very good knife, with a file in it, as well as a corkscrew and other things – and he did not come down at once, because he was detained by having to make an apple-pie bed for Dicky. Dicky came up after him to see what he was up to, and when he did see he buzzed a pillow at Oswald, and the fight began. The others, hearing the noise of battle from afar, hastened to the field of action, all except Dora, who couldn't, because of being laid up with her foot, and Daisy, because she is a little afraid of us still, when we are all together. She thinks we are rough. This comes of having only one brother.[5]

Well, the fight was a very fine one. Alice backed me up, and Noël and H.O. backed Dicky, and Denny heaved a pillow or two; but he cannot shy straight, so I don't know which side he was on.

And just as the battle raged most fiercely, Mrs Pettigrew came in and snatched the pillows away, and shook those of the warriors who were small enough for it. *She* was rough if you like. She also used language I should have thought she would be above. She said, 'Drat you!' and 'Drabbit you!' The last is a thing I have never heard said before. She said:

'There's no peace of your life with you children. Drat your antics! And that poor, dear, patient gentleman right underneath, with his headache and his handwriting: and you rampaging about over his head like young bull-calves. I wonder you haven't more sense, a great girl like you.'

She said this to Alice, and Alice answered gently, as we are told to do:

'I really am awfully sorry; we forgot about the headache. Don't be cross, Mrs Pettigrew; we didn't mean to; we didn't think.'

'You never do,' she said, and her voice, though grumpy, was no longer violent. 'Why on earth you can't take yourselves off for the day I don't know.'

We all said, 'But may we?'

She said, 'Of course you may. Now put on your boots and go for a good long walk. And I'll tell you what – I'll put you up a snack, and you can have an egg to your tea to make up for missing your dinner. Now don't go clattering about the stairs and passages, there's good children. See if you can't be quiet this once, and give the good gentleman a chance with his copying.'

She went off. Her bark is worse than her bite. She does not understand anything about writing books, though. She thinks Albert's uncle copies things out of printed books, when he is really writing new ones. I wonder how she thinks printed books get made first of all. Many servants are like this.

She gave us the 'snack' in a basket, and sixpence to buy milk with. She said any of the farms would let us have it, only most likely it would be skim. We thanked her politely, and she hurried us out of the front door as if we'd been chickens on a pansy bed.

(I did not know till after I had left the farm gate open, and the hens had got into the garden, that these feathered bipeds display a great partiality for the young buds of plants of the genus *viola*, to which they are extremely destructive. I was told that by the gardener. I looked it up in the gardening book afterwards to be sure he was right. You do learn a lot of things in the country.)

We went through the garden as far as the church, and then we rested a bit in the porch, and just looked into the basket to see what the 'snack' was. It proved sausage rolls, and queen cakes, and a Lent pie in a round tin dish, and some hard-boiled eggs, and some apples. We all ate the apples at once, so as not to have to carry them about with us. The church-yard smells awfully good. It is the wild thyme that grows on the graves. This is another thing we did not know before we came into the country.

Then the door of the church tower was ajar, and we all went up; it had always been locked before when we had tried it.

We saw the ringer's loft where the ends of the bell-ropes hang down with long, furry handles to them like great caterpillars, some red, and some blue and white, but we did not pull them. And then we went up to where the bells are, very big and dusty among large dirty beams; and four windows with no glass, only shutters like Venetian blinds, but they won't pull up. There were heaps of straws and sticks on the window ledges. We think they were owls' nests, but we did not see any owls.

Then the tower stairs got very narrow and dark, and we went on up, and we came to a door and opened it suddenly, and it was like being hit in the face, the light was so sudden. And there we were on the top of the tower, which is flat, and people have cut their names on it, and a turret at one corner, and a low wall all round, up and down, like castle battlements. And we looked down and saw the roof of the church, and the leads, and the church-yard, and our garden, and the Moat House, and the farm, and Mrs Simpkins's cottage, looking very small, and other farms looking like toy things out of boxes, and we saw corn-fields and meadows and pastures. A pasture is not the same thing as a meadow, what-ever you may think. And we saw the tops of trees and hedges, looking like the map of the United States, and villages, and a tower that did not look very far away standing by itself on the top of a hill.

Alice pointed to it, and said:

'What's that?'

'It's not a church,' said Noël, 'because there's no church-yard. Perhaps it's a tower of mystery that covers the entrance to a sub-terranean vault with treasure in it.'

Dicky said, 'Subterranean fiddlestick!' and 'A water-works, more likely.'

Alice thought perhaps it was a ruined castle, and the rest of its crumbling walls were concealed by ivy, the growth of years.

Oswald could not make his mind up what it was, so he said, 'Let's go and see! We may as well go there as anywhere.'

So we got down out of the church tower and dusted ourselves, and set out.

The Tower of Mystery showed quite plainly from the road, now that we knew where to look for it, because it was on the top of a hill. We began to walk. But the tower did not seem to get any nearer. And it was very hot.

So we sat down in a meadow where there was a stream in the ditch and ate the 'snack.' We drank the pure water from the brook out of our hands, because there was no farm to get milk at just there, and it was too much fag to look for one – and, besides, we thought we might as well save the sixpence.

Then we started again, and still the tower looked as far off as ever. Denny began to drag his feet, though he had brought a walking-stick which none of the rest of us had,[6] and said:

'I wish a cart would come along. We might get a lift.'

He knew all about getting lifts, of course, from having been in the country before. He is not quite the white mouse we took him for at first. Of course when you live in Lewisham or Blackheath you learn other things. If you asked for a lift in Lewisham, High Street, your only reply would be jeers. We sat down on a heap of stones, and decided that we would ask for a lift from the next cart, whichever way it was going. It was while we were waiting that Oswald found out about plantain seeds being good to eat.

When the sound of wheels came we remarked with joy that the cart was going towards the Tower of Mystery. It was a cart a man was going to fetch a pig home in. Denny said:

'I say, you might give us a lift. Will you?'

The man who was going for the pig said:

'What, all that little lot?' but he winked at Alice, and we saw that he meant to aid us on our way. So we climbed up, and he whipped up the horse and asked us where we were going. He was a kindly old man, with a face like a walnut shell, and white hair and beard like a jack-in-the-box.

'We want to get to the tower,' Alice said. 'Is it a ruin, or not?'

'It ain't no ruin,' the man said; 'No fear of that! The man wot built it he left so much a year to be spent on repairing of it! Money that might have put bread in honest folks' mouths.'

We asked was it a church then, or not.

'Church?' he said. 'Not it. It's more of a tombstone, from all I can make out. They do say there was a curse on him that built it, and he wasn't to rest in earth or sea. So he's buried half-way up the tower – if you can call it buried.'

'Can you go up it?' Oswald asked.

'Lord love you! yes; a fine view from the top, they say. I've never been up myself, though I've lived in sight of it, boy and man, these sixty-three years come harvest.'

Alice asked whether you had to go past the dead and buried person to get to the top of the tower, and could you see the coffin.

'No, no,' the man said; 'that's all hid away behind a slab of stone, that is, with reading on it. You've no call to be afraid, missy.

It's daylight all the way up. But I wouldn't go there after dark, so I wouldn't. It's always open, day and night, and they say tramps sleep there now and again. Anyone who likes can sleep there, but it wouldn't be me.'

We thought that it would not be us either, but we wanted to go more than ever, especially when the man said:

'My own great-uncle of the mother's side, he was one of the masons that set up the stone slab. Before then it was thick glass, and you could see the dead man lying inside, as he'd left it in his will. He was lying there in a glass coffin with his best clothes – blue satin and silver, my uncle said, such as was all the go in his day, with his wig on, and his sword beside him, what he used to wear. My uncle said his hair had grown out from under his wig, and his beard was down to the toes of him. My uncle he always upheld that that dead man was no deader than you and me, but was in a sort of fit, a transit, I think they call it, and looked for him to waken into life again some day. But the doctor said not. It was only something done to him like Pharaoh in the Bible afore he was buried.'[7]

Alice whispered to Oswald that we should be late for tea, and wouldn't it be better to go back now directly. But he said:

'If you're afraid, say so; and you needn't come in anyway – but I'm going on.'

The man who was going for the pig put us down at a gate quite near the tower – at least it looked so until we began to walk again. We thanked him, and he said:

'Quite welcome,' and drove off.

We were rather quiet going through the wood. What we had heard made us very anxious to see the tower – all except Alice, who would keep talking about tea, though not a greedy girl by nature. None of the others encouraged her, but Oswald thought himself that we had better be home before dark.

As we went up the path through the wood we saw a poor way-farer with dusty bare feet sitting on the bank.

He stopped us and said he was a sailor, and asked for a trifle to help him to get back to his ship.

I did not like the look of him much myself, but Alice said, 'Oh, the poor man, do let's help him, Oswald.' So we held a hurried council, and decided to give him the milk sixpence. Oswald had it in his purse, and he had to empty the purse into his hand to find the sixpence, for that was not all the money he had, by any means. Noël said afterwards that he saw the wayfarer's eyes fastened greedily upon the shining pieces as Oswald returned them to his purse. Oswald has to own that he purposely let the man see that he had more money, so that the man might not feel shy about accepting so large a sum as sixpence.

The man blessed our kind hearts and we went on.

The sun was shining very brightly, and the Tower of Mystery did not look at all like a tomb when we got to it. The bottom story was on arches, all open, and ferns and things grew underneath. There was a round stone stair going up in the middle. Alice began to gather ferns while we went up, but when we had called out to her that it was as the pig-man had said, and daylight all the way up, she said:

'All right. I'm not afraid. I'm only afraid of being late home,' and came up after us. And perhaps, though not downright manly truthfulness, this was as much as you could expect from a girl.

There were holes in the little tower of the staircase to let light in. At the top of it was a thick door with iron bolts. We shot these back, and it was not fear but caution that made Oswald push open the door so very slowly and carefully.

Because, of course, a stray dog or cat might have got shut up there by accident, and it would have startled Alice very much if it had jumped out on us.

When the door was opened we saw that there was no such thing. It was a room with eight sides. Denny says it is the shape called octogenarian, because a man named Octagius invented it. There were eight large arched windows with no glass, only stone-work, like in churches. The room was full of sunshine, and you could see the blue sky through the windows, but nothing else, because they were so high up. It was so bright we began to think the pig-man had been kidding us. Under one of the windows was a door. We went through, and there was a little passage and then a turret-twisting stair, like in the church, but quite light with windows. When we had gone some way up this, we came to a sort of landing, and there was a block of stone let into the wall – polished – Denny said it was Aberdeen graphite, with gold letters cut in it.[8] It said –

> 'Here lies the body of Mr Richard Ravenal
> Born 1720.   Died 1779.'

And a verse of poetry:

> 'Here lie I, between earth and sky,
> Think upon me, dear passers-by,
> And you who do my tombstone see
> Be kind to say a prayer for me.'

'How horrid!' Alice said. 'Do let's get home.'

'We may as well go to the top,' Dicky said, 'just to say we've been.'

And Alice is no funk – so she agreed; though I could see she did not like it.

Up at the top it was like the top of the church tower, only octogenarian in shape, instead of square.

Alice got all right there; because you cannot think much about ghosts and nonsense when the sun is shining bang down on you at four o'clock in the afternoon, and you can see red farm-roofs between the trees, and the safe white roads, with people in carts like black ants crawling.

It was very jolly, but we felt we ought to be getting back, because tea is at five, and we could not hope to find lifts both ways.

So we started to go down. Dicky went first, then Oswald, then Alice – and H.O. had just stumbled over the top step and saved himself by Alice's back, which nearly upset Oswald and Dicky, when the hearts of all stood still, and then went on by leaps and bounds, like the good work in missionary magazines.

For, down below us, in the tower where the man whose beard grew down to his toes after he was dead was buried,[9] there was a noise – a loud noise. And it was like a door being banged and bolts fastened. We tumbled over each other to get back into the open sunshine on the top of the tower, and Alice's hand got jammed between the edge of the doorway and H.O.'s boot; it was bruised black and blue, and another part bled, but she did not notice it till long after.

We looked at each other, and Oswald said in a firm voice (at least, I hope it was):

'What was that?'

'He *has* waked up,' Alice said. 'Oh, I know he has. Of course there is a door for him to get out by when he wakes. He'll come up here. I know he will.'

Dicky said, and his voice was not at all firm (I noticed that at the time), 'It doesn't matter, if he's *alive*.'

'Unless he's come to life a raving lunatic,' Noël said, and we all stood with our eyes on the doorway of the turret – and held our breath to hear.

But there was no more noise.

Then Oswald said – and nobody ever put it in the Golden Deed book, though they own that it was brave and noble of him – he said:

'Perhaps it was only the wind blowing one of the doors to. I'll go down and see, if you will, Dick.'

Dicky only said:

'The wind doesn't shoot bolts.'

'A bolt from the blue,' said Denny to himself, looking up at the sky. His father is a sub-editor. He had gone very red, and he was holding on to Alice's hand. Suddenly he stood up quite straight and said:

'I'm not afraid. I'll go and see.'

This was afterwards put in the Golden Deed book. It ended in Oswald and Dicky and Denny going. Denny went first because he said he would rather – and Oswald understood this and let him. If Oswald had pushed first it would have been like Sir Launcelot refusing to let a young knight win his spurs. Oswald took good care to go second himself, though. The others never understood this. You don't expect it from girls; but I did think father would have understood without Oswald telling him, which of course he never could.

We all went slowly.

At the bottom of the turret stairs we stopped short. Because the door there was bolted fast and would not yield to shoves, however desperate and united.

Only now somehow we felt that Mr Richard Ravenal was all right and quiet, but that some one had done it for a lark, or perhaps not known about anyone being up there. So we rushed up, and Oswald told the others in a few hasty but well-chosen words, and we all leaned over between the battlements, and shouted, 'Hi! you there!'

Then from under the arches of the quite-downstairs part of the tower a figure came forth – and it was the sailor who had had our milk sixpence. He looked up and he spoke to us. He did not speak loud, but he spoke loud enough for us to hear every word quite plainly. He said:

'Drop that.'

Oswald said, 'Drop what?'

He said, 'That row.'

Oswald said, 'Why?'

He said, 'Because if you don't I'll come up and make you, and pretty quick too, so I tell you.'

Dicky said, 'Did you bolt the door?'

The man said, 'I did so, my young cock.'

Alice said – and Oswald wished to goodness she had held her tongue, because he saw right enough the man was not friendly – 'Oh, do come and let us out – do, please.'

While she was saying it Oswald suddenly saw that he did not want the man to come up. So he scurried down the stairs because he thought he had seen something on the door on the top side, and sure enough there were two bolts, and he shot them into their sockets. This bold act was not put in the Golden Deed book, because when Alice wanted to, the others said it was not *good* of Oswald to think of this, but only *clever*. I think sometimes, in moments of danger and disaster, it is as good to be clever as it is to be good. But Oswald would never demean himself to argue about this.

When he got back the man was still standing staring up. Alice said:

'Oh, Oswald, he says he won't let us out unless we give him all our money. And we might be here for days and days and all night as well. No one knows where we are to come and look for us. Oh, do let's give it him *all*.'[10]

She thought the lion of the English nation, which does not know when it is beaten, would be ramping in her brother's breast. But Oswald kept calm. He said:

'All right,' and he made the others turn out their pockets. Denny had a bad shilling, with a head on both sides, and three halfpence. H.O. had a halfpenny. Noël had a French penny, which is only good for chocolate machines at railway stations. Dicky had tenpence halfpenny, and Oswald had a two-shilling piece of his own that he was saving up to buy a gun with.[11] Oswald tied the whole lot up in his handkerchief, and looking over the battlements, he said:

'You are an ungrateful beast. We gave you sixpence freely of our own will.'

The man did look a little bit ashamed, but he mumbled something about having his living to get.

Then Oswald said:

'Here you are. Catch!' and he flung down the handkerchief with the money in it.

The man muffed the catch – butter-fingered idiot! – but he picked up the handkerchief and undid it, and when he saw what was in it he swore dreadfully. The cad!

'Look here,' he called out, 'this won't do, young shaver. I want those there shiners I see in your pus! Chuck 'em along!'

Then Oswald laughed. He said:

'I shall know you again anywhere, and you'll be put in prison for this. Here are the *shiners*.' And he was so angry he chucked down purse and all. The shiners were not real ones, but only card-counters that looked like sovereigns on one side. Oswald used to carry them in his purse so as to look affluent. He does not do this now.

When the man had seen what was in the purse he disappeared under the tower, and Oswald was glad of what he had done about the bolts – and he hoped they were as strong as the ones on the other side of the door.

They were.

We heard the man kicking and pounding at the door, and I am not ashamed to say that we were all holding on to each other very tight. I am proud, however, to relate that nobody screamed or cried.

After what appeared to be long years, the banging stopped, and presently we saw the brute going away among the trees.

Then Alice did cry, and I do not blame her.

Then Oswald said:

'It's no use. Even if he's undone the door, he may be in ambush. We must hold on here till somebody comes.'

Then Alice said, speaking chokily because she had not quite done crying:

'Let's wave a flag.'

By the most fortunate accident she had on one of her Sunday petticoats, though it was Monday. This petticoat is white. She tore it out at the gathers, and we tied it to Denny's stick, and took turns to wave it. We had laughed at his carrying a stick before, but we were very sorry now that we had done so.

And the tin dish the Lent pie was baked in we polished with our handkerchiefs, and moved it about in the sun so that the sun might strike on it and signal our distress to some of the outlying farms.

This was perhaps the most dreadful adventure that had then ever happened to us. Even Alice had now stopped thinking of Mr Richard Ravenal, and thought only of the lurker in ambush.[12]

We all felt our desperate situation keenly. I must say Denny behaved like anything but a white mouse. When it was the others' turn to wave, he sat on the leads of the tower and held Alice's and Noël's hands, and said poetry to them – yards and yards of it. By some strange fatality it seemed to comfort them. It wouldn't have me.

He said 'The Battle of the Baltic,' and 'Gray's Elegy,' right through, though I think he got wrong in places, and the 'Revenge,' and Macaulay's thing about Lars Porsena and the Nine Gods.[13] And when it was his turn he waved like a man.

I will try not to call him a white mouse any more. He was a brick that day, and no mouse.[14]

The sun was low in the heavens, and we were sick of waving and very hungry, when we saw a cart in the road below. We waved like mad, and shouted, and Denny screamed exactly like a railway whistle, a thing none of us had known before that he could do.

And the cart stopped. And presently we saw a figure with a white beard among the trees. It was our pig-man.

We bellowed the awful truth to him, and when he had taken it in – he thought at first we were kidding – he came up and let us out.[15]

He had got the pig; luckily it was a very small one – and we were not particular. Denny and Alice sat on the front of the cart with the pig-man, and the rest of us got in with the pig, and the man drove us right home. You may think we talked it over on the way. Not us. We went to sleep, among the pig, and before long the pig-man stopped and got us to make room for Alice and Denny. There was a net over the cart. I never was so sleepy in my life, though it was not more than bed-time.[16]

Generally, after anything exciting, you are punished – but this could not be, because we had only gone for a walk, exactly as we were told.

There was a new rule made, though. No walks, except on the high-roads, and we were always to take Pincher, and either Lady, the deer-hound, or Martha, the bull-dog. We generally hate rules, but we did not mind this one.[17]

Father gave Denny a gold pencil-case because he was first to go down into the tower. Oswald does not grudge Denny this, though some might think he deserved at least a silver one.

But Oswald is above such paltry jealousies.

✳ ✳ ✳

Chapter 5
The Water-Works

This is the story of one of the most far-reaching and influentially naughty things we ever did in our lives. We did not mean to do such a deed. And yet we did do it. These things will happen with the best-regulated consciences.[1]

The story of this rash and fatal act is intimately involved – which means all mixed up anyhow – with a private affair of Oswald's, and the one cannot be revealed without the other. Oswald does not particularly want his story to be remembered,[2] but he wishes to tell the truth, and perhaps it is what father calls a wholesome discipline to lay bare the awful facts.

It was like this.

On Alice's and Noël's birthday we went on the river for a picnic. Before that we had not known that there was a river so near us. Afterwards father said he wished we had been allowed to remain on our pristine ignorance, whatever that is. And perhaps the dark hour did dawn when we wished so too. But a truce to vain regrets.

It was rather a fine thing in birthdays. The uncle sent a box of toys and sweets, things that were like a vision from another and a brighter world. Besides that Alice had a knife, a pair of shut-up scissors, a silk handkerchief, a book – it was *The Golden Age* and is A1 except where it gets mixed with grown-up nonsense.[3] Also a work-case lined with pink plush, and a boot-bag, which no one in their senses would use because it had flowers in wool all over it.[4] And she had a box of chocolates and a musical box that played 'The Man Who Broke' and two other tunes, and two pairs of kid gloves for church, and a box of writing-paper – pink – with 'Alice' on it in gold writing, and an egg colored red that said 'A. Bastable' in ink on one side.[5] These gifts were the offerings of Oswald, Dora, Dicky, Albert's uncle, Daisy, Mr Foulkes (our own robber), Noël, H.O., father, and Denny.[6] Mrs Pettigrew gave the egg. It was a kindly housekeeper's friendly token.

I shall not tell you about the picnic on the river, because the happiest times form but dull reading when they are written down. I will merely state that it was prime. Though happy, the day was uneventful. The only thing exciting enough to write about was in one of the locks, where there was a snake – a viper. It was asleep in a warm sunny corner of the lock gate, and when the gate was shut it fell off into the water.

Alice and Dora screamed hideously. So did Daisy, but her screams were thinner.

The snake swam round and round all the time our boat was in the lock. It swam with four inches of itself – the head end – reared up out of the water, exactly like Kaa in *The Jungle Book* – so we know Kipling is a true author and no rotter. We were careful to keep our hands well inside the boat. A snake's eyes strike terror into the boldest breast.

When the lock was full father killed the viper with a boat-hook. I was sorry for it myself. It was indeed a venomous serpent. But it was the first we had ever seen, except at the Zoo. And it did swim most awfully well.

Directly the snake had been killed H.O. reached out for its corpse, and the next moment the body of our little brother was seen wriggling conclusively on the boat's edge. This exciting spectacle was not of a lasting nature. He went right in. Father clawed him out. H.O. is very unlucky with water.

Being a birthday, but little was said. H.O. was wrapped in everybody's coats, and did not take any cold at all.

This glorious birthday ended with an iced cake and ginger wine, and drinking healths. Then we played whatever we liked. There had been rounders during the afternoon.[7] It was a day to be forever marked by memory's brightest what's-its-name.

I should not have said anything about the picnic but for one thing. It was the thin edge of the wedge. It was the all-powerful lever that moved but too many events. You see, *we were no longer strangers to the river.*

And we went there whenever we could. Only we had to take the dogs, and to promise no bathing without grown-ups. But paddling in back waters was allowed. I say no more.

I have not numerated Noël's birthday presents because I wish to leave something to the imagination of my young readers.[8] (The best authors always do this.) If you will take the large, red catalogue of the Army and Navy Stores, and just make a list of about fifteen of the things you would like best – prices from 2*s.* to 25*s.*[9] – you will get a very good idea of Noël's presents, and it will help you to make up your mind in case you are asked just before your next birthday what you really *need*.

One of Noël's birthday presents was a cricket-ball. He cannot bowl for nuts, and it was a first-rate ball. So some days after the birthday Oswald offered him to exchange it for a cocoanut he had won at the fair, and two pencils (new), and a brand-new notebook. Oswald thought, and he still thinks, that this was a fair exchange, and so did Noël at the time, and he agreed to it, and was quite pleased till the girls said it wasn't fair, and Oswald had the best of it. And then that young beggar Noël wanted the ball back, but Oswald, though not angry, was firm.

'You said it was a bargain, and you shook hands on it,' he said, and he said it quite kindly and calmly.

Noël said he didn't care. He wanted his cricket-ball back.

And the girls said it was a horrid shame.

If they had not said that, Oswald might yet have consented to let Noël have the beastly ball, but now, of course, he was not going to. He said:

'Oh yes, I daresay. And then you would be wanting the cocoanut and things again the next minute.'

'No, I shouldn't,' Noël said. It turned out afterwards that he and H.O. had eaten the cocoanut, which only made it worse. And it made them worse too – which is what the book calls poetic justice.[10]

Dora said, 'I don't think it was fair,' and even Alice said:

'Do let him have it back, Oswald.' I wish to be just to Alice. She did not know then about the cocoanut having been secretly wolfed up.

We were in the garden. Oswald felt all the feelings of the hero when the opposing forces gathered about him are opposing as hard as ever they can. He knew he was not unfair, and he did not like to be jawed at just because Noël had eaten the cocoanut and then wanted the ball back.[11] Though Oswald did not know then about the eating of the cocoanut, but he felt the injustice in his soul all the same.

Noël said afterwards he meant to offer Oswald something else to make up for the cocoanut, but he said nothing about this at the time.

'Give it me, I say,' Noël said.

And Oswald said, 'Sha'n't!'

Then Noël called Oswald names, and Oswald did not answer back but just kept smiling pleasantly, and carelessly throwing up the ball and catching it again with an air of studied indifference.

It was Martha's fault that what happened happened. She is the bull-dog, and very stout and heavy. She had just been let loose and she came bounding along in her clumsy way, and jumped up on Oswald, who is beloved by all dumb animals. (You know how sagacious they are.) Well, Martha knocked the ball out of Oswald's hands, and it fell on the grass, and Noël pounced on it like a hooded falcon on its prey. Oswald would scorn to deny that he was not going to stand this, and the next moment the two were rolling over on the grass, and very soon Noël was made to bite the dust. And serve him right. He is old enough to know his own mind.

Then Oswald walked slowly away with the ball, and the others picked Noël up, and consoled the beaten, but Dicky would not take either side.

And Oswald went up into his own room and lay on his bed, and reflected gloomy reflections about unfairness.

Presently he thought he would like to see what the others were doing without their knowing he cared. So he went into the linen-room and looked out of its window, and he saw they were playing Kings and Queens – and Noël had the biggest paper crown and the longest stick sceptre.

Oswald turned away without a word, for it really was sickening.

Then suddenly his weary eyes fell upon something they had not before beheld. It was a square trap-door in the ceiling of the linen-room.

Oswald never hesitated. He crammed the cricket-ball into his pocket and climbed up the shelves and unbolted the trap-door, and shoved it up, and pulled himself up through it. Though above all was dark and smelt of spiders, Oswald fearlessly shut the trap-door down again before he struck a match. He always carries matches. He is a boy fertile in every subtle expedient. Then he saw he was in the wonderful, mysterious place between the ceiling and the roof of the house. The roof is beams and tiles. Slits of light show through the tiles here and there. The ceiling, on its other and top side, is made of rough plaster and beams. If you walk on the beams it is all right – if you walk on the plaster you go through with your feet. Oswald found this out later, but some fine instinct now taught the young explorer where he ought to tread and where not. It was splendid. He was still very angry with the others, and he was glad he had found out a secret they jolly well didn't know.

He walked along a dark, narrow passage. Every now and then cross-beams barred his way, and he had to creep under them. At last a small door loomed before him with cracks of light under and over. He drew back the rusty bolts and opened it. It opened straight on to the leads, a flat place between two steep red roofs, with a parapet two feet high back and front, so that no one could see you. It was a place no one could have invented better than, if they had tried, for hiding in.

Oswald spent the whole afternoon there. He happened to have a volume of *Percy's Anecdotes* in his pocket, the one about lawyers, as well as a few apples. While he read he fingered the cricket ball, and presently it rolled away, and he thought he would get it by-and-by.[12]

When the tea-bell rang he forgot the ball and went hurriedly down, for apples do not keep the inside from the pangs of hunger.

Noël met him on the landing, got red in the face, and said:

'It wasn't *quite* fair about the ball, because H.O. and I had eaten the cocoanut. *You* can have it.'

'I don't want your beastly ball,' Oswald said, 'Only I hate unfairness. However, I don't know where it is just now. When I find it you shall have it to bowl with as often as you want.'

'Then you're not waxy?'

And Oswald said 'No,' and they went in to tea together. So that was all right. There were raisin cakes for tea.

Next day we happened to want to go down to the river quite early. I don't know why; this is called Fate, or Destiny. We dropped in at the 'Rose and Crown' for some ginger-beer on our way. The landlady is a friend of ours and lets us drink it in her back parlour, instead of in the bar, which would be improper for girls.

We found her awfully busy, making pies and jellies, and her two sisters were hurrying about with great hams and pairs of chickens and rounds of cold beef and lettuces and pickled salmon and trays of crockery and glasses.

'It's for the angling competition,' she said.

We said, 'What's that?'

'Why,' she said, slicing cucumber like beautiful machinery while she said it, 'a lot of anglers come down some particular day and fish one particular bit of the river. And the one that catches most fish gets the prize. They're fishing the pen above Stoneham Lock.[13] And they all come here to dinner. So I've got my hands full and a trifle over.'

We said, 'Couldn't we help?'

But she said, 'Oh no, thank you. Indeed not, please.[14] I really am so busy I don't know which way to turn. Do run along, like dears.'

So we ran along like these timid but graceful animals.

Need I tell the intellectual reader that we went straight off to the pen above Stoneham Lock to see the anglers competing? Angling is the same thing as fishing.

I am not going to try and explain locks to you. If you've never seen a lock you could never understand even if I wrote it in words of one syllable and pages and pages long. And if you have, you'll understand without my telling you. It is harder than Euclid if you don't know beforehand. But you might get a grown-up person to explain it to you with books or wooden bricks.

I will tell you what a pen is because that is easy. It is the bit of river between one lock and the next. In some rivers 'pens' are called 'reaches,' but pen is the proper word.

We went along the towing-path; it is shady with willows, aspens, alders, elders, oaks and other trees. On the banks are flowers – yarrow, meadow-sweet, willow herb, loose-strife, and lady's bed-straw. Oswald learned the names of all these trees and plants on the day of the picnic. The others didn't remember them, but Oswald did. He is a boy of what they call relenting memory.

The anglers were sitting here and there on the shady bank among the grass and the different flowers I have named. Some had dogs with them, and some umbrellas, and some had only their wives and families.

We should have liked to talk to them and ask how they liked their lot, and what kinds of fish there were, and whether they were nice to eat, but we did not like to.

Denny had seen anglers before and he knew they liked to be talked to, but though he spoke to them quite like to equals he did not ask the things we wanted to know. He just asked whether they'd had any luck, and what bait they used.

And they answered him back politely. I am glad I am not an angler. It is an immovable amusement, and, as often as not, no fish to speak of after all.

Daisy and Dora had stayed at home: Dora's foot was nearly well, but they seem really to like sitting still. I think Dora likes to have a little girl to order about. Alice never would stand it.[15] When we got to Stoneham Lock, Denny said he should go home and fetch his fishing-rod. H.O. went with him. This left four of us – Oswald, Alice, Dicky, and Noël. We went on down the towing-path.

The lock shuts up (that sounds as if it was like the lock on a door, but it is very otherwise) between one pen of the river and the next; the pen where the anglers were was full right up over the roots of the grass and flowers.

But the pen below was nearly empty.

'You can see the poor river's bones,' Noël said.

And so you could.

Stones and mud and dried branches, and here and there an old kettle or a tin pail with no bottom to it, that some bargee had chucked in.

From walking so much along the river we knew many of the bargees. Bargees are the captains and crews of the big barges that are pulled up and down the river by slow horses. The horses do not swim. They walk on the towing-path, with a rope tied to them, and the other end to the barge. So it gets pulled along. The bargees we knew were a good friendly sort, and used to let us go all over the barges when they were in a good temper. They were not at all the sort of bullying, cowardly fiends in human form that the young hero at Oxford fights a crowd of, single-handed, in books.

The river does not smell nice when its bones are showing. But we went along down, because Oswald wanted to get some cobbler's wax in Falding village for a bird-net he was making.[16]

But just above Falding Lock, where the river is narrow and straight, we saw a sad and gloomy sight – a big barge sitting flat on the mud because there was not water enough to float her.

There was no one on board, but we knew by a red flannel waistcoat that was spread out to dry on top that the barge belonged to friends of ours.

Then Alice said, 'They have gone to find the man who turns on the water to fill the pen. I dare say they won't find him. He's gone to his dinner, I shouldn't wonder. What a lovely surprise it would be if they came back to find their barge floating high and dry on a lot of water! *Do* let's do it. It's a long time since any of us did a kind action deserving of being put in the Book of Golden Deeds.'

We had given that name to the minute-book of that beastly 'Society of the Wouldbegoods.' Then you could think of the book if you wanted to without remembering the Society. I always tried to forget both of them.[17]

Oswald said, 'But how? *You* don't know how. And if you did we haven't got a crow-bar.'

I cannot help telling you that locks are opened with crow-bars. You push and push till a thing goes up and the water runs through. It is rather like the little sliding-door in the big door of a hen-house.

'I know where the crow-bar is,' Alice said. 'Dicky and I were down here yesterday when you were su – ' She was going to say sulking, I know, but she remembered manners ere too late, so Oswald bears her no malice. She went on: 'Yesterday, when you were upstairs. And we saw the water-tender open the lock and the weir sluices. It's quite easy, isn't it, Dicky?'

'As easy as kiss your hand,' said Dicky; 'and what's more, I know where he keeps the other thing he opens the sluices with. I votes we do.'

'Do let's, if we can,' Noël said, 'and the bargees will bless the names of their unknown benefactors. They might make a song about us, and sing it on winter nights as they pass round the wassail bowl in front of the cabin fire.'

Noël wanted to very much; but I don't think it was altogether for generousness, but because he wanted to see how the sluices opened. Yet perhaps I do but wrong the boy.

We sat and looked at the barge a bit longer, and then Oswald said, well, he didn't mind going back to the lock and having a look at the crow-bars. You see Oswald did not propose this; he did not even care very much about it when Alice suggested it.

But when we got to Stoneham Lock, and Dicky dragged the two heavy crow-bars from among the elder bushes behind a fallen tree, and began to pound away at the sluice of the lock, Oswald felt it would not be manly to stand idly apart. So he took his turn.

It was very hard work, but we opened the lock sluices, and we did not drop the crow-bar into the lock either, as I have heard of being done by older and sillier people.

The water poured through the sluices all green and solid, as if it had been cut with a knife, and where it fell on the water underneath the white foam spread like a moving counterpane. When we had finished the lock we did the weir – which is wheels and chains – and the water pours through over the stones in a magnificent water-fall and sweeps out all round the weir-pool.

The sight of the foaming water-falls was quite enough reward for our heavy labours, even without the thought of the unspeakable gratitude that the bargees would feel to us when they got back to their barge and found her no longer a stick-in-the-mud, but bounding on the free bosom of the river.

When we had opened all the sluices we gazed awhile on the beauties of nature, and then went home, because we thought it would be more truly noble and good not to wait to be thanked for our kind and devoted action – and besides, it was nearly dinner-time, and Oswald thought it was going to rain.

On the way home we agreed not to tell the others, because it would be like boasting of our good acts.

'They will know all about it,' Noël said, 'when they hear us being blessed by the grateful bargees, and the tale of the Unknown Helpers is being told by every village fireside. And then they can write it in the Golden Deed book.'

So we went home. Denny and H.O. had thought better of it, and they were fishing in the moat. They did not catch anything.

Oswald is very weather-wise – at least, so I have heard it said, and he had thought there would be rain. There was. It came on while we were at dinner – a great, strong, thundering rain, coming down in sheets – the first rain we had had since we came to the Moat House.

We went to bed as usual. No presentiment of the coming awfulness clouded our young mirth. I remember Dicky and Oswald had a wrestling match, and Oswald won.

In the middle of the night Oswald was awakened by a hand on his face. It was a wet hand and very cold. Oswald hit out, of course, but a voice said, in a hoarse, hollow whisper:

'Don't be a young ass! Have you got any matches? My bed's full of water; it's pouring down from the ceiling.'

Oswald's first thought was that perhaps by opening those sluices we had flooded some secret passage which communicated with the top of Moat House, but when he was properly awake he saw that this could not be, on account of the river being so low.

He had matches. He is, as I said before, a boy full of resources. He struck one and lit a candle, and Dicky, for it was indeed he, gazed with Oswald at the amazing spectacle.

Our bedroom floor was all wet in patches. Dicky's bed stood in a pond, and from the ceiling water was dripping in rich profusion at a dozen different places. There was a great wet patch in the ceiling, and that was blue, instead of white like the dry part, and the water dripped from different parts of it.

For a moment Oswald was quite unmanned.

'Krikey!' he said, in a heart-broken tone, and remained an instant plunged in thought.

'What on earth are we to do?' Dicky said.

And really for a short time even Oswald did not know. It was a blood-curdling event, a regular facer. Albert's uncle had gone to London that day to stay till the next. Yet something must be done.

The first thing was to rouse the unconscious others from their deep sleep, because the water was beginning to drip on to their beds, and though as yet they knew it not, there was quite a pool on Noël's bed, just in the hollow behind where his knees were doubled up, and one of H.O.'s boots was full of water, that surged wildly out when Oswald happened to kick it over.

We woke them – a difficult task, but we did not shrink from it.

Then we said, 'Get up, there is a flood! Wake up, or you will be drowned in your beds! And it's half-past two by Oswald's watch.'

They awoke slowly and very stupidly. H.O. was the slowest and stupidest.

The water poured faster and faster from the ceiling.

We looked at each other and turned pale, and Noël said:

'Hadn't we better call Mrs Pettigrew?'

But Oswald simply couldn't consent to this. He could not get rid of the feeling that this was our fault somehow for meddling with the river, though of course the clear star of reason told him it could not possibly be the case.

We all devoted ourselves, heart and soul, to the work before us. We put the bath under the worst and wettest place, and the jugs and basins under lesser streams, and we moved the beds away to the dry end of the room. Ours is a long attic that runs right across the house.

But the water kept coming in worse and worse. Our night-shirts were wet through, so we got into our other shirts and knickerbockers, but preserved bareness in our feet. And the floor kept on being half an inch deep in water, however much we mopped it up.

We emptied the basins out of the window as fast as they filled, and we baled the bath with a jug without pausing to complain how hard the work was. All the same, it was more exciting than you can think.[18] But in Oswald's dauntless breast he began to see that they would *have* to call Mrs Pettigrew.

A new water-fall broke out between the fire-grate and the mantel-piece, and spread in devastating floods. Oswald is full of ingenious devices. I think I have said this before, but it is quite true; and perhaps even truer this time than it was last time I said it.

He got a board out of the box-room next door, and rested one end in the chink between the fireplace and the mantel-piece, and laid the other end on the back of a chair, then we stuffed the rest of the chink with our night-gowns, and laid a towel along the plank, and behold, a noble stream poured over the end of the board right into the bath we put there ready. It was like Niagara, only not so round in shape. The first lot of water that came down the chimney was very dirty. The wind whistled outside. Noël said, 'If it's pipes burst, and not the rain, it will be nice for the water-rates.' Perhaps it was only natural after this for Denny to begin with his everlasting poetry. He stopped mopping up the water to say:

> 'By this the storm grew loud apace,
> The water-rates were shrieking,
> And in the howl of Heaven each face
> Grew black as they were speaking.'[19]

Our faces were black, and our hands too, but we did not take any notice; we only told him not to gas but to go on mopping. And he did. And we all did.

But more and more water came pouring down. You would not believe so much could come off one roof.

When at last it was agreed that Mrs Pettigrew must be awakened at all hazards, we went and woke Alice to do the fatal errand.

When she came back, with Mrs Pettigrew in a night-cap and a red flannel petticoat, we held our breath.

But Mrs Pettigrew did not even say, 'What on earth have you children been up to *now*?' as Oswald had feared.

She simply sat down on my bed and said:

'Oh, dear! oh, dear! oh, dear!' ever so many times.

Then Denny said, 'I once saw holes in a cottage roof. The man told me it was done when the water came through the thatch. He said if the water lies all about on the top of the ceiling it breaks it down, but if you make holes the water will only come through the holes and you can put pails under the holes to catch it.'

So we made nine holes in the ceiling with the poker, and put pails, baths and tubs under, and now there was not so much water on the floor. But we had to keep on working like niggers, and Mrs Pettigrew and Alice worked the same.[20]

About five in the morning the rain stopped; about seven the water did not come in so fast, and presently it only dripped slowly. Our task was done.

This is the only time I was ever up all night. I wish it happened oftener. We did not go back to bed then, but dressed and went down. We all went to sleep in the afternoon, though. Quite without meaning to.

Oswald went up on the roof, before breakfast, to see if he could find the hole where the rain had come in. He did not find any hole, but he found the cricket-ball jammed in the top of a gutter-pipe, which he afterwards knew ran down inside the wall of the house and ran into the moat below. It seems a silly dodge, but so it was.

When the men went up after breakfast to see what had caused the flood they said there must have been a good half-foot of water on the leads the night before for it to have risen high enough to go above the edge of the lead, and of course when it got above the lead there was nothing to stop it running down under it, and soaking through the ceiling. The parapet and the roofs kept it from tumbling off down the sides of the house in the natural way. They said there must have been some obstruction in the pipe which ran down into the house, but whatever it was the water had washed it away, for they put wires down, and the pipe was quite clear.

While we were being told this Oswald's trembling fingers felt at the wet cricket-ball in his pocket. And he *knew*, but he *could* not tell. He heard them wondering what the obstruction could have been, and all the time he had the obstruction in his pocket, and never said a single word.

I do not seek to defend him. But it really was an awful thing to have been the cause of; and Mrs Pettigrew is but harsh and hasty. But this, as Oswald knows too well, is no excuse for his silent conduct.

That night at tea Albert's uncle was rather silent too. At last he looked upon us with a glance full of intelligence, and said:

'There was a queer thing happened yesterday. You know there was an angling competition. The pen was kept full on purpose. Some mischievous busybody went and opened the sluices and let all the water out. The anglers' holiday was spoiled. No, the rain wouldn't have spoiled it anyhow, Alice; anglers *like* rain. The 'Rose and Crown' dinner was half of it wasted because the anglers were so furious that a lot of them took the next train to town. And this is the worst of all – a barge, that was on the mud in the pen below, was lifted and jammed across the river, and then the water tilted her over, and her cargo is on the river bottom. It was coals.'

During this speech there were four of us who knew not where to turn our agitated glances. Some of us tried bread-and-butter, but it seemed dry and difficult, and those who tried tea choked and spluttered and were sorry they had not let it alone.

When the speech stopped Alice said, 'It was us.'

And with deepest feelings she and the rest of us told all about it.

Oswald did not say much. He was turning the obstruction round and round in his pocket, and wishing with all his sentiments that he had owned up like a man when Albert's uncle asked him before tea to tell him all about what had happened during the night.

When they had told all, Albert's uncle told us four still more plainly, and exactly, what we had done, and how much pleasure we had spoiled, and how much of my father's money we had wasted – because he would have to pay for the coals being got up from the bottom of the river, if they could be, and if not, for the price of the coals. And we saw it *all*.

And when he had done Alice burst out crying over her plate and said:

'It's no use! We *have* tried to be good since we've been down here. You don't know how we've tried! And it's all no use. I believe we are the wickedest children in the whole world, and I wish we were all dead!'

This was a dreadful thing to say, and of course the rest of us were all very shocked. But Oswald could not help looking at Albert's uncle to see how he would take it.

He said very gravely, 'My dear kiddie, you ought to be sorry, and I wish you to be sorry for what you've done. And you will be punished for it.' (We were; our pocket-money was stopped and we were forbidden to go near the river, besides impositions miles long.) 'But,' he went on, 'You mustn't give up trying to be good. You are extremely naughty and tiresome, as you know very well.'

Alice, Dicky, and Noël began to cry at about this time.

'But you are not the wickedest children in the world by any means.'

Then he stood up and straightened his collar, and put his hands in his pockets.

'You're very unhappy now,' he said, 'and you deserve to be. But I will say one thing to you.'

Then he said a thing which Oswald at least will never forget (though but little he deserved it, with the obstruction in his pocket, unowned up to all the time).

He said, 'I have known you all for four years – and you know as well as I do how many scrapes I've seen you in and out of – but I've never known one of you tell a lie, and I've never known one of you do a mean or dishonourable action. And when you have done wrong you are always sorry. Now this is something to stand firm on. You'll learn to be good in the other ways some day.'

He took his hands out of his pockets, and his face looked different, so that three of the four guilty creatures knew he was no longer adamant, and they threw themselves into his arms. Dora, Denny, Daisy, and H.O., of course, were not in it, and I think they thanked their stars.

Oswald did not embrace Albert's uncle. He stood there and made up his mind he would go for a soldier. He gave the wet ball one last squeeze, and took his hand out of his pocket, and said a few words before going to enlist. He said:

'The others may deserve what you say. I hope they do, I'm sure. But *I* don't, because it was my rotten cricket-ball that stopped up the pipe and caused the midnight flood in our bedroom. And I knew it quite early this morning. And I didn't own up.'

Oswald stood there covered with shame, and he could feel the hateful cricket-ball heavy and cold against the top of his leg, through the pocket.

Albert's uncle said – and his voice made Oswald hot all over, but not with shame – he said:

I shall not tell you what he said. It is no one's business but Oswald's; only I will own it made Oswald not quite so anxious to run away for a soldier as he had been before.

That owning up was the hardest thing I ever did. They did put that in the Book of Golden Deeds, though it was not a kind or generous act, and did no good to any one or anything except Oswald's own inside feelings. I must say I think they might have let it alone. Oswald would rather forget it. Especially as Dicky wrote it in and put this:

'Oswald acted a lie, which, he knows, is as bad as telling one. But he owned up when he needn't have, and this condones his sin. We think he was a thorough brick to do it.'

Alice scratched this out afterwards and wrote the record of the incident in more flattering terms. But Dicky had used Father's ink, and she used Mrs Pettigrew's, so anyone can read *his* underneath the scratching outs.

The others were awfully friendly to Oswald, to show they agreed with Albert's uncle in thinking I deserved as much share as anyone in any praise there might be going.

It was Dora who said it all came from my quarrelling with Noël about that rotten cricket-ball; but Alice, gently yet firmly, made her shut up.

I let Noël have the ball. It had been thoroughly soaked, but it dried all right. But it could never be the same to me after what *it* had done and what *I* had done.

I hope you will try to agree with Albert's uncle and not think foul scorn of Oswald because of this story. Perhaps you have done things nearly as bad yourself sometimes. If you have, you will know how 'owning up' soothes the savage breast and alleviates the gnawings of remorse.[21]

If you have never done naughty acts I expect it is only because you never had the sense to think of anything.

* * *

Chapter 6
The Circus

The ones of us who had started the Society of the Wouldbegoods began, at about this time, to bother.

They said we had not done anything really noble – not worth speaking of, that is – for over a week, and that it was high time to begin again – 'With earnest endeavour,' Daisy said. So then Oswald said:

'All right; but there ought to be an end to everything. Let's each of us think of one really noble and unselfish act, and the others shall help to work it out, like we did when we were Treasure Seekers. Then when everybody's had their go-in we'll write every single thing down in the Golden Deed book, and we'll draw two lines in red ink at the bottom, like father does at the end of an account. And after that, if any one wants to be good they can jolly well be good on our own, if at all.'

The ones who had made the Society did not welcome this wise idea, but Dicky and Oswald were firm.

So they had to agree. When Oswald is really firm, opposingness and obstinacy have to give way.

Dora said, 'It would be a noble action to have all the school-children from the village and give them tea and games in the paddock. They would think it so nice and good of us.'

But Dicky showed her that this would not be *our* good act, but father's, because he would have to pay for the tea, and he had already stood us the keepsakes for the soldiers, as well as having to stump up heavily over the coal barge. And it is in vain being noble and generous when some one else is paying for it all the time, even if it happens to be your father. Then three others had ideas at the same time and began to explain what they were.

We were all in the dining-room, and perhaps we were making a bit of a row.[1] Anyhow, Oswald, for one, does not blame Albert's uncle for opening his door and saying:

'I suppose I must not ask for complete silence. That were too much. But if you could whistle, or stamp with your feet, or shriek or howl – anything to vary the monotony of your well-sustained conversation.'

Oswald said, kindly, 'We're awfully sorry. Are you busy?'

'Busy?' said Albert's uncle.[2] 'My heroine is now hesitating on the verge of an act which, for good or ill, must influence her whole subsequent career. You wouldn't like her to decide in the middle of such a row that she can't hear herself think?'

We said, 'No, we wouldn't.'

Then he said, 'If any outdoor amusement should commend itself to you this bright midsummer day – '

So we all went out.

Then Daisy whispered to Dora – they always hang together. Daisy is not nearly so white-micey as she was at first, but she still seems to fear the deadly ordeal of public speaking. Dora said:

'Daisy's idea is a game that'll take us all day. She thinks keeping out of the way when he's making his heroine decide right would be a noble act, and fit to write in the Golden Book; and we might as well be playing something at the same time.'

We all said 'Yes, but what?'

There was a silent interval.

'Speak up, Daisy, my child,' Oswald said; 'fear not to lay bare the utmost thoughts of that faithful heart.'

Daisy giggled. Our own girls never giggle; they laugh right out or hold their tongues. Their kind brothers have taught them this. Then Daisy said:

'If we could have a sort of play to keep us out of the way? I once read a story about an animal race. Everybody had an animal, and they had to go how they liked, and the one that got in first got the prize. There was a tortoise in it, and a rabbit, and a peacock, and sheep, and dogs, and a kitten.'[3]

This proposal left us cold, as Albert's uncle says, because we knew there could not be any prize worth bothering about. And though you may be ever ready and willing to do anything for nothing, yet if there's going to be a prize there must *be* a prize and there's an end of it.

Thus the idea was not followed up. Dicky yawned and said, 'Let's go into the barn and make a fort.'

So we did, with straw. It does not hurt straw to be messed about with like it does hay.

The down-stairs – I mean down-ladder – part of the barn was fun too, especially for Pincher. There was as good ratting there as you could wish to see. Martha tried it, but she could not help running kindly beside the rat, as if she was in double harness with it. This is the noble bull-dog's gentle and affectionate nature coming out. We all enjoyed the ratting that day, but it ended, as usual, in the girls crying because of the poor rats. Girls cannot help this; we must not be waxy with them on account of it, they have their nature, the same as bull-dogs have, and it is this that makes them so useful in smoothing the pillows of the sick-bed and tending wounded heroes.

However, the forts, and Pincher, and the girls crying, and having to be thumped on the back, passed the time very agreeably till dinner. There was roast mutton with onion sauce, and a roly-poly pudding.

Albert's uncle said we had certainly effaced ourselves effectually, which means we hadn't bothered.

So we determined to do the same during the afternoon, for he told us his heroine was by no means out of the wood yet.

And at first it was easy. Jam roly gives you a peaceful feeling and you do not at first care if you never play any runabout game ever any more. But after a while the torpor begins to pass away. Oswald was the first to recover from his.

He had been lying on his front part in the orchard, but now he turned over on his back and kicked his legs up, and said:

'I say, look here; let's do something.'[4]

Daisy looked thoughtful. She was chewing the soft yellow parts of grass, but I could see she was still thinking about that animal race. So I explained to her that it would be very poor fun without a tortoise and a peacock, and she saw this, though not willingly.

It was H.O. who said:

'Doing anything with animals is prime! if they only will. Let's have a circus!'[5]

At the word the last thought of the pudding faded from Oswald's memory, and he stretched himself, sat up, and said:

'Bully for H.O. Let's!'

The others also threw off the heavy weight of memory, and sat up and said 'Let's!' too.

Never, never in all our lives had we had such a gay galaxy of animals at our command. The rabbits and the guinea-pigs, and even all the bright, glass-eyed, stuffed denizens of our late-lamented Jungle, paled into insignificance before the number of live things on the farm.

(I hope you do not think that the words I use are getting too long. I know they are the right words. And Albert's uncle says your style is always altered a bit by what you read. And I have been reading the Vicomte de Bragelonne.[6] Nearly all my new words come out of those.)

'The worst of a circus is,' Dora said, 'that you've got to teach the animals things. A circus where the performing creatures hadn't learned performing would be a bit silly. Let's give up a week to teaching them and then have the circus.'

Some people have no idea of the value of time. And Dora is one of those who do not understand that when you want to do a thing you *do* want to, and not to do something else, and perhaps your own thing, a week later.

Oswald said the first thing was to collect the performing animals.

'Then perhaps,' he said, 'we may find that they have hidden talents hitherto unsuspected by their harsh masters.'

So Denny took a pencil and wrote a list of the animals required.

This is it:

LIST OF ANIMALS REQUISITE FOR THE
CIRCUS WE ARE GOING TO HAVE

1 Bull for bull-fight.

1 Horse for ditto (if possible).

1 Goat to do Alpine feats of daring.

1 Donkey to play see-saw.

2 White pigs – one to be Learned, and the other to play with the clown.

Turkeys – as many as possible, because they can make a noise that sounds like the audience applauding.

The dogs – for any odd parts.

1 large black pig – to be the Elephant in the procession.

Calves (several) to be camels, and to stand on tubs.

Daisy ought to have been captain because it was partly her idea, but she let Oswald be, because she is of a retiring character. Oswald said:

'The first thing is to get all the creatures together; the paddock at the side of the orchard is the very place, because the hedge is good all round. When we've got the performers all there we'll make a programme, and then dress for our parts. It's a pity there won't be any audience but the turkeys.'

We took the animals in their right order, according to Denny's list. The bull was the first. He is black. He does not live in the cow-house with the other horned people; he has a house all to himself two fields away.

Oswald and Alice went to fetch him. They took a halter to lead the bull by, and a whip, not to hurt the bull with, but just to make him mind.

The others were to try to get one of the horses while we were gone.

Oswald, as usual, was full of bright ideas.

'I dare say,' he said, 'the bull will be shy at first, and he'll have to be goaded into the arena.'

'But goads hurt,' Alice said.

'They don't hurt the bull,' Oswald said; 'his powerful hide is too thick.'

'Then why does he attend to it,' Alice asked, 'if it doesn't hurt?'

'Properly brought-up bulls attend because they know they ought,' Oswald said. 'I think I shall ride the bull,' the brave boy went on. 'A bull-fight, where an intrepid rider appears on the bull, sharing its joys and sorrows. It would be something quite new.'

'You can't ride bulls,' Alice said; 'at least, not if their backs are sharp like cows.'

But Oswald thought he could. The bull lives in a house made of wood and prickly furze-bushes, and he has a yard to his house. You cannot climb on the roof of his house at all comfortably.

When we got there he was half in his house and half out in his yard, and he was swinging his tail because of the flies which bothered. It was a very hot day.

'You'll see,' Alice said, 'he won't want a goad. He'll be so glad to get out for a walk he'll drop his head in my hand like a tame fawn, and follow me lovingly all the way.'

Oswald called to him. He said, 'Bull! Bull! Bull! Bull!' because we did not know the animal's real name.[7] The bull took no notice; then Oswald picked up a stone and threw it at the bull, not angrily, but just to make it pay attention. But the bull did not pay a far-thing's worth of it. So then Oswald leaned over the iron gate of the bull's yard and just flicked the bull with the whip lash. And then the bull *did* pay attention. He started when the lash struck him, then suddenly he faced round, uttering a roar like that of the wounded King of Beasts, and putting his head down close to his feet he ran straight at the iron gate where we were standing.

Alice and Oswald mechanically turned away; they did not wish to annoy the bull any more, and they ran as fast as they could across the field so as not to keep the others waiting.

As they ran across the field Oswald had a dream-like fancy that perhaps the bull had rooted up the gate with one paralysing blow, and was now tearing across the field after him and Alice, with the broken gate balanced on its horns. We climbed the stile quickly and looked back; the bull was still on the right side of the gate.

Oswald said, 'I think we'll do without the bull. He did not seem to want to come. We must be kind to dumb animals.'

Alice said, between laughing and crying:

'Oh, Oswald, how can you!' But we did do without the bull, and we did not tell the others how we had hurried to get back. We just said, 'The bull didn't seem to care about coming.'

The others had not been idle. They had got old Clover, the cart-horse, but she would do nothing but graze, so we decided not to use her in the bull-fight, but to let her be the Elephant. The Elephant's is a nice, quiet part, and she was quite big enough for a young one. Then the black pig could be Learned, and the other two pigs could be something else. They had also got the goat; he was tethered to a young tree.

The donkey was there. Denny was leading him in the halter.

The dogs were there, of course – they always are.

So now we only had to get the turkeys for the applause, and the calves and pigs.

The calves were easy to get, because they were in their own house. There were five. And the pigs were in their houses too. We got them out after long and patient toil, and persuaded them that they wanted to go into the paddock, where the circus was to be. This is done by pretending to drive them the other way. A pig only knows two ways – the way you want him to go and the other. But the turkeys knew thousands of different ways, and tried them all. They made such an awful row we had to drop all ideas of ever hearing applause from their lips, so we came away and left them.

'Never mind,' H.O. said, 'they'll be sorry enough afterwards, nasty, unobliging things, because now they won't see the circus. I hope the other animals will tell them about it.'

While the turkeys were engaged in baffling the rest of us, Dicky had found three sheep who seemed to wish to join the glad throng, so we let them.

Then we shut the gate of the paddock, and left the dumb circus performers to make friends with each other while we dressed.

Oswald and H.O. were to be clowns. It is quite easy with Albert's uncle's pyjamas, and flour on your hair and face, and the red they do the brick-floors with.

Alice had very short pink and white skirts, and roses in her hair and round her dress. Her dress was the pink calico and white muslin stuff off the dressing-table in the girls' room fastened with pins and tied round the waist with a small bath towel. She was to be the Dauntless Equestrienne, and to give her enhancing act of barebacked daring, riding either a pig or a sheep, whichever we found was freshest and most skittish. Dora was dressed for the *Haute école*, which means a riding-habit and a high hat.[8] She took Dick's topper that he wears with his Etons, and a skirt of Mrs Pettigrew's. Daisy dressed the same as Alice, taking the muslin from Mrs Pettigrew's dressing-table without saying anything beforehand. None of us would have advised this, and indeed we were thinking of trying to put it back, when Denny and Noël, who were wishing to look like highwaymen, with brown paper top-boots and slouch hats and Turkish towel cloaks, suddenly stopped dressing and gazed out of the window.[9]

'Krikey!' said Dick; 'come on, Oswald!' and he bounded like an antelope from the room.

Oswald and the rest followed, casting a hasty glance through the window. Noël had got brown paper boots too, and a Turkish towel cloak. H.O. had been waiting for Dora to dress him up for the other clown. He had only his shirt and knickerbockers and his braces on. He came down as he was – as indeed we all did. And no wonder, for in the paddock, where the circus was to be, a blood-thrilling thing had transpired. The dogs were chasing the sheep. And we had now lived long enough in the country to know the fell nature of our dogs' improper conduct.

We all rushed into the paddock, calling to Pincher, and Martha, and Lady. Pincher came almost at once. He is a well-brought-up dog – Oswald trained him. Martha did not seem to hear. She is awfully deaf, but she did not matter so much, because the sheep could walk away from her easily. She has no pace and no wind. But Lady is a deer-hound. She is used to pursuing that fleet and antlered pride of the forest – the stag – and she can go like billyo. She was now far away in a distant region of the paddock, with a fat sheep just before her in full flight. I am sure if ever anybody's eyes did start out of their heads with horror, like in narratives of adventure, ours did then.

There was a moment's pause of speechless horror. We expected to see Lady pull down her quarry, and we know what a lot of money a sheep costs, to say nothing of its own personal feelings.

Then we started to run for all we were worth. It is hard to run swiftly as the arrow from the bow when you happen to be wearing pyjamas belonging to a grown-up person – as I was – but even so I beat Dicky.[10] He said afterwards it was because his brown paper boots came undone and tripped him up. Alice came in third. She held up the dressing-table muslin and ran jolly well. But ere we reached the fatal spot all was very nearly up with the sheep. We heard a plop; Lady stopped and looked round. She must have heard us bellowing to her as we ran. Then she came towards us, prancing with happiness, but we said, 'Down!' and 'Bad dog!' and ran sternly on.

When we came to the brook which forms the northern boundary of the paddock we saw the sheep struggling in the water. It is not very deep, and I believe the sheep could have stood up, and been well in its depth, if it had liked, but it would not try.

It was a steepish bank. Alice and I got down and stuck our legs into the water, and then Dicky came down, and the three of us hauled that sheep up by its shoulders till it could rest on Alice and me as we sat on the bank. It kicked all the time we were hauling. It gave one extra kick at last, that raised it up, and I tell you that sopping wet, heavy, panting, silly donkey of a sheep sat there on our laps like a pet dog; and Dicky got his shoulder under it at the back and heaved constantly to keep it from flumping off into the water again, while the others fetched the shepherd.

When the shepherd came he called us every name you can think of, and then he said:

'Good thing master didn't come along. He would ha' called you some tidy names.'

He got the sheep out, and took it and the others away. And the calves too. He did not seem to care about the other performing animals.

Alice, Oswald, and Dick had had almost enough circus for just then, so we sat in the sun and dried ourselves and wrote the programme of the circus. This was it:

PROGRAMME

1. Startling leap from the lofty precipice by the performing sheep. Real water, and real precipice. The gallant rescue.[11] O., A., and D. Bastable. (We thought we might as well put that in, though it was over and had happened accidentally.)
2. Graceful bare-backed equestrienne act on the trained pig, Eliza. A. Bastable.
3. Amusing clown interlude, introducing trained dog, Pincher, and the other white pig. H.O. and O. Bastable.
4. The See-saw. Trained donkeys. (H.O. said we had only one donkey, so Dicky said H.O. could be the other. When peace was restored we went on to 5.)
5. Elegant equestrian act by D. Bastable. *Haute école*, on Clover, the incomparative trained elephant from the plains of Venezuela.
6. Alpine feat of daring. The climbing of the Andes, by Billy, the well-known acrobatic goat. (We thought we could make the Andes out of hurdles and things, and so we could have but for what always happens. (This is the unexpected. (This is a saying Father told me – but I see I am three deep in brackets, so I will close them before I get into any more.).).).
7. The Black but Learned Pig. ('I daresay he knows something,' Alice said, 'If we can only find out what.' We *did* find out all too soon.)

We could not think of anything else, and our things were nearly dry – all except Dick's brown paper top-boots, which were mingled with the gurgling waters of the brook.

We went back to the seat of action – which was the iron trough where the sheep have their salt put – and began to dress up the creatures. We had just tied the Union Jack we made out of Daisy's flannel petticoat and cetera, when we gave the soldiers the baccy,[12] round the waist of the Black and Learned Pig, when we heard screams from the back part of the house; and suddenly we saw that Billy, the acrobatic goat, had got loose from the tree we had tied him to. (He had eaten all the parts of its bark that he could get at, but we did not notice it until next day, when led to the spot by a grown-up.)

The gate of the paddock was open. The gate leading to the bridge that goes over the moat to the back door was open too.[13] We hastily proceeded in the direction of the screams, and, guided by the sound, threaded our way into the kitchen. As we went, Noël, ever fertile in melancholy ideas, said he wondered whether Mrs Pettigrew was being robbed, or only murdered.

In the kitchen we saw that Noël was wrong as usual. It was neither. Mrs Pettigrew, screaming like a steam-siren and waving a broom, occupied the foreground. In the distance the maid was shrieking in a hoarse and monotonous way, and trying to shut herself up inside a clothes-horse on which washing was being aired. On the dresser – which he had ascended by a chair – was Billy, the acrobatic goat, doing his Alpine daring act. He had found out his Andes for himself, and even as we gazed he turned and tossed his head in a way that showed us some mysterious purpose was hidden beneath his calm exterior. The next moment he put his off-horn neatly behind the end plate of the next to the bottom row, and ran it along against the wall. The plates fell crashing on to the soup tureen and vegetable dishes which adorned the lower range of the Andes.

Mrs Pettigrew's screams were almost drowned in the discording crash and crackle of the falling avalanche of crockery.

Oswald, though stricken with horror and polite regret, preserved the most dauntless coolness.

Disregarding the mop which Mrs Pettigrew kept on poking at the goat in a timid yet cross way, he sprang forward, crying out to his trusty followers, 'Stand by to catch him!'

But Dick had thought of the same thing, and ere Oswald could carry out his long-cherished and general-like design, Dicky had caught the goat's legs and tripped it up. The goat fell against another row of plates, righted itself hastily in the gloomy ruins of the soup tureen and the sauce-boats, and then fell again, this time towards Dicky. The two fell heavily on the ground together. The trusty followers had been so struck by the daring of Dicky and his lion-hearted brother that they had not stood by to catch anything. The goat was not hurt, but Dicky had a sprained thumb and a lump on his head like a black marble door-knob. He had to go to bed.

I will draw a veil and asterisks over what Mrs Pettigrew said. Also Albert's uncle, who was brought to the scene of ruin by her screams. Few words escaped our lips. There are times when it is not wise to argue; however, little what has occurred is really our fault.[14]

When they had said what they deemed enough, and we were let go, we all went out. Then Alice said distractedly, in a voice which she vainly strove to render firm:

'Let's give up the circus. Let's put the toys back in the boxes – no, I don't mean that – the creatures in their places – and drop the whole thing. I want to go and read to Dicky.'

Oswald has a spirit that no reverses can depreciate. He hates to be beaten. But he gave in to Alice, as the others said so too, and we went out to collect the performing troop and sort it out into its proper places.

Alas! we came too late. In the interest we had felt about whether Mrs Pettigrew was the abject victim of burglars or not, we had left both gates open again. The old horse – I mean the trained elephant from Venezuela – was there all right enough. The dogs we had beaten and tied up after the first act, when the intrepid sheep bounded, as it says in the programme. The two white pigs were there, but the donkey was gone. We heard his hoofs down the road, growing fainter and fainter, in the direction of the 'Rose and Crown.'[15] And just round the gate-post we saw a flash of red and white and blue and black that told us, with dumb significa-tion, that the pig was off in exactly the opposite direction. Why couldn't they have gone the same way? But no, one was a pig and the other was a donkey, as Denny said afterwards.

Daisy and H.O. started after the donkey; the rest of us, with one accord, pursued the pig – I don't know why.[16] It trotted quietly down the road; it looked very black against the white road, and the ends on the top, where the Union Jack was tied, bobbed brightly as it trotted. At first we thought it would be easy to catch up to it. This was an error.

When we ran faster it ran faster; when we stopped it stopped and looked round at us, and nodded. (I dare say you won't swallow this, but you may safely. It's as true as true, and so's all that about the goat. I give you my sacred word of honour.) I tell you the pig nodded as much as to say:

'Oh, yes. You think you will, but you won't!' and then as soon as we moved again off it went. That pig led us on and on, o'er miles and miles of strange country. One thing, it did keep to the roads. When we met people, which wasn't often, we called out to them to help us, but they only waved their arms and roared with laughter. One chap on a bicycle almost tumbled off his machine, and then he got off it and propped it against a gate and sat down in the hedge to laugh properly. You remember Alice was still dressed up as the gay equestrienne in the dressing-table pink and white, with rosy garlands, now very droopy, and she had no stockings on, only white sand-shoes, because she thought they would be easier than boots for balancing on the pig in the graceful bare-backed act.

Oswald was attired in red paint and flour and pyjamas, for a clown. It is really *impossible* to run speedfully in another man's pyjamas, so Oswald had taken them off, and wore his own brown knickerbockers belonging to his Norfolks. He had tied the pyjamas round his neck to carry them easily. He was afraid to leave them in a ditch, as Alice suggested, because he did not know the roads, and for aught he recked they might have been infested with footpads. If it had been his own pyjamas, it would have been different. (I'm going to ask for pyjamas next winter, they are so useful in many ways.)

Noël was a highwayman in brown paper gaiters and bath towels and a cocked hat of newspaper. I don't know how he kept it on. And the pig was encircled by the dauntless banner of our country. All the same, I think if I had seen a band of youthful travellers in bitter distress about a pig I should have tried to lend a helping hand and not sat roaring in the hedge, no matter how the travellers and the pig might have been dressed.

It was hotter than any one would believe who has never had occasion to hunt the pig when dressed for quite another part. The flour got out of Oswald's hair into his eyes and his mouth. His brow was wet with what the village blacksmith's was wet with, and not his fair brow alone.[17] It ran down his face and washed the red off in streaks, and when he rubbed his eyes he only made it worse. Alice had to run holding the equestrienne skirts on with both hands, and I think the brown paper boots bothered Noël from the first. Dora had her skirt over her arm and carried the topper in her hand. It was no use to tell ourselves it was a wild boar hunt – we were long past that.

At last we met a man who took pity on us. He was a kind-hearted man. I think, perhaps, he had a pig of his own – or, perhaps, children. Honour to his name!

He stood in the middle of the road and waved his arms. The pig right-wheeled through a gate into a private garden and cantered up the drive. We followed. What else were we to do, I should like to know?

The Learned Black Pig seemed to know its way.[18] It turned first to the right and then to the left, and emerged on a lawn.

'Now, all together!' cried Oswald, mustering his failing voice to give the word of command. 'Surround him! – cut off his retreat!'

We almost surrounded him. He edged off towards the house.

'Now we've got him!' cried the crafty Oswald, as the pig got onto a bed of yellow pansies close against the red house wall.

All would even then have been well, but Denny, at the last, shrank from meeting the pig face to face in a manly way. He let the pig pass him, and the next moment, with a squeak that said 'There now!' as plain as words, the pig bolted into a French window. The pursuers halted not. This was no time for trivial ceremony. In another moment the pig was a captive. Alice and Oswald had their arms round him under the ruins of a table that had had teacups on it, and around the hunters and their prey stood the startled members of a parish society for making clothes for the poor heathen, that that pig had led us into the very midst of. They were reading a missionary report or something when we ran our quarry to earth under their table. Even as he crossed the threshold I heard something about 'black brothers being already white to the harvest.'[19] All the ladies had been sewing flannel things for the poor blacks while the curate read aloud to them. You think they screamed when they saw the Pig and Us? You are right.

On the whole, I cannot say that the missionary people behaved badly. Oswald explained that it was entirely the pig's doing, and asked pardon quite properly for any alarm the ladies had felt; and Alice said how sorry we were, but really it was *not* our fault this time. The curate looked a bit nasty, but the presence of ladies made him keep his hot blood to himself.[20]

When we had explained, we said, 'Might we go?'

The curate said, 'The sooner the better.' But the Lady of the House asked for our names and addresses, and said she should write to our father. (She did, and we heard of it too.) They did not do anything to us, as Oswald at one time believed to be the curate's idea. They let us go.

And we went, after we had asked for a piece of rope to lead the pig by.

'In case it should come back into your nice room,' Alice said. 'And that would be such a pity, wouldn't it?'

A little girl in a starched pinafore was sent for the rope. And as soon as the pig had agreed to let us tie it round his neck we came away. The scene in the drawing-room had not been long.

The pig went slowly,

'Like the meandering brook,'

Denny said.[21] Just by the gate the shrubs rustled and opened, and the little girl came out. Her pinafore was full of cake.

'Here,' she said. 'You must be hungry if you've come all that way. I think they might have given you some tea after all the trouble you've had.'

We took the cake with correct thanks.

'I wish *I* could play at circuses,' she said. 'Tell me about it.'

We told her while we ate the cake; and when we had done she said perhaps it was better to hear about than do, especially the goat's part and Dicky's.

'But I do wish auntie had given you tea,' she said.[22]

We told her not to be too hard on her aunt, because you have to make allowances for grown-up people.

When we parted she said she would never forget us, and Oswald gave her his pocket button-hook and corkscrew combined for a keepsake.

Dicky's act with the goat (which is true, and no kid) was the only thing out of that day that was put in the Golden Deed Book, and he put that in himself while we were hunting the pig.

Alice and me capturing the pig was never put in. We would scorn to write our own good actions, but I suppose Dicky was dull with us all away; and you must pity the dull, and not blame them.

I will not seek to unfold to you how we got the pig home, or how the donkey was caught (that was poor sport compared to the pig). Nor will I tell you a word of all that was said and done to the intrepid hunters of the Black and Learned. I have told you all the interesting part. Seek not to know the rest. It is better buried in obliquity.

∗ ∗ ∗

Chapter 7
Being Beavers; or, The Young Explorers (Arctic or Otherwise)

You read in books about the pleasures of London, and about how people who live in the country long for the gay whirl of fashion in town because the country is so dull. I do not agree with this at all. In London, or at any rate Lewisham, nothing happens unless you make it happen; or if it happens it doesn't happen to you, and you don't know the people it does happen to. But in the country the most interesting events occur quite freely, and they seem to happen to you as much as to any one else. Very often quite without your doing anything to help.

The natural and right ways of earning your living in the country are much jollier than town ones, too; sowing and reaping, and doing things with animals, are much better sport than fishmongering or bakering or oil-shopping, and those sort of things, except, of course, a plumber's and gasfitter's, and he is the same, town or country – most interesting and like an engineer.

I remember what a nice man it was that came to cut the gas off once at our old house in Lewisham, when my father's business was feeling so poorly. He was a true gentleman, and gave Oswald and Dicky over two yards and a quarter of good lead piping, and a brass tap that only wanted a washer, and a whole handful of screws to do what we liked with. We screwed the back door up with the screws, I remember, one night when Eliza was out without leave. There was an awful row. We did not mean to get her into trouble. We only thought it would be amusing for her to find the door screwed up when she came down to take in the milk in the morning. But I must not say any more about the Lewisham house. It is only the pleasures of memory, and nothing to do with being beavers, or any sort of exploring.

I think Dora and Daisy are the kind of girls who will grow up very good, and perhaps marry missionaries. I am glad Oswald's destiny looks at present as if it might be different.

We made two expeditions to discover the source of the Nile (or the north pole), and owing to their habit of sticking together and doing dull and praiseable things – like sewing, and helping with the cooking, and taking invalid delicacies to the poor and indignant – Daisy and Dora were wholly out of it both times, though Dora's foot was now quite well enough to have gone to the north pole or the equator either.[1] They said they did not mind the first time, because they like to keep themselves clean; it is another of their queer ways. And they said they had had a better time than us. (It was only a clergyman and his wife who called, and hot cakes for tea.) The second time they said they were lucky not to have been in it. And perhaps they were right. But let me to my narrating. I hope you will like it. I am going to try to write it a different way, like the books they give you for a prize at a girls' school – I mean a 'young ladies' school,' of course – not a high school. High schools are not nearly so silly as some other kinds. Here goes:

'"Ah, me!" sighed a slender maiden of twelve summers, removing her elegant hat and passing her tapery fingers lightly through her fair tresses, "how sad it is – is it not? – to see able-bodied youths and young ladies wasting the precious summer hours in idleness and luxury."[2]

'The maiden frowned reproachingly, but yet with earnest gentleness, at the group of youths and maidens who sat beneath an umbragiferous beech-tree and ate blackcurrants.

' "Dear brothers and sisters," the blushing girl went on, "could we not, even now, at the eleventh hour, turn to account these wasted lives of ours, and seek some occupation at once improving and agreeable?"

' "I do not quite follow your meaning, dear sister," replied the cleverest of her brothers, on whose brow – '

It's no use. I can't write like these books. I wonder how the books' authors can keep it up.

What really happened was that we were all eating black currants in the orchard, out of a cabbage leaf, and Alice said:

'I say, look here, let's do something. It's simply silly to waste a day like this. It's just on eleven. Come on!'

And Oswald said, 'Where to?'

This was the beginning of it.

The moat that is all round our house is fed by streams. One of them is a sort of open overflow pipe from a good-sized stream that flows at the other side of the orchard.

It was this stream that Alice meant when she said:

'Why not go and discover the source of the Nile?'

Of course Oswald knows quite well that the source of the real live Egyptian Nile is no longer buried in that mysteriousness where it lurked undisturbed for such a long time. But he was not going to say so. It is a great thing to know when not to say things.[3]

'Why not have it an arctic expedition?' said Dicky; 'then we could take an ice-axe and live on blubber and things. Besides, it sounds cooler.'

'Vote! vote!' cried Oswald. So we did.

Oswald, Alice, Noël, and Denny voted for the river of the ibis and the crocodile. Dicky, H.O., and the other girls for the region of perennial winter and rich blubber.

So Alice said, 'We can decide as we go. Let's start, anyway.'

The question of supplies had now to be gone into. Everybody wanted to take something different, and nobody thought the other people's things would be the slightest use. It is sometimes thus even with grown-up expeditions. So then Oswald, who is equal to the hardest emergency that ever emerged yet, said:

'Let's each get what we like. The secret storehouse can be the shed in the corner of the stable-yard where we got the door for the raft.[4] Then the captain can decide who's to take what.'

This was done. You may think it but the work of a moment to fit out an expedition, but this is not so, especially when you know not whether your exploring party is speeding to Central Africa or merely to the world of icebergs and the polar bear.

Dicky wished to take the wood-axe, the coal hammer, a blanket, and a mackintosh.

H.O. brought a large faggot in case we had to light fires, and a pair of old skates he had happened to notice in the box-room, in case the expedition turned out icy.[5]

Noël had nicked a dozen boxes of matches, a spade, and a trowel, and had also obtained – I know not by what means – a jar of pickled onions.

Denny had a walking-stick – we can't break him of walking with it[6] – a book to read in case he got tired of being a discoverer, a butterfly net and a box with a cork in it, a tennis ball, if we happened to want to play rounders in the pauses of exploring, two towels and an umbrella in the event of camping or if the river got big enough to bathe in or to be fallen into.

Alice had a comforter for Noël in case we got late, a pair of scissors and needle and cotton, two whole candles in case of caves. And she had thoughtfully brought the table-cloth off the small table in the dining-room, so that we could make all the things up into one bundle and take it in turns to carry it.

Oswald had fastened his master mind entirely on grub. Nor had the others neglected this.

All the stores for the expedition were put down on the table-cloth and the corners tied up. Then it was more than even Oswald's muscley arms could raise from the ground, so we decided not to take it, but only the best selected grub. The rest we hid in the straw loft, for there are many ups and downs in life, and grub *is* grub at any time, and so are stores of all kinds. The pickled onions we had to leave, but not forever.[7]

Then Dora and Daisy came along with their arms round each other's necks as usual, like a picture on a grocer's almanac, and said they weren't coming.[8]

It was, as I have said, a blazing hot day, and there were differences of opinion among the explorers about what eatables we ought to have taken, and H.O. had lost one of his garters and wouldn't let Alice tie it up with her handkerchief, which the gentle sister was quite willing to do. So it was a rather gloomy expedition that set off that bright sunny day to seek the source of the river where Cleopatra sailed in Shakespeare (or the frozen plains Mr Nansen wrote that big book about).[9]

But the balmy calm of peaceful nature soon made the others less cross – Oswald had not been cross exactly, but only disinclined to do anything the others wanted – and by the time we had followed the stream a little way, and had seen a water-rat and shied a stone or two at him, harmony was restored. We did not hit the rat.

You will understand that we were not the sort of people to have lived so long near a stream without plumbing its depths. Indeed, it was the same stream the sheep took its daring jump into the day we had the circus.[10] And of course we had often paddled in it – in the shallower parts. But now our hearts were set on exploring. At least they ought to have been, but when we got to the place where the stream goes under a wooden sheep-bridge, Dicky cried, 'A camp! a camp!' and we were all glad to sit down at once. Not at all like real explorers, who know no rest, day or night, till they have got there (whether it's the north pole, or the central point of the part marked '*Desert of Sahara*' on old-fashioned maps).[11]

The food supplies obtained by various members were good, and plenty of it. Cake, hard eggs, sausage-rolls, currants, lemon cheesecakes, raisins, and cold apple dumplings.[12] It was all very decent, but Oswald could not help feeling that the source of the Nile (or north pole) was a long way off, and perhaps nothing much when you got there.

So he was not wholly displeased when Denny said, as he lay kicking into the bank when the things to eat were all gone:

'I believe this is clay: did you ever make huge platters and bowls out of clay and dry them in the sun? Some people did in a book called *Foul Play*, and I believe they baked turtles, or oysters, or something, at the same time.'[13]

He took up a bit of clay and began to mess it about, like you do putty when you get hold of a bit. And at once the heavy gloom that had hung over the explorers became expelled, and we all got under the shadow of the bridge and messed about with clay.

'It will be jolly!' Alice said, 'and we can give the huge platters to poor cottagers who are short of the usual sorts of crockery. That would really be a very golden deed.'

It is harder than you would think when you read about it, to make huge platters with clay. It flops about as soon as you get it any size, unless you keep it much too thick, and then when you turn up the edges they crack.[14] Yet we did not mind the trouble. And we had all got our shoes and stockings off. It is impossible to go on being cross when your feet are in cold water; and there is something in the smooth messiness of clay, and not minding how dirty you get, that would soothe the savagest breast that ever beat.

After a bit, though, we gave up the idea of the huge platter and tried little things. We made some platters – they were like flower-pot saucers; and Alice made a bowl by doubling up her fists and getting Noël to slab the clay on outside. Then they smoothed the thing inside and out with wet fingers, and it was a bowl – at least they said it was. When we'd made a lot of things we set them in the sun to dry, and then it seemed a pity not to do the thing thoroughly. So we made a bonfire, and when it had burned down we put our pots on the soft, white, hot ashes among the little red sparks, and kicked the ashes over them and heaped more fuel over the top. It was a fine fire.

Then tea-time seemed as if it ought to be near, and we decided to come back next day and get our pots.

As we went home across the fields Dicky looked back and said:

'The bonfire's going pretty strong.'

We looked. It was. Great flames were rising to heaven against the evening sky. And we had left it a smouldering, flat heap.

'The clay must have caught alight,' H.O. said. 'Perhaps it's the kind that burns. I know I've heard of fire-clay. And there's another sort you can eat.'[15]

'Oh, shut up!' Dicky said, with anxious scorn.

With one accord we turned back. We all felt *the* feeling – the one that means something fatal being up and it being your fault.

'Perhaps,' Alice said, 'a beautiful young lady in a muslin dress was passing by, and a spark flew on to her, and now she is rolling in agony enveloped in flames.'

We could not see the fire now, because of the corner of the wood, but we hoped Alice was mistaken.

But when we got in sight of the scene of our pottering industry we saw it was as bad nearly as Alice's wild dream. For the wooden fence leading up to the bridge had caught fire, and it was burning like billyo.

Oswald started to run; so did the others. As he ran he said to himself, 'This is no time to think about your clothes. Oswald, be bold!'

And he was.

Arrived at the site of the conflagration, he saw that caps or straw hats full of water, however quickly and perseveringly given, would never put the bridge out, and his eventful past life made him know exactly the sort of wigging you get for an accident like this.

So he said, 'Dicky, soak your jacket and mine in the stream and chuck them along. Alice, stand clear, or your silly girl's clothes 'll catch as sure as fate.'

Dicky and Oswald tore off their jackets, so did Denny, but we would not let him and H.O. wet theirs. Then the brave Oswald advanced warily to the end of the burning rails and put his wet jacket over the end bit, like a linseed poultice on the throat of a suffering invalid who has got bronchitis. The burning wood hissed and smouldered, and Oswald fell back, almost choked with the smoke. But at once he caught up the other wet jacket and put it on another place, and of course it did the trick, as he had known it would do. But it was a long job, and the smoke in his eyes made the young hero obliged to let Dicky and Denny take a turn as they had bothered to do from the first. At last all was safe; the devouring element was conquered. We covered up the beastly bonfire with clay to keep it from getting into mischief again, and then Alice said:

'Now we must go and tell.'

'Of course,' Oswald said shortly. He had meant to tell all the time.

So we went to the farmer who has the Moat House Farm, and we went at once,[16] because if you have any news like that to tell it only makes it worse if you wait about. When we had told him he said:

'You little – ' I shall not say what he said besides that, because I am sure he must have been sorry for it next Sunday when he went to church, if not before.

We did not take any notice of what he said, but just kept on saying how sorry we were; and he did not take our apology like a man, but only said he dare said, just like a woman does. Then he went to look at his bridge, and we went in to our tea. The jackets were never quite the same again.

Really great explorers would never be discouraged by the dare saying of a farmer, still less by his calling them names he ought not to. Albert's uncle was away, so we got no double slating; and next day we started again to discover the source of the river of cataracts (or the region of mountain-like icebergs).

We set out heavily provisioned with a large cake Daisy and Dora had made themselves and six bottles of ginger-beer. I think real explorers most likely have their ginger-beer in something lighter to carry than stone bottles. Perhaps they have it by the cask, which would come cheaper; and you could make the girls carry it on their back, like in pictures of the daughters of regiments.[17]

We passed the scene of the devouring conflagration, and the thought of the fire made us so thirsty we decided to drink the ginger-beer and leave the bottles in a place of concealment. Then we went on, determined to reach our destination, tropic or polar, that day.

Denny and H.O. wanted to stop and try to make a fashionable watering-place at that part where the stream spreads out like a small-sized sea, but Noël said, 'No.' We did not like fashionableness.

'*You* ought to, at any rate,' Denny said. 'A Mr Collins wrote an "Ode to the Fashions," and he was a great poet.'[18]

'The poet Milton wrote a long book about Satan,' Noël said, 'but I'm not bound to like *him*.' I think it was smart of Noël.

'People aren't obliged to like everything they write about even, let alone read,' Alice said. 'Look at "Ruin seize thee, ruthless king!" and all the pieces of poetry about war and tyrants and slaughtered saints – and the one you made yourself about the black beetle, Noël.'[19]

By this time we had got by the pondy place and the danger of delay was past; but the others went on talking about poetry for quite a field and a half, as we walked along by the banks of the stream. The stream was broad and shallow at this part, and you could see the stones and gravel at the bottom, and millions of baby fishes, and a sort of skating-spiders walking about on the top of the water. Denny said the water must be ice for them to be able to walk on it, and this showed we were getting near the north pole. But Oswald had seen a kingfisher by the wood, and he said it was an ibis, so this was even.

When Oswald had had as much poetry as he could bear, he said, 'Let's be beavers and make a dam.'

And everybody was so hot they agreed joyously, and soon our clothes were tucked up as far as they could go and our legs looked green through the water, though they were pink out of it.

Making a dam is jolly good fun, though laborious, as books about beavers take care to let you know.

Dicky said it must be Canada if we were beavers, and so it was on the way to the polar system, but Oswald pointed to his heated brow, and Dicky owned it was warm for polar regions. He had brought the ice-axe (it is called the wood-chopper sometimes), and Oswald, ever ready and able to command, set him and Denny to cut turfs from the bank while we heaped stones across the stream. It was clayey here, or of course dam making would have been vain, even for the best-trained beaver.

When we had made a ridge of stones we laid turfs against them – nearly across the stream, leaving about two feet for the water to go through – then more stones, and then lumps of clay stamped down as hard as we could. The industrious beavers spent hours over it, with only one easy to eat cake in. And at last the dam rose to the level of the bank. Then the beavers collected a great heap of clay, and four of them lifted it and dumped it down in the opening where the water was running. It did splash a little, but a true-hearted beaver knows better than to mind a bit of a wetting, as Oswald told Alice at the time. Then with more clay the work was completed. We must have used tons of clay; there was quite a big long hole in the bank above the dam where we had taken it out.

When our beaver task was performed we went on, and Dicky was so hot he had to take his jacket off and shut up about icebergs.

I cannot tell you about all the windings of the stream; it went through fields and woods and meadows, and at last the banks got steeper and higher, and the trees overhead darkly arched their mysterious branches, and we felt like the princes in a fairy tale who go out to seek their fortunes.

And then we saw a thing that was well worth coming all that way for; the stream suddenly disappeared under a dark stone archway, and however much you stood in the water and stuck your head down between your knees you could not see any light at the other end.

The stream was much smaller than where we had been beavers.

Gentle reader, you will guess in a moment who it was that said:

'Alice, you've got a candle. Let's explore.'

This gallant proposal met but a cold response.

The others said they didn't care much about it, and what about tea?

I often think the way people try to hide their cowardliness behind their teas is simply beastly.

Oswald took no notice. He just said, with that dignified manner, not at all like sulking, which he knows so well how to put on:

'All right. *I'm* going. If you funk it you'd better cut along home and ask your nurses to put you to bed.'

So then, of course, they agreed to go. Oswald went first with the candle. It was not comfortable; the architect of that dark, subterranean passage had not imagined anyone would ever be brave enough to lead a band of beavers into its inky recesses, or he would have built it high enough to stand upright in. As it was, we were bent almost at a right angle, and this is very awkward if for long.

But the leader pressed dauntlessly on, and paid no attention to the groans of his faithful followers, nor to what they said about their backs.

It really was a very long tunnel, though, and even Oswald was not sorry to say, 'I see daylight.' The followers cheered as well as they could as they splashed after him. The floor was stone as well as the roof, so it was easy to walk on. I think the followers would have turned back if it had been sharp stones or gravel.

And now the spot of daylight at the end of the tunnel grew larger and larger, and presently the intrepid leader found himself blinking in the full sun, and the candle he carried looked simply silly. He emerged, and the others too, and they stretched their backs, and the word 'Krikey' fell from more than one lip. It had indeed been a cramping adventure. Bushes grew close to the mouth of the tunnel, so we could not see much landscape, and when we had stretched our backs we went on up stream, and nobody said they'd had jolly well enough of it, though in more than one young heart this was thought.

It was jolly to be in the sunshine again. I never knew before how cold it was underground. The stream was getting smaller and smaller.

Dicky said, 'This can't be the way. I expect there was a turning to the north pole inside the tunnel, only we missed it. It was cold enough there.'

But here a twist in the stream brought us out from the bushes, and Oswald said:

'Here is strange, wild, tropical vegetation in the richest profusion. Such blossoms as these never opened in a frigid what's-its-name.'

It was indeed true. We had come out into a sort of marshy, swampy place like, I think, a jungle is, that the stream ran through, and it was simply crammed with queer plants and flowers we never saw before or since. And the stream was quite thin. It was torridly hot and softish to walk on. There were rushes and reeds and small willows, and it was all tangled over with different sorts of grasses – and pools here and there. We saw no wild beasts, but there were more different kinds of wild flies and beetles than you could believe anybody could bear, and dragon-flies and gnats. The girls picked a lot of flowers. I know the names of some of them, but I will not tell you them because this is not meant to be instructing. So I will only name meadow-sweet, yarrow, loose-strife, lady's bed-straw, and willow herb – both the larger and the lesser.

Every one now wished to go home. It was much hotter there than in natural fields. It made you want to tear all your clothes off and play at savages, instead of keeping respectable in your boots.

But we had to bear the boots because it was so brambly.

It was Oswald who showed the others how flat it would be to go home the same way we came; and he pointed out the telegraph wires in the distance and said:

'There must be a road there, let's make for it,' which was quite a simple and ordinary thing to say, and he does not ask for any credit for it.

So we sloshed along, scratching our legs with the brambles, and the water squelched in our boots, and Alice's blue muslin frock was torn all over in those criss-cross tears which are considered so hard to darn.

We did not follow the stream any more. It was only a trickle now, so we knew we had tracked it to its source. And we got hotter and hotter and hotter, and the dews of agony stood in beads on our brows and rolled down our noses and off our chins. And the flies buzzed and the gnats stung, and Oswald bravely sought to keep up Dicky's courage, when he tripped on a snag and came down on a bramble-bush, by saying:

'You see it *is* the source of the Nile we've discovered. What price north poles now?'

Alice said, 'Ah, but think of ices! I expect Oswald wishes it *had* been the pole, anyway – '

Oswald is naturally the leader, especially when following up what is his own idea, but he knows that leaders have other duties besides just leading. One is to assist weak or wounded members of the expedition, whether polar or equatorish.

So the others had got a bit ahead through Oswald lending the tottering Denny a hand over the rough places. Denny's feet hurt him, because when he was a beaver his stockings had dropped out of his pocket, and boots without stockings are not a bed of luxuriousness. And he is often unlucky with his feet.[20]

Presently we came to a pond, and Denny said:

'Let's paddle.'

Oswald likes Denny to have ideas; he knows it is healthy for the boy, and generally he backs him up, but just now it was getting late and the others were ahead, so he said:

'Oh, rot! come on.'

Generally the Dentist would have; but even worms will turn if they are hot enough, and if their feet are hurting them.

'I don't care, I shall!' he said.

Oswald overlooked the mutiny and did not say who was leader. He just said:

'Well, don't be all day about it,' for he is a kind-hearted boy and can make allowances.

So Denny took off his boots and went into the pool.

'Oh, it's ripping!' he said. 'You ought to come in.'

'It looks beastly muddy,' said his tolerating leader.

'It is a bit,' Denny said, 'but the mud's just as cool as the water, and so soft it squeezes between your toes quite different to boots.'

And so he splashed about, and kept asking Oswald to come along in.

But some unseen influence prevented Oswald doing this; or it may have been because both his bootlaces were in hard knots.

Oswald had cause to bless the unseen influence, or the boot-laces, or whatever it was.

Denny had got to the middle of the pool, and he was splashing about, and getting his clothes very wet indeed, and altogether you would have thought his was a most envious and happy state. But alas! the brightest cloud has a waterproof lining. He was just saying:

'You *are* a silly, Oswald. You'd much better – ' when he gave a blood-piercing scream, and began to kick about.

'What's up?' cried the ready Oswald; he feared the worst from the way Denny screamed, but he knew it could not be an old meat tin in this quiet and jungular spot, like it was in the moat when the shark bit Dora.

'I don't know, it's biting me. Oh, it's biting me all over my legs! Oh, what shall I do? Oh, it does hurt! Oh! oh! oh!' remarked Denny, among his screams, and he splashed towards the bank. Oswald went into the water and caught hold of him and helped him out. It is true that Oswald had his boots on, but I trust he would not have funked the unknown terrors of the deep, even without his boots, I am almost sure he would not have.

When Denny had scrambled and been hauled ashore, we saw with horror and amaze that his legs were stuck all over with large black slug-looking things. Denny turned green in the face – and even Oswald felt a bit queer, for he knew in a moment what the black dreadfulnesses were. He had read about them in a book called *Magnet Stories*, where there was a girl called Theodosia, and she could play brilliant trebles on the piano in duets, but the other girl knew all about leeches, which is much more useful and golden deedy.[21] Oswald tried to pull the leeches off, but they wouldn't, and Denny howled so he had to stop trying. He remembered from the *Magnet Stories* how to make the leeches begin biting – the girl did it with cream – but he could not remember how to stop them, and they had not wanted any showing how to begin.

'Oh, what shall I do? What shall I do? Oh, it does hurt! Oh, oh!' Denny observed, and Oswald said:

'Be a man! Buck up! If you won't let me take them off you'll just have to walk home in them.'

At this thought the unfortunate youth's tears fell fast. But Oswald gave him an arm, and carried his boots for him, and he consented to buck up, and the two struggled on towards the others, who were coming back, attracted by Denny's yells. He did not stop howling for a moment, except to breathe. No one ought to blame him till they have had eleven leeches on their right leg and six on their left, making seventeen in all, as Dicky said, at once.

It was lucky he did yell, as it turned out, because a man on the road – where the telegraph wires were – was interested by his howls, and came across the marsh to us as hard as he could.

When he saw Denny's legs he said:

'Blest if I didn't think so,' and he picked Denny up and carried him under one arm, where Denny went on saying 'Oh!' and 'It does hurt' as hard as ever.

Our rescuer, who proved to be a fine big young man in the bloom of youth, and a farm-labourer by trade, in corduroys, carried the wretched sufferer to the cottage where he lived with his aged mother; and then Oswald found that what he had forgotten about the leeches was *salt*. The young man in the bloom of youth's mother put salt on the leeches, and they squirmed off, and fell with sickening, slug-like flops on the brick floor.

Then the young man in corduroys and the bloom, etc., carried Denny home on his back, after his legs had been bandaged up, so that he looked like 'Wounded warriors returning.'[22]

It was not far by the road, though such a long distance by the way the young explorers had come.

He was a good young man, and though, of course, acts of goodness are their own reward, still I was glad he had the two half-crowns Albert's uncle gave him, as well as his own good act. But I am not sure Alice ought to have put him in the Golden Deed book which was supposed to be reserved for Us.[23]

Perhaps you will think this was the end of the source of the Nile (or north pole). If you do, it only shows how mistaken the gentlest reader may be.

The wounded explorer was lying with his wounds and bandages on the sofa, and we were all having our tea, with raspberries and white currants, which we richly needed after our torrid adventures, when Mrs Pettigrew, the housekeeper, put her head in at the door and said:

'Please could I speak to you half a moment, sir,' to Albert's uncle. And her voice was the kind that makes you look at each other when the grown-up has gone out, and you are silent, with your bread-and-butter half way to the next bite, or your teacup in mid flight to your lips.

It was as we supposed. Albert's uncle did not come back for a long while. We did not keep the bread-and-butter on the wing all that time, of course, and we thought we might as well finish the raspberries and white currants. We kept some for Albert's uncle, of course, and they were the best ones too; but when he came back he did not notice our thoughtful unselfishness.

He came in, and his face wore the look that means bed, and very likely no supper.

He spoke, and it was the calmness of white-hot iron, which is something like the calmness of despair. He said:

'You have done it again. What on earth possessed you to make a dam?'

'We were being beavers,' said H.O., in proud tones. He did not see as we did where Albert's uncle's tone pointed to.

'No doubt,' said Albert's uncle, rubbing his hands through his hair. 'No doubt! no doubt! Well, my beavers, you may go and build dams with your bolsters. Your dam stopped the stream; the clay you took for it left a channel through which it has run down and ruined about seven pounds' worth of freshly reaped barley. Luckily the farmer found it out in time or you might have spoiled seventy pounds' worth. And you burned a bridge yesterday.'

We said we were sorry. There was nothing else to say, only Alice added, 'We didn't *mean* to be naughty.'

'Of course not,' said Albert's uncle, 'you never do. Oh, yes, I'll kiss you – but it's bed and it's two hundred lines to-morrow, and the line is – "Beware of Being Beavers and Burning Bridges. Dread Dams." It will be a capital exercise in capital B's and D's.'

We knew by that that, though annoyed, he was not furious; we went to bed.

I got jolly sick of capital B's and D's before sunset on the morrow. That night, just as the others were falling asleep, Oswald said:

'I say.'

'Well,' retorted his brother.

'There is one thing about it,' Oswald went on, 'it does show it was a rattling good dam anyhow.'

And filled with this agreeable thought, the weary beavers (or explorers, polar or otherwise) fell asleep.

* * *

Chapter 8
The High-born Babe

It really was not such a bad baby – for a baby. Its face was round and quite clean, which babies' faces are not always, as I dare say you know by your own youthful relatives; and Dora said its cape was trimmed with real lace, whatever that may be – I don't see myself how one kind of lace can be realler than another. It was in a very swagger sort of perambulator when we saw it; and the perambulator was standing quite by itself in the lane that leads to the mill.

'I wonder whose baby it is,' Dora said. 'Isn't it a darling, Alice?'

Alice agreed to its being one, and said she thought it was most likely the child of noble parents stolen by gypsies.

'These two, as likely as not,' Noël said. 'Can't you see something crime-like in the very way they're lying?'

They were two tramps, and they were lying on the grass at the edge of the lane on the shady side fast asleep, only a very little further on than where the Baby was. They were very ragged, and their snores did have a sinister sound.

'I expect they stole the titled heir at dead of night, and they've been travelling hot-foot ever since, so now they're sleeping the sleep of exhaustedness,' Alice said. 'What a heartrending scene when the patrician mother wakes in the morning and finds the infant aristocrat isn't in bed with his mamma.'

The Baby was fast asleep or else the girls would have kissed it. They are strangely fond of kissing. The author never could see anything in it himself.

'If the gypsies *did* steal it,' Dora said, 'perhaps they'd sell it to us. I wonder what they'd take for it.'

'What could you do with it if you'd got it?' H.O. asked.

'Why, adopt it, of course,' Dora said. 'I've often thought I should enjoy adopting a baby. It would be a golden deed, too. We've hardly got any in the book yet.'[1]

'I should have thought there were enough of us,' Dicky said.

'Ah, but you're none of you babies,' said Dora.

'Unless you count H.O. as a baby: he behaves jolly like one sometimes.'

This was because of what had happened that morning when Dicky found H.O. going fishing with a box of worms, and the box was the one Dicky keeps his silver studs in, and the medal he got at school, and what is left of his watch and chain. The box is lined with red velvet and it was not nice afterwards. And then H.O. said Dicky had hurt him, and he was a beastly bully, and he cried. We thought all this had been made up, and were sorry to see it threaten to break out again. So Oswald said:

'Oh, bother the Baby! Come along, do!'

And the others came.

We were going to the miller's with a message about some flour that hadn't come, and about a sack of sharps for the pigs.

After you go down the lane you come to a clover-field, and then a cornfield, and then another lane, and then it is the mill. It is a jolly fine mill: in fact, it is two – water and wind ones – one of each kind – with a house and farm buildings as well. I never saw a mill like it, and I don't believe you have either.

If we had been in a story-book the miller's wife would have taken us into the neat sanded kitchen where the old oak settle was black with time and rubbing, and dusted chairs for us – old brown Windsor chairs – and given us each a glass of sweet-scented cowslip wine and a thick slice of rich home-made cake. And there would have been fresh roses in an old china bowl on the table. As it was, she asked us all into the parlour and gave us Eiffel Tower lemonade and Marie biscuits.[2] The chairs in her parlour were 'bent wood,' and no flowers, except some wax ones under a glass shade, but she was very kind, and we were very much obliged to her. We got out to the miller, though, as soon as we could; only Dora and Daisy stayed with her, and she talked to them about her lodgers and about her relations in London.

The miller is a MAN. He showed us all over the mills – both kinds – and let us go right up into the very top of the wind-mill, and showed us how the top moved round so that the sails could catch the wind, and the great heaps of corn, some red and some yellow (the red is English wheat), and the heaps slice down a little bit at a time into a square hole and go down to the millstones. The corn makes a rustling, soft noise that is very jolly – something like the noise of the sea – and you can hear it through all the other mill noises.

Then the miller let us go all over the water-mill. It is fairy palaces inside a mill. Everything is powdered over white, like sugar on pancakes when you are allowed to help yourself. And he opened a door and showed us the great water-wheel working on slow and sure, like some great, round dripping giant, Noël said, and then he asked us if we fished.[3]

'Yes,' was our immediate reply.

'Then why not try the mill-pool?' he said, and we replied politely; and when he was gone to tell his man something we owned to each other that he was a trump.

He did the thing thoroughly. He took us out and cut us ash saplings for rods; he found us in lines and hooks, and several different sorts of bait, including a handsome handful of meal-worms, which Oswald put loose in his pocket.

When it came to bait, Alice said she was going home with Dora and Daisy. Girls are strange, mysterious, silly things. Alice always enjoys a rat hunt until the rat is caught, but she hates fishing from beginning to end. We boys have got to like it. We don't feel now as we did when we turned off the water and stopped the competition of the competing anglers. We had a grand day's fishing that day. I can't think what made the miller so kind to us. Perhaps he felt a thrill of fellow-feeling in his manly breast for his fellow-sportsmen, for he was a noble fisherman himself.

We had glorious sport – eight roach, six dace, three eels, seven perch, and a young pike, but he was so very young the miller asked us to put him back, and of course we did.

'He'll live to bite another day,' said the miller.

The miller's wife gave us bread and cheese and more Eiffel Tower lemonade, and we went home at last, a little damp, but full of successful ambition, with our fish on a string.

It had been a strikingly good time – one of those times that happen in the country quite by themselves. Country people are much more friendly than town people. I suppose they don't have to spread their friendly feelings out over so many persons, so it's thicker, like a pound of butter on one loaf is thicker than on a dozen. Friendliness in the country is not scrape, like it is in London. Even Dicky and H.O. forgot the affair of honour that had taken place in the morning. H.O. changed rods with Dicky because H.O.'s was the best rod, and Dicky baited H.O.'s hook for him, just like loving, unselfish brothers in Sunday-school magazines.[4]

We were talking fishlikely as we went along down the lane and through the cornfield and the cloverfield, and then we came to the other lane where we had seen the Baby. The tramps were gone, and the perambulator was gone, and, of course, the Baby was gone too.

'I wonder if those gypsies *had* stolen the Baby?' Noël said, dreamily. He had not fished much, but he had made a piece of poetry. It was this:

> 'How I wish
> I was a fish.
> I would not look
> At your hook,
> But lie still and be cool
> At the bottom of the pool.
> And when you went to look
> At your cruel hook,
> You would not find me there,
> So there!'

'If they did steal the Baby,' Noël went on, 'they will be tracked by the lordly perambulator. You can disguise a baby in rags and walnut juice, but there isn't any disguise dark enough to conceal a perambulator's person.'

'You might disguise it as a wheel-barrow,' said Dicky.

'Or cover it with leaves,' said H.O., 'like the robins.'[5]

We told him to shut up and not gibber, but afterwards we had to own that even a young brother may sometimes talk sense by accident.

For we took the short cut home from the lane – it begins with a large gap in the hedge and the grass and weeds trodden down by the hasty feet of persons who were late for church and in too great a hurry to go round by the road. Our house is next to the church, as I think I have said before, some time.[6]

The short cut leads to a stile at the edge of a bit of wood (the Parson's Shave, they call it, because it belongs to him). The wood has not been shaved for some time, and it has grown out beyond the stile; and here, among the hazels and chestnuts and young dog-wood bushes, we saw something white. We felt it was our duty to investigate, even if the white was only the under side of the tail of a dead rabbit caught in a trap. It was not – it was part of the perambulator. I forget whether I said that the perambulator was enamelled white – not the kind of enamelling you do at home with Aspinall's and the hairs of the brush come out and it is gritty-looking, but smooth, like the handles of ladies' very best lace parasols.[7] And whoever had abandoned the helpless perambulator in that lonely spot had done exactly as H.O. said, and covered it with leaves, only they were green and some of them had dropped off.

The others were wild with excitement. Now or never, they thought, was a chance to be real detectives. Oswald alone retained a calm exterior. It was he who would not go straight to the police station.

He said: 'Let's try and ferret out something for ourselves before we tell the police. They always have a clue directly they hear about the finding of the body. And besides, we might as well let Alice be in anything there is going. And besides, we haven't had our dinners yet.'

This argument of Oswald's was so strong and powerful – his arguments are often that, as I dare say you have noticed – that the others agreed. It was Oswald, too, who showed his artless brothers why they had much better not take the deserted perambulator home with them.

'The dead body, or whatever the clew is, is always left exactly as it is found,' he said, 'till the police have seen it, and the coroner, and the inquest, and the doctor, and the sorrowing relations. Besides, suppose some one saw us with the beastly thing, and thought we had stolen it; then they would say, *"What have you done with the Baby?"* and then where should we be?' Oswald's brothers could not answer this question, and once more Oswald's native eloquence and far-seeing discerningness conquered.

'Anyway,' Dicky said, 'let's shove the derelict a little further under cover.'

So we did.

Then we went on home. Dinner was ready and so were Alice and Daisy, but Dora was not there.

'She's got a – well, she's not coming to dinner anyway,' Alice said when we asked. 'She can tell you herself afterwards what it is she's got.'

Oswald thought it was headache, or pain in the temper, or in the pinafore, so he said no more, but as soon as Mrs Pettigrew had helped us and left the room he began the thrilling tale of the forsaken perambulator. He told it with the greatest thrillingness any one could have, but Daisy and Alice seemed almost unmoved. Alice said:

'Yes, very strange,' and things like that, but both the girls seemed to be thinking of something else. They kept looking at each other and trying not to laugh, so Oswald saw they had got some silly secret, and he said:

'Oh, all right! I don't care about telling you. I only thought you'd like to be in it. It's going to be a real big thing, with policemen in it, and perhaps a judge.'

'In what?' H.O. said; 'the perambulator?'

Daisy choked and then tried to drink, and spluttered and got purple, and had to be thumped on the back. But Oswald was not appeased. When Alice said, 'Do go on, Oswald. I'm sure we all like it very much,' he said:

'Oh, no, thank you,' very politely. 'As it happens,' he went on, 'I'd just as soon go through with this thing without having any girls in it.'

'In the perambulator?' said H.O. again.

'It's a man's job,' Oswald went on, without taking any notice of H.O.

'Do you really think so,' said Alice, 'when there's a baby in it?'

'But there isn't,' said H.O., 'if you mean in the perambulator.'

'Blow you and your perambulator,' said Oswald, with gloomy forbearance.

Alice kicked Oswald under the table and said:

'Don't be waxy, Oswald. Really and truly Daisy and I *have* got a secret, only it's Dora's secret, and she wants to tell you herself. If it was mine or Daisy's we'd tell you this minute, wouldn't we, Mouse?'

'This very second,' said the White Mouse.

And Oswald consented to take their apologies.

Then the pudding came in, and no more was said except asking for things to be passed – sugar and water, and bread and things.

Then when the pudding was all gone, Alice said:

'Come on.'

And we came on. We did not want to be disagreeable, though really we were keen on being detectives and sifting that perambulator to the very dregs. But boys have to try to take an interest in their sisters' secrets, however silly. This is part of being a good brother.

Alice led us across the field where the sheep once fell into the brook, and across the brook by the plank. At the other end of the next field there was a sort of wooden house on wheels, that the shepherd sleeps in at the time of year when lambs are being born, so that he can see that they are not stolen by gypsies before the owners have counted them.

To this hut Alice now led her kind brothers and Daisy's kind brother. 'Dora is inside,' she said, 'with the Secret. We were afraid to have it in the house in case it made a noise.'

The next moment the Secret was a secret no longer, for we all beheld Dora, sitting on a sack on the floor of the hut, with the Secret in her lap.

It was the High-born Babe!

Oswald was so overcome that he sat down suddenly, just like Betsy Trotwood did in *David Copperfield*, which just shows what a true author Dickens is.[8]

'You've done it this time,' he said. 'I suppose you know you're a baby-stealer?'

'I'm not,' Dora said. 'I've adopted him.'

'Then it was you,' Dicky said, 'who scuttled the perambulator in the wood?'

'Yes,' Alice said; 'we couldn't get it over the stile unless Dora put down the Baby, and we were afraid of the nettles for his legs. His name is to be Lord Edward.'

'But, Dora – really, don't you think – '

'If you'd been there you'd have done the same,' said Dora, firmly. 'The gypsies had gone. Of course something had frightened them, and they fled from justice. And the little darling was awake and held out his arms to me. No, he hasn't cried a bit, and I know all about babies; I've often nursed Mrs Simpkins's daughter's baby when she brings it up on Sundays.[9] They have bread and milk to eat. You take him, Alice, and I'll go and get some bread and milk for him.'

Alice took the noble brat. It was horribly lively, and squirmed about in her arms, and wanted to crawl on the floor. She could only keep it quiet by saying things to it a boy would be ashamed even to think of saying, such as 'Goo goo,' and 'Did ums was,' and 'Ickle ducksums then.'

When Alice used these expressions the Baby laughed and chuckled and replied:

'Daddadda,' 'Bababa,' or 'Glueglue.'

But if Alice stopped her remarks for an instant the thing screwed its face up as if it was going to cry, but she never gave it time to begin.

It was a rummy little animal.

Then Dora came back with the bread and milk, and they fed the noble infant. It was greedy and slobbery, but all three girls seemed unable to keep their eyes and hands off it. They looked at it exactly as if it was pretty.

We boys stayed watching them. There was no amusement left for us now, for Oswald saw that Dora's Secret knocked the bottom out of the perambulator.

When the infant aristocrat had eaten a hearty meal it sat on Alice's lap and played with the amber heart she wears that Albert's uncle brought her from Hastings after the business of the bad sixpence and the nobleness of Oswald.

'Now,' said Dora, 'this is a council, so I want to be business-like. The Duckums Darling has been stolen away; its wicked stealers have deserted the Precious. We've got it. Perhaps its ancestral halls are miles and miles away. I vote we keep the little Lovey Duck till it's advertised for.'

'If Albert's uncle lets you,' said Dicky darkly.

'Oh, don't say "you" like that,' Dora said; 'I want it to be all of our baby. It will have five fathers and three mothers, and a grand-father and a great Albert's uncle, and a great grand-uncle. I'm sure Albert's uncle will let us keep it – at any rate till it's advertised for.'

'And suppose it never is,' Noël said.

'Then so much the better,' said Dora, 'the little Duckywux.'

She began kissing the baby again. Oswald, ever thoughtful, said:

'Well, what about your dinner?'

'Bother dinner!' Dora said – so like a girl. 'Will you all agree to be his fathers and mothers?'

'Anything for a quiet life,' said Dicky, and Oswald said:

'Oh yes, if you like. But you'll see we sha'n't be allowed to keep it.'

'You talk as if he was rabbits or white rats,' said Dora, 'and he's not – he's a little man, he is.'

'All right, he's no rabbit, but a man. Come on and get some grub, Dora,' rejoined the kind-hearted Oswald, and Dora did, with Oswald and the other boys. Only Noël stayed with Alice. He really seemed to like the baby. When I looked back he was standing on his head to amuse it, but the baby did not seem to like him any better whichever end of him was up.

Dora went back to the shepherd's house on wheels directly she had had her dinner. Mrs Pettigrew was very cross about her not being in to it, but she had kept her some mutton hot all the same. She is a decent sort. And there were stewed prunes. We had some to keep Dora company. Then we boys went fishing again in the moat, but we caught nothing.

Just before tea-time we all went back to the hut, and before we got half across the last field we could hear the howling of the Secret.

'Poor little beggar,' said Oswald, with manly tenderness. 'They must be sticking pins in it.'

We found the girls and Noël looking quite pale and breathless. Daisy was walking up and down with the Secret in her arms. It looked like Alice in Wonderland nursing the baby that turned into a pig.[10] Oswald said so, and added that its screams were like it too.

'What on earth is the matter with it?' he said.

'*I* don't know,' said Alice. 'Daisy's tired, and Dora and I are quite worn out. He's been crying for hours and hours. *You* take him a bit.'

'Not me,' replied Oswald, firmly, withdrawing a pace from the Secret.

Dora was fumbling with her waistband in the furthest corner of the hut.

'I think he's cold,' she said. 'I thought I'd take off my flannelette petticoat, only the horrid strings got into a hard knot. Here, Oswald, let's have your knife.'

With the word she plunged her hand into Oswald's jacket pocket, and next moment she was rubbing her hand like mad on her dress, and screaming almost as loud as the Baby. Then she began to laugh and to cry at the same time. This is called hysterics.

Oswald was sorry, but he was annoyed too. He had forgotten that his pocket was half full of the meal-worms the miller had kindly given him. And, anyway, Dora ought to have known that a man always carries his knife in his trousers pocket and not in his jacket one.

Alice and Daisy rushed to Dora. She had thrown herself down on the pile of sacks in the corner. The titled infant delayed its screams for a moment to listen to Dora's, but almost at once it went on again.

'Oh, get some water!' said Alice. 'Daisy, run!'

The White Mouse, ever docile and obedient, shoved the baby into the arms of the nearest person, who had to take it or it would have fallen a wreck to the ground. This nearest person was Oswald.

He tried to pass it on to the others, but they wouldn't. Noël would have, but he was busy kissing Dora and begging her not to.

So our hero, for such I may perhaps term him, found himself the degraded nursemaid of a small but furious kid.

He was afraid to lay it down, for fear in its rage it should beat its brains out against the hard earth, and he did not wish, however innocently, to be the cause of its hurting itself at all. So he walked earnestly up and down with it, thumping it unceasingly on the back, while the others attended to Dora, who presently ceased to yell.

Suddenly it struck Oswald that the High-born also had ceased to yell. He looked at it, and could hardly believe the glad tidings of his faithful eyes. With bated breath he hastened back to the sheep-house.

The others turned on him, full of reproaches about the mealworms and Dora, but he answered without anger.

'Shut up,' he said in a whisper of imperial command. 'Can't you see it's *gone to sleep?*'

As exhausted as if they had all taken part in all the events of a very long Athletic Sports, the youthful Bastables and their friends dragged their weary limbs back across the fields. Oswald was compelled to go on holding the titled infant, for fear it should wake up if it changed hands, and begin to yell again. Dora's flannelette petticoat had been got off somehow – how I do not seek to inquire – and the Secret was covered with it. The others surrounded Oswald as much as possible, with a view to concealment if we met Mrs Pettigrew. But the coast was clear. Oswald took the Secret up into his bedroom. Mrs Pettigrew doesn't come there much; it's too many stairs.

With breathless precaution Oswald laid it down on his bed. It sighed, but did not wake. Then we took it in turns to sit by it and see that it did not get up and fling itself out of bed, which, in one of its furious fits, it would just as soon have done as not.

We expected Albert's uncle every minute.

At last we heard the gate, but he did not come in, so we looked out and saw that there he was talking to a distracted-looking man on a piebald horse – one of the miller's horses.

A shiver of doubt coursed through our veins. We could not remember having done anything wrong at the miller's. But you never know. And it seemed strange his sending a man up on his own horse. But when we had looked a bit longer our fears went down and our curiosity got up. For we saw that the distracted one was a gentleman.

Presently he rode off, and Albert's uncle came in. A deputation met him at the door – all the boys and Dora, because the baby was her idea.

'We've found something,' Dora said, 'and we want to know whether we may keep it.'

The rest of us said nothing. We were not so very extra anxious to keep it after we had heard how much and how long it could howl. Even Noël had said he had no idea a baby could yell like it. Dora said it only cried because it was sleepy, but we reflected that it would certainly be sleepy once a day, if not oftener.

'What is it?' said Albert's uncle. 'Let's see this treasure-trove. Is it a wild beast?'

'Come and see,' said Dora, and we led him to our room.

Alice turned down the pink flannelette petticoat with silly pride, and showed the youthful heir fatly and pinkly sleeping.

'A baby!' said Albert's uncle. '*The* Baby! Oh, my cats alive!'

That is an expression which he uses to express despair unmixed with anger.

'Where did you? – but that doesn't matter. We'll talk of this later.'

He rushed from the room, and in a moment or two we saw him mount his bicycle and ride off.

Quite shortly he returned with the distracted horseman.

It was *his* baby, and not titled at all. The horseman and his wife were the lodgers at the mill. The nursemaid was a girl from the village.

She *said* she only left the Baby five minutes while she went to speak to her sweetheart, who was gardener at the Red House. But *we* knew she left it over an hour, and nearly two.

I never saw anyone so pleased as the distracted horseman.

When we were asked we explained about having thought the Baby was the prey of gypsies, and the distracted horseman stood hugging the Baby, and actually thanked us.

But when he had gone we had a brief lecture on minding our own business. But Dora still thinks she was right. As for Oswald and most of the others, they agreed that they would rather mind their own business all their lives than mind a baby for a single hour.

If you have never had to do with a baby in the frenzied throes of sleepiness you can have no idea what its screams are like.

If you have been through such a scene you will understand how we managed to bear up under having no baby to adopt.

Oswald insisted on having the whole thing written in the Golden Deed book. Of course his share could not be put in without telling about Dora's generous adopting of the forlorn infant outcast, and Oswald could not and cannot forget that he was the one who did get that baby to sleep.

What a time Mr and Mrs Distracted Horseman must have of it, though – especially now they've sacked the nursemaid.

If Oswald is ever married – I suppose he must be some day – he will have ten nurses to each baby. Eight is not enough. We know that because we tried, and the whole eight of us were not enough for the needs of that deserted infant, who was not so extra high-born after all.

* * *

Chapter 9
Hunting the Fox

It is idle to expect every one to know everything in the world without being told. If we had been brought up in the country we should have known that it is not done – to hunt the fox in August. But in the Lewisham Road the most observing boy does not notice the dates when it is proper to hunt foxes.

And there are some things you cannot bear to think that anybody would think you would do; that is why I wish to say plainly at the very beginning that none of us would have shot a fox on purpose even to save our skins.[1] Of course, if a man were at bay in a cave, and had to defend girls from the simultaneous attack of a herd of savage foxes it would be different. A man is bound to protect girls and take care of them – they can jolly well take care of themselves really it seems to me – still, this is what Albert's uncle calls one of the 'rules of the game,' so we are bound to defend them and fight for them to the death, if needful.

Denny knows a quotation which says:

> 'What dire offence from harmless causes springs,
> What mighty contests rise from trefoil things.'[2]

He says this means that all great events come from three things – three-fold, like the clover or trefoil, and the causes are always harmless. Trefoil is short for three-fold.

There were certainly three things that led up to the adventure which is now going to be told you. The first was our Indian uncle coming down to the country to see us. The second was Denny's tooth. The third was only our wanting to go hunting; but if you count it in it makes the thing about the trefoil come right. And all these causes were harmless.

It is a flattering thing to say, and it was not Oswald who said it, but Dora.[3] She said she was certain our uncle missed us, and that he felt he could no longer live without seeing his dear ones (that was us).

Anyway, he came down, without warning, which is one of the few bad habits that excellent Indian man has, and this habit has ended in unpleasantness more than once, as when we played Jungles.[4]

However, this time it was all right. He came on rather a dull kind of day, when no one had thought of anything particularly amusing to do. So that, as it happened to be dinner-time and we had just washed our hands and faces, we were all spotlessly clean (compared with what we are sometimes, I mean, of course).

We were just sitting down to dinner, and Albert's uncle was just plunging the knife into the hot heart of the steak pudding, when there was the rumble of wheels, and the station fly stopped at the garden gate. And in the fly, sitting very upright, with his hands on his knees, was our Indian relative so much beloved. He looked very smart, with a rose in his buttonhole. How different from what he looked in other days when he helped us to pretend that our currant pudding was a wild boar we were killing with our forks. Yet, though tidier, his heart still beat kind and true. You should not judge people harshly because their clothes are tidy. He had dinner with us, and then we showed him round the place, and told him everything we thought he would like to hear, and about the Tower of Mystery, and he said:

'It makes my blood boil to think of it.'

Noël said he was sorry for that, because everyone else we had told it to had owned, when we asked them, that it froze their blood.

'Ah,' said the Uncle, 'But in India we learn how to freeze our blood and boil it at the same time.'

In those hot longitudes, perhaps, the blood is always near boiling-point, which accounts for Indian tempers, though not for the curry and pepper they eat. But I must not wander; there is no curry at all in this story. About temper I will not say.

The Uncle let us all go with him to the station when the fly came back for him; and when we said good-bye he tipped us all half a quid, without any insidious distinctions about age or considering whether you were a boy or a girl. Our Indian uncle is a true-born Briton, with no nonsense about him.

We cheered him like one man as the train went off, and then we offered the fly-driver a shilling to take us back to the four cross-roads, and the grateful creature did it for nothing because, he said, the gent had tipped him something like. How scarce is true gratitude! So we cheered the driver too for this rare virtue, and then went home to talk about what we should do with our money.

I cannot tell you all that we did with it, because money melts away 'like snow-wreaths in thaw-jean,' as Denny says, and somehow the more you have the more quickly it melts.[5] We all went into Maidstone, and came back with the most beautiful lot of brown paper parcels, with things inside that supplied long-felt wants. But none of them belongs to this narration,[6] except what Oswald and Denny clubbed to buy.

This was a pistol, and it took all the money they both had, but when Oswald felt the uncomfortable inside sensation that reminds you who it is and his money that are soon parted he said to himself:[7]

'I don't care. We ought to have a pistol in the house, and one that will go off, too – not those rotten flint-locks. Suppose there should be burglars and us totally unarmed?'

We took it in turns to have the pistol, and we decided always to practise with it far from the house, so as not to frighten the grown-ups, who are always much nervouser about firearms than we are.

It was Denny's idea getting it; and Oswald owns it surprised him, but the boy was much changed in his character.[8] We got it while the others were grubbing at the pastry-cook's in the High Street, and we said nothing till after tea, though it was hard not to fire at the birds on the telegraph wires as we came home in the train.

After tea we called a council in the straw-loft, and Oswald said:

'Denny and I have got a secret.'

'I know what it is,' Dicky said, contemptibly. 'You've found out that shop in Maidstone where peppermint rock is four ounces a penny. H.O. and I found it out before you did.'

Oswald said, 'You shut up. If you don't want to hear the secret you'd better bunk. I'm going to administer the secret oath.'

This is a very solemn oath, and only used about real things, and never for pretending ones, so Dicky said:

'Oh, all right; go ahead! I thought you were only rotting.'

So they all took the secret oath. Noël made it up long before, when he had found the first thrush's nest we ever saw in the Blackheath garden:

> 'I will not tell, I will not reveal,
> I will not touch, or try to steal;
> And may I be called a beastly sneak,
> If this great secret I ever repeat.'

It is a little wrong about the poetry, but it is a very binding promise. They all repeated it, down to H.O.

'Now then,' Dicky said, 'what's up?'

Oswald, in proud silence, drew the pistol from his breast and held it out, and there was a murmur of awful amazement and respect from every one of the council. The pistol was not loaded, so we let even the girls have it to look at.

And then Dicky said, 'Let's go hunting.'

And we decided that we would. H.O. wanted to go down to the village and get penny horns at the shop for the huntsmen to wind, like in the song, but we thought it would be more modest not to wind horns or anything noisy, at any rate not until we had run down our prey.[9] But his talking of the song made us decide that it was the fox we wanted to hunt. We had not been particular which animal we hunted before that.

Oswald let Denny have first go with the pistol, and when we went to bed he slept with it under his pillow, but not loaded, for fear he should have a nightmare and draw his fell weapon before he was properly awake.

Oswald let Denny have it, because Denny had toothache, and a pistol is consoling though it does not actually stop the pain of the tooth. The toothache got worse, and Albert's uncle looked at it, and said it was very loose, and Denny owned he had tried to crack a peach-stone with it. Which accounts. He had creosote and camphor, and went to bed early, with his tooth tied up in red flannel.

Oswald knows it is right to be very kind when people are ill, and he forbore to wake the sufferer next morning by buzzing a pillow at him, as he generally does. He got up and went over to shake the invalid, but the bird had flown and the nest was cold. The pistol was not in the nest either, but Oswald found it afterwards under the looking-glass on the dressing-table. He had just awakened the others (with a hair-brush because they had not got anything the matter with their teeth), when he heard wheels, and, looking out, beheld Denny and Albert's uncle being driven from the door in the farmer's high cart with the red wheels.

We dressed extra quick, so as to get down-stairs to the bottom of the mystery. And we found a note from Albert's uncle. It was addressed to Dora, and said:

'Denny's toothache got him up in the small hours. He's off to the dentist to have it out with him, man to man. Home to dinner.'[10]

Dora said, 'Denny's gone to the dentist.'

'I expect it's a relation,' H.O. said. 'Denny must be short for Dentist.'

I suppose he was trying to be funny – he really does try very hard. He wants to be a clown when he grows up. The others laughed.

'I wonder,' said Dicky, 'whether he'll get a shilling or half-a-crown for it.'

Oswald had been meditating in gloomy silence, now he cheered up and said:

'Of course! I'd forgotten that. He'll get his tooth money, and the drive too. So it's quite fair for us to have the fox-hunt while he's gone. I was thinking we should have to put it off.'

The others agreed that it would not be unfair.

'We can have another one another time if he wants to,' Oswald said.

We know foxes are hunted in red coats and on horseback – but we could not do this – but H.O. had the old red football jersey that was Albert's uncle's when he was at Loretto.[11] He was pleased.

'But I do wish we'd had horns,' he said, grievingly. 'I should have liked to wind the horn.'

'We can pretend horns,' Dora said; but he answered, 'I didn't want to pretend. I wanted to wind something.'

'Wind your watch,' Dicky said. And that was unkind, because we all know H.O.'s watch is broken, and when you wind it, it only rattles inside without going in the least.

We did not bother to dress up much for the hunting expedition – just cocked hats and lath swords; and we tied a card on to H.O.'s chest with 'Moat House Fox-Hunters' on it; and we tied red flannel round all the dogs' necks to show they were fox-hounds. Yet it did not seem to show it plainly; somehow it made them look as if they were not fox-hounds, but their own natural breeds – only with sore throats.[12]

Oswald slipped the pistol and a few cartridges into his pocket. He knew, of course, that foxes are not shot; but as he said:

'Who knows whether we may not meet a bear or a crocodile.'

We set off gaily. Across the orchard and through two cornfields, and along the hedge of another field, and so we got into the wood, through a gap we had happened to make a day or two before, playing 'follow my leader.'

The wood was very quiet and green; the dogs were happy and most busy. Once Pincher started a rabbit. We said, 'View Halloo!' and immediately started in pursuit; but the rabbit went and hid, so that even Pincher could not find him, and we went on. But we saw no foxes.

So at last we made Dicky be a fox, and chased him down the green rides. A wide walk in a wood is called a ride, even if people never do anything but walk in it.

We had only three hounds – Lady, Pincher, and Martha – so we joined the glad throng and were being hounds as hard as we could, when we suddenly came barking round a corner in full chase and stopped short, for we saw that our fox had stayed his hasty flight. The fox was stooping over something reddish that lay beside the path, and he said:

'I say, look here!' in tones that thrilled us throughout.

Our fox – whom we must now call Dicky, so as not to muddle the narration – pointed to the reddy thing that the dogs were sniffing at.

'It's a real live fox,' he said. And so it was. At least it was real – only it was quite dead – and when Oswald lifted it up its head was bleeding. It had evidently been shot through the brain and expired instantly. Oswald explained this to the girls when they began to cry at the sight of the poor beast; I do not say he did not feel a bit sorry himself.

The fox was cold, but its fur was so pretty, and its tail and its little feet. Dicky strung the dogs on the leash; they were so much interested we thought it was better.

'It does seem horrid to think it'll never see again out of its poor little eyes,' Dora said, blowing her nose.

'And never run about through the wood again; lend me your hanky, Dora,' said Alice.

'And never be hunted or get into a hen-roost or a trap or anything exciting, poor little thing,' said Dicky.

The girls began to pick green chestnut leaves to cover up the poor fox's fatal wound, and Noël began to walk up and down making faces, the way he always does when he's making poetry. He cannot make one without the other. It works both ways, which is a comfort.[13]

'What are we going to do now?' H.O. said; 'the huntsman ought to cut off its tail, I'm quite certain. Only, I've broken the big blade of my knife, and the other never was any good.'

The girls gave H.O. a shove, and even Oswald said, 'Shut up.' For somehow we all felt we did not want to play fox-hunting any more that day. When his deadly wound was covered the fox hardly looked dead at all.

'Oh, I wish it wasn't true!' Alice said.

Daisy had been crying all the time, and now she said, 'I should like to pray God to make it not true.'

But Dora kissed her, and told her that was no good – only she might pray God to take care of the fox's poor little babies, if it had had any, which I believe she has done ever since.

'If only we could wake up and find it was a horrid dream,' Alice said. It seems silly that we should have cared so much when we had really set out to hunt foxes with dogs, but it is true. The fox's feet looked so helpless. And there was a dusty mark on its side that I know would not have been there if it had been alive and able to wash itself.

Noël now said, 'This is the piece of poetry:

> 'Here lies poor Reynard who is slain,
> He will not come to life again.
> I never will the huntsman's horn
> Wind since the day that I was born
> Until the day I die.
> For I don't like hunting, and this is why.'

'Let's have a funeral,' said H.O. This pleased everybody, and we got Dora to take off her petticoat to wrap the fox in, so that we could carry it to our garden and bury it without bloodying our jackets. Girls' clothes are silly in one way, but I think they are useful too. A boy cannot take off more than his jacket and waistcoat in any emergency, or he is at once entirely undressed. But I have known Dora take off two petticoats for useful purposes and look just the same outside afterwards.

We boys took it in turns to carry the fox. It was very heavy.

When we got near the edge of the wood Noël said:

'It would be better to bury it here, where the leaves can talk funeral songs over its grave forever, and the other foxes can come and cry if they want to.' He dumped the fox down on the moss under a young oak-tree as he spoke.

'If Dicky fetched the spade and fork we could bury it here, and then he could tie up the dogs at the same time.'

'You're sick of carrying it,' Dicky remarked, 'that's what it is.' But he went on condition the rest of us boys went too.

While we were gone the girls dragged the fox to the edge of the wood; it was a different edge to the one we went in by – close to a lane – and while they waited for the digging or fatigue party to come back, they collected a lot of moss and green things to make the fox's long home soft for it to lie in. There are no flowers in the woods in August, which is a pity.

When we got back with the spade and fork we dug a hole to bury the fox in. We did not bring the dogs back, because they were too interested in the funeral to behave with real, respectable calmness.

The ground was loose and soft and easy to dig when we had scraped away the broken bits of sticks and the dead leaves and the wild honeysuckle; Oswald used the fork and Dicky had the spade. Noël made faces and poetry – he was struck so that morning – and the girls sat stroking the clean parts of the fox's fur till the grave was deep enough. At last it was; then Daisy threw in the leaves and grass, and Alice and Dora took the poor dead fox by his two ends, and we helped to put him in the grave. We could not lower him slowly – he was dropped in, really. Then we covered the furry body with leaves, and Noël said the Burial Ode he had made up. He says this was it, but it sounds better now than it did then, so I think he must have done something to it since:[14]

THE FOX'S BURIAL ODE.
'Dear Fox, sleep here, and do not wake.
We picked these leaves for your sake.
You must not try to rise or move,
We give you this grave with our love.
Close by the wood where once you grew
Your mourning friends have buried you.
If you had lived you'd not have been
(Been proper friends with us, I mean),
But now you're laid upon the shelf,
Poor fox, you cannot help yourself,
So, as I say, we are your loving friends
And here your Burial Ode, dear Foxy, ends.

P.S. – When in the moonlight bright
The foxes wander of a night,
They'll pass your grave and fondly think of you,
Exactly like we mean to always do.
So now, dear fox, adieu!
Your friends are few
But true
To you.
Adieu!'

When this had been said we filled in the grave and covered the top of it with dry leaves and sticks to make it look like the rest of the wood. People might think it was treasure, and dig it up, if they thought there was anything buried there, and we wished the poor fox to sleep sound and not to be disturbed.

The interring was over. We folded up Dora's bloodstained pink cotton petticoat, and turned to leave the sad spot.

We had not gone a dozen yards down the lane when we heard footsteps and a whistle behind us, and a scrabbling and whining, and a gentleman with two fox-terriers had called a halt just by the place where we had laid low the 'little red rover.'[15]

The gentleman stood in the lane, but the dogs were digging – we could see their tails wagging and see the dust fly. And we *saw where*. We ran back.

'Oh, please, do stop your dogs digging there!' Alice said.

The gentleman said 'Why?'

'Because we've just had a funeral, and that's the grave.'

The gentleman whistled, but the fox-terriers were not trained like Pincher, who was brought up by Oswald.[16] The gentleman took a stride through the hedge gap.

'What have you been burying – a pet dicky bird, eh?' said the gentleman, kindly. He had riding breeches and white whiskers.

We did not answer, because now, for the first time, it came over all of us, in a rush of blushes and uncomfortableness, that burying a fox is a suspicious act. I don't know why we felt this, but we did.

Noël said, dreamily:

'We found his murdered body in the wood,
And dug a grave by which the mourners stood.'[17]

But no one heard him except Oswald, because Alice and Dora and Daisy were all jumping about with the jumps of unstrained anguish, and saying, 'Oh, call them off! Do! do! – oh, don't, don't! Don't let them dig.'

Alas! Oswald was, as usual, right. The ground of the grave had not been trampled down hard enough, and he had said so plainly at the time, but his prudent counsels had been overruled. Now these busy-bodying, meddling, mischief-making fox-terriers (how different from Pincher, who minds his own business unless told otherwise) had scratched away the earth and laid bare the reddish tip of the poor corpse's tail.

We all turned to go without a word, it seemed to be no use staying any longer.

But in a moment the gentleman with the whiskers had got Noël and Dicky each by an ear – they were nearest him. H.O. hid in the hedge. Oswald, to whose noble breast sneakishness is, I am thankful to say, a stranger, would have scorned to escape, but he ordered his sisters to bunk in a tone of command which made refusal impossible.

'And bunk sharp, too,' he added sternly. 'Cut along home.'

So they cut.

The white-whiskered gentleman now encouraged his mangy fox-terriers, by every means at his command, to continue their vile and degrading occupation; holding on all the time to the ears of Dicky and Noël, who scorned to ask for mercy. Dicky got purple and Noël got white. It was Oswald who said:

'Don't hang on to them, sir. We won't cut. I give you my word of honour.'

'*Your* word of honour,' said the gentleman, in tones for which, in happier days, when people drew their bright blades and fought duels, I would have had his heart's dearest blood. But now Oswald remained calm and polite as ever.

'Yes, on my honour,' he said, and the gentleman dropped the ears of Oswald's brothers at the sound of his firm, unswerving tones. He dropped the ears and pulled out the body of the fox and held it up.

The dogs jumped up and yelled.

'Now,' he said, 'you talk very big about words of honour. Can you speak the truth?'

Dicky said, 'If you think we shot it, you're wrong. We know better than that.'

The white-whiskered one turned suddenly to H.O. and pulled him out of the hedge.

'And what does that mean?' he said, and he was pink with fury to the ends of his large ears, as he pointed to the card on H.O.'s breast, which said, 'Moat House Fox-Hunters.'

Then Oswald said, 'We *were* playing at fox-hunting, but we couldn't find anything but a rabbit that hid, so my brother was being the fox; and then we found the fox shot dead, and I don't know who did it; and we were sorry for it and we buried it – and that's all.'

'Not quite,' said the riding-breeches gentleman, with what I think you call a bitter smile, 'Not quite. This is my land, and I'll have you up for trespass and damage. Come along now, no nonsense! I'm a magistrate and I'm Master of the Hounds. A vixen, too! What did you shoot her with? You're too young to have a gun. Sneaked your father's revolver, I suppose?'

Oswald thought it was better to be goldenly silent. But it was vain. The Master of the Hounds made him empty his pockets, and there was the pistol and the cartridges.

The magistrate laughed a harsh laugh of successful disagreeableness.

'All right,' said he, 'Where's your licence? You come with me. A week or two in prison.'

I don't believe now he could have done it, but we all thought then he could and would, what's more.

So H.O. began to cry, but Noël spoke up. His teeth were chattering, yet he spoke up like a man.

He said, 'You don't know us. You've no right not to believe us till you've found us out in a lie. We don't tell lies. You ask Albert's uncle if we do.'

'Hold your tongue,' said the White Whiskered.

But Noël's blood was up.

'If you do put us in prison without being sure,' he said, trembling more and more, 'you are a horrible tyrant like Caligula, and Herod, or Nero, and the Spanish Inquisition, and I will write a poem about it in prison, and people will curse you forever.'

'Upon my word,' said White Whiskers, 'we'll see about that,' and he turned up the lane with the fox hanging from one hand and Noël's ear once more reposing in the other.

I thought Noël would cry or faint. But he bore up nobly – exactly like an early Christian martyr.

The rest of us came along too. I carried the spade and Dicky had the fork, H.O. had the card, and Noël had the magistrate. At the end of the lane there was Alice. She had bunked home, obeying the orders of her thoughtful brother, but she had bottled back again like a shot, so as not to be out of the scrape. She is almost worthy to be a boy for some things.

She spoke to Mr Magistrate and said:

'Where are you taking him?'

The outraged majesty of the magistrate said, 'To prison, you naughty little girl.'

Alice said, 'Noël will faint. Somebody once tried to take him to prison before – about a dog. Do please come to our house and see our uncle – at least he's not – but it's the same thing. We didn't kill the fox, if that's what you think – indeed we didn't. Oh, dear, I do wish you'd think of your own little boys and girls if you've got any, or else about when you were little. You wouldn't be so horrid if you did.'

I don't know which, if either, of these objects the fox-hound master thought of, but he said:

'Well, lead on,' and he let go Noël's ear and Alice snuggled up to Noël and put her arm round him.

It was a frightened procession, whose cheeks were pale with alarm – except those between white whiskers, and they were red – that wound in at our gate and into the hall among the old oak furniture and black and white marble floor and things.[18]

Dora and Daisy were at the door. The pink petticoat lay on the table, all stained with the gore of the departed. Dora looked at us all, and she saw that it was serious. She pulled out the big oak chair and said:

'Won't you sit down?' very kindly to the white-whiskered magistrate.

He grunted, but did as she said.

Then he looked about him in a silence that was not comforting, and so did we.[19]

At last he said:

'Come, you didn't try to bolt. Speak the truth, and I'll say no more.'

We said we had.

Then he laid the fox on the table, spreading out the petticoat under it, and he took out a knife and the girls hid their faces. Even Oswald did not care to look. Wounds in battle are all very well, but it's different to see a dead fox cut into with a knife.

Next moment the magistrate wiped something on his handkerchief and then laid it on the table and put one of my cartridges beside it. It was the bullet that had killed the fox.

'Look here!' he said. And it was too true. The bullets were the same.

A thrill of despair ran through Oswald. He knows now how a hero feels when he is innocently accused of a crime and the judge is putting on the black cap, and the evidence is convulsive and all human aid is despaired of.

'I can't help it,' he said, 'we didn't kill it, and that's all there is to it.'

The white-whiskered magistrate may have been master of the fox-hounds, but he was not master of his temper, which is more important, I should think, than a lot of beastly dogs.

He said several words which Oswald would never repeat, much less use in his own conversing, and besides that he called us 'obstinate little beggars.'

Then suddenly Albert's uncle entered in the midst of a silence freighted with despairing reflections. The M. F. H. got up and told his tale: it was mainly lies, or, to be more polite, it was hardly any of it true, though I suppose he believed it.

'I am very sorry, sir,' said Albert's uncle, looking at the bullets. 'You'll excuse my asking for the children's version?'

'Oh, certainly, sir, certainly,' fuming, the fox-hound magistrate replied.

Then Albert's uncle said, 'Now, Oswald, I know I can trust you to speak the exact truth.'

So Oswald did.

Then the white-whiskered fox-master laid the bullets before Albert's uncle, and I felt this would be a trial to his faith far worse than the rack or the thumbscrew in the days of the Armada.[20]

And then Denny came in. He looked at the fox on the table.

'You found it, then?' he said.

The M. F. H. would have spoken but Albert's uncle said, 'One moment, Denny; you've seen this fox before?'

'Rather,' said Denny; 'I – '

But Albert's uncle said, 'Take time. Think before you speak and say the exact truth. No, don't whisper to Oswald. This boy,' he said to the injured fox-master, 'has been with me since seven this morning. His tale, whatever it is, will be independent evidence.'

But Denny would not speak, though again and again Albert's uncle told him to.

'I can't till I've asked Oswald something,' he said at last.

White Whiskers said, 'That looks bad – eh?'

But Oswald said, 'Don't whisper, old chap. Ask me whatever you like, but speak up.'

So Denny said, 'I can't without breaking the secret oath.'

So then Oswald began to see, and he said, 'Break away for all you're worth, it's all right.' And Denny said, drawing relief's deepest breath, 'Well, then, Oswald and I have got a pistol – shares – and I had it last night. And when I couldn't sleep last night because of the toothache I got up and went out early this morning. And I took the pistol. And I loaded it just for fun. And down in the wood I heard a whining like a dog, and I went, and there was the poor fox caught in an iron trap with teeth. And I went to let it out and it bit me – look, here's the place – and the pistol went off and the fox died, and I am so sorry.'

'But why didn't you tell the others?'

'They weren't awake when I went to the dentist's.'

'But why didn't you tell your uncle if you've been with him all the morning?'

'It was the oath,' H.O. said:

'May I be called a beastly sneak
If this great secret I ever repeat.'

White Whiskers actually grinned.

'Well,' he said, 'I see it was an accident, my boy.' Then he turned to us and said:

'I owe you an apology for doubting your word – all of you. I hope it's accepted.'

We said it was all right and he was to never mind.

But all the same we hated him for it. He tried to make up for his unbelievingness afterwards by asking Albert's uncle to shoot rabbits; but we did not really forgive him till the day when he sent the fox's brush to Alice, mounted in silver, with a note about her plucky conduct in standing by her brothers.

We got a lecture about not playing with firearms, but no punishment, because our conduct had not been exactly sinful, Albert's uncle said, but merely silly.

The pistol and the cartridges were confiscated.

I hope the house will never be attacked by burglars. When it is, Albert's uncle will only have himself to thank if we are rapidly overpowered, because it will be his fault that we shall have to meet them totally unarmed, and be their almost unresisting prey.

∗ ∗ ∗

Chapter 10
The Sale of Antiquities

It began one morning at breakfast. It was the fifteenth of August – the birthday of Napoleon the Great, Oswald Bastable, and another very nice writer.[1] Oswald was to keep his birthday on the Saturday, so that his father could be there. A birthday when there are only many happy returns is a little like Sunday or Christmas Eve. Oswald had a birthday-card or two – that was all; but he did not repine, because he knew they always make it up to you for putting off keeping your birthday, and he looked forward to Saturday.

Albert's uncle had a whole stack of letters as usual, and presently he tossed one over to Dora, and said, 'What do you say, little lady? Shall we let them come?'

But Dora, butter-fingered as ever, missed the catch, and Dick and Noël both had a try for it, so that the letter went into the place where the bacon had been, and where now only a frozen-looking lake of bacon fat was slowly hardening, and then somehow it got into the marmalade, and then H.O. got it, and Dora said:

'I don't want the nasty thing now – all grease and stickiness.' So H.O. read it aloud:

'MAIDSTONE SOCIETY OF ANTIQUITIES AND FIELD CLUB[2]

'Aug. 14, 1900.

'DEAR SIR, – At a meeting of the – '

H.O. stuck fast here, and the writing was really very bad, like a spider that has been in the ink-pot crawling in a hurry over the paper without stopping to rub its feet properly on the mat. So Oswald took the letter. He is above minding a little marmalade or bacon. He began to read. It ran thus:

'It's not Antiquities, you little silly,' he said; 'it's *Antiquaries*.'

'The other's a very good word,' said Albert's uncle, 'and I never call names at breakfast myself – it upsets the digestion, my egregious Oswald.'

'That's a name though,' said Alice, 'and you got it out of "Stalky," too.[3] Go on, Oswald.'

So Oswald went on where he had been interrupted:

'MAIDSTONE SOCIETY OF ANTIQUARIES AND FIELD CLUB,

'Aug. 14, 1900.

'DEAR SIR, – At a meeting of the Committee of this Society it was agreed that a field day should be held on Aug. 20, when the Society proposes to visit the interesting church of Ivybridge and also the Roman remains in the vicinity. Our president, Mr Longchamps, F.R.S., has obtained permission to open a barrow in the Three Trees pasture. We venture to ask whether you would allow the members of the Society to walk through your grounds and to inspect – from without, of course – your beautiful house, which is, as you are doubtless aware, of great historic interest, having been for some years the residence of the celebrated Sir Thomas Wyatt.[4] – I am, dear Sir, yours faithfully,

'EDWARD K. TURNBULL (*Hon. Sec.*).'

'Just so,' said Albert's uncle; 'well, shall we permit the eye of the Maidstone Antiquities to profane these sacred solitudes, and the foot of the Field Club to kick up a dust on our gravel?'

'Our gravel is all grass,' H.O. said. And the girls said, 'Oh, do let them come!' It was Alice who said:

'Why not ask them to tea? They'll be very tired coming all the way from Maidstone.'

'Would you really like it?' Albert's uncle asked. 'I'm afraid they'll be but dull dogs, the Antiquities, stuffy old gentlemen with amphoræ in their button-holes instead of orchids, and pedigrees poking out of all their pockets.'

We laughed – because we knew what an amphoræ is.[5] If you don't you might look it up in the dicker. It's not a flower, though it sounds like one out of the gardening book, the kind you never hear of any one growing.

Dora said she thought it would be splendid.

'And we could have out the best china,' she said, 'and decorate the table with flowers. We could have tea in the garden. We've never had a party since we've been here.'

'I warn you that your guests may be boresome; however, have it your own way,' Albert's uncle said; and he went off to write the invitation to tea to the Maidstone Antiquities. I know that is the wrong word – but somehow we all used it whenever we spoke of them, which was often.

In a day or two Albert's uncle came in to tea with a lightly clouded brow.

'You've let me in for a nice thing,' he said. 'I asked the Antiquities to tea, and I asked casually how many we might expect. I thought we might need at least the full dozen of the best teacups. Now the secretary writes accepting my kind invitation – '

'Oh, good!' we cried. 'And how many are coming?'

'Oh, only about sixty,' was the groaning rejoinder. 'Perhaps more, should the weather be exceptionally favourable.'

Though stunned at first, we presently decided that we were pleased. We had never, never given such a big party.

The girls were allowed to help in the kitchen, where Mrs Pettigrew made cakes all day long without stopping. They did not let us boys be there, though I cannot see any harm in putting your finger in a cake before it is baked, and then licking your finger, if you are careful to put a different finger in the cake next time. Cake before it is baked is delicious – like a sort of cream.

Albert's uncle said he was the prey of despair. He drove in to Maidstone one day. When we asked him where he was going, he said:

'To get my hair cut: if I keep it this length I shall certainly tear it out by double handfuls in the extremity of my anguish every time I think of those innumerable Antiquities.'

But we found out afterwards that he really went to borrow china and things to give the Antiquities their tea out of; though he did have his hair cut too, because he is the soul of truth and honour.

Oswald had a very good sort of birthday, with bows and arrows as well as other presents. I think these were meant to make up for the pistol that was taken away after the adventure of the fox-hunting.[6] These gave us boys something to do between the birthday-keeping, which was on the Saturday, and the Wednesday when the Antiquities were to come.

We did not allow the girls to play with the bows and arrows, because they had the cakes that we were cut off from: there was little or no unpleasantness over this.

On the Tuesday we went down to look at the Roman place where the Antiquities were going to dig. We sat on the Roman wall and ate nuts. And as we sat there, we saw coming through the beet-field two labourers with picks and shovels, and a very young man with thin legs and a bicycle. It turned out afterwards to be a free wheel, the first we had ever seen.[7]

They stopped at a mound inside the Roman wall, and the men took their coats off and spat on their hands.

We went down at once, of course. The thin-legged bicyclist explained his machine to us very fully and carefully when we asked him, and then we saw the men were cutting turfs and turning them over and rolling them up and putting them in a heap. So we asked the gentleman with the thin legs what they were doing. He said:

'They are beginning the preliminary excavation in readiness for to-morrow.'

'What's up to-morrow?' H.O. asked.

'To-morrow we propose to open this barrow and examine it.'

'Then *you're* the Antiquities?' said H.O.

'I'm the secretary,' said the gentleman, smiling, but narrowly.

'Oh, you're all coming to tea with us,' Dora said, and added anxiously, 'how many of you do you think there'll be?'

'Oh, not more than eighty or ninety, I should think,' replied the gentleman.

This took our breath away and we went home. As we went, Oswald, who notices many things that would pass unobserved by the light and careless, saw Denny frowning hard.

So he said, 'What's up?'

'I've got an idea,' the Dentist said. 'Let's call a council.' The Dentist had grown quite used to our ways now. We had called him Dentist ever since the fox-hunt day.[8] He called a council as if he had been used to calling such things all his life, and having them come, too; whereas we all know that his former existing was that of a white mouse in a trap, with that cat of a Murdstone aunt watching him through the bars.

(That is what is called a figure of speech. Albert's uncle told me.)

Councils are held in the straw-loft.

As soon as we were all there and the straw had stopped rustling after our sitting down, Dicky said:

'I hope it's nothing to do with the Wouldbegoods?'

'No,' said Denny in a hurry: 'quite the opposite.'

'I hope it's nothing wrong,' said Dora and Daisy together.

'It's – it's "Hail to thee, blithe spirit – bird thou never wert,"' said Denny.[9] 'I mean, I think it's what is called a lark.'

'You never know your luck. Go on, Dentist,' said Dick.

'Well, then, do you know a book called *The Daisy Chain*?'[10]

We didn't.

'It's by Miss Charlotte M. Yonge,' Daisy interrupted, 'and it's about a family of poor motherless children who tried so hard to be good, and they were confirmed, and had a bazaar, and went to church at the Minster, and one of them got married and wore black watered silk and silver ornaments. So her baby died, and then she was sorry she had not been a good mother to it. And – '

Here Dicky got up and said he'd got some snares to attend to, and he'd receive a report of the Council after it was over. But he only got as far as the trap-door, and then Oswald, the fleet of foot, closed with him, and they rolled together on the floor – while all the others called out 'Come back! Come back!' like guinea-hens on a fence.

Through the rustle and bustle and hustle of the struggle with Dicky, Oswald heard the voice of Denny murmuring one of his everlasting quotations:

> ' "Come back, come back!" he cried in Greek,
>   "Across the stormy water,
> And I'll forgive your Highland cheek,
>   My daughter, O my daughter!' "[11]

When quiet was restored and Dicky had agreed to go through with the Council, Denny said:

'*The Daisy Chain* is not a bit like that really. It's a ripping book. One of the boys dresses up like a lady and comes to call, and another tries to hit his little sister with a hoe. It's jolly fine, I tell you.'

Denny is learning to say what he thinks, just like other boys. He would never have learned such words as 'Ripping' and 'Jolly fine' while under the auntal tyranny.

Since then I have read *The Daisy Chain*. It is a first-rate book for girls and little boys.

But we did not want to talk about *The Daisy Chain* just then, so Oswald said:

'But what's your lark?'

Denny got pale pink and said:

'Don't hurry me. I'll tell you directly. Let me think a minute.'

Then he shut his pale pink eyelids a moment in thought, and then opened them and stood up on the straw and said very fast:

'Friends, Romans, countrymen, lend me your ears, or if not ears, pots.[12] You know we've been told that they are going to open the barrow, to look for Roman remains to-morrow. Don't you think it seems a pity they shouldn't find any?'

'Perhaps they will,' Dora said.

But Oswald *saw*, and he said, 'Primus! Go ahead, old man.'

The Dentist went ahead.

'In *The Daisy Chain*,' he said, 'they dug in a Roman encampment, and the children went first and put some pottery there they'd made themselves, and Harry's old medal of the Duke of Wellington. The doctor helped them to some stuff to partly efface the inscription, and all the grown-ups were sold. I thought we might:

> 'You may break, you may shatter
> The vase if you will;
> But the scent of the Romans
> Will cling round it still.'[13]

Denny sat down amid applause. It really was a great idea, at least for *him*. It seemed to add just what was wanted to the visit of the Maidstone Antiquities. To sell the Antiquities thoroughly would be indeed splendiferous. Of course, Dora made haste to point out that we had not got an old medal of the Duke of Wellington, and that we hadn't any doctor who would 'help us to stuff to efface,' and etcetera; but we sternly bade her stow it. We weren't going to do *exactly* like those *Daisy Chain* kids.

The pottery was easy. We had made a lot of it by the stream – which was the Nile when we discovered its source – and dried it in the sun, and then baked it under a bonfire, like in *Foul Play*. And most of the things were such queer shapes that they would have done for almost anything – Roman or Greek, or even Egyptian or antediluvian, or household milk-jugs of the cave-men, Albert's uncle said.[14] The pots were, fortunately, quite ready and dirty, because we had already buried them in mixed sand and river mud to improve the colour, and not remembered to wash it off.

So the Council at once collected it all – and some rusty hinges and some brass buttons and a file without a handle; and the girl Councillors carried it all concealed in their pinafores, while the men members carried digging tools. H.O. and Daisy were sent on ahead as scouts to see if the coast was clear. We have learned the true usefulness of scouts from reading about the Transvaal War.[15] But all was still in the hush of evening sunset on the Roman ruin.

We posted sentries, who were to lie on their stomachs on the walls and give a long, low, signifying whistle if aught approached.

Then we dug a tunnel, like the one we once did after treasure, when we happened to bury a boy. It took some time; but never shall it be said that a Bastable grudged time or trouble when a lark was at stake. We put the things in as naturally as we could, and shoved the dirt back, till everything looked just as before. Then we went home, late for tea. But it was in a good cause; and there was no hot toast, only bread-and-butter, which does not get cold with waiting.

That night Alice whispered to Oswald on the stairs, as we went up to bed:

'Meet me outside your door when the others are asleep. Hist! Not a word.'

Oswald said, 'No kid?' And she replied in the affirmation.

So he kept awake by biting his tongue and pulling his hair – for he shrinks from no pain if it is needful and right.

And when the others all slept the sleep of innocent youth, he got up and went out, and there was Alice dressed.

She said, 'I've found some broken things that look ever so much more Roman – they were on top of the cupboard in the library. If you'll come with me, we'll bury them – just to see how surprised the others will be.'

It was a wild and daring act, but Oswald did not mind.

He said:

'Wait half a shake.' And he put on his knickerbockers and jacket, and slipped a few peppermints into his pocket in case of catching cold. It is these thoughtful expedients which mark the born explorer and adventurer.

It *was* a little cold; but the white moonlight was very fair to see, and we decided we'd do some other daring moonlight act some other day. We got out of the front door, which is never locked till Albert's uncle goes to bed at twelve or one, and we ran swiftly and silently across the bridge and through the fields to the Roman ruin.

Alice told me afterwards she should have been afraid if it had been dark. But the moonlight made it as bright as day is in your dreams.

Oswald had taken the spade and a sheet of newspaper.

We did not take all the pots Alice had found – but just the two that weren't broken – two crooked jugs, made of stuff like flower-pots are made of. We made two long cuts with the spade and lifted the turf up and scratched the earth under, and took it out very carefully in handfuls on to the newspaper, till the hole was deepish. Then we put in the jugs, and filled it up with earth and flattened the turf over. Turf stretches like elastic. This we did a couple of yards from the place where the mound was dug into by the men, and we had been so careful with the newspaper that there was no loose earth about.

Then we went home in the wet moonlight – at least, the grass was very wet – chuckling through the peppermint, and got up to bed without any one knowing a single thing about it.

The next day the Antiquities came. It was a jolly hot day, and the tables were spread under the trees on the lawn, like a large and very grand Sunday-school treat. There were dozens of different kinds of cake, and bread-and-butter, both white and brown, and gooseberries and plums and jam sandwiches. And the girls decorated the tables with flowers – blue larkspur and white canterbury bells. And at about three there was a noise of people walking in the road, and presently the Antiquities began to come in at the front gate, and stood about on the lawn by twos and threes and sixes and sevens, looking shy and uncomfy, exactly like a Sunday-school treat. Presently some gentlemen came, who looked like the teachers; they were not shy, and they came right up to the door. So Albert's uncle, who had not been too proud to be up in our room with us watching the people on the lawn through the netting of our short blinds, said:

'I suppose that's the Committee. Come on!'

So we all went down – we were in our Sunday things – and Albert's uncle received the Committee like a feudal system baron, and we were his retainers.

He talked about dates, and king-posts and gables, and mullions, and foundations, and records, and Sir Thomas Wyatt, and poetry, and Julius Caesar, and Roman remains, and lych-gates and churches, and dog's-tooth moulding till the brain of Oswald reeled. I suppose that Albert's uncle remarked that all our mouths were open, which is a sign of reels in the brain, for he whispered:

'Go hence, and mingle unsuspected with the crowd!'

So we went out on to the lawn, which was now crowded with men and women and one child. This was a girl; she was fat, and we tried to talk to her, though we did not like her. (She was covered in red velvet like an arm-chair.) But she wouldn't. We thought at first she was from a deaf-and-dumb asylum, where her kind teachers had only managed to teach the afflicted to say 'Yes' and 'No.' But afterwards we knew better, for Noël heard her say to her mother, 'I wish you hadn't brought me, mamma. I didn't have a pretty teacup, and I haven't enjoyed my tea one bit.' And she had had five pieces of cake, besides little cakes and nearly a whole plate of plums, and there were only twelve pretty teacups altogether.

Several grown-ups talked to us in a most uninterested way, and then the President read a paper about the Moat House, which we couldn't understand, and other people made speeches we couldn't understand either, except the part about kind hospitality, which made us not know where to look.

Then Dora and Alice and Daisy and Mrs Pettigrew poured out the tea, and we handed cups and plates.

Albert's uncle took me behind a bush to see him tear what was left of his hair when he found there were one hundred and twenty-three Antiquities present, and I heard the President say to the Secretary that 'tea always fetched them.'

Then it was time for the Roman ruin, and our hearts beat high as we took our hats – it was exactly like Sunday – and joined the crowded procession of eager Antiquities. Many of them had umbrellas and overcoats, though the weather was fiery and without a cloud. That is the sort of people they were. The ladies all wore stiff bonnets, and no one took their gloves off, though, of course, it was quite in the country, and it is not wrong to take your gloves off there.

We had planned to be quite close when the digging went on; but Albert's uncle made us a mystic sign and drew us apart.

Then he said: 'The stalls and dress-circle are for the guests. The hosts and hostesses retire to the gallery, whence, I am credibly informed, an excellent view may be obtained.'

So we all went up on the Roman walls, and thus missed the cream of the lark; for we could not exactly see what was happening. But we saw that things were being taken from the ground as the men dug, and passed round for the Antiquities to look at. And we knew they must be our Roman remains: but the Antiquities did not seem to care for them much, though we heard sounds of pleased laughter. And at last Alice and I exchanged meaning glances when the spot was reached where we had put in the extras. Then the crowd closed up thick, and we heard excited talk and we knew we really *had* sold the Antiquities this time.

Presently the bonnets and coats began to spread out and trickle towards the house, and we were aware that all would soon be over. So we cut home the back way, just in time to hear the President saying to Albert's uncle:

'A genuine find – most interesting. Oh, really, you ought to have *one*. Well, if you insist – '

And so, by slow and dull degrees, the thick sprinkling of Antiquities melted off the lawn; the party was over, and only the dirty teacups and plates, and the trampled grass and the pleasures of memory were left.

We had a very beautiful supper – out-of-doors, too – with jam sandwiches and cakes and things that were over; and as we watched the setting monarch of the skies – I mean the sun – Alice said:

'Let's tell.'

We let the Dentist tell, because it was he who hatched the lark, but we helped him a little in the narrating of the fell plot, because he has yet to learn how to tell a story straight from the beginning.

When he had done, and we had done, Albert's uncle said, 'Well, it amused you; and you'll be glad to learn that it amused your friends the Antiquities.'

'Didn't they think they were Roman?' Daisy said; 'they did in *The Daisy Chain*.'

'Not in the least,' said Albert's uncle; 'but the Treasurer and Secretary were charmed by your ingenious preparations for their reception.'

'We didn't want them to be disappointed,' said Dora.

'They weren't,' said Albert's uncle. 'Steady on with those plums, H.O. A little way beyond the treasure you had prepared for them they found two specimens of *real* Roman pottery which sent every man-jack of them home thanking his stars he had been born a happy little Antiquary child.'[16]

'Those were *our* jugs,' said Alice, 'and we really *have* sold the Antiquities.' She unfolded the tale about our getting the jugs and burying them in the moonlight, and the mound; and the others listened with deeply respectful interest. 'We really have done it this time, haven't we?' she added in tones of well-deserved triumph.

But Oswald had noticed a queer look about Albert's uncle from almost the beginning of Alice's recital; and he now had the sensation of something being up, which has on other occasions frozen his noble blood. The silence of Albert's uncle now froze it yet more Arcticly.

'Haven't we?' repeated Alice, unconscious of what her sensitive brother's delicate feelings had already got hold of. 'We have done it this time, haven't we?'

'Since you ask me thus pointedly,' answered Albert's uncle at last, 'I cannot but confess that I think you have indeed done it. Those pots on the top of the library cupboard *are* Roman pottery. The amphoræ which you hid in the mound are probably – I can't say for certain, mind – priceless. They are the property of the owner of this house. You have taken them out and buried them. The President of the Maidstone Antiquarian Society has taken them away in his bag. Now what are you going to do?'

Alice and I did not know what to say, or where to look. The others added to our pained position by some ungenerous murmurs about our not being so jolly clever as we thought ourselves.

There was a very far from pleasing silence. Then Oswald got up. He said:

'Alice, come here a sec., I want to speak to you.'

As Albert's uncle had offered no advice, Oswald disdained to ask him for any.

Alice got up too, and she and Oswald went into the garden, and sat down on the bench under the quince-tree, and wished they had never tried to have a private lark of their very own with the Antiquities – 'A Private Sale,' Albert's uncle called it afterwards. But regrets, as nearly always happens, were vain. Something had to be done.

But what?

Oswald and Alice sat in silent desperateness, and the voices of the gay and careless others came to them from the lawn, where, heartless in their youngness, they were playing tag. I don't know how they could. Oswald would not like to play tag when his brother and sister were in a hole, but Oswald is an exception to some boys. But Dicky told me afterwards he thought it was only a joke of Albert's uncle's.

The dusk grew dusker, till you could hardly tell the quinces from the leaves, and Alice and Oswald still sat exhausted with hard thinking, but they could not think of anything. And it grew so dark that the moonlight began to show.

Then Alice jumped up – just as Oswald was opening his mouth to say the same thing – and said, 'Of course – how silly! I know. Come on in, Oswald.'

And they went on in.

Oswald was still far too proud to consult any one else. But he just asked carelessly if Alice and he might go into Maidstone the next day to buy some wire-netting for a rabbit-hutch, and to see after one or two things.

Albert's uncle said certainly. And they went by train with the bailiff from the farm, who was going in about some sheep-dip and to buy pigs. At any other time Oswald would not have been able to bear to leave the bailiff without seeing the pigs bought. But now it was different. For he and Alice had the weight on their bosoms of being thieves without having meant it – and nothing, not even pigs, had power to charm the young but honourable Oswald till that stain had been wiped away.

So he took Alice to the Secretary of the Maidstone Antiquities' house, and Mr Turnbull was out, but the maid-servant kindly told us where the President lived, and ere long the trembling feet of the unfortunate brother and sister vibrated on the spotless gravel of Camperdown Villa.

When they asked, they were told that Mr Longchamps was at home. Then they waited, paralysed with undescribed emotions, in a large room with books and swords and glass book-cases with rotten-looking odds and ends in them. Mr Longchamps was a collector. That means he stuck to anything, no matter how ugly and silly, if only it was old.

He came in rubbing his hands, and very kind. He remembered us very well, he said, and asked what he could do for us.

Oswald for once was dumb. He could not find words in which to own himself the ass he had been.

But Alice was less delicately moulded. She said:

'Oh, if you please, we are most awfully sorry, and we hope you'll forgive us, but we thought it would be such a pity for you and all the other poor dear Antiquities to come all that way and then find nothing Roman – so we put some pots and things in the barrow for you to find.'

'So I perceived,' said the President, stroking his white beard and smiling most agreeably at us; 'a harmless joke, my dear! Youth's the season for jesting. There's no harm done – pray think no more about it. It's very honourable of you to come and apologize, I'm sure.'

His brow began to wear the furrowed, anxious look of one who would fain be rid of his guests and get back to what he was doing before they interrupted him.

Alice said, 'We didn't come for that. It's *much* worse. Those were two *real* true Roman jugs you took away; we put them there; they aren't ours. We didn't know they were real Roman. We wanted to sell the Antiquities – I mean Antiquaries – and we were sold ourselves.'

'This is serious,' said the gentleman. 'I suppose you'd know the – the "jugs" if you saw them again?'

'Anywhere,' said Oswald, with the confidential rashness of one who does not know what he is talking about.

Mr Longchamps opened the door of a little room leading out of the one we were in, and beckoned us to follow. We found ourselves amid shelves and shelves of pottery of all sorts; and two whole shelves – small ones – were filled with the sort of jug we wanted.

'Well,' said the President, with a veiled, menacing sort of smile, like a wicked cardinal, 'which is it?'

Oswald said, 'I don't know.'

Alice said, 'I should know if I had it in my hand.'

The President patiently took the jugs down one after another, and Alice tried to look inside them. And one after another she shook her head and gave them back.

At last she said, 'You didn't *wash* them?'

Mr Longchamps shuddered and said 'No.'

'Then,' said Alice, 'there is something written with lead-pencil inside both the jugs. I wish I hadn't. I would rather you didn't read it. I didn't know it would be a nice old gentleman like you would find it. I thought it would be the younger gentleman with the thin legs and the narrow smile.'

'Mr Turnbull.' The President seemed to recognize the description unerringly. 'Well, well – boys will be boys – girls, I mean. I won't be angry. Look at all the "jugs" and see if you can find yours.'

Alice did – and the next one she looked at she said, 'This is one' – and two jugs further on she said, 'This is the other.'

'Well,' the President said, 'these are certainly the specimens which I obtained yesterday. If your uncle will call on me I will return them to him. But it's a disappointment. Yes. I think you must let me look inside.'

He did. And at the first one he said nothing. At the second he laughed.

'Well, well,' he said, 'we can't expect old heads on young shoulders. You're not the first who went forth to shear and returned shorn. Nor, it appears, am I. Next time you have a Sale of Antiquities, take care that you yourself are not "sold". Good-day to you, my dear. Don't let the incident prey on your mind,' he said to Alice. 'Bless your heart, I was a boy once myself, unlikely as you may think it. Good-bye.'

We were in time to see the pigs bought, after all.

I asked Alice what on earth it was she'd scribbled inside the beastly jugs, and she owned that just to make the lark complete she had written 'Sucks' in one of the jugs, and 'Sold again, silly,' in the other.

But we know well enough who it was that was sold. And if ever we have any Antiquities to tea again, they sha'n't find so much as a Greek waistcoat button if we can help it.

Unless it's the President, for he did not behave at all badly. For a man of his age I think he behaved exceedingly well. Oswald can picture a very different scene having been enacted over those rotten pots if the President had been an otherwise sort of man.

But that picture is not pleasing, so Oswald will not distress you by drawing it for you. You can most likely do it easily for yourself.

* * *

Chapter 11
The Benevolent Bar

The tramp was very dusty about the feet and legs, and his clothes were very ragged and dirty, but he had cheerful twinkly grey eyes, and he touched his cap to the girls when he spoke to us, though a little as though he would rather not.

We were on the top of the big wall of the Roman ruin in the Three Tree pasture. We had just concluded a severe siege with bows and arrows – the ones that were given us to make up for the pistol that was confiscated after the sad but not sinful occasion when it shot a fox.

To avoid accidents that you would be sorry for afterwards, Oswald, in his thoughtfulness, had decreed that everyone was to wear wire masks.

Luckily there were plenty of these, because a man who lived in the Moat House once went to Rome, where they throw hundreds and thousands at each other in play, and call it a Comfit Battle or Battaglia di Confetti (that's real Italian).[1] And he wanted to get up that sort of thing among the village people – but they were too beastly slack, so he chucked it.

And in the attic were the wire masks he brought home with him from Rome, which people wear to prevent the nasty comfits getting in their mouths and eyes.

So we were all armed to the teeth with masks and arrows, but in attacking or defending a fort your real strength is not in your equipment, but in your power of Shove. Oswald, Alice, Noël and Denny defended the fort. We were much the strongest side, but that was how Dicky and Oswald picked up.

The others got in, it is true, but that was only because an arrow hit Dicky on the nose, and it bled quarts as usual, though hit only through the wire mask. Then he put into dock for repairs, and while the defending party weren't looking he sneaked up the wall at the back and shoved Oswald off, and fell on top of him, so that the fort, now that it had lost its gallant young leader, the life and soul of the besieged party, was of course soon overpowered and had to surrender.

Then we sat on the top and ate some peppermints Albert's uncle brought us a bag of from Maidstone when he went to fetch away the Roman pottery we tried to sell the Antiquities with.[2]

The battle was over, and peace raged among us as we sat in the sun on the big wall and looked at the fields, all blue and swimming in the heat.

We saw the tramp coming through the beet-field. He made a dusty blot on the fair scene.

When he saw us he came close to the wall, and touched his cap, as I have said, and remarked:

'Excuse me interrupting of your sports, young gentlemen and ladies, but if you could so far oblige as to tell a labouring man the way to the nearest pub. It's a dry day and no error.'

'The "Rose and Crown" is the best pub,' said Dicky, 'and the landlady is a friend of ours.[3] It's about a mile if you go by the field path.'

'Lor' love a duck!' said the tramp, 'a mile's a long way, and walking's a dry job this 'ere weather.' We said we agreed with him.

'Upon my sacred,' said the tramp, 'if there was a pump handy I believe I'd take a turn at it – I would indeed, so help me if I wouldn't! Though water always upsets me and makes my 'and shaky.'

We had not cared much about tramps since the adventure of the villainous sailor-man and the Tower of Mystery, but we had the dogs on the wall with us (Lady was awfully difficult to get up, on account of her long deer-hound legs), and the position was a strong one, and easy to defend. Besides, the tramp did not look like that bad sailor, nor talk like it. And we considerably outnumbered the tramp, anyway.[4]

Alice nudged Oswald and said something about Sir Philip Sidney and the tramp's need being greater than his, so Oswald was obliged to go to the hole in the top of the wall where we store provisions during sieges, and get out the bottle of ginger-beer which he had gone without when the others had theirs so as to drink it when he got really thirsty.[5]

Meanwhile Alice said:

'We've got some ginger-beer; my brother's getting it. I hope you won't mind drinking out of our glass. We can't wash it, you know – unless we rinse it out with a little ginger-beer.'

'Don't ye do it, miss,' he said eagerly; 'never waste good liquor on washing.'

The glass was beside us on the wall. Oswald filled it with ginger-beer and handed down the foaming tankard to the tramp. He had to lie on his young stomach to do this.

The tramp was really quite polite – one of Nature's gentlemen, and a man as well, we found out afterwards. He said:

'Here's to you!' before he drank. Then he drained the glass till the rim rested on his nose.

'Swelp me, but I *was* dry,' he said. 'Don't seem to matter much what it is, this weather, do it? so long as it's suthink wet. Well, here's thanking you.'

'You're very welcome,' said Dora; 'I'm glad you liked it.'

'Like it?' said he. 'I don't suppose you know what it's like to have a thirst on you. Talk of free schools and free libraries, and free baths and wash-houses and such! Why don't some one start free *drinks*? He'd be a 'ero, he would. I'd vote for him any day of the week and one over. Ef yer don't objec I'll set down a bit and put on a pipe.'

He sat down on the grass and began to smoke. We asked him questions about himself, and he told us many of his secret sorrows – especially about there being no work nowadays for an honest man. At last he dropped asleep in the middle of a story about a vestry he worked for that hadn't acted fair and square by him like he had by them, or it (I don't know if vestry is singular or plural), and we went home. But before we went we held a hurried council and collected what money we could from the little we had with us (it was ninepence half-penny), and wrapped it in an old envelope Dicky had in his pocket and put it gently on the billowing middle of the poor tramp's sleeping waistcoat, so that he would find it when he woke. None of the dogs said a single syllable while we were doing this, so we knew they believed him to be poor but honest, and we always find it safe to take their word for things like that.

As we went home a brooding silence fell upon us; we found out afterwards that those words of the poor tramp's about free drinks had sunk deep in all our hearts, and rankled there.

After dinner we went out and sat with our feet in the stream. People tell you it makes your grub disagree with you to do this just after meals, but it never hurts us. There is a fallen willow across the stream that just seats the eight of us, only the ones at the end can't get their feet into the water properly because of the bushes, so we keep changing places. We had got some liquorice root to chew. This helps thought. Dora broke a peaceful silence with this speech:

'Free drinks.'

The words awoke a response in every breast.

'I wonder some one doesn't,' H.O. said, leaning back till he nearly toppled in, and was only saved by Oswald and Alice at their own deadly peril.

'Do for goodness sake sit still, H.O.,' observed Alice. 'It would be a glorious act! I wish *we* could.'

'What, sit still?' asked H.O.

'No, my child,' replied Oswald, 'most of us can do that when we try. Your angel sister was only wishing to set up free drinks for the poor and thirsty.'

'Not for all of them,' Alice said, 'Just a few. Change places now, Dicky. My feet aren't properly wet at all.'

It is very difficult to change places safely on the willow. The changers have to crawl over the laps of the others, while the rest sit tight and hold on for all they're worth. But the hard task was accomplished and then Alice went on:

'And we couldn't do it for always, only a day or two – just while our money held out. Eiffel Tower lemonade's the best, and you get a jolly lot of it for your money too.[6] There must be a great many sincerely thirsty persons go along the Dover Road every day.'

'It wouldn't be bad. We've got a little chink between us,' said Oswald.

'And then think how the poor grateful creatures would linger and tell us about their inmost sorrows. It would be most frightfully interesting. We could write all their agonied life histories down afterwards like *All the Year Round* Christmas numbers.[7] Oh, do let's!'

Alice was wriggling so with earnestness that Dicky thumped her to make her calm.

'We might do it, just for one day,' Oswald said, 'but it wouldn't be much – only a drop in the ocean compared with the enormous dryness of all the people in the whole world. Still, every little helps, as the mermaid said when she cried into the sea.'

'I know a piece of poetry about that,' Denny said.

> ' "Small things are best.
> Care and unrest
> To wealth and rank are given,
> But little things
> On little wings – "

Do something or other, I forget what, but it means the same as Oswald was saying about the mermaid.'[8]

'What are you going to call it?' asked Noël coming out of a dream.

'Call what?'

'The Free Drinks game.

> 'It's a horrid shame
> If the Free Drinks game
> Doesn't have a name.
> You would be to blame
> If anyone came
> And – '

'Oh, shut up!' remarked Dicky. 'You've been making that rot up all the time we've been talking instead of listening properly.' Dicky hates poetry. I don't mind it so very much myself, especially Macaulay's and Kipling's and Noël's.

'There was a lot more – "lame" and "dame" and "name" and "game" and things – and now I've forgotten it,' Noël said, in gloom.[9]

'Never mind,' Alice answered, 'it'll come back to you in the silent watches of the night; you see if it doesn't. But really, Noël's right, it *ought* to have a name.'

'Free Drinks Company.'

'Thirsty Travellers' Rest.'

'The Travellers' Joy.'

These names were suggested, but not cared for extra.

Then some one said – I think it was Oswald:

'Why not "The House Beautiful"?'

'It can't be a house, it must be in the road. It'll only be a stall.'

'The "Stall Beautiful" is simply silly,' Oswald said.

'The "Bar Beautiful" then,' said Dicky, who knows what the 'Rose and Crown' bar is like inside, which of course is hidden from girls.

'Oh, wait a minute,' cried the Dentist, snapping his fingers like he always does when he is trying to remember things. 'I thought of something, only Daisy tickled me and it's gone – I know – let's call it the Benevolent Bar!'

It was exactly right, and told the whole truth in two words. 'Benevolent' showed it was free, and 'Bar' showed what was free; *e.g.*, things to drink.[10] The 'Benevolent Bar' it was.

We went home at once to prepare for the morrow, for of course we meant to do it the very next day. Procrastination is you know what – and delays are dangerous.[11] If we had waited long we might have happened to spend our money on something else.

The utmost secrecy had to be observed, because Mrs Pettigrew hates tramps. Most people do who keep fowls. Albert's uncle was in London till the next evening, so we could not consult him, but we know he is always chock full of intelligent sympathy with the poor and needy.

Acting with the deepest disguise, we made an awning to cover the Benevolent Bar keepers from the searching rays of the monarch of the skies. We found some old striped sun-blinds in the attic, and the girls sewed them together. They were not very big when they were done, so we added the girls' striped petticoats. I am sorry their petticoats turn up so constantly in my narrative, but they really are very useful, especially when the band is cut off. The girls borrowed Mrs Pettigrew's sewing-machine; they could not ask her leave without explanations, which we did not wish to give just then, and she had lent it to them before. They took it into the cellar to work it, so that she should not hear the noise and ask bothering questions. They had to balance it on one end of the beer-stand. It was not easy. While they were doing the sewing we boys went out and got willow poles and chopped the twigs off, and got ready as well as we could to put up the awning.

When we returned a detachment of us went down to the shop in the village for Eiffel Tower lemonade. We bought seven-and-sixpence worth; then we made a great label to say what the bar was for. Then there was nothing else to do except to make rosettes out of a blue sash of Daisy's to show we belonged to the Benevolent Bar.

The next day was as hot as ever. We rose early from our inno-cent slumbers, and went out to the Dover Road to the spot we had marked down the day before. It was at a cross-roads, so as to be able to give drinks to as many people as possible.

We hid the awning and poles behind the hedge and went home to brekker.

After brek we got the big zinc bath they wash clothes in, and after filling it with clean water we just had to empty it again, because it was too heavy to lift. So we carried it vacant to the trysting-spot and left H.O. and Noël to guard it while we went and fetched separate pails of water; very heavy work, and no one who wasn't really benevolent would have bothered about it for an instant. Oswald alone carried three pails. So did Dicky and the Dentist. Then we rolled down some empty barrels and stood up three of them by the road-side, and put planks on them. This made a very first-class table, and we covered it with the best table-cloth we could find in the linen cupboard. We brought out sev-eral glasses and some teacups – not the best ones, Oswald was firm about that – and the kettle and spirit-lamp and the teapot, in case any weary tramp-woman fancied a cup of tea instead of Eiffel Tower. H.O. and Noël had to go down to the shop for tea; they need not have grumbled; they had not carried any of the water. And their having to go the second time was only because we forgot to tell them to get some real lemons to put on the bar to show what the drink would be like when you got it. The man at the shop kindly gave us tick for the lemons, and we cashed up out of our next week's pocket-money.

Two or three people passed while we were getting things ready, but no one said anything except the man who said, 'Bloomin' Sunday-school treat,' and as it was too early in the day for any one to be thirsty we did not stop the wayfarers to tell them their thirst could be slaked without cost at our Benevolent Bar.

But when everything was quite ready, and our blue rosettes fas-tened on our breasts over our benevolent hearts, we stuck up the great placard we had made with 'Benevolent Bar. Free Drinks to all Weary Travellers,' in white wadding on red calico, like Christmas decorations in church. We had meant to fasten this to the edge of the awning, but we had to pin it to the front of the table-cloth, because I am sorry to say the awning went wrong from the first. We could not drive the willow poles into the road; it was much too hard. And in the ditch it was too soft, besides being no use. So we had just to cover our benevolent heads with our hats, and take it in turns to go into the shadow of the tree on the other side of the road. For we had pitched our table on the sunny side of the way, of course, relying on our broken-reed-like awning, and wishing to give it a fair chance.

Everything looked very nice, and we longed to see somebody really miserable come along so as to be able to allicve their distress.[12]

A man and woman were the first: they stopped and stared, but when Alice said, 'Free drinks! Free drinks! Aren't you thirsty?' they said, 'No, thank you,' and went on. Then came a person from the village; he didn't even say 'Thank you' when we asked him, and Oswald began to fear it might be like the awful time when we wandered about on Christmas Day trying to find poor persons and persuade them to eat our Conscience pudding.

But a man in a blue jersey and a red bundle eased Oswald's fears by being willing to drink a glass of lemonade, and even to say, 'Thank you, I'm sure,' quite nicely.

After that it was better. As we had foreseen, there were plenty of thirsty people walking along the Dover Road, and even some from the cross-road.

We had had the pleasure of seeing nineteen tumblers drained to the dregs ere we tasted any ourselves. Nobody asked for tea.

More people went by than we gave lemonade to. Some wouldn't have it because they were too grand. One man told us he could pay for his own liquor when he was dry, which, praise be, he wasn't over and above, at present; and others asked if we hadn't any beer, and when we said 'No,' they said it showed what sort we were – as if the sort was not a good one, which it is.

And another man said, 'Slops again! You never get nothing for nothing, not this side heaven you don't. Look at the bloomin' blue ribbon on 'em! Oh, Lor'!' and went on quite sadly without having a drink.[13]

Our Pig-man who helped us on the Tower of Mystery day went by and we hailed him, and explained it all to him and gave him a drink, and asked him to call as he came back. He liked it all, and said we were a real good sort. How different from the man who wanted the beer. Then he went on.

One thing I didn't like, and that was the way boys began to gather. Of course we could not refuse to give drinks to any traveller who was old enough to ask for it, but when one boy had had three glasses of lemonade and asked for another, Oswald said:

'I think you've had jolly well enough. You can't be really thirsty after all that lot.'

The boy said, 'Oh, can't I? You'll just see if I can't,' and went away. Presently he came back with four other boys, all bigger than Oswald; and they all asked for lemonade. Oswald gave it to the four new ones, but he was determined in his behaviour to the other one, and wouldn't give him a drop. Then the five of them went and sat on a gate a little way off and kept laughing in a nasty way, and whenever a boy went by they called out:

'I say, 'ere's a go,' and as often as not the new boy would hang about with them. It was disquieting, for though they had nearly all had lemonade, we could see it had not made them friendly.

A great glorious glow of goodness gladdened (those go all together and are called alliteration) our hearts when we saw our own tramp coming down the road. The dogs did not growl at him as they had at the boys or the beer-man. (I did not say before that we had the dogs with us, but of course we had, because we had promised never to go out without them.)

Oswald said, 'Hullo,' and the tramp said, 'Hullo.'

Then Alice said, 'You see we've taken your advice; we're giving free drinks. Doesn't it all look nice?'

'It does that,' said the tramp. 'I don't mind if I do.'

So we gave him two glasses of lemonade succeedingly, and thanked him for giving us the idea. He said we were very welcome, and if we'd no objection he'd sit down a bit and put on a pipe. He did, and after talking a little more he fell asleep. Drinking anything seemed to end in sleep with him. I always thought it was only beer and things made people sleepy, but he was not so. When he was asleep he rolled into the ditch, but it did not wake him up.

The boys were getting very noisy, and they began to shout things, and to make silly noises with their mouths, and when

Oswald and Dicky went over to them and told them to just chuck it, they were worse than ever. I think perhaps Oswald and Dicky might have fought and settled them – though there were eleven, yet back to back you can always do it against overwhelming numbers in a book – only Alice called out:

'Oswald, here's some more, come back!'

We went. Three big men were coming down the road, very red and hot, and not amiable-looking. They stopped in front of the Benevolent Bar and slowly read the wadding and red-stuff label.

Then one of them said he was blessed, or something like that, and another said he was too. The third one said, 'Blessed or not, a drink's a drink. Blue ribbon, though, by – ' (a word you ought not to say, though it is in the Bible and the catechism as well). 'Let's have a liquor, little missy.'

The dogs were growling, but Oswald thought it best not to take any notice of what the dogs said, but to give these men each a drink. So he did. They drank, but not as if they cared about it very much, and then they set their glasses down on the table, a liberty no one else had entered into, and began to try and chaff Oswald. Oswald said in an undervoice to H.O.:

'Just take charge. I want to speak to the girls a sec. Call if you want anything.' And then he drew the others away, to say he thought there'd been enough of it, and considering the boys and the new three men, perhaps we'd better chuck it and go home. We'd been benevolent nearly four hours anyway.

While this conversation and the objections of the others were going on, H.O. perpetuated an act which nearly wrecked the Benevolent Bar.

Of course Oswald was not an eye or ear witness of what happened, but from what H.O. said in the calmer moments of later life, I think this was about what happened:

One of the big disagreeable men said to H.O.:

'Ain't got such a thing as a drop o' spirit, 'ave yer?'

H.O. said no, we hadn't, only lemonade and tea.

'Lemonade and tea! blank' (bad word I told you about) 'and blazes,' replied the bad character, for such he afterwards proved to be. 'What's *that* then?'

He pointed to a bottle labelled Dewar's whiskey, which stood on the table near the spirit-kettle.[14]

'Oh, is *that* what you want?' said H.O., kindly.

The man is understood to have said he should bloomin' well think so, but H.O. is not sure about the bloomin'.

He held out his glass with about half the lemonade in it, and H.O. generously filled up the tumbler out of the bottle labelled Dewar's whiskey. The man took a great drink, and then suddenly he spat out what happened to be left in his mouth just then, and began to swear.[15] It was then that Oswald and Dicky rushed upon the scene. The man was shaking his fist in H.O.'s face, and H.O. was still holding on to the bottle we had brought out the methylated spirit in for the lamp, in case of anyone wanting tea, which they hadn't.

'If I was Jim,' said the second ruffian, for such indeed they were, when he had snatched the bottle from H.O. and smelt it, 'I'd chuck the whole show over the hedge, so I would, and you young gutter-snipes after it, so I wouldn't.'

Oswald saw in a moment that in point of strength, if not numbers, he and his party were outmatched, and the unfriendly boys were drawing gladly near. It is no shame to signal for help when in distress – the best ships do it every day. Oswald shouted 'Help, help!' Before the words were out of his brave yet trembling lips our own tramp leaped like an antelope from the ditch and said:

'Now then, what's up?'

The biggest of the three men immediately knocked him down. He lay still.

The biggest then said, 'Come on – any more of you? Come on!'

Oswald was so enraged at this cowardly attack that he actually hit out at the big man – and he really got one in just above the belt. Then he shut his eyes, because he felt that now all was indeed up. There was a shout and a scuffle, and Oswald opened his eyes in astonishment at finding himself still whole and unimpaired. Our own tramp had artfully stimulated insensible-ness, to get the men off their guard, and then had suddenly got his arms round a leg each of two of the men, and pulled them to the ground, helped by Dicky, who saw his game and rushed in at the same time, exactly like Oswald would have done if he had not had his eyes shut ready to meet his doom.

The unpleasant boys shouted, and the third man tried to help his unrespectable friends, now on their backs, involved in a desperate struggle with our own tramp, who was on top of them, accompanied by Dicky. It all happened in a minute, and it was all mixed up. The dogs were growling and barking – Martha had one of the men by the trouser leg and Pincher had another; the girls were screaming like mad and the strange boys shouted and laughed (little beasts!), and then suddenly our Pig-man came round the corner, and two friends of his with him. He had gone and fetched them to take care of us if anything unpleasant occurred. It was very thoughtful, and just like him.

'Fetch the police!' cried the Pig-man in noble tones, and H.O. started running to do it. But the scoundrels struggled from under Dicky and our tramp, shook off the dogs and some bits of trouser, and fled heavily down the road.

Our Pig-man said, 'Get along home!' to the disagreeable boys, and 'Shoo'd' them as if they were hens, and they went. H.O. ran back when they began to go up the road, and there we were, all standing breathless and in tears on the scene of the late desperate engagement. Oswald gives you his word of honour that his and Dicky's tears were tears of pure rage. There are such things as tears of pure rage. Any one who knows will tell you so.

We picked up our own tramp and bathed the lump on his forehead with lemonade. The water in the zinc bath had been upset in the struggle. Then he and the Pig-man and his kind friends helped us carry our things home.

The Pig-man advised us on the way not to try these sort of kind actions without getting a grown-up to help us. We've been advised this before, but now I really think we shall never try to be benevolent to the poor and needy again. At any rate not unless we know them very well first.

We have seen our own tramp often since. The Pig-man gave him a job. He has got work to do at last. The Pig-man says he is not such a very bad chap, only he will fall asleep after the least drop of drink. We know that is his failing. We saw it at once. But it was lucky for us he fell asleep that day near our benevolent bar.

I will not go into what my father said about it all. There was a good deal in it about minding your own business – there generally is in most of the talkings to we get. But he gave our tramp a sovereign, and the Pig-man says he went to sleep on it for a solid week.

* * *

Chapter 12
The Canterbury Pilgrims

The author of these few lines really does hope to goodness that no one will be such an owl as to think from the number of things we did when we were in the country, that we were wretched, neglected little children, whose grown-up relations sparkled in the bright haunts of pleasure, and whirled in the giddy what's-its-name of fashion, while we were left to weep forsaken at home. It was nothing of the kind, and I wish you to know that my father was with us a good deal – and Albert's uncle gave up a good many of his valuable hours to us. And the father of Denny and Daisy came now and then, and other people, quite as many as we wished to see. And we had some very decent times with them; and enjoyed ourselves very much indeed, thank you. In some ways the good times you have with grown-ups are better than the ones you have by yourselves. At any rate, they are safer. It is almost impossible, then, to do anything fatal without being pulled up short by a grown-up ere yet the deed is done. And, if you are careful, anything that goes wrong can be looked on as the grown-up's fault. But these secure pleasures are not so interesting to tell about as the things you do when there is no one to stop you on the edge of the rash act.

It is curious, too, that many of our most interesting games happened when grown-ups were far away. For instance, when we were pilgrims.

It was just after the business of the benevolent bar, and it was a wet day.[1] It is not so easy to amuse yourself in-doors on a wet day as older people seem to think, especially when you are far removed from your own home, and haven't got all your own books and things. The girls were playing Halma – which is a beastly game – Noël was writing poetry, H.O. was singing 'I don't know what to do' to the tune of 'Canaan's happy shore.'[2] It goes like this, and is very tiresome to listen to:

'I don't know what to do – oo – oo!
I don't know what to do – oo – oo!

> It *is* a beastly rainy day
> And I don't know what to do.'

The rest of us were trying to make him shut up. We put a carpet-bag over his head, but he went on inside it; and then we sat on him, but he sang under us; we held him upside down and made him crawl head first under the sofa, but when, even there, he kept it up, we saw that nothing short of violence would induce him to silence, so we let him go. And then he said we had hurt him, and we said we were only in fun, and he said if we were he wasn't, and ill feeling might have grown up even out of a playful brotherly act like ours had been, only Alice chucked the Halma and said:

'Let dogs delight.[3] Come on – let's play something.'

Then Dora said, 'Yes, but look here. Now we're all together, I do want to say something. What about the Wouldbegoods Society?'

Many of us groaned, and one said, 'Hear! hear!' I will not say which one, but it was not Oswald.

'No, but really,' Dora said, 'I don't want to be preachy – but you know we *did* say we'd try to be good. And it says in a book I was reading only yesterday that *not* being naughty is not enough. You must *be* good. And we've hardly done anything. The Golden Deed book's almost empty.'

'Couldn't we have a book of leaden deeds?' said Noël, coming out of his poetry, 'then there'd be plenty for Alice to write about if she wants to, or brass or zinc or aluminium deeds? We sha'n't ever fill the book with golden ones.'

H.O. had rolled himself in the red table-cloth and said Noël was only advising us to be naughty, and again peace waved in the balance. But Alice said, 'Oh, H.O., *don't* – he didn't mean that; but really and truly, I wish wrong things weren't so interesting. You begin to do a noble act, and then it gets so exciting, and before you know where you are you are doing something wrong as hard as you can lick.'

'And enjoying it too,' Dicky said.

'It's very curious,' Denny said, 'but you don't seem to be able to be certain inside yourself whether what you're doing is right if you happen to like doing it, but if you don't like doing it you know quite well. I only thought of that just now. I wish Noël would make a poem about it.'

'I am,' Noël said; 'it began about a crocodile, but it is finishing itself up quite different from what I meant it to at first. Just wait a minute.'

He wrote very hard while his kind brothers and sisters and his little friends waited the minute he had said, and then he read:

> 'The crocodile is very wise,
> He lives in the Nile with little eyes,
> He eats the hippopotamus too,
> And if he could he would eat up you.

> 'The lovely woods and starry skies
> He looks upon with glad surprise;
> He sees the riches of the east,
> And the tiger and lion, kings of beast.

> 'So let all be good and beware
> Of saying sha'n't and won't and don't care;
> For doing wrong is easier far
> Than any of the right things I know about are.

And I couldn't make it king of beasts because of it not rhyming with east, so I put the s off beasts on to king. It comes even in the end.'

We all said it was a very nice piece of poetry. Noël gets really ill if you don't like what he writes, and then he said, 'If it's trying that's wanted, I don't care how hard we *try* to be good, but we may as well do it some nice way. Let's be Pilgrim's Progress, like I wanted to at first.'

And we were all beginning to say we didn't want to, when suddenly Dora said, 'Oh, look here! I know. We'll be the Canterbury Pilgrims. People used to go pilgrimages to make themselves good.'

'With pease in their shoes,' the Dentist said. 'It's in a piece of poetry – only the man boiled his pease – which is quite unfair.'[4]

'Oh, yes,' said H.O., 'and cocked hats.'

'Not cocked – cockled' – it was Alice who said this. 'And they had staffs and scrips, and they told each other tales. We might as well.'

Oswald and Dora had been reading about the Canterbury Pilgrims in a book called *A Short History of the English People*.[5] It is not at all short really – three fat volumes – but it has jolly good pictures. It was written by a gentleman named Green. So Oswald said:

'All right. I'll be the Knight.'

'I'll be the wife of Bath,' Dora said. 'What will you be, Dicky?'

'Oh, I don't care, I'll be Mr Bath if you like.'

'We don't know much about the people,' Alice said. 'How many were there?'

'Thirty,' Oswald replied, 'but we needn't be all of them. There's the Nun-Priest.'

'Is that a man or a woman?'

Oswald said he could not be sure by the picture, but Alice and Noël could be it between them. So that was settled. Then we got the book and looked at the dresses to see if we could make up dresses for the parts. At first we thought we would, because it would be something to do, and it was a very wet day; but they looked difficult, especially the Miller's. Denny wanted to be the Miller, but in the end he was the Doctor, because it was next door to Dentist, which is what we call him for short. Daisy was to be the Prioress – because she is good, and has 'a soft little red mouth,' and H.O. *would* be the Manciple (I don't know what that is), because the picture of him is bigger than most of the others, and he said Manciple was a nice portmanteau word – half mandarin and half disciple.

'Let's get the easiest parts of the dresses ready first,' Alice said – 'the pilgrims' staffs and hats and the cockles.'

So Oswald and Dicky braved the fury of the elements and went into the wood beyond the orchard to cut ash-sticks. We got eight jolly good long ones. Then we took them home, and the girls bothered till we changed our clothes, which were indeed sopping with the elements we had faced.

Then we peeled the sticks. They were nice and white at first, but they soon got dirty when we carried them. It is a curious thing: however often you wash your hands they always seem to come off on anything white. And we nailed paper rosettes to the tops of them. That was the nearest we could get to cockle-shells.

'And we may as well have them there as on our hats,' Alice said. 'And let's call each other by our right names to-day, just to get into it. Don't you think so, Knight?'

'Yea, Nun-Priest,' Oswald was replying, but Noël said she was only half the Nun-Priest, and again a threat of unpleasantness darkened the air. But Alice said:

'Don't be a piggy-wiggy, Noël, dear; you can have it all, I don't want it. I'll just be a plain pilgrim, or Henry who killed Becket.'[6]

So she was called the Plain Pilgrim, and she did not mind.

We thought of cocked hats, but they are warm to wear, and the big garden hats that make you look like pictures on the covers of plantation songs did beautifully. We put cockle-shells on them. Sandals we did try, with pieces of oil-cloth cut the shape of soles and fastened with tape, but the dust gets into your toes so, and we decided boots were better for such a long walk. Some of the pilgrims who were very earnest decided to tie their boots with white tape crossed outside to pretend sandals. Denny was one of these earnest palmers. As for dresses, there was no time to make them properly, and at first we thought of nightgowns; but we decided not to, in case people in Canterbury were not used to that sort of pilgrim nowadays. We made up our minds to go as we were – or as we might happen to be next day.

You will be ready to believe we hoped next day would be fine. It was.

Fair was the morn when the pilgrims arose and went down to breakfast. Albert's uncle had had brekker early and was hard at work in his study. We heard his quill-pen squeaking when we listened at the door. It is not wrong to listen at doors when there is only one person inside, because nobody would tell itself secrets aloud when it was alone.

We got lunch from the housekeeper, Mrs Pettigrew. She seems almost to *like* us all to go out and take our lunch with us. Though I should think it must be very dull for her all alone. I remember, though, that Eliza, our late general at Lewisham, was just the same.[7] We took the dear dogs, of course. Since the Tower of Mystery happened we are not allowed to go anywhere without the escort of these faithful friends of man. We did not take Martha, because bull-dogs do not like long walks. Remember this if you ever have one of those valuable animals.

When we were all ready, with our big hats and cockle-shells, and our staves and our tape sandals, the pilgrims looked very nice.

'Only we haven't any scrips,' Dora said.

'What is a scrip?'

'I think it's something to read. A roll of parchment or something.'

So we had old newspapers rolled up, and carried them in our hands. We took the *Globe* and the *Westminster Gazette* because they are pink and green. The Dentist wore his white sandshoes, sandalled with black tape, and bare legs. They really looked almost as good as bare feet.

'We *ought* to have peas in our shoes,' he said. But we did not think so. We knew what a very little stone in your boot will do, let alone peas.

Of course we knew the way to go to Canterbury, because the old Pilgrims' Road runs just above our house. It is a very pretty road, narrow, and often shady. It is nice for walking, but carts do not like it because it is rough and rutty; so there is grass growing in patches on it.

I have said that it was a fine day, which means that it was not raining, but the sun did not shine all the time.

''Tis well, O Knight,' said Alice, 'that the orb of day shines not in undi – what's-its-name? – splendour.'[8]

'Thou sayest sooth, Plain Pilgrim,' replied Oswald. ''Tis jolly warm even as it is.'

'I wish I wasn't two people,' Noël said, 'it seems to make me hotter. I think I'll be a Reeve or something.'

But we would not let him, and we explained that if he hadn't been so beastly particular Alice would have been half of him, and he had only himself to thank if being all of a Nun-Priest made him hot.

But it *was* warm certainly, and it was some time since we'd gone so far in boots. Yet when H.O. complained we did our duty as pilgrims and made him shut up. He did as soon as Alice said that about whining and grizzling being below the dignity of a Manciple.

It was so warm that the Prioress and the wife of Bath gave up walking with their arms round each other in their usual silly way (Albert's uncle calls it Laura Matildaing), and the Doctor and Mr Bath had to take their jackets off and carry them.[9]

I am sure if an artist or a photographer, or any person who liked pilgrims, had seen us he would have been very pleased. The paper cockle-shells were first-rate, but it was awkward having them on the top of the staffs, because they got in your way when you wanted the staff to use as a walking-stick.

We stepped out like a man all of us, and kept it up as well as we could in book-talk, and at first all was merry as a dinner-bell; but presently Oswald, who was the 'very perfect gentle knight,' could not help noticing that one of us was growing very silent and rather pale, like people are when they have eaten something that disagrees with them before they are quite sure of the fell truth.[10]

So he said, 'What's up, Dentist, old man?' quite kindly and like a perfect knight, though, of course, he was annoyed with Denny. It is sickening when people turn pale in the middle of a game and everything is spoiled, and you have to go home, and tell the spoiler how sorry you are that he is knocked up, and pretend not to mind about the game being spoiled.

Denny said, 'Nothing,' but Oswald knew better.

Then Alice said, 'Let's rest a bit, Oswald, it *is* hot.'

'Sir Oswald, if you please, Plain Pilgrim,' returned her brother, dignifiedly. 'Remember I'm a knight.'

So then we sat down and had lunch, and Denny looked better. We played adverbs, and twenty questions, and apprenticing your son, for a bit in the shade, and then Dicky said it was time to set sail if we meant to make the port of Canterbury that night. Of course, pilgrims reck not of ports, but Dicky never does play the game thoughtfully.[11]

We went on. I believe we should have got to Canterbury all right and quite early, only Denny got paler and paler, and presently Oswald saw, beyond any doubt, that he was beginning to walk lame.

'Shoes hurt you, Dentist?' he said, still with kind, striving cheerfulness.

'Not much – it's all right,' returned the other.

So on we went – but we were all a bit tired now – and the sun was hotter and hotter; the clouds had gone away. We had to begin to sing to keep up our spirits. We sang 'The British Grenadiers' and 'John Brown's Body,' which is grand to march to, and a lot of others. We were just starting on 'Tramp, tramp, tramp, the boys are marching,' when Denny stopped short.[12] He stood first on one foot and then on the other, and suddenly screwed up his face and put his knuckles in his eyes and sat down on a heap of stones by the road-side.

When we pulled his hands down he was actually crying. The author does not wish to say it is babyish to cry.

'Whatever is up?' we all asked, and Daisy and Dora petted him to get him to say, but he only went on howling, and said it was nothing, only would we go on and leave him, and call for him as we came back.

Oswald thought very likely something had given Denny the stomach-ache, and he did not like to say so before all of us, so he sent the others away and told them to walk on a bit.

Then he said, 'Now, Denny, don't be a young ass. What is it? *Is* it stomach-ache?'

And Denny stopped crying to say 'No!' as loud as he could.

'Well, then,' Oswald said, 'look here, you're spoiling the whole thing. Don't be a jackape, Denny. What is it?'

'You won't tell the others if I tell you?'

'Not if you say not,' Oswald answered in kindly tones.

'Well, it's my shoes.'

'Take them off, man.'

'You won't laugh?'

'NO!' cried Oswald, so impatiently that the others looked back to see why he was shouting. He waved them away, and with humble gentleness began to undo the black tape sandals. Denny let him, crying hard all the time.

When Oswald had got off the first shoe the mystery was made plain to him.

'Well! Of all the – ' he said in proper indignation.

Denny quailed – though he says he did not – but then he doesn't know what quailing is, and if Denny did not quail then Oswald does not know what quailing is either.

For when Oswald took the shoe off he naturally chucked it down and gave it a kick, and a lot of little pinky yellow things rolled out. And Oswald looked closer at the interesting sight. And the little things were *split peas*.

'Perhaps you'll tell me,' said the gentle knight, with the politeness of despair, 'why on earth you've played the goat like this?'

'Oh, don't be angry,' Denny said; and now his shoes were off, he curled and uncurled his toes and stopped crying. 'I *knew* pilgrims put peas in their shoes – and – oh, I wish you wouldn't laugh!'

'I'm not,' said Oswald, still with bitter politeness.

'I didn't want to tell you I was going to, because I wanted to be better than all of you, and I thought if you knew I was going to you'd want to too, and you wouldn't when I said it first. So I just put some pease in my pocket and dropped one or two at a time into my shoes when you weren't looking.'

In his secret heart Oswald said, 'Greedy young ass.' For it *is* greedy to want to have more of anything than other people, even goodness.

Outwardly Oswald said nothing.

'You see,' – Denny went on, – 'I do want to be good. And if pilgriming is to do you good, you ought to do it properly. I shouldn't mind being hurt in my feet if it would make me good for ever and ever. And besides, I wanted to play the game thoroughly. You always say I don't.'

The breast of the kind Oswald was touched by these last words.

'I think you're quite good enough,' he said. 'I'll fetch back the others – no, they won't laugh.'

And we all went back to Denny, and the girls made a fuss with him. But Oswald and Dicky were grave and stood aloof. They were old enough to see that being good was all very well, but after all you had to get the boy home somehow.

When they said this, as agreeably as they could, Denny said:

'It's all right – some one will give me a lift.'

'You think everything in the world can be put right with a lift,' Dicky said, and he did not speak lovingly.

'So it can,' said Denny, 'when it's your feet. I shall easily get a lift home.'

'Not here you won't,' said Alice. 'No one goes down this road; but the high-road's just round the corner, where you see the telegraph wires.'

Dicky and Oswald made a sedan-chair and carried Denny to the high-road, and we sat down in a ditch to wait. For a long time nothing went by but a brewer's dray. We hailed it, of course, but the man was so sound asleep that our hails were vain, and none of us thought soon enough about springing like a flash to the horses' heads, though we all thought of it directly the dray was out of sight.

So we had to keep on sitting there by the dusty road, and more than one pilgrim was heard to say it wished we had never come. Oswald was not one of those who uttered this useless wish.

At last, just when despair was beginning to eat into the vital parts of even Oswald, there was a quick tap-tapping of horses' feet on the road, and a dog-cart came in sight with a lady in it all alone.

We hailed her like the desperate shipwrecked mariners in the long-boat hail the passing sail.

She pulled up. She was not a very old lady – twenty-five we found out afterwards her age was – and she looked jolly.

'Well,' she said, 'what's the matter?'

'It's this poor little boy,' Dora said, pointing to the Dentist, who had gone to sleep in the dry ditch, with his mouth open as usual. 'His feet hurt him so, and will you give him a lift?'

'But why are you all rigged out like this?' asked the lady, looking at our cockle-shells and sandals and things. We told her.

'And how has he hurt his feet?' she asked.

And we told her that.

She looked very kind. 'Poor little chap,' she said. 'Where do you want to go?'

We told her that too. We had no concealments from this lady.

'Well,' she said, 'I have to go on to – what is its name?'

'Canterbury,' said H.O.

'Well, yes, Canterbury,' she said; 'it's only about half a mile.[13] I'll take the poor little pilgrim – and, yes, the three girls. You boys must walk. Then we'll have tea and see the sights, and I'll drive you home – at least some of you. How will that do?'

We thanked her very much indeed, and said it would do very nicely.

Then we helped Denny into the cart, and the girls got up, and the red wheels of the cart spun away through the dust.

'I wish it had been an omnibus the lady was driving,' said H.O., 'then we could all have had a ride.'

'Don't you be so discontented,' Dicky said.

And Noël said:

'You ought to be jolly thankful you haven't got to carry Denny all the way home on your back. You'd have had to if you'd been out alone with him.'

When we got to Canterbury it was much smaller than we expected, and the cathedral not much bigger than the church that is next to the Moat House.[14] There seemed to be only one big street, but we supposed the rest of the city was hidden away somewhere.

There was a large inn, with a green before it, and the red-wheeled dogcart was standing in the stable-yard, and the lady, with Denny and the others, sitting on the benches in the porch looking out for us. The inn was called the 'George and Dragon,' and it made me think of the days when there were coaches and highwaymen and footpads and jolly landlords, and adventures at country inns like you read about.[15]

'We've ordered tea,' said the lady. 'Would you like to wash your hands?' We saw that she wished us to, so we said yes, we would. The girls and Denny were already much cleaner than when we parted from them.

There was a court-yard to the inn and a wooden staircase out-side the house. We were taken up this, and washed our hands in a big room with a fourpost wooden bed and dark red hangings – just the sort of hangings that would not show the stains of gore in the dear old adventurous times.

Then we had tea in a great big room with wooden chairs and tables, very polished and old.

It was a very nice tea, with lettuces and cold meat and three kinds of jam, as well as cake, and new bread, which we are not allowed at home.[16]

While tea was being had the lady talked to us. She was very kind. There are two sorts of people in the world, besides others; one sort understand what you're driving at and the other don't. This lady was the one sort.

After every one had had as much to eat as they could possibly want, the lady said, 'What was it you particularly wanted to see at Canterbury?'

'The cathedral,' Alice said, 'and the place where Thomas à Becket was murdered.'

'And the Danejohn,' said Dicky.

Oswald wanted to see the walls, because he likes the story of St. Alphege and the Danes.[17]

'Well, well,' said the lady, and she put on her hat; it was a really sensible one – not a blob of fluffy stuff and feathers put on side-ways and stuck on with long pins, and no shade to your face, but almost as big as ours, with a big brim and red flowers, and black strings to tie under your chin to keep it from blowing off.

Then we went out all together to see Canterbury. Dicky and Oswald took it in turns to carry Denny on their backs. The lady called him 'The Wounded Comrade.'

We went first to the church. Oswald, whose quick brain was easily aroused to suspicions, was afraid the lady might begin talking in the church, but she did not. The church door was open. I remember mother telling us once it was right and good for churches to be left open all day, so that tired people could go in and be quiet, and say their prayers, if they wanted to. But it does not seem respectful to talk out loud in church. (*See* Note A.)[18]

When we got outside the lady said, 'You can imagine how on the chancel steps began the mad struggle in which Becket, after hurling one of his assailants, armour and all, to the ground – '

'It would have been much cleverer,' H.O. interrupted, 'to hurl him without his armour, and leave that standing up.'

'Go on,' said Alice and Oswald, when they had given H.O. a withering glance. And the lady did go on. She told us all about Becket, and then about St. Alphege, who had bones thrown at him till he died, because he wouldn't tax his poor people to please the beastly rotten Danes.

And Denny recited a piece of poetry he knows called 'The Ballad of Canterbury.'[19]

It begins about Danish warships snake-shaped, and ends about doing as you'd be done by. It is long, but it has all the beef-bones in it, and all about St. Alphege.

Then the lady showed us the Danejohn, and it was like an oast-house. And Canterbury walls that Alphege defied the Danes from looked down on a quite common farm-yard. The hospital was like a barn, and other things were like other things, but we went all about and enjoyed it very much. The lady was quite amusing, besides sometimes talking like a real cathedral guide I met afterwards. (*See* Note B.) When at last we said we thought Canterbury was very small considering, the lady said:

'Well, it seemed a pity to come so far and not at least *hear* something about Canterbury.'

And then at once we knew the worst, and Alice said:

'What a horrid sell!'

But Oswald, with immediate courteousness, said:

'I don't care. You did it awfully well.'

And he did not say, though he owns he thought of it:

'I knew it all the time,' though it was a great temptation. Because really it was more than half true. He had felt from the first that this was too small for Canterbury. (*See* Note C.)

The real name of the place was Hazelbridge, and not Canterbury at all. We went to Canterbury another time. (*See* Note D.)

We were not angry with the lady for selling us about it being Canterbury, because she had really kept it up first-rate. And she asked us if we minded, very handsomely, and we said we liked it. But now we did not care how soon we got home. The lady saw this, and said:

'Come, our chariots are ready, and our horses caparisoned.'

That is a first-rate word out of a book. It cheered Oswald up, and he liked her for using it, though he wondered why she said chariots. When we got back to the inn I saw her dog-cart was there, and a grocer's cart too, with B. Munn, grocer, Hazelbridge, on it. She took the girls in her cart, and the boys went with the grocer. His horse was a very good one to go, only you had to hit it with the wrong end of the whip. But the cart was very bumpety.

The evening dews were falling – at least, I suppose so, but you do not feel dew in a grocer's cart – when we reached home. We all thanked the lady very much, and said we hoped we should see her again some day. She said she hoped so.

The grocer drove off, and when we had all shaken hands with the lady and kissed her, according as we were boys or girls, or little boys, she touched up her horse and drove away.

She turned at the corner to wave to us, and just as we had done waving, and were turning into the house, Albert's uncle came into our midst like a whirling wind. He was in flannels, and his shirt had no stud in at the neck, and his hair was all rumpled up and his hands were inky, and we knew he had left off in the middle of a chapter by the wildness of his eye.

'Who was that lady?' he said. 'Where did you meet her?'

Mindful, as ever, of what he was told, Oswald began to tell the story from the beginning.

'The other day, protector of the poor,' he began, 'Dora and I were reading about the Canterbury pilgrims – '[20]

Oswald thought Albert's uncle would be pleased to find his instructions about beginning at the beginning had borne fruit, but instead he interrupted.

'Stow it, you young duffer! Where did you meet her?'

Oswald answered briefly, in wounded accents, 'Hazelbridge.'

Then Albert's uncle rushed up-stairs three at a time, and as he went he called out to Oswald:

'Get out my bike, old man, and blow up the back tyre.'

I am sure Oswald was as quick as any one could have been, but long ere the tyre was thoroughly blowed Albert's uncle appeared, with a collar-stud and tie and blazer, and his hair tidy, and wrenched the unoffending machine from Oswald's surprised fingers.

Albert's uncle finished pumping up the tyre, and then, flinging himself into the saddle, he set off, scorching down the road at a pace not surpassed by any highwayman, however black and high-mettled his steed.

We were left looking at each other.

'He must have recognized her,' Dicky said.

'Perhaps,' Noël said, 'she is the old nurse who alone knows the dark secret of his high-born birth.'

'Not old enough, by chalks,' Oswald said.

'I shouldn't wonder,' said Alice, 'if she holds the secret of the will that will make him rolling in long-lost wealth.'[21]

'I wonder if he'll catch her,' Noël said. 'I'm quite certain all his future depends on it. Perhaps she's his long-lost sister, and the estate was left to them equally, only she couldn't be found, so it couldn't be shared up.'

'Perhaps he's only in love with her,' Dora said; 'parted by cruel fate at an early age, he has ranged the wide world ever since trying to find her.'

'I hope to goodness he hasn't – anyway, he's not ranged since we knew him – never further than Hastings,' Oswald said. 'We don't want any of that rot.'

'What rot?' Daisy asked. And Oswald said:

'Getting married, and all that sort of rubbish.'

And Daisy and Dora were the only ones that didn't agree with him.[22] Even Alice owned that being bridesmaids must be fairly good fun. It's no good. You may treat girls as well as you like, and give them every comfort and luxury, and play fair just as if they were boys, but there is something unmanly about the best of girls. They go silly, like milk goes sour, without any warning.

When Albert's uncle returned he was very hot, with a beaded brow, but pale as the Dentist when the peas were at their worst.

'Did you catch her?' H.O. asked.

Albert's uncle's brow looked black as the cloud the thunder will presently break from.

'No,' he said.

'Is she your long-lost nurse?' H.O. went on, before we could stop him.

'Long-lost grandmother! I knew the lady long ago in India,' said Albert's uncle, as he left the room, slamming the door in a way we should be forbidden to.

And that was the end of the Canterbury Pilgrimage.

As for the lady, we did not then know whether she was his long-lost grandmother that he had known in India or not, though we thought she seemed youngish for the part. We found out afterwards whether she was or not, but that comes in another tale. His manner was not the one that makes you go on asking questions.

The Canterbury Pilgriming did not exactly make us good, but then, as Dora said, we had not done anything wrong that day. So we were twenty-four hours to the good.

Note A. – Afterwards we went and saw real Canterbury. It is very large. A disagreeable man showed us round the cathedral, and jawed all the time quite loud as if it wasn't a church. I remember one thing he said. It was this:

'This is the Dean's Chapel; it was the Lady Chapel in the wicked days when people used to worship the Virgin Mary.'

And H.O. said, 'I suppose they worship the Dean now?'

Some strange people who were there laughed out loud. I think this is worse in church than not taking your cap off when you come in, as H.O. forgot to do, because the cathedral was so big he didn't think it was a church.

> *Note B.* (*See* Note C.)
> *Note C.* (*See* Note D.)
> *Note D.* (*See* Note E.)
> *Note E.* (*See* Note A.)

This ends the Canterbury Pilgrims.

* * *

Chapter 13
The Dragon's Teeth; or, Army-seed

Albert's uncle was out on his bicycle as usual. After the day when we became Canterbury Pilgrims and were brought home in the dog-cart with red wheels by the lady he told us was his long-lost grandmother he had known years ago in India, he spent not nearly so much of his time in writing, and he used to shave every morning instead of only when requisite, as in earlier days. And he was always going out on his bicycle in his new Norfolk suit. We are not so unobserving as grown-up people make out. We knew well enough he was looking for the long-lost. And we jolly well wished he might find her. Oswald, always full of sympathy with misfortune, however undeserved, had himself tried several times to find the lady. So had the others. But all this is what they call a digression; it has nothing to do with the dragon's teeth I am now narrating.

It began with the pig dying – it was the one we had for the circus, but it having behaved so badly that day had nothing to do with its illness and death, though the girls said they felt remorse, and perhaps if we hadn't made it run so that day it might have been spared to us. But Oswald cannot pretend that people were right just because they happen to be dead, and as long as that pig was alive we all knew well enough that it was it that made us run – and not us it.

The pig was buried in the kitchen garden. Bill, that we made the tombstone for, dug the grave, and while he was away at his dinner we took a turn at digging, because we like to be useful, and besides, when you dig you never know what you may turn up.[1] I knew a man once that found a gold ring on the point of his fork when he was digging potatoes, and you know how we found two half-crowns ourselves once when we were digging for treasure.

Oswald was taking his turn with the spade, and the others were sitting on the gravel and telling him how to do it.

'Work with a will,' Dicky said, yawning.

Alice said: 'I wish we were in a book. People in books never dig without finding something. I think I'd rather it was a secret passage than anything.'

Oswald stopped to wipe his honest brow ere replying.

'A secret's nothing when you've found it out. Look at the secret staircase. It's no good, not even for hide-and-seek, because of its squeaking. I'd rather have the pot of gold we used to dig for when we were little.' It was really only last year, but you seem to grow old very quickly after you have once passed the prime of your youth, which is at ten, I believe.

'How would you like to find the mouldering bones of Royalist soldiers foully done to death by nasty Ironsides?' Noël asked, with his mouth full of plum.

'If they were really dead it wouldn't matter,' Dora said. 'What I'm afraid of is a skeleton that can walk about and catch at your legs when you're going up-stairs to bed.'

'Skeletons can't walk,' Alice said in a hurry; 'you know they can't, Dora.'

And she glared at Dora till she made her sorry she had said what she had. The things you are frightened of, or even those you would rather not meet in the dark, should never be mentioned before the little ones, or else they cry when it comes to bedtime, and say it was because of what you said.

'We sha'n't find anything. No jolly fear,' said Dicky.

And just then my spade I was digging with struck on something hard, and it felt hollow. I did really think for one joyful space that we had found that pot of gold. But the thing, whatever it was, seemed to be longish; longer, that is, than a pot of gold would naturally be. And as I uncovered it I saw that it was not at all pot-of-gold-colour, but like a bone Pincher has buried. So Oswald said:

'It *is* the skeleton.'

The girls all drew back, and Alice said, 'Oswald, I wish you wouldn't.'

A moment later the discovery was unearthed, and Oswald lifted it up with both hands.

'It's a dragon's head,' Noël said, and it certainly looked like it. It was long and narrowish and bony, and with great yellow teeth sticking in the jaw.

Bill came back just then and said it was a horse's head, but H.O. and Noël would not believe it, and Oswald owns that no horse he has ever seen had a head at all that shape.

But Oswald did not stop to argue, because he saw a keeper who showed me how to set snares going by, and he wanted to talk to him about ferrets, so he went off, and Dicky and Denny and Alice with him. Also Daisy and Dora went off to finish reading *Ministering Children*.[2] So H.O. and Noël were left with the bony head. They took it away.

The incident had quite faded from the mind of Oswald next day. But just before breakfast Noël and H.O. came in, looking hot and anxious. They had got up early and had not washed at all – not even their hands and faces. Noël made Oswald a secret signal. All the others saw it, and with proper delicate feeling pretended not to have.

When Oswald had gone out with Noël and H.O., in obedience to the secret signal, Noël said:

'You know that dragon's head yesterday?'

'Well?' Oswald said, quickly, but not crossly – the two things are quite different.

'Well, you know what happened in Greek history when some chap sowed dragon's teeth?'[3]

'They came up armed men,' said H.O.; but Noël sternly bade him shut up, and Oswald said 'Well,' again. If he spoke impatiently it was because he smelled the bacon being taken in to breakfast.

'Well,' Noël went on, 'what do you suppose would have come up if we'd sowed those dragon's teeth we found yesterday?'

'Why, nothing, you young duffer,' said Oswald, who could now smell the coffee. 'All that isn't History – it's Humbug. Come on in to brekker.'

'It's *not* humbug,' H.O. cried, 'it *is* history. We *did* sow – '

'Shut up,' said Noël again. 'Look here, Oswald. We did sow those dragon's teeth in Randall's ten-acre meadow, and what do you think has come up?'

'Toadstools, I should think,' was Oswald's contemptible rejoinder.

'They have come up a camp of soldiers,' said Noël – *'armed men.* So you see it *was* history. We have sowed army-seed, just like Cadmus, and it has come up. It was a very wet night. I daresay that helped it along.'

Oswald could not decide which to disbelieve – his brother or his ears. So, disguising his doubtful emotions without a word, he led the way to the bacon and the banqueting hall.

He said nothing about the army-seed then, neither did Noël and H.O. But after the bacon we went into the garden, and then the good elder brother said:

'Why don't you tell the others your cock-and-bull story?'

So they did, and their story was received with warm expressions of doubt. It was Dicky who observed:

'Let's go and have a squint at Randall's ten-acre, anyhow. I saw a hare there the other day.'

We went. It is some little way, and as we went disbelief reigned superb in every breast except Noël's and H.O.'s, so you will see that even the ready pen of the present author cannot be expected to describe to you his variable sensations when he got to the top of the hill and suddenly saw that his little brothers had spoken the truth. I do not mean that they generally tell lies, but people make mistakes sometimes, and the effect is the same as lies if you believe them.

There *was* a camp there with real tents and soldiers in grey and red tunics. I daresay the girls would have said coats. We stood in ambush, too astonished even to think of lying in it, though of course we know that this is customary. The ambush was the wood on top of the little hill, between Randall's ten-acre meadow and Sugden's Waste Wake pasture.

'There would be cover here for a couple of regiments,' whispered Oswald, who was, I think, gifted by Fate with the far-seeingness of a born general.

Alice merely said 'Hist,' and we went down to mingle with the troops as though by accident, and seek for information.

The first man we came to at the edge of the camp was cleaning a sort of cauldron thing like witches brew bats in.

We went up to him and said, 'Who are you? Are you English, or are you the enemy?'

'We're the enemy,' he said, and he did not seem ashamed of being what he was. And he spoke English with quite a good accent for a foreigner.

'The enemy!' Oswald echoed in shocked tones. It is a terrible thing to a loyal and patriotic youth to see an enemy cleaning a pot in an English field, with English sand, and looking as much at home as if he was in his foreign fastnesses.

The enemy seemed to read Oswald's thoughts with deadly unerringness. He said:

'The English are somewhere over on the other side of the hill. They are trying to keep us out of Maidstone.'

After this our plan of mingling with the troops did not seem worth going on with. This soldier, in spite of his unerringness in reading Oswald's inmost heart, seemed not so very sharp in other things, or he would never have given away his secret plans like this, for he must have known from our accents that we were Britons to the backbone. Or perhaps (Oswald thought this, and it made his blood at once boil and freeze, which our uncle had told us was possible, but only in India), perhaps he thought that Maidstone was already as good as taken and it didn't matter what he said. While Oswald was debating within his intellect what to say next, and how to say it so as to discover as many as possible of the enemy's dark secrets, Noël said:

'How did you get here? You weren't here yesterday at tea-time.'

The soldier gave the pot another sandy rub, and said:

'I dare say it does seem quick work – the camp seems as if it had sprung up in the night, doesn't it? – like a mushroom.'

Alice and Oswald looked at each other, and then at the rest of us. The words '*sprung up in the night*' seemed to touch a string in every heart.

'You see,' whispered Noël, 'he won't tell us how he came here. *Now*, is it humbug or history?'

Oswald, after whisperedly requesting his young brother to dry up and not bother, remarked:

'Then you're an invading army?'

'Well,' said the soldier, 'we're a skeleton battalion, as a matter of fact, but we're invading all right enough.'

And now indeed the blood of the stupidest of us froze, just as the quick-witted Oswald's had done earlier in the interview. Even H.O. opened his mouth and went the colour of mottled soap; he is so fat that this is the nearest he can go to turning pale.[4]

Denny said, 'But you don't look like skeletons.'

The soldier stared, then he laughed and said: 'Ah, that's the padding in our tunics. You should see us in the grey dawn taking our morning bath in a bucket.'

It was a dreadful picture for the imagination. A skeleton, with its bones all loose most likely, bathing anyhow in a pail. There was a silence while we thought it over.

Now, ever since the cleaning-cauldron soldier had said that about taking Maidstone, Alice had kept on pulling at Oswald's jacket behind, and he had kept on not taking any notice. But now he could not stand it any longer, so he said, 'Well, what is it?'

Alice drew him aside, or rather, she pulled at his jacket so that he nearly fell over backwards, and then she whispered, 'Come along, don't stay parlaying with the foe. He's only talking to you to gain time.'

'What for?' said Oswald.

'Why, so that we shouldn't warn the other army, you silly,' Alice said, and Oswald was so upset by what she said that he forgot to be properly angry with her for the wrong word she used.

'But we ought to warn them at home,' she said; 'suppose the Moat House was burned down, and all the supplies commandeered for the foe?'[5]

Alice turned boldly to the soldier. '*Do* you burn down farms?' she asked.

'Well, not as a rule,' he said, and he had the cheek to wink at Oswald, but Oswald would not look at him. 'We've not burned a farm since – oh, not for years.'

'A farm in Greek history it was, I expect,' Denny murmured.

'Civilized warriors do not burn farms nowadays,' Alice said, sternly, 'whatever they did in Greek times. You ought to know that.'[6]

The soldier said things had changed a good deal since Greek times. So we said good-morning as quickly as we could: it is proper to be polite even to your enemy, except just at the moments when it has really come to rifles and bayonets or other weapons.

The soldier said 'So long!' in quite a modern voice, and we retraced our footsteps in silence to the ambush – I mean the wood. Oswald did think of lying in the ambush then, but it was rather wet, because of the rain the night before, that H.O. said had brought the army-seed up. And Alice walked very fast, saying nothing but 'Hurry up, can't you!' and dragging H.O. by one hand and Noël by the other. So we got into the road.

Then Alice faced round and said, 'This is all our fault. If we hadn't sowed those dragon's teeth there wouldn't have been any invading army.'

I am sorry to say Daisy said, 'Never mind, Alice, dear. *We* didn't sow the nasty things, did we, Dora?'

But Denny told her it was just the same. It was *we* had done it, so long as it was any of us, especially if it got any of us into trouble.[7] Oswald was very pleased to see that the Dentist was beginning to understand the meaning of true manliness, and about the honour of the house of Bastable, though of course he is only a Foulkes. Yet it is something to know he does his best to learn.

If you are very grown-up, or very clever, I dare say you will now have thought of a great many things. If you have you need not say anything, especially if you're reading this aloud to anybody. It's no good putting in what you think in this part, because none of us thought anything of the kind at the time.

We simply stood in the road without any of your clever thoughts, filled with shame and distress to think of what might happen owing to the dragon's teeth being sown. It was a lesson to us never to sow seed without being quite sure what sort it is. This is particularly true of the penny packets, which sometimes do not come up at all, quite unlike dragon's teeth.

Of course H.O. and Noël were more unhappy than the rest of us. This was only fair.

'How can we possibly prevent their getting to Maidstone?' Dicky said.[8] 'Did you notice the red cuffs on their uniforms? Taken from the bodies of dead English soldiers, I shouldn't wonder.'

'If they're the old Greek kind of dragon's-teeth soldiers, they ought to fight each other to death,' Noël said; 'at least, if we had a helmet to throw among them.'

But none of us had, and it was decided that it would be of no use for H.O. to go back and throw his straw hat at them, though he wanted to.

Denny said suddenly:

'Couldn't we alter the sign-posts, so that they wouldn't know the way to Maidstone?'

Oswald saw that this was the time for true generalship to be shown. He said:

'Fetch all the tools out of your chest – Dicky go too, there's a good chap, and don't let him cut his legs with the saw.' He did once, tumbling over it. 'Meet us at the cross-roads, you know, where we had the Benevolent Bar. Courage and dispatch, and look sharp about it.'

When they had gone we hastened to the cross-roads, and there a great idea occurred to Oswald. He used the forces at his command so ably that in a very short time the board in the field which says 'No thoroughfare. Trespassers will be prosecuted' was set up in the middle of the road to Maidstone. We put stones, from a heap by the road, behind it to make it stand up.

Then Dicky and Denny came back, and Dicky shinned up the sign-post and sawed off the two arms, and we nailed them up wrong, so that it said 'To Maidstone' on the Dover Road, and 'To Dover' on the road to Maidstone. We decided to leave the Trespassers board on the real Maidstone road, as an extra guard.

Then we settled to start at once to warn Maidstone.

Some of us did not want the girls to go, but it would have been unkind to say so. However, there was at least one breast that felt a pang of joy when Dora and Daisy gave out that they would rather stay where they were and tell anybody who came by which was the real road.

'Because it would be so dreadful if some one was going to buy pigs or fetch a doctor or anything in a hurry and then found they had got to Dover instead of where they wanted to go to,' Dora said. But when it came to dinner-time they went home, so that they were entirely out of it. This often happens to them by some strange fatalism.[9]

We left Martha to take care of the two girls, and Lady and Pincher went with us. It was getting late in the day, but I am bound to remember no one said anything about their dinners, whatever they may have thought. We cannot always help our thoughts. We happened to know it was roast rabbits and currant jelly that day.

We walked two and two, and sang the 'British Grenadiers' and 'Soldiers of the Queen' so as to be as much part of the British Army as possible. The Cauldron-Man had said the English were the other side of the hill. But we could not see any scarlet any-where, though we looked for it as carefully as if we had been fierce bulls.

But suddenly we went round a turn in the road and came plump into a lot of soldiers. Only they were not red-coats. They were dressed in grey and silver. And it was a sort of furzy-common place, and three roads branching out. The men were lying about, with some of their belts undone, smoking pipes and cigarettes.

'It's not British soldiers,' Alice said. 'Oh, dear, oh, dear, I'm afraid it's more enemy. You didn't sow the army-seed anywhere else, did you, H.O., dear?'

H.O. was positive he hadn't. 'But perhaps lots more came up where we did sow them,' he said; 'they're all over England by now, very likely. *I* don't know how many men can grow out of one dragon's tooth.'

Then Noël said, 'It was my doing, anyhow, and I'm not afraid,' and he walked straight up to the nearest soldier, who was cleaning his pipe with a piece of grass, and said:

'Please, are you the enemy?' The man said:

'No, young commander-in-chief, we're the English.'

Then Oswald took command.

'Where is the General?' he said.

'We're out of generals just now, field-marshal,' the man said, and his voice was a gentleman's voice. 'Not a single one in stock. We might suit you in majors now – and captains are quite cheap. Competent corporals going for a song.[10] And we have a very nice colonel, too – quiet to ride or drive.'

Oswald does not mind chaff at proper times. But this was not one.

'You seem to be taking it very easy,' he said with disdainful expression.

'This *is* an easy,' said the grey soldier, sucking at his pipe to see if it would draw.

'I suppose *you* don't care if the enemy gets into Maidstone or not!' exclaimed Oswald bitterly. 'If I were a soldier I'd rather die than be beaten.'

The soldier saluted. 'Good old patriotic sentiment,' he said, smiling at the heartfelt boy. But Oswald could bear no more.

'Which is the Colonel?' he asked.

'Over there – near the grey horse.'

'The one lighting a cigarette?' H.O. asked.

'Yes – but I say, kiddie, he won't stand any jaw. There's not an ounce of vice about him, but he's peppery.[11] He might kick out. You'd better bunk.'

'Better what?' asked H.O.

'Bunk, bottle, scoot, skip, vanish, exit,' said the soldier.

'That's what you'd do when the fighting begins,' said H.O. He is often rude like that – but it was what we all thought, all the same. The soldier only laughed.

A spirited but hasty altercation among ourselves in whispers ended in our allowing Alice to be the one to speak to the Colonel. It was she who wanted to. 'However peppery he is he won't kick a girl,' she said, and perhaps this was true.

But of course we all went with her. So there were six of us to stand in front of the Colonel. And as we went along we agreed that we would salute him on the word three. So when we got near, Dick said, 'One, two, three,' and we all saluted very well – except H.O., who chose that minute to trip over a rifle a soldier had left lying about, and was only saved from falling by a man in a cocked hat who caught him deftly by the back of his jacket and stood him up on his legs.

'Let go, can't you,' said H.O. 'Are you the general?'

Before the Cocked Hat had time to frame a reply, Alice spoke to the Colonel. I knew what she meant to say, because she had told me as we threaded our way among the resting soldiery. What she really said was:

'Oh, how *can* you!'

'How can I *what*?' said the Colonel, rather crossly.

'Why, *smoke*?' said Alice.

'My good children, if you're an infant Band of Hope, let me recommend you to play in some other back yard,' said the Cocked-Hatted Man.[12]

H.O. said, 'Band of Hope yourself' – but no one noticed it.[13]

'We're *not* a Band of Hope,' said Noël. 'We're British, and the man over there told us you are. And Maidstone's in danger, and the enemy not a mile off, and you stand *smoking*.' Noël was standing crying, himself, or something very like it.

'It's quite true,' Alice said.

The Colonel said, 'Fiddle de dee.'

But the Cocked-Hatted Man said, 'What was the enemy like?'

We told him exactly. And even the Colonel then owned there might be something in it.

'Can you show me the place where they are on the map?' he asked.

'Not on the map, we can't,' said Dicky; 'at least, I don't think so, but on the ground we could. We could take you there in a quarter of an hour.'

The Cocked-Hatted One looked at the Colonel, who returned his scrutiny; then he shrugged his shoulders.

'Well, we've got to do something,' he said, as if to himself. 'Lead on, Macduff!'[14]

The Colonel roused his soldiery from their stupor of pipes by words of command which the present author is sorry he can't remember.

Then he bade us boys lead the way. I tell you it felt fine, marching at the head of a regiment. Alice got a lift on the Cocked-Hatted One's horse. It was a red-roan steed of might, exactly as if it had been in a ballad. They call a grey-roan a 'blue' in South Africa, the Cocked-Hatted One said.

We led the British army by unfrequented lanes till we got to the gate of Sugden's Waste Wake pasture. Then the Colonel called a whispered halt, and choosing two of us to guide him, the daunt-less and discerning commander went on, on foot, with an orderly. He chose Dicky and Oswald as guides.[15] So we led him to the ambush, and we went through it as quietly as we could. But twigs do crackle and snap so when you are reconnoitring, or anxious to escape detection for whatever reason.

Our Colonel's orderly crackled most. If you're not near enough to tell a colonel by the crown and stars on his shoulder-strap, you can tell him by the orderly behind him, like 'follow my leader.'

'Look out!' said Oswald in a low but commanding whisper, 'the camp's down in that field. You can see if you take a squint through this gap.'

The speaker took a squint himself as he spoke, and drew back, baffled beyond the power of speech. While he was struggling with his baffledness the British Colonel had his squint. He also drew back, and said a word that he must have known was not right – at least when he was a boy.

'I don't care,' said Oswald, 'they were there this morning. White tents like mushrooms, and an enemy cleaning a cauldron.'

'With sand,' said Dicky.

'That's most convincing,' said the Colonel, and I did not like the way he said it.

'I say,' Oswald said, 'let's get to the top corner of the ambush – the wood, I mean. You can see the cross-roads from there.'

We did, and quickly, for the crackling of branches no longer dismayed our almost despairing spirits.

We came to the edge of the wood, and Oswald's patriotic heart really did give a jump, and he cried, 'There they are, on the Dover Road.'

Our miscellaneous sign-board had done its work.

'By Jove, young un, you're right! And in quarter column, too! We've got 'em on toast – on toast – egad!'

I never heard any one not in a book say 'egad' before, so I saw something really out of the way was indeed up.

The Colonel was a man of prompt and decisive action. He sent the orderly to tell the Major to advance two companies on the left flank and take cover. Then we led him back through the wood the nearest way, because he said he must rejoin the main body at once. We found the main body very friendly with Noël and H.O.

and the others, and Alice was talking to the Cocked-Hatted One as if she had known him all her life.[16] 'I think he's a general in disguise,' Noël said. 'He's been giving us chocolate out of a pocket in his saddle.' Oswald thought about the roast rabbit then – and he is not ashamed to own it – yet he did not say a word. But Alice is really not a bad sort. She had saved two bars of chocolate for him and Dicky. Even in war girls can sometimes be useful in their humble way.

The Colonel fussed about and said, 'Take cover there!' and everybody hid in the ditch, and the horses and the Cocked Hat, with Alice, retreated down the road out of sight. We were in the ditch too. It was muddy – but nobody thought of their boots in that perilous moment. It seemed a long time we were crouching there. Oswald began to feel the water squelching in his boots; so we held our breath and listened.[17] Oswald laid his ear to the road like a Red Indian. You would not do this in time of peace, but when your country is in danger you care but little about keeping your ears clean. His backwoods strategy was successful. He rose and dusted himself and said:

'They're coming!'

It was true. The footsteps of the approaching foe were now to be heard quite audibly, even by ears in their natural position. The wicked enemy approached. They were marching with a careless swaggeringness that showed how little they suspected the horrible doom which was about to teach them England's might and supremeness. Just as the enemy turned the corner so that we could see them, the Colonel shouted:

'Right section, fire!' and there was a deafening banging.

The enemy's officer said something, and then the enemy got confused and tried to get into the fields through the hedges. But all was vain. There was firing now from our men, on the left as well as the right. And then our Colonel strode nobly up to the enemy's Colonel and demanded surrender. He told me so afterwards. His exact words are only known to himself and the other Colonel. But the enemy's Colonel said, 'I would rather die than surrender,' or words to that effect.

Our Colonel returned to his men and gave the order to fix bayonets, and even Oswald felt his manly cheek turn pale at the thought of the amount of blood about to be shed. What would have happened can never now be revealed. For at this moment a man on a piebald horse came clattering over a hedge – as carelessly as if the air was not full of lead and steel at all. Another man rode behind him with a lance and a red pennon on it. I think he must have been the enemy's General coming to tell his men not to throw away their lives on a forlorn hope, for directly he said they were captured the enemy gave in and owned that they were. The enemy's Colonel saluted and ordered his men to form quarter column again. I should have thought he would have had about enough of that myself.

He had now given up all thought of sullen resistance to the bitter end. He rolled a cigarette for himself, and had the foreign cheek to say to our Colonel:

'By Jove, old man, you got me clean that time! Your scouts seem to have marked us down uncommonly neatly.'

It was a proud moment when our Colonel laid his military hand on Oswald's shoulder and said:

'This is my chief scout,' which were high words, but not undeserved, and Oswald owns he felt red with gratifying pride when he heard them.

'So you are the traitor, young man,' said the wicked Colonel, going on with his cheek.

Oswald bore it because our Colonel had, and you should be generous to a fallen foe, but it is hard to be called a traitor when you haven't.

He did not treat the wicked Colonel with silent scorn as he might have done, but he said:

'We aren't traitors. We are the Bastables and one of us is a Foulkes. We only mingled unsuspected with the enemy's soldiery and learned the secret of their acts, which is what Baden-Powell always does when the natives rebel in South Africa; and Denis Foulkes thought of altering the sign-posts to lead the foe astray.[18] And if we did cause all this fighting, and get Maidstone threatened with capture and all that, it was only because we didn't believe Greek things could happen in Great Britain and Ireland, even if you sow dragon's teeth, and besides, some of us were not asked about sowing them.'

Then the Cocked-Hatted One led his horse and walked with us and made us tell him all about it, and so did the Colonel. The wicked Colonel listened too, which was only another proof of his cheek.

And Oswald told the tale in the modest yet manly way that some people think he has, and gave the others all the credit they deserved.[19] His narration was interrupted no less than four times by shouts of 'Bravo!' in which the enemy's Colonel once more showed his cheek by joining. By the time the story was told we were in sight of another camp. It was the British one this time. The Colonel asked us to have tea in his tent, and it only shows the magnanimosity of English chivalry in the field of battle that he asked the enemy's Colonel too. With his usual cheek he accepted. We were jolly hungry.

When everyone had had as much tea as they possibly could, the Colonel shook hands with us all, and to Oswald he said:

'Well, good-bye, my brave scout. I must mention your name in my despatches to the War Office.'

H.O. interrupted him to say, 'His name's Oswald Cecil Bastable, and mine is Horace Octavius.' I wish H.O. would learn to hold his tongue. No one ever knows Oswald was christened Cecil as well, if he can possibly help it. *You* didn't know it till now.

'Mr Oswald Bastable,' the Colonel went on – he had the decency not to take any notice of the 'Cecil' – 'you would be a credit to any regiment. No doubt the War Office will reward you properly for what you have done for your country. But meantime, perhaps, you'll accept five shillings from a grateful comrade-in-arms.' Oswald felt heart-feltly sorry to wound the good Colonel's feelings, but he had to remark that he had only done his duty, and he was sure no British scout would take five bob for doing that. 'And besides,' he said, with that feeling of justice which is part of his young character, 'it was the others just as much as me.'

'Your sentiments, sir,' said the Colonel, who was one of the politest and most discerning colonels I ever saw, 'your sentiments do you honour. But, Bastables all, and – and non-Bastables' (he couldn't remember Foulkes; it's not such an interesting name as Bastable, of course) – 'at least you'll accept a soldier's pay?'

'Lucky to touch it, a shilling a day!' Alice and Denny said together.[20] And the Cocked-Hatted Man said something about knowing your own mind and knowing your own Kipling.

'A soldier,' said the Colonel, 'would certainly be lucky to touch it. You see there are deductions for rations. Five shillings is exactly right, deducting twopence each for six teas.'

This seemed cheap for the three cups of tea and the three eggs and all the strawberry-jam and bread-and-butter Oswald had had, as well as what the others ate, and Lady's and Pincher's teas, but I suppose soldiers get things cheaper than civilians, which is only right.[21]

Oswald took the five shillings then, there being no longer any scruples why he should not.

Just as we had parted from the brave Colonel and the rest we saw a bicycle coming. It was Albert's uncle. He got off and said:

'What on earth have you been up to? What were you doing with those volunteers?'

We told him the wild adventures of the day, and he listened, and then he said he would withdraw the word volunteers if we liked.

But the seeds of doubt were sown in the breast of Oswald. He was now almost sure that we had made jolly fools of ourselves without a moment's pause throughout the whole of this eventful day. He said nothing at the time, but after supper he had it out with Albert's uncle about the word which had been withdrawn.

Albert's uncle said, of course, no one could be sure that the dragon's teeth hadn't come up in the good old-fashioned way, but that, on the other hand, it was barely possible that both the British and the enemy were only volunteers having a field-day or sham fight, and he rather thought the Cocked-Hatted Man was not a general, but a doctor. And the man with a red pennon carried behind him *might* have been the umpire.

Oswald never told the others a word of this. Their young breasts were all panting with joy because they had saved their country; and it would have been but heartless unkindness to show them how silly they had been. Besides, Oswald felt he was much too old to have been so taken in – if he *had* been. Besides, Albert's uncle did say that no one could be sure about the dragon's teeth.

The thing that makes Oswald feel most that, perhaps, the whole thing was a beastly sell is that we didn't see any wounded. But he tries not to think of this. And if he goes into the army when he grows up, he will not go quite green. He has had experience of the arts of war and the tented field. And a real colonel has called him 'Comrade-in-Arms,' which is exactly what Lord Roberts called his own soldiers when he wrote home about them.[22]

∗   ∗   ∗

Chapter 14
Albert's Uncle's Grandmother; or, the Long-lost[1]

The shadow of the termination now descended in sable thunder-clouds upon our devoted nobs. As Albert's uncle said, 'School now gaped for its prey.' In a very short space of time we should be wending our way back to Blackheath, and all the variegated delightfulness of the country would soon be only preserved in memory's faded flowers. (I don't care for that way of writing very much. It would be an awful swot to keep it up – looking out the words and all that.)

To speak in the language of every-day life, our holiday was jolly nearly up. We had had a ripping time, but it was all but over. We really did feel sorry – though, of course, it was rather decent to think of getting back to father and being able to tell the other chaps about our raft, and the dam, and the Tower of Mystery, and things like that.

When but a brief time was left to us, Oswald and Dicky met by chance in an apple-tree. (That sounds like 'consequences,' but it is mere truthfulness.[2]) Dicky said:

'Only four more days.' Oswald said, 'Yes.'

'There's one thing,' Dicky said, 'that beastly society. We don't want that smarming all over everything when we get home. We ought to dissolve it before we leave here.'

The following dialogue now took place:

Oswald – 'Right you are. I always said it was piffling rot.'

Dicky – 'So did I.'

Oswald – 'Let's call a council. But don't forget we've jolly well got to put our foot down.'

Dicky assented, and the dialogue concluded with apples.

The council, when called, was in but low spirits. This made Oswald's and Dicky's task easier. When people are sunk in gloomy despair about one thing, they will agree to almost anything about something else. (Remarks like this are called philosophic generalizations, Albert's uncle says.) Oswald began by saying:

'We've tried the society for being good in, and perhaps it's done us good. But now the time has come for each of us to be good or bad on his own, without hanging on to the others.'

> 'The race is run by one and one,
>   But never by two and two,'

the Dentist said.[3] The others said nothing. Oswald went on: 'I move that we chuck – I mean dissolve – the Wouldbegoods Society; its appointed task is done. If it's not well done, that's *its* fault and not ours.'

Dicky said, 'Hear! hear! I second this prop.'

The unexpected Dentist said, 'I third it. At first I thought it would help, but afterwards I saw it only made you want to be naughty, just because you were a Wouldbegood.'

Oswald owns he was surprised. We put it to the vote at once, so as not to let Denny cool. H.O. and Noël and Alice voted with us, so Daisy and Dora were what is called a hopeless minority. We tried to cheer their hopelessness by letting them read the things out of the Golden Deed book aloud. Noël hid his face in the straw so that we should not see the faces he made while he made poetry instead of listening, and when the Wouldbegoods was by vote dissolved forever he sat up, with straws in his hair, and said:

> 'THE EPITAPH
> 'The Wouldbegoods are dead and gone,
> But not the golden deeds they have done.
> These will remain upon Glory's page
> To be an example to every age,
> And by this we have got to know
> How to be good upon our ow – N.

'N is for Noël, that makes the rhyme and the sense both right. O, W, N, own; do you see?'

We saw it, and said so, and the gentle poet was satisfied. And the council broke up. Oswald felt that a weight had been lifted from his expanding chest, and it is curious that he never felt so inclined to be good and a model youth as he did then.

As he went down the ladder out of the loft he said:

'There's one thing we ought to do, though, before we go home. We ought to find Albert's uncle's long-lost grandmother for him.'

Alice's heart beat true and steadfast. She said: 'That's just exactly what Noël and I were saying this morning. Look out, Oswald, you wretch, you're kicking chaff into my eyes.' She was going down the ladder just under me.

Oswald's young sister's thoughtful remark ended in another council. But not in the straw loft. We decided to have a quite new place, and disregarded H.O.'s idea of the dairy and Noël's of the cellars. We had the new council on the secret staircase, and there we settled exactly what we ought to do. This is the same thing, if you really wish to be good, as what you are going to do. It was a very interesting council, and when it was over Oswald was so pleased to think that the Wouldbegoods was unrecoverishly dead that he gave Denny and Noël, who were sitting on the step below him, a good-humoured, playful, gentle, loving, brotherly shove, and said, 'Get along down, it's tea-time!'

No reader who understands justice and the real rightness of things, and who is to blame for what, will ever think it could have been Oswald's fault that the two other boys got along down by rolling over and over each other, and bursting the door at the bottom of the stairs open by their revolving bodies. And I should like to know whose fault it was that Mrs Pettigrew was just on the other side of that door at that very minute? The door burst open, and the impetuous bodies of Noël and Denny rolled out of it into Mrs Pettigrew, and upset her and the tea-tray. Both revolving boys were soaked with tea and milk, and there were one or two cups and things smashed. Mrs Pettigrew was knocked over, but none of her bones were broken. Noël and Denny were going to be sent to bed, but Oswald said it was all his fault. He really did this to give the others a chance of doing a refined, golden deed by speaking the truth and saying it was *not* his fault. But you cannot really count on any one. They did not say anything, but only rubbed the lumps on their late-revolving heads. So it was bed for Oswald, and he felt the injustice hard.

But he sat up in bed and read *The Last of the Mohicans,* and then he began to think.[4] When Oswald really thinks he almost always thinks of something. He thought of something now, and it was miles better than the idea we had decided on in the secret staircase, of advertising in the *Kentish Mercury* and saying if Albert's uncle's long-lost grandmother would call at the Moat House she might hear of something much to her advantage.[5]

What Oswald thought of was that if we went to Hazelbridge and asked Mr B. Munn, grocer, that drove us home in the cart with the horse that liked the wrong end of the whip best, he would know who the lady was in the red hat and red wheels that paid him to drive us home that Canterbury night. He must have been paid, of course, for even grocers are not generous enough to drive perfect strangers, and five of them too, about the country for nothing.

Thus we may learn that even unjustness and sending the wrong people to bed may bear useful fruit, which ought to be a great comfort to every one when they are unfairly treated. Only it most likely won't be. For if Oswald's brothers and sisters had nobly stood by him, as he expected, he would not have had the solitudy reflections that led to the great scheme for finding the grandmother.

Of course when the others came up to roost they all came and squatted on Oswald's bed and said how sorry they were. He waived their apologies with noble dignity, because there wasn't much time, and said he had an idea that would knock the council's plan into a cocked hat. But he would not tell them what it was. He made them wait till next morning. This was not sulks, but kind feeling. He wanted them to have something else to think of besides the way they hadn't stood by him in the bursting of the secret staircase door and the tea-tray and the milk.

Next morning Oswald kindly explained, and asked who would volunteer for a forced march to Hazelbridge. The word volunteer cost the young Oswald a pang as soon as he had said it, but I hope he can bear pangs with any man living. 'And mind,' he added, hiding the pang under a general-like severeness, 'I won't have anyone in the expedition who has anything in his shoes except his feet.'

This could not have been put more delicately and decently. But Oswald is often misunderstood. Even Alice said it was unkind to throw the pease up at Denny. When this little unpleasantness had passed away (it took some time, because Daisy cried, and Dora said, 'There now, Oswald!') there were seven volunteers, which, with Oswald, made eight, and was, indeed, all of us. There were no cockle-shells, or tape-sandals, or staves, or scrips, or anything romantic and pious about the eight persons who set out for Hazelbridge that morning, more earnestly wishful to be good and deedful – at least Oswald, I know, was – than ever they had been in the days of the beastly Wouldbegood Society. It was a fine day. Either it was fine nearly all last summer, which is how Oswald remembers it, or else nearly all the interesting things we did came on fine days.

With hearts light and gay, and no pease in anyone's shoes, the walk to Hazelbridge was perseveringly conducted. We took our lunch with us, and the dear dogs. Afterwards we wished for a time that we had left one of them at home. But they did so want to come, all of them, and Hazelbridge is not nearly as far as Canterbury, really, so even Martha was allowed to put on her things – I mean her collar – and come with us. She walks slowly, but we had the day before us, so there was no extra hurry.

At Hazelbridge we went into B. Munn's grocer's shop and asked for ginger-beer to drink. They gave it us, but they seemed sur-prised at us wanting to drink it there, and the glass was warm – it had just been washed. We only did it, really, so as to get into con-versation with B. Munn, grocer, and extract information without rousing suspicion. You cannot be too careful.

However, when we had said it was first-class ginger-beer, and paid for it, we found it not so easy to extract anything more from B. Munn, grocer; and there was an anxious silence while he fid-dled about behind the counter among the tinned meats and sauce bottles, with a fringe of hob-nailed boots hanging over his head.

H.O. spoke suddenly. He is like the sort of person who rushes in where angels fear to tread, as Denny says (I do not say what sort of person that is).[6] He said:

'I say, you remember driving us home that day. Who paid for the cart?'

Of course B. Munn, grocer, was not such a nincompoop (I like that word, it means so many people I know) as to say right off. He said:

'I was paid all right, young gentleman. Don't you terrify yourself.'

People in Kent say terrify when they mean worry.

So Dora shoved in a gentle oar. She said:

'We want to know the kind lady's name and address, so that we can write and thank her for being so jolly that day.'

B. Munn, grocer, muttered something about the lady's address being goods he was often asked for. Alice said, 'But do tell us. We forgot to ask her. She's a relation of a second-hand uncle of ours, and I do so want to thank her properly. And if you've got any extra strong peppermints at a penny an ounce, we should like a quarter of a pound.'

This was a master-stroke. While he was weighing out the peppermints his heart got soft, and just as he was twisting up the corner of the paper bag, Dora said, 'What lovely fat peppermints! Do tell us.'

And B. Munn's heart was now quite melted, and he said:

'It's Miss Ashleigh, and she lives at The Cedars – about a mile down the Maidstone Road.'

We thanked him, and Alice paid for the peppermints. Oswald was a little anxious when she ordered such a lot, but she and Noël had got the money all right, and when we were outside on Hazelbridge Green (a good deal of it is gravel, really), we stood and looked at each other.

Then Dora said:

'Let's go home and write a beautiful letter and all sign it.'

Oswald looked at the others. Writing is all very well, but it's such a beastly long time to wait for anything to happen afterwards.

The intelligent Alice divined his thoughts, and the Dentist divined hers – he is not clever enough yet to divine Oswald's – and the two said together:

'Why not go and see her?'

'She *did* say she would like to see us again some day,' Dora replied. So after we had argued a little about it we went.

And before we had gone a hundred yards down the dusty road Martha began to make us wish with all our hearts we had not let her come. She began to limp, just as a pilgrim, who I will not name, did when he had the split pease in his silly palmering shoes.

So we called a halt and looked at her feet. One of them was quite swollen and red. Bulldogs almost always have something the matter with their feet, and it always comes on when least required. They are not the right breed for emergencies.

There was nothing for it but to take it in turns to carry her. She is very stout, and you have no idea how heavy she is. A half-hearted, unadventurous person (I name no names, but Oswald, Alice, Noël, H.O., Dicky, Daisy, and Denny will understand me) said, why not go straight home and come another day without Martha? But the rest agreed with Oswald when he said it was only a mile, and perhaps we might get a lift home with the poor invalid. Martha was very grateful to us for our kindness. She put her fat white arms round the person's neck who happened to be carrying her. She is very affectionate, but by holding her very close to you you can keep her from kissing your face all the time. As Alice said, 'Bulldogs do give you such large, wet, pink kisses.'

A mile is a good way when you have to take your turn at carrying Martha.

At last we came to a hedge with a ditch in front of it, and chains swinging from posts to keep people off the grass and out of the ditch, and a gate with 'The Cedars' on it in gold letters. All very neat and tidy, and showing plainly that more than one gardener was kept. There we stopped. Alice put Martha down, grunting with exhaustedness, and said:

'Look here, Dora and Daisy, I don't believe a bit that it's his grandmother. I'm sure Dora was right, and it's only his horrid sweetheart. I feel it in my bones. Now, don't you really think we'd better chuck it; we're sure to catch it for interfering. We always do.'

'The cross of true love never did come smooth,' said the Dentist.[7] 'We ought to help him to bear his cross.'

'But if we find her for him, and she's not his grandmother, he'll *marry* her,' Dicky said, in tones of gloominess and despair.

Oswald felt the same, but he said, 'Never mind. We should all hate it, but perhaps Albert's uncle *might* like it. You can never tell. If you want to do a really unselfish action and no kid, now's your time, my late Wouldbegoods.'

No one had the face to say right out that they didn't want to be unselfish.

But it was with sad hearts that the unselfish seekers opened the long gate and went up the gravel drive between the rhododendrons and other shrubberies towards the house.

I think I have explained to you before that the eldest son of anybody is called the representative of the family if his father isn't there. This was why Oswald now took the lead. When we got to the last turn of the drive it was settled that the others were to noiselessly ambush in the rhododendrons, and Oswald was to go on alone and ask at the house for the grandmother from India – I mean Miss Ashleigh.

So he did, but when he got to the front of the house and saw how neat the flower-beds were with red geraniums, and the windows all bright and speckless with muslin blinds and brass rods, and a green parrot in a cage in the porch, and the doorstep newly whited, lying clean and untrodden in the sunshine, he stood still and thought of his boots and how dusty the roads were, and wished he had not gone into the farm-yard after eggs before starting that morning. As he stood there in anxious uncertainness he heard a low voice among the bushes. It said, 'Hist! Oswald, here!' and it was the voice of Alice.

So he went back to the others among the shrubs, and they all crowded round their leader, full of impartable news.

'She's not in the house; she's *here*,' Alice said, in a low whisper that seemed nearly all S's. 'Close by – she went by just this minute with a gentleman.'

'And they're sitting on a seat under a tree on a little lawn, and she's got her head on his shoulder, and he's holding her hand. I never saw anyone look so silly in all my born,' Dicky said.

'It's sickening,' Denny said, trying to look very manly with his legs wide apart.

'I don't know,' Oswald whispered. 'I suppose it wasn't Albert's uncle?'

'Not much,' Dicky briefly replied.

'Then don't you see it's all right. If she's going on like that with this other fellow, she'll want to marry him, and Albert's uncle is safe. And we've really done an unselfish action without having to suffer for it afterwards.' With a stealthy movement Oswald rubbed his hands as he spoke in real joyfulness. We decided that we had better bunk unnoticed. But we had reckoned without Martha. She had strolled off limping to look about her a bit in the shrubbery. 'Where's Martha?' Dora suddenly said.

'She went that way,' pointingly remarked H.O.

'Then fetch her back, you young duffer! What did you let her go for?' Oswald said. 'And look sharp. Don't make a row.'

He went. A minute later we heard a hoarse squeak from Martha – the one she always gives when suddenly collared from behind – and a little squeal in a lady-like voice, and a man say 'Hallo!' and then we knew that H.O. had once more rushed in where angels might have thought twice about it. We hurried to the fatal spot, but it was too late. We were just in time to hear H.O. say:

'I'm sorry if she frightened you. But we've been looking for you. Are you Albert's uncle's long-lost grandmother?'

'*No*,' said our lady, unhesitatingly.

It seemed vain to add seven more agitated actors to the scene now going on. We stood still. The man was standing up. He was a clergyman, and I found out afterwards he was the nicest we ever knew, except our own Mr Bristow at Lewisham, who is now a canon, or a dean, or something grand that no one ever sees. At present I did not like him. He said: 'No, this lady is nobody's grandmother. May I ask in return how long it is since you escaped from the lunatic asylum, my poor child, and where your keeper is?'

H.O. took no notice of this at all, except to say: 'I think you are very rude, and not at all funny, if you think you are.'

The lady said: 'My dear, I remember you now perfectly. How are all the others, and are you pilgrims again to-day?'

H.O. does not always answer questions. He turned to the man and said:

'Are you going to marry the lady?'

'Margaret,' said the clergyman, 'I never thought it would come to this: he asks me my intentions.'

'If you *are*,' said H.O., 'it's all right; because if you do, Albert's uncle can't – at least, not till you're dead. And we don't want him to.'

'Flattering, upon my word,' said the clergyman, putting on a deep frown. 'Shall I call him out, Margaret, for his poor opinion of you, or shall I send for the police?'

Alice now saw that H.O., though firm, was getting muddled and rather scared. She broke cover and sprang into the middle of the scene.

'Don't let him rag H.O. any more,' she said, 'it's all our faults. You see, Albert's uncle was so anxious to find you, we thought perhaps you were his long-lost heiress sister or his old nurse who alone knew the secret of his birth, or something, and we asked him, and he said you were his long-lost grandmother he had known in India. And we thought that must be a mistake and that really you were his long-lost sweetheart. And we tried to do a really unselfish act and find you for him. Because we don't want him to be married at all.'

'It isn't because we don't like *you*,' Oswald cut in, now emerging from the bushes; 'and if he must marry, we'd sooner it was you than any one. Really we would.'

'A generous concession, Margaret,' the strange clergyman uttered, 'most generous, but the plot thickens. It's almost pea-soup-like now. One or two points clamour for explanation. Who are these visitors of yours? Why this Red Indian method of paying morning calls? Why the lurking attitude of the rest of the tribe which I now discern among the undergrowth? Won't you ask the rest of the tribe to come out and join the glad throng?'[8]

Then I liked him better. I always like people who know the same songs we do, and books and tunes and things.

The others came out. The lady looked very uncomfy, and partly as if she was going to cry. But she couldn't help laughing, too, as more and more of us came out.

'And who,' the clergyman went on – 'who in fortune's name is Albert? And who is his uncle? And what have they or you to do in this *galère* – I mean garden?'

We all felt rather silly, and I don't think I ever felt more than then what an awful lot there were of us.

'Three years' absence in Calcutta and elsewhere may explain my ignorance of these details, but still – '

'I think we'd better go,' said Dora. 'I'm sorry if we've done anything rude or wrong. We didn't mean to. Good-bye. I hope you'll be happy with the gentleman, I'm sure.'

'I *hope* so too,' said Noël, and I know he was thinking how much nicer Albert's uncle was. We turned to go. The lady had been very silent compared with what she was when she pretended to show us Canterbury. But now she seemed to shake off some dreamy silliness, and caught hold of Dora by the shoulder.

'No, dear, no,' she said, 'it's all right, and you must have some tea – we'll have it on the lawn. John, don't tease them any more. Albert's uncle is the gentleman I told you about. And, my dear children, this is my brother that I haven't seen for three years.'

'Then he's a long-lost too,' said H.O.

The lady said 'Not now,' and smiled at him. And the rest of us were dumb with confounding emotions. Oswald was particularly dumb. He might have known it was her brother, because in rotten grown-up books if a girl kisses a man in a shrubbery that is not the man you think she's in love with, it always turns out to be a brother, though generally the disgrace of the family and not a respectable chaplain from Calcutta.

The lady now turned to her reverend and surprising brother and said: 'John, go and tell them we'll have tea on the lawn.'

When he was gone she stood quite still a minute. Then she said: 'I'm going to tell you something, but I want to put you on your honour not to talk about it to other people. You see it isn't every one I would tell about it. He, Albert's uncle, I mean, has told me a lot about you, and I know I can trust you.'

We said 'Yes,' Oswald with a brooding sentiment of knowing all too well what was coming next.

The lady then said, 'Though I am not Albert's uncle's grandmother, I did know him in India once, and we were going to be married, but we had a – a – misunderstanding.'

'Quarrel?' 'Row?' said Noël and H.O. at once.

'Well, yes, a quarrel, and he went away. He was in the Navy then. And then … well, we were both sorry; but well, anyway, when his ship came back we'd gone to Constantinople, then to England, and he couldn't find us. And he says he's been looking for me ever since.'

'Not you for him?' said Noël.

'Well, perhaps,' said the lady.

And the girls said 'Ah!' with deep interest. The lady went on more quickly, 'and then I found you, and then he found me, and now I must break it to you.[9] Try to bear up …'

She stopped. The branches crackled, and Albert's uncle was in our midst. He took off his hat. 'Excuse my tearing my hair,' he said to the lady, 'but has the pack really hunted you down?'

'It's all right,' she said, and when she looked at him she got miles prettier quite suddenly. 'I was just breaking to them ...'

'Don't take that proud privilege from me,' he said. 'Kiddies, allow me to present you to the future Mrs Albert's uncle, or shall we say Albert's new aunt?'

* * *

There was a good deal of explaining done before tea – about how we got there, I mean, and why. But after the first bitterness of disappointment we felt not nearly so sorry as we had expected to. For Albert's uncle's lady was very jolly to us, and her brother was awfully decent, and showed us a lot of first-class native curiosities and things, unpacking them on purpose: skins of beasts, and beads, and brass things, and shells from different savage lands besides India. And the lady told the girls that she hoped they would like her as much as she liked them, and if they wanted a new aunt she would do her best to give satisfaction in the new situation. And Alice thought of the Murdstone aunt belonging to Daisy and Denny, and how awful it would have been if Albert's uncle had married *her*. And she decided, she told me afterwards, that we might think ourselves jolly lucky it was no worse.

Then the lady led Oswald aside, pretending to show him the parrot, which he had explored thoroughly before, and told him she was not like some people in books. When she was married she would never try to separate her husband from his bachelor friends, she only wanted them to be her friends as well.

Then there was tea, and thus all ended in amicableness, and the reverend and friendly drove us home in a wagonette. But for Martha we shouldn't have had tea, or explanations, or lift, or anything. So we honoured her, and did not mind her being so heavy and walking up and down constantly on our laps as we drove home.

* * *

And that is all the story of the long-lost grandmother and Albert's uncle. I am afraid it is rather dull, but it was very important (to him), so I felt it ought to be narrated. Stories about lovers and getting married are generally slow. I like a love-story where the hero parts with the girl at the garden-gate in the gloaming and goes off and has adventures, and you don't see her any more till he comes home to marry her at the end of the book. And I suppose people have to marry. Albert's uncle is awfully old – more than thirty, and the lady is advanced in years – twenty-six next Christmas. They are to be married then. The girls are to be bridesmaids in white frocks with fur. This quite consoles them. If Oswald repines sometimes, he hides it. What's the use? We all have to meet our fell destiny, and Albert's uncle is not extirpated from this awful law.

Now the finding of the long-lost was the very last thing we did for the sake of its being a noble act, so that is the end of the Wouldbegoods, and there are no more chapters after this. But Oswald hates books that finish up without telling you the things you might want to know about the people in the book. So here goes. We went home to the beautiful Blackheath house. It seemed very stately and mansion-like after the Moat House, and every one was most frightfully pleased to see us.

Mrs Pettigrew *cried* when we went away. I never was so astonished in my life. She made each of the girls a fat red pincushion like a heart, and each of us boys had a knife bought out of the housekeeping (I mean housekeeper's own) money.

Bill Simpkins is happy as sub-under-gardener to Albert's uncle's lady's mother. They do keep three gardeners – I knew they did. And our tramp still earns enough to sleep well on from our dear old Pig-man.

Our last three days were entirely filled up with visits of farewell sympathy to all our many friends who were so sorry to lose us. We promised to come and see them next year. I hope we shall.

Denny and Daisy went back to live with their father at Forest Hill. I don't think they'll ever be again the victims of the Murdstone aunt – who is really a great-aunt and about twice as much in the autumn of her days as our new Albert's uncle aunt. I think they plucked up spirit enough to tell their father they didn't like her – which they'd never thought of doing before. Our own robber says their holidays in the country did them both a great deal of good. And he says us Bastables have certainly taught Daisy and Denny the rudiments of the art of making home happy. I believe they have thought of several quite new naughty things entirely on their own – and done them too – since they came back from the Moat House.

I wish you didn't grow up so quickly. Oswald can see that ere long he will be too old for the kind of games we can all play, and he feels grown-upness creeping inordiously upon him. But enough of this.

And now, gentle reader, farewell. If anything in these chronicles of the Wouldbegoods should make you try to be good yourself, the author will be very glad, of course. But take my advice and don't make a society for trying in. It is much easier without.

And do try to forget that Oswald has another name besides Bastable. The one beginning with C., I mean. Perhaps you have not noticed what it was. If so, don't look back for it. It is a name no manly boy would like to be called by – if he spoke the truth. Oswald is said to be a very manly boy, and he despises that name, and will never give it to his own son when he has one. Not if a rich relative offered to leave him an immense fortune if he did. Oswald would still be firm. He would, on the honour of the House of Bastable.

Notes

The Story of the Treasure Seekers

1. **Oswald Barron**: Journalist Arthur Oswald Barron (1868–1939) was a fellow member of the Fabian Society and a writing (and probably romantic) partner of Nesbit's before his marriage in 1899. According to Julia Briggs's biography of Nesbit, *A Woman of Passion: The Life of E. Nesbit 1858–1924* (New York: New Amsterdam, 1987), he exerted an important influence over *The Treasure Seekers*.

Chapter 1   The Council of Ways and Means

1. *in the Lewisham Road:* We learn later that the family's address is 150 Lewisham Road in London, which places them at the intersection of Lewisham Road and Blackheath Rise, a few blocks from the southwest corner of Greenwich Park. During the infancy of her first child, Paul, Nesbit lived nearby at 28 Elswick Road.
2. *a General: i.e.*, a maid-of-all-work.
3. *Fifth of November:* the first of a number of references to the celebrations connected with Guy Fawkes Day, 5 November, on which British children traditionally create and burn a 'guy' stuffed with newspapers and wearing a mask. The event commemorates the foiling of the 1605 Gunpowder Plot, led by Fawkes, to blow up the Palace of Westminster and assassinate the king and members of Parliament.
4. *'Eat H.O.':* an advertising slogan for Hornby's Oatmeal.
5. *'We aren't playing Babel':* While the name 'The Tower of Babel' could refer to a nineteenth-century board game or a form of solitaire, this comment seems to suggest a parlour game in which participants compete to be heard. I have not been able to trace such a game.
6. *Dick Turpin and Claude Duval:* Of these two famous highwaymen, Turpin (ca. 1705–39) was executed for stealing horses; the French-born Duval (or Du Vall, 1643–70), known for his elegant clothing and polite demeanour, was hanged for robbery. The exploits of these popular antiheroes were chronicled in such mid-nineteenth-century penny dreadfuls as William Harrison Ainsworth's *Rookwood* (1834) and James Malcolm Rymer's *Nightshade, or Claude Duval, the Dashing Highwayman* (1865). Duval resurfaces in chapter 13, where Dicky terms him 'very generous to the poor and needy.'

Chapter 3   Being Detectives

1. *The (original) version of this chapter in* Pall Mall begins 'If you have
   not read about us in this Magazine before, you will need to be told that
   we are of the family of Bastable, and that we desired, above all things,
   to restore the fallen fortunes of our house. There are six of us, Dora,
   who is the good elder sister, and Dicky, who is good at sums. Oswald
   is very clever, some people say, but he is not one, because he is humble
   and modest. Then Alice and Noël are twins – they are clever. Noël is a
   poet, and Alice is a dear. And then there is H. O., whose name is Horace
   Octavius, but we call him H. O. because of the advertisement, and he
   is never quite sure that people won't take the advertisement's advice,
   and eat him. But I need not say we elder ones know better.'
2. *Mr Sherlock Holmes ... Dick Diddlington:* Arthur Conan Doyle
   (1859–1930) began publishing his Sherlock Holmes stories in *Beeton's
   Christmas Annual* in 1887; like many of Nesbit's works, they eventually (1891) found a home in the *Strand Magazine*, where they were
   extremely popular. Émile Gaboriau (1832–73) was a French writer
   of detective stories whose hero, Monsieur Lecoq, gained interna-
   tional renown before being eclipsed by Holmes; crime fiction was
   among the many genres in which Nesbit worked. The reference to
   Rudyard Kipling (1865–1936) is the first of many tributes in the
   Bastable stories to Nesbit's fellow author, a major literary influence
   upon her. 'Dick Diddlington' may refer to Ralph Rollington (John
   Allingham), who founded *The Boys' World*, a sensational story paper
   for working-class readers, in 1879. *Pall Mall* ends this paragraph after
   'bookstall.'
3. *'poor little children':* Pall Mall inserts 'pallid' before 'children.'
4. *'too much of a man':* Pall Mall has 'not going.'
5. *Pall Mall* contains neither 'the blood and things, and' nor the paragraph following this one.
6. *'But we might watch':* Pall Mall precedes this sentence with 'And they
   might not have had time to get away.'
7. *'equi-what's-its-name':* one of many occasions on which Oswald for-
   gets or misapprehends a grown-up word, in this case 'equilibrium.'

Chapter 4   Good Hunting

1. *'Good Hunting' was the first instalment to appear in* Pall Mall. There
   the opening paragraph reads 'We wanted money very badly to restore
   the fallen fortunes of our house. We knew the fortunes were fallen
   because we hardly ever have any pocket money now and father is so
   worried. So when we happened to have some money we meant to
   answer the advertisement which says "Ladies and gentlemen can make
   £5 a week in their leisure time"; but when we had got a shilling each
   we all found that there were things that we wanted.'

2. *Pall Mall* omits 'first of all' and adds 'His name is Horace Octavius, but we call him H.O. because of the poster-advertisement.'
3. *Pall Mall* adds 'Oswald is very just.'
4. *Pall Mall* has 'H.O. agreed – he's not a mean kid – but I found out afterwards that Dora had paid his share herself.'
5. *Pall Mall* has 'Then we wanted some new paints, and Noël wanted a pencil, and it does seem hard never to have any apples; so somehow or other most of the money got spent and we agreed that we must let the advertisement wait.'
6. *Pall Mall*'s version of this paragraph reads 'Then when all the money was gone except a halfpenny of mine and fourpence of Noël's and a few pennies that the girls had kept, we held another council' and adds as another paragraph 'There are six of us. Dora, Oswald, Alice, Dicky, Nöel, and H. O. I shan't tell you which I am, but you may guess, and I bet you don't.'
7. *Pall Mall* adds 'to try the blade.'
8. *Pall Mall* omits this sentence and, from the preceding paragraph, 'We had made a fire on purpose, though it was rather warm' and 'or you are a dirty boy.'
9. *Pall Mall* has '...said Noël proudly; "but I shall look for the Princess all by myself. But I'll let you see her when we're married."'
10. **'Wreck of the Malabar':** The steamship *Malabar* was lost off Point de Galle in 1860 while travelling to China. Journalist Thomas William Bowlby, who survived the event, wrote an account of it. *Pall Mall* has 'Revival Preacher' for the malapropism 'Reviving Preacher.'
11. **the Jungle Book:** Kipling's *The Jungle Book* and *The Second Jungle Book* appeared in volume form in 1894 and 1895 respectively and inspire the children's game in Chapter 1 of *The Wouldbegoods*. Bagheera, the panther mentioned here by Mrs Leslie, is a major character in the Mowgli stories, which constitute an important part of the Jungle Books.
12. **'So Oswald said.... stories':** *Pall Mall* has instead 'so we told her all about where we were going. She was awfully jolly, and when I told her Noël was a poet she laughed and said she was a sort of poet too, and the long strips of paper were the proofs of her new book.'
13. *Pall Mall* omits the poem and the two paragraphs preceding it; here the transition is 'She was a very jolly lady, and she talked to us all the way up, and when we got near to Cannon Street she said:'

Chapter 5   The Poet and the Editor

1. **Gordon:** Charles George Gordon (1833–85) was a flamboyant military leader known during his lifetime as 'Chinese' Gordon for quelling the Taiping rebellion and after his death in Sudan (at the hands of the forces of the 'Mad Mahdi') as 'Gordon of Khartoum.' *Pall Mall* has 'considering what a great man he was.'

2. *'They don't burn people any more there now':* Smithfield was histori-
   cally used as an execution site; it is famous for its association with the
   Smithfield Martyrs, Protestants brought to the stake under Mary I.
   Pall Mall has 'They don't burn people there any more now, and it was
   a rather long way, and Noël got very tired.'
3. *'jolly Bovril sign':* one of Nesbit's many references to advertising
   images or slogans. Bovril, developed in the 1870s, is a meat extract.
4. *Pall Mall* omits the final two sentences.
5. *'since the coal strike':* Oswald may be referring to an 1898 strike by
   the colliers of south Wales.
6. *Pall Mall* ends this sentence after 'Noël would do it.'
7. *Pall Mall* has 'We came at last to a door, and the boy opened it and let
   us in. There was a large room with a big soft red and blue carpet and a
   roaring fire, and a table with papers all littered over it like the one in
   father's study. A gentleman was sitting one side of the table; he had a
   light moustache and light eyes, and he looked tired, as if he had got
   up very early; but he was kind, and Oswald thought he looked clever.
   Oswald is considered a judge of faces.'
8. *Pall Mall* omits this sentence.
9. *Pall Mall* omits this sentence.
10. *'The mad old Protectionist':* From the mid-1840s through the early
    1930s, Britain embraced free trade policies under which tariffs were
    levied on only a handful of imported products. From the early 1870s
    onward, however, the anti-free trade position, or protectionism,
    found increasing support, especially from Conservatives.
11. *'a black cloak like Lord Tennyson's':* Poet Laureate Alfred, Lord
    Tennyson (1809–92) favoured a long black cloak and broad-brimmed
    hat on his walks, a costume that would appeal to Oswald's sense of
    the dramatic.
12. *'a beastly paper one!':* Disposable paper collars were considered
    déclassé.
13. *Mecænas:* Corrected in later editions to Mæcenas. Roman statesman
    Caius Cilnius Mæcenas was the patron of Horace, Virgil, and other
    notable poets.
14. *Pall Mall* has 'But he never put Noël's poetry in the *Daily Recorder*. It
    was quite a long time after we saw a sort of story in a magazine on the
    station bookstall, and the Editor had written it, I suppose. It said a lot
    about Noël and me, describing us all wrong and saying how we had
    tea with the Editor; and all Noël's poems were in the story thing. I
    think the Editor made game of them, but Noël was quite pleased – so
    that's all right.'

Chapter 6   Noël's Princess

1. *In Pall Mall* these two paragraphs are 'Noël always said he meant to
   marry a Princess, and one day he did it. This is a curious thing –

because very often when people say things are going to happen it does not turn out to be so. It was different with the prophets of old.'

2. *Pall Mall* has 'I often wish the Park was nearer our house; but I suppose it would be difficult to move it, and besides, trees do take such an awful time to grow.'

3. *Pall Mall* adds 'His name is Horace Octavius, so we call him H. O., like the advertisement' and omits 'wrought by enchanted gnomes' from the next sentence.

4. **Croom's Hill:** The Croom's Hill Gate to Greenwich Park adjoins Lewisham, the area of London where the Bastables live.

5. **Count Folko of Mont Faucon:** Like the others mentioned in this exchange, Folko features in Friedrich de la Motte Fouqué's chivalric romance *Sintram and His Companions*, first published in Britain in 1820. *Pall Mall* adds '(which is me)' after 'Oswald' in this sentence and has Alice say ' "and Noël and H. O. can be the Pilgrim and the little Master," ' while Dicky responds, ' "Oh, I can be Rolf, or the Chaplain." ' Oswald, characteristically, takes a particularly glamorous part.

6. *Pall Mall* ends this sentence after 'bronchitis.'

7. *Pall Mall* has 'She was like a china doll; she had a white face, and long yellow hair, done up very tight in two pigtails. Her forehead was very big and lumpy, and her cheeks came high up, like little shelves under her eyes. Her eyes were small and blue. She had on a funny black frock trimmed with blue braid, and buttoned boots with a lot of buttons. Her hands and face were fat, but her legs were very thin.'

8. **Prince Camaralzaman:** Also known as Camar al Zaman, Camaralzaman is a Persian prince in *The Arabian Nights* who falls in love with the Chinese princess Badoura.

9. *Pall Mall* gives this line to Alice.

10. *Pall Mall* has 'so that she should not walk off the grass. When we got to the other grass we all sat down, and the Princess asked us if we liked "dragées" (I know that's how you spell it because I asked my father).'

11. *Pall Mall* has 'Princess of Schmudeldorf-Pumphosen.'

12. *Pall Mall* has 'he said he was Noël Camaralzaman Ivan Constantine Charlemagne James John Edward Biggs Maximilian Bastable, Prince of New Cross. But when she asked him to say it again, of course he couldn't, because he'd only made it up as he went on, so the Princess said – .' New Cross is a district in the London borough of Lewisham.

13. *Pall Mall* has ' "Never mind," said Noël. "Come out and have a ride now. I will pay for it. I've got fourpence." '

14. *Pall Mall* assigns this remark to Dora.

15. **'cross-touch.... les graces':** games of the era; those preferred by the Bastables are more active than those with which the Princess is familiar. Cross-touch is a form of tag in which the player who is It must pursue whomever has crossed the trajectory of his pursuit of

his previous prey. In Les Graces, two players toss hoops to each other, catching them on crossed sticks.

16. *Pall Mall* has 'Princess Pauline' here and 'Royal Highness' below.

Chapter 7   Being Bandits

1. *'where the big guns are with the iron fence round them':* Oswald may refer to Lewisham Hill, then capped with a flagstaff and two cannon within an enclosure.

2. *'Board School children':* The Education Act of 1870 established local school boards, which took over a number of erstwhile religious schools as Board Schools. Initially the education of the poorest pupils was subsidized; after 1891 such schools were free to all children. From the standpoint of the middle-class Oswald, Board School attendance betokens poverty.

3. *'we call Blackheath the village, I don't know why':* Blackheath was originally a village separate from London, but by Oswald's day had long been subsumed into the metropolis.

Chapter 8   Being Editors

1. *'what it says in the copy-books about Virtue being its own Reward':* Copy books, designed to teach penmanship by having users copy short texts, often used as examples moral sayings so that children would simultaneously internalize good principles.

2. **Quentin Durward:** Walter Scott's 1823 novel *The Adventures of Quentin Durward* takes as its protagonist a Scottish archer in the service of Louis XI of France.

3. *'The Assyrian came down...':* Noël has been inspired by Byron's 'The Destruction of Sennacherib' (1815), which begins, 'The Assyrian came down like the wolf on the fold, / And his cohorts were gleaming in purple and gold; / And the sheen of their spears was like stars on the sea, / When the blue wave rolls nightly on deep Galilee.'

4. *'quand...away':* Dora has translated (perhaps as a schoolroom exercise) a variant of the traditional English song 'Over the Hills and Far Away' that begins 'When I was young and had no sense, / I bought a fiddle for eighteen pence. / The only tune that I could play / Was "Over the hills and far away."'

5. *'Mercie...boire':* Another nursery poem, this one by Jane Taylor. The original version begins: 'Thank you, pretty cow, that made / Pleasant milk to soak my bread. / Every day and every night, / Warm, and fresh, and sweet, and white.' Dora's translation, which misspells 'merci,' is looser than her first effort.

6. *'The Bush Ranger's Burial':* Through Dicky's serial, with its mixture of Australian and American Western local colour with detective fiction, Nesbit spoofs the style of Edwin Brett's *The Boys of England*, a popular downmarket story paper of the 1860s and after.

7. **'a good way to make a slate-pencil squeak':** Presumably this knowledge is desirable as a distraction from lessons.
8. **'the Oxford Local':** The Oxford University Delegacy of Local Examinations, given at both Junior (through age fifteen) and Senior levels, was established in 1857 to measure attainment in the liberal arts by middle-class boys who were leaving school and did not plan to attend university. Achieving the year's second highest score in the Oxford Local would have conferred considerable standing upon the examinee.

Chapter 9   The G.B.

1. *Windsor* begins 'We thought of all sorts of ways to restore the fallen fortunes of our house. You see, we had been rich once. Oswald and Dora can remember when father was always bringing nice things home from London, and there used to be game and wine and cigars sent as Christmas presents, and boxes of candied fruit, and French plums in boxes with silk and velvet and gilt on them. They were called prunes; but the prunes you buy at the grocer's are quite different. But now there is very seldom anything nice at Christmas or any other time. I suppose the people have forgotten father's address; so we used to look at the advertisements in the *Daily Chronicle*, and one day Dickie read out this: – "£100 secures partnership in lucrative business for sale of useful patent. £10 weekly. No personal attendance necessary. Jepson, 106, Old Street Road."'
2. **Bice:** from French *bis*, dark, applied in English to green but also to blue colours.
3. *Windsor* inserts after 'mouth': ' – his name is Horace Octavius, but the other is shorter – .'
4. **'Generous Benefactor, like in Miss Edgeworth':** Maria Edgeworth (1768–1849) uses the phrase 'generous benefactor' in more than one novel, including *Ennui, or Memoirs of the Earl of Glenthorn* (1809) and *Ormond* (1817).
5. *Windsor* adds 'Of course we all wanted to go' and omits 'with a bath-towel turban.'
6. *Windsor* has 'a girl' for 'our elder sister' and 'a row' for 'a little disagreeableness.'
7. *Windsor* has 'Grafton Street' for 'Brook Street, Bond Street' and 'Vauxhall' for 'Waterloo,' adding 'Palace' after 'St. James's.' Both Brook Street and Grafton Street were and continue to be expensive locations. Charing Cross Station is about a mile and a half from Brook Street; the Bastables' detour to the two palaces of Whitehall and St James adds about a mile to their walk.
8. **Klondike:** The 1897 discovery of gold in Klondike (Yukon Territory, Canada) sparked one of the major gold rushes of the nineteenth century. *Windsor* uses 'Klondyke' and omits 'some day.'

9. ***Then he took out a sovereign:*** In this episode Nesbit draws on stereotypes of Jews then current, including Mr Rosenbaum's 'hooky' nose, his respect for academic achievement, his love of money, and his high rate of interest (the common European association of Jews with money-lending dates from medieval times).

10. *Windsor* omits this sentence.

11. *Windsor* gives this line to Noël.

12. *Windsor* ends the instalment here.

Chapter 10   Lord Tottenham

1. *Pall Mall* opens 'I had always thought that the books were right, and that the best way to make your fortune was to rescue an old gentleman in distress.'

2. *Pall Mall* has 'The others did not seem to care much about the rescue.'

3. ***'New every morning':*** John Keble's six-stanza hymn (1827) begins 'New ev'ry morning is the love / Our waking and uprising prove; / Through sleep and darkness safely brought, / Restored to life, and pow'r, and thought.'

4. *Pall Mall* omits this sentence.

5. *Pall Mall* has 'Pincher is our fox-terrier. He is very well bred, and he does know one or two things, though we never could teach him to beg.'

6. *Pall Mall* has '…she went and sat in the dining-room, so as to be able to say she didn't have anything to do with it if we got into trouble.'

7. ***a beastly fox eating his inside:*** Many children have been raised on the story of the Spartan boy who, having stolen a fox, hides it in his garments to evade detection. Although the fox gnaws at the boy's flesh (and, in Hélène Guerber's 1896 version, widely used in schools, ultimately kills him), the stoical boy conceals his agony. *Pall Mall* omits 'It was his knees – he wears socks' and 'who were walking about.'

8. ***'the mad Protectionist':*** Lord Tottenham supports tariffs to give British-made goods an advantage. See Chapter 5, note 10.

9. *Pall Mall* attributes this line to Oswald.

10. *Pall Mall* ends this sentence after 'up.'

11. *Pall Mall* has ' "and in the books if you rescue an old gentleman from deadly peril he makes your fortune; and there wasn't any deadly peril, so we made Pincher into one – and so – ." '

12. *Pall Mall* has 'Then Alice slid along the bench close to him, and said, "I think you're very good to forgive us. […] But we *are* sorry, very sorry. […] Directly you said that about a tip I began to feel bad inside, and I whispered to H.O. that I wished we hadn't." '

13. ***the Death of Nelson:*** the subject of many history paintings, including one (1807) by Arthur William Devis, who was present on Nelson's

flagship during the event. Devis shows the fallen hero (clean-shaven, as Oswald notes) reclining in the midst of a small group of men who are leaning over him solicitously.

14. *Pall Mall* has 'And when we meet him he nods to us; so he can't really be going on thinking us ungentlemanly any more.'

Chapter 11   Castilian Amoroso

1. *Pall Mall* begins 'We suddenly found we had half a crown, and we said now was the time to send for sample and instructions how to earn two pounds a week in our Spare Time.'
2. *'"Quis?"... "Ego"':* Latin for 'Who?' 'I,' a reflection of the classical curriculum traditional in Britain for the sons of the well-to-do.
3. *'the poisonous printing ink':* Nineteenth-century newspaper ink contained lead.
4. **Punch-and-Judy show:** a slapstick travelling puppet show featuring Mr Punch, his wife Judy, and their baby.
5. *'"the drinking of wine and spirits"':* In the late nineteenth century in Britain and the USA, temperance was a dynamic social movement with strong religious affiliations. Nesbit herself was no teetotaller. For additional temperance references, see *Wouldbegoods* Chapter 11, note 13, and Chapter 13, note 12.
6. *Pall Mall* has 'said Alice: she did not see that the game was up.'
7. *Pall Mall* has 'Mother taught me to call her Sissy when we were very little, but I don't often somehow, now we are old,' and uses 'story' for 'chapter' above.
8. *Pall Mall* has 'can sit on the others if they need it.'
9. *'wine that maketh glad the heart of man':* see Psalm 104:15, 'And wine that maketh glad the heart of man, and oil to make his face to shine, and bread which strengtheneth man's heart.'
10. *Pall Mall* ends 'But when he had done laughing he spoke. "It's all right, kids. Only don't do it again. The wine trade is overcrowded," father said.'

Chapter 12   The Nobleness of Oswald

1. *Windsor* has 'just then' for 'about that time' and omits the next five sentences.
2. *Windsor* omits this sentence.
3. **the Children of the New Forest:** In Frederick Marryat's 1847 historical novel by that title, Cavalier children go into hiding in the New Forest during the Interregnum of 1649–60.
4. *Windsor* has 'Then we had some liquorice water to wind up with, and then Dicky said, "This reminds me."'
5. *Windsor* omits this and the preceding six paragraphs.

6. ***It is not right…the same as men:*** Nesbit (a smoker) has Oswald voice a standard antifeminist argument of the day. *Windsor* omits this paragraph.

7. *Windsor* ends this paragraph 'Be quiet, H. O.'

8. *Windsor* ends this sentence after 'settled.'

9. ***a 'heated discussion ensued':*** This phrase remains a cliché of parliamentary reportage.

10. ***Rosabella soap:*** apparently an invention of Nesbit's, although the reference to a 'complexion fair as the lily' recalls numerous romantic works of the early nineteenth century. *Windsor* has 'we remembered what her face was like when she washed it with coal tar soap, and she agreed that perhaps it was better not.'

11. ***It kills parrots to eat parsley:*** This piece of lore (also featured in Giacomo Puccini's 1896 opera *La Bohème*) remains current among some parrot owners today, since ingesting parsley can bring about a photosensitivity reaction if the bird is then exposed to excessive sunlight. Others hold that eaten in moderation, parsley is healthy for parrots and other conures.

12. ***Couleurs non Vénéneuses:*** French for 'nontoxic paints.'

13. *Windsor* adds 'He is never unkind to those in distress.'

14. *Windsor* casts this paragraph in third person.

15. *Windsor* has instead of this sentence 'And he blinked as he came in, because we had made up such a jolly good fire.'

16. ***'Ye have my leave to depart':*** Albert's uncle may be quoting a line from Kipling's 1891 story 'Namgay Doola,' ' "You have my leave to go," said the king.'

17. *Windsor* omits 'but the cold had gone to Noël instead' and, from the next paragraph, ' "You might have killed your little brother with your precious medicines." '

18. *Windsor* adds: 'and though Oswald was very anxious to be noble, he could not think of any good way,' and has as the next sentence 'It was quite late in the afternoon when Oswald met his friend Mrs. Leslie on the Parade.'

19. *Windsor* omits this sentence and has 'Oswald' for 'me' in the next sentence.

20. *Windsor* has: 'I do not say he was a noble boy – that is what others said of the way he behaved.'

Chapter 13   The Robber and the Burglar

1. *Pall Mall* has 'There was snow that day; it was jolly.'

2. ***'Water Rates':*** a metonymy for the representative of the water company, who is collecting payment. The size of the bill depended on the value of the house being supplied.

3. *Pall Mall* omits 'and he is very generous.'

4. ***Ali Baba:*** In 'Ali Baba and the Forty Thieves,' the clever slave Morgiana saves Ali Baba by pouring boiling oil into the jars in which the murderous thieves have hidden. This is one of several references that Nesbit makes to *The Arabian Nights.*

5. *Pall Mall* omits 'politely and quietly.'

6. *Pall Mall* has 'Gentle reader, have you ever been playing Red Indians in blankets round a fire...' and concludes the paragraph with '...and the insides of Oswald's hands got hot and wet, and his nose was cold like a dog's, and his ears were burning,' following this sentence with a new paragraph reading 'The girls said afterwards that they shivered with terror, and their teeth chattered, but we did not see this.'

7. *Pall Mall* has '...and then perhaps to hear it, whatever it was, come creeping slowly up the stairs with the stairs creaking....'

8. *Pall Mall* has 'a matchbox' instead of 'three boxes of matches.'

9. *Pall Mall* assigns to Alice the comment here given to Noël.

10. ***Balliol:*** one of the colleges composing Oxford University; Mr Bastable is also a Balliol product, and in *The Wouldbegoods* Oswald mentions his ambition to attend Balliol as well. This reference establishes that the 'robber' belongs to the educated classes.

11. ***Nelson:*** Horatio, Lord Nelson (1758–1805), British admiral and hero of the battle of Trafalgar, was killed during the latter victory; his surgeon, William Beatty, reported that on his deathbed, he told Thomas Masterman Hardy, 'Take care of my dear Lady Hamilton, Hardy, take care of poor Lady Hamilton. Kiss me, Hardy. Now I am satisfied. Thank God I have done my duty.' The children re-enact this death scene at the beginning of Chapter 14. See also Chapter 9, note 13.

12. ***'interesting stranger'...'Light Sparkling Family':*** The term 'interesting stranger' appears in many romantic novels from the eighteenth and nineteenth centuries; *Pall Mall* has 'speaker.' Various breweries, including Burke's and M. B. Foster & Sons, marketed 'light sparkling' ales.

13. *Pall Mall* ends this sentence after 'days' and has 'penny' for 'stiver' in the preceding paragraph.

14. ***'Bank-ollerday show':*** Bank Holiday shows, which featured competitions in such areas as vegetable-growing and the cooking of tasty but economical Sunday dinners, were designed chiefly for the working classes. The burglar's use of this metaphor seems intended as a criticism of Mr Bastable's inferior tableware. *Pall Mall* omits this phrase and has 'stiver' for 'haporth' (halfpennyworth) earlier in the paragraph.

15. *Pall Mall* ends the sentence after 'away.'

16. ***see some rich people...letter:*** Contributors to hospitals received documents authorizing admission to the medical facility for treatment; such documents could be transferred to deserving cases.

17. ***cold wreck of mutton, Father called it:*** Mr Bastable is punning on 'cold rack of lamb,' a more elegant dish. *Pall Mall* omits this phrase.

18. ***but that comes in another story:*** *Pall Mall* adds 'as good old Kipling says'; the line 'But that's another story,' used in *Plain Tales from the Hills* (1888), became a catchphrase across the British Empire.

Chapter 14   The Divining Rod

1. *Pall Mall* has 'The house was very uncomfortable' and ends the paragraph after 'doctor.'
2. ***while every man was doing his duty:*** The mention of Hardy (see Chapter 12, note 11) identifies this as a reference to Horatio, Lord Nelson's famous encouragement of his fleet, 'England expects that every man this day shall do his duty.'
3. *Pall Mall* has 'Before mother died people often came to dinner, and father's business was not such a bother, and we used to sit on the stairs and get nice things to eat as they came out of the dining-room.'
4. *Pall Mall* ends this sentence after 'ago' and spells Dicky's name 'Dickie' throughout.
5. *Pall Mall* ends this sentence after 'any way.'
6. ***'Let dogs delight':*** Noël is invoking a didactic poem by Isaac Watts, 'Against Quarreling and Fighting' (1715), which begins 'Let dogs delight to bark and bite, / For God hath made them so.' The line is also quoted in *Wouldbegoods* Chapter 12, note 3.
7. *Pall Mall* has 'But that piece is quite true. You begin to quarrel, and then you can't stop. Often, long before the others are ready to cry and make it up, I see how silly it is; but it doesn't do to say so, for it only makes the others crosser than they were before.'
8. ***carcanet:*** Both carcanets and ouches are archaic terms for bejeweled ornaments.
9. *Pall Mall* has ' "Do ye desire to fashion of it helms and hauberks?" said Alice. "Yea," said I, "and fair goblets." "To drink cocoanut milk out of," said Noël. "And we desire to build stately palaces of it," said Dickie. "And to buy things," said Dora – "a great many things." Then Alice put on the nursery tablecloth and tied an antimacassar over her head – and she said, "If your intentions are correct, fear nothing and follow me."'
10. ***'Heroes':*** Edna Dean Proctor's poem by this title (included in her 1867 volume *Poems*) begins, 'The winds that once the Argo bore / Have died by Neptune's ruined shrines: / And her hull is the drift of the deep-sea floor, / Though shaped of Pelion's tallest pines.'
11. *Pall Mall* has ' "You mustn't say anything – and when there is gold underneath, the magic rod will twist in the hand of the priestess like a live thing. Then you will dig, and the gold will be revealed."'
12. *Pall Mall* has ' "The magic rod has spoken," said Alice; "dig here, and that with dispatch. [...] for ere sundown the dragon who guards this spot will return and make you his prey."'
13. ***'And there it was ... cracked at the top':*** *Pall Mall* has 'And there it was, and it was a half-sovereign. We can't think how it came there, but

Dora thinks she remembers once, when H. O. was very little, mother gave him some money to hold, and he dropped it, and it rolled all over the floor. So we think perhaps this was part of it. We were very glad. H. O. wanted to go out at once and buy a mask he had seen for fourpence. It had been a shilling, but now it was going to be very cheap, because Guy Fawkes Day was over, and it was a little cracked at the top.'

14. *Pall Mall* has ' "I will leave him to meditate on his actions while I enjoy the pleasure of your conversation. It will be a lesson to him." '

15. *Pall Mall* omits the preceding sentence and uses 'It was him who showed us how to make people talk like books when you're playing things, and to tell a story straight from the beginning, not beginning in the middle like most people do.'

16. *'"Ye have my leave to depart"':* See Chapter 11, note 16. *Pall Mall* has 'You' for 'ye.'

17. *Pall Mall* omits this sentence.

18. *Pall Mall* has 'We talked it over all that evening, and we decided to have a feast. The next day we went out and bought the things. We got figs and almonds and raisins, and a real rabbit, and Eliza promised to cook it for us if we could wait till next day, because of the Indian uncle coming to dinner; she was very busy cooking nice things for him to eat. We got the rabbit because we are so tired of beef and mutton, and father hasn't a bill at the poultry shop. And we got hard-bake, and raspberry noyau, and peppermint rock, and oranges, and a cocoanut, with other nice things. We put it all in the top long drawer. It is H. O.'s drawer, and we made him turn his things out and put them in father's old portmanteau.' Hardbake, known in Italy as 'pan forte di Siena,' is a candy related to toffee; raspberry noyau is a layered candy made partly of fresh fruit paste. In the final paragraph, *Pall Mall* has 'tale' rather than 'chapter.'

Chapter 15   'Lo, the Poor Indian!'

1. *Pall Mall* ends this paragraph after 'hardly any soles to them.'

2. *Pall Mall* omits this sentence.

3. ***an imposition he had learned:*** a term from boys' schools; *Pall Mall* has 'a lesson.'

4. *Pall Mall* adds 'and we went into the nursery,' omitting the first, second, and fourth of the paragraphs following.

5. ***'Lo, the poor Indian!':*** a line from 'An Essay on Man' (1744), by Alexander Pope, 'Lo! the poor Indian, whose untutor'd mind / Sees God in clouds, or hears him in the wind.'

6. *Pall Mall* has 'The table was very nice.'

7. *Pall Mall* ends this paragraph after 'dishonourable' and begins the next ' "And the Brussels sprouts were all wet and swimming," Dora went on.'

8. *Pall Mall* omits this paragraph.
9. *Pall Mall* omits this paragraph.
10. *Pall Mall* omits this and the preceding paragraph.
11. *Pall Mall* omits 'with currents in it' and ends the paragraph with this sentence.
12. *Pall Mall* has 'H.O. kicked Oswald under the table, to make me ...'
13. *Pall Mall* has ' "Will you take it, please, because we do like you so very much? And we don't want it, really." And I held it out to him. "I'll take the threepenny-bit," said he, 'but I couldn't rob you of the rest. By the way, where did you get the money for this most royal spread – eh?" We told him all about the different ways we had looked for treasure, and we told him how Alice had played at the divining rod, and how it really had found a half-sovereign.'
14. *'A contented mind is a continual feast'*: Dora is quoting an American proverb.

Chapter 16   The End of the Treasure-Seeking

1. *Pall Mall* omits much of this material. It runs this instalment into the previous one and begins 'The next day father got one of his awful colds, and it was a wet day, so Dora persuaded him not to go to London, and she made him some gruel. [...] We kept as quiet as we could, and I made H.O. do some lessons, but it was very dull. Dicky said if things went on like this he should run away to sea, and Alice said she thought it would be nice to go into a convent. H.O. was rather disagreeable because of the powder Eliza had given him, so he tried to read two books at once, one with each eye, just because Noël wanted one of them – which was very selfish of him, and so it only made his head ache more ... .'
2. *Pall Mall* has 'Then, as we were looking out at the rain, we saw a four-wheeled cab come lumbering up from the way the station is. [...] Oswald had only said that about stopping, but the cab really did stop. It had boxes on the top, and knobbly parcels sticking out of the window, and it was something like going away to the seaside, and something like the gentleman who takes things in a carriage with the wooden windows up to sell to the drapers' shops. The cabman got down, and some one inside handed out ever so many parcels of different shapes, and the cabman stood holding them in his arms.'
3. *'If he's not a man, I'm a nigger!'*: The uncle's comment, like a similar remark by Oswald in *The Wouldbegoods*, illustrates the casualness with which this slur was used in turn-of-the-century society, as is also reflected in its inclusion in the large-circulation *Pall Mall* instalment.
4. *Pall Mall* has 'Some of them were done up in old dirty newspaper, and some in brown paper and string from the shop, and there were boxes.'

5. *Pall Mall* omits this and the preceding paragraph.

6. **'elephant-and-castles. There is a railway station called that':** The Elephant and Castle railway station in south London was built in 1863 and was supplemented by a Tube station in 1890. The name comes most immediately from an inn sign (in turn inspired by the symbol of the Worshipful Company of Cutlers, which had formerly occupied the inn site) depicting an elephant bearing a castle. Dicky's chess set makes reference to the game's roots in sixth-century India, when the pieces now known as bishops represented elephants; war elephants, which carried towers containing archers, were used by the Romans.

7. *Pall Mall* has 'He got Eliza to help, and we took all the parcels into the nursery, and he undid them. Father came too, and sat in the Guy Fawkes chair. There were toys for the kids, and model engines for Dick and me, and china tea-sets for the girls; there were sweets by the pound and by the box, and lovely long yards and yards of soft silk from India, to make frocks for the girls; a real Indian sword for Oswald, a book of Japanese pictures for Noël, and some ivory chess-men for Dick – the castles of the chessmen are elephant-and-castles. There is a railway station called that. I never knew what it meant before. The brown-paper-and-string parcels had boxes of games in them, and big cases of preserved fruits and things; and the shabby old newspaper parcels and the boxes had the Indian things in. I never saw so many beautiful things before. There were carved fans, and silver bangles, and strings of amber beads, and shawls and scarves of silk, and cabinets of brown and gold, and ivory boxes, and silver trays, and brass things. The uncle kept undoing them and handing them round, saying, "This is for you, young man," or "Little Alice will like this fan," or "Miss Dora would look well in this green silk, I think – eh – what?"'

8. *Pall Mall* ends this paragraph after 'cigars.'

9. *Pall Mall* has 'That was a wonderful day. There were heaps of presents, like things out of a fairy-tale – and even Eliza had a shawl.'

10. **Crystal Palace:** Originally erected in Hyde Park as the venue for the 1851 Great Exhibition, the Crystal Palace, a glass-and-iron marvel of Victorian engineering, was rebuilt on Penge Common in 1854, where it housed public events such as concerts and, by the 1890s, served partly as a shopping mall with stalls for vendors. In place of this paragraph and the ten that follow it, *Pall Mall* has 'The Indian Uncle came to see us often after that. And at Christmas he invited us all to dine with him. We went, of course; and it was a big house on the Heath, and there was everything nice you could think of for dinner, and a real stuffed fox with a duck in its mouth in a glass case in the hall. He gave us Christmas presents. You must be tired [...].'

11. **'Flint. Ashford. 1776':** William Flint was a late eighteenth-century clockmaker in Ashford, Kent.

12. ***a Waterbury, 'To match his boots':*** The Waterbury (Connecticut) Clock Company, now Timex, produced an inexpensive and popular watch; Nesbit refers to Waterbury watches in a number of her novels, including *Five Children and It, The Story of the Amulet,* and *The Railway Children.* Connecticut was also a centre for rubber manufacturing in the 1890s, so that boots were a major industry in the state.

13. ***'What happened to the guinea-pig?':*** Alice may be citing a riddle that I have not been able to trace; *Pall Mall* omits this sentence. In referring to 'the honourable member opposite,' the Uncle is invoking Parliamentary speechifying.

14. *Pall Mall* has 'He had our threepenny-bit on his watch-chain, and he is as rich as rich; and because he is our uncle he is going to give us everything we want' and eliminates the next seventeen paragraphs. Like the book version, the *Pall Mall* serial ends with Noël's poem and the Uncle's response.

The Wouldbegoods

1. ***Fabian Bland***: Born in 1885, Nesbit's youngest child, named for the Fabian Society, had died in 1900 of asphyxiation after a tonsillectomy.

Chapter 1   The Jungle

1. *Pall Mall* includes a subtitle, 'Being a Passage from the Life of Master Oswald Bastable,' with this and other instalments published in this periodical.

2. *Pall Mall* ends this sentence after 'furniture.'

3. *Pall Mall* ends this sentence after 'family,' adds 'boy' after 'eldest,' and uses 'we all felt this so much that' instead of 'we all knew this, so that' in the preceding sentence.

4. *Pall Mall* adds 'But you must not expect me to tell you all the hard words.' Earlier in the paragraph, *Pall Mall* uses 'be naughty' for 'do anything wrong' and 'exactly pleased' for 'quite pleased,' omitting 'when we had done with them.'

5. ***Blackheath:*** a southeastern suburb that underwent significant development in the late Victorian era. During their early married life, Nesbit and her husband occupied various houses in this general area of London. *Pall Mall* omits 'red'; cf. Nesbit's 1902 adult novel *The Red House*, in which the Bastables make an appearance.

6. ***Dyer & Hilton:*** William Dyer and John Hilton were the principals in the Blackheath firm of Dyer, Son and Hilton, auctioneers and estate agents. *Pall Mall* omits 'big.'

7. *Pall Mall* has 'the most agreeable meals every day, and heaps of pocket-money.'

8 **Bennett's:** Serving such notables as Charles Dickens, Bennett's was a family firm of watch- and clockmakers with several shops, including the one in Blackheath that Oswald mentions.

9. *Pall Mall* adds 'and it led to the adventure of "The Soldier's Mother."'

10. **Blackheath High School...Prop.:** The Blackheath High School, affiliated with the 'Prop.,' opened in 1880 as one of 26 schools run by the Girls' Public Day School Trust to provide high-quality education to girls. The Blackheath Proprietary School, which closed in 1907, was founded in 1830 as a day school competitive with elite boarding institutions. *Pall Mall* uses 'the Red House' for 'Morden House.'

11. *Pall Mall* adds 'and then we went into the country, and "The Soldier's Mother" happened.' Instead of 'vac.', *Pall Mall* uses 'holidays.'

12. **They teach botany at girls' schools:** Although botany was often included in girls' curricula, throughout the nineteenth century it was both a popular pastime and a subject of serious scientific inquiry for men as well.

13. **Ramsgate:** A popular beach resort in Kent; presumably sea air was prescribed for Denis's health.

14. **black with beady things:** *Pall Mall* has 'a black cape with beady things.'

15. **Miss Murdstone...Mangnall's Questions:** Miss Murdstone is the sister of David Copperfield's stepfather in Dickens's 1849–50 novel; both Murdstones are such a byword for hostility to the young that *Pall Mall* omits the novel's title, confident that readers will catch the reference. A standard textbook, *A History of England from the First Invasion of the Romans to the End of the Reign of George the Third, with Conversations at the End of Each Chapter*, by 'Mrs. Markham' (Elizabeth Penrose), was first published in 1823 and reprinted throughout the century; although continued and updated by later writers after Penrose's 1837 death, this text's style and outlook would have seemed old-fashioned to many of Oswald's generation. Finally, of Richmal Mangnall's *Historical and Miscellaneous Questions for the Use of Young People* (1800), another work frequently used in educating Victorian girls, Robert Hebert Quick wrote, 'The long-continued success of this book is a melancholy proof of the stupidity which is at work, vigorously destroying the intelligence of youthful minds' (*Essays on Educational Reformers* [1868], Cincinnati, OH: Robert Clarke & Co., 1879, p. 317). *Pall Mall* omits *Mangnall's Questions* and 'in *David Copperfield*.'

16. *Pall Mall* omits this phrase.

17. *Pall Mall* omits 'or Indians' and has 'we are all strangers to them.'

18. **apple-pie bed:** also known as short-sheeting, the apple-pie bed is a practical joke wherein the victim's sheet is folded in half to make lying at full length impossible. In the preceding sentence, Oswald is unable to remember the word 'lethargy.'

19. **if they didn't like it they could jolly well do the other thing:** A euphemistic reference to an earthy variant of the expression 'like it or lump it.'

20. ***Jungle Book...Mowgli:*** Mowgli is the central figure in many stories in *The Jungle Book* (1893–94) and *The Second Jungle Book* (1895), by Rudyard Kipling. Nesbit and Kipling admired one another's works for children, each sometimes finding inspiration in the other's ideas. *Pall Mall* ends the second sentence of this paragraph after 'like.'

21. *Pall Mall* omits 'conscious' and ends this sentence after 'mice'; it also uses 'his father' for 'Albert's uncle' at the beginning of the paragraph.

22. ***the 'White Seal' and 'Rikki Tikki':*** that is, not stories featuring the jungle setting in which Oswald is interested.

23. *Pall Mall* ends this sentence after 'let her' and uses 'clever' rather than 'handy' in the preceding sentence.

24. ***crème d'Amande pour la barbe et les mains:*** 'almond cream for the beard and hands,' a slogan for a Victorian shaving cream.

25. *Pall Mall* omits this phrase.

26. ***not the fox, of course:*** Shooting foxes, as opposed to using dogs to kill them during a hunt, was a cardinal sin in upper-class country life, a point that drives much of the action of Chapter 9 of this novel. *Pall Mall* omits 'tremendous.'

27. ***The duck-bill – what's its name?:*** Here and later in the chapter, Oswald mislays the word 'platypus.' *Pall Mall* has 'Duck-bill-what's-his-name.'

28. ***Condy's fluid:*** An oxidant used as an antiseptic; it generates a brown stain. *Pall Mall* omits 'I think this was thoughtful' and notes, 'H.O. painted his legs and his arms, hands and face with Condy's fluid, to make himself brown [...].'

29. *Pall Mall* has ' "I don't want to be beavers," he said.'

30. *Pall Mall* omits this phrase.

31. *Pall Mall* omits this sentence.

32. *Pall Mall* ends this sentence after 'oyster' and uses 'twisted' instead of 'a horrid violet-colour.'

33. *Pall Mall* has 'we were to go to the same house as him, Daisy and Denny too; we were glad of this.'

34. *Pall Mall* has 'so very good.'

Chapter 2   The Wouldbegoods

1. ***The Wouldbegoods:*** The *Illustrated London News* (*ILN*) titles this instalment 'The Perils of the Deep.'

2. *ILN* uses 'to be better children' for 'to be good,' omits 'really,' and has 'our parlour-maid' for 'Mrs. Blake.'

3. *ILN* inserts here the following: 'There are six of us Bastables, Dora, Oswald, Dickie, Alice, Noël, and H. O. – his name is Horace Octavius, but the other is shorter, and like the advertisement. Dora is goodish; Oswald is modest, so I will say no more about his merits; Dickie is common-sense; Alice and Noël are twins, and Noël is a poet; and H. O. is young enough to wear socks instead of stockings. Daisy and

Denny are the white-mouse-like children of a friend of father's, a very nice man we once took for a robber – and they were staying with us when we went into the country. One of us tells the story, I will not say which one. Albert's uncle is the uncle of Albert, a muff who used to live next door to us once. All this is dull, but it will be better later on if you know quite clearly who we are.'

4. ***The Moat House:*** The Moat House is based on Well Hall in Eltham, Kent, which Nesbit occupied from 1899 until 1921. *ILN* omits 'in ancient centuries – I don't remember which.'

5. *ILN* omits 'watery' and adds at the end of the sentence 'and another to the back door.' The oast-houses mentioned in the next sentence were used for drying hops as part of the brewing process; they were a distinctive feature of the Kentish landscape during Nesbit's time.

6. *ILN* has 'my father and Albert's uncle took it.'

7. *ILN* omits mention of the farm-worker and his warning, using instead '...and had a jolly good time all of us. Then we turned the handle of the chaff-cutting machine, and nobody got hurt.'

8. ***You see he wears socks:*** Short pants and socks were associated with younger boys.

9. ***S.P.G.:*** the Society for the Propagation of the Gospel in Foreign Parts, founded in 1701.

10. *ILN* has ' "Oh, do let me go on," Alice said. We let her, and she did.'

11. ***Make this earth an eagle:*** Denny's mistake for 'Make this world an Eden, / Like the Heaven above,' lines from one version of a popular mid-nineteenth-century American children's hymn by Julia Fletcher Carney.

12. ***Mr Greatheart:*** a slayer of giants and monsters, Mr Greatheart is the hero of the second part of John Bunyan's Christian allegory *The Pilgrim's Progress* (1684).

13. ***Ministering Children:*** Maria Louisa Charlesworth's didactic children's novel by this title, first published in 1854, was often used as a Sunday School prize book.

14. *ILN* omits 'like the head had in its mouth.'

15. *ILN* ends this sentence after 'morning.'

16. *ILN* omits 'all by itself' and 'most.'

17. *ILN* has ' "It's nothing naughty?" the White Mouse Girl asked [...].'

18. *ILN* has 'There were green apples on the trees, but we did not take any till we had asked if we might[....] Mrs. Pettigrew said, "Lor! [...]"'

19. *ILN* omits this sentence.

20. *ILN* has 'We had some blackcurrants while they were gone.'

21. *ILN* uses 'The White Mouse Boy' for 'Denny.'

22. *ILN* uses 'The White Mice did not want to go on it, so that was all right.'

23. *ILN* has 'because Noël does catch cold so, and we knew well [...].'

24. ***Battle of the Revenge:*** Alfred Tennyson's 'The "Revenge": A Ballad of the Fleet' (1878) memorializes Sir Richard Grenville's death in a 1591 naval battle against Spain.

25. **Ladywell Swimming Baths:** constructed in 1884 and located in Lewisham.
26. **like Venus in the Latin verses:** Venus (the Greek Aphrodite) was born of the sea foam after Kronos castrated his father, the sky-god Uranus. *ILN* has 'Venus in the "Heathen Gods."'
27. *ILN* has 'Of course, we knew it could not be a shark or a crocodile; but I thought of pikes, who are large and cruel fish, and I caught hold of Dora, who screamed without stopping.'
28. *ILN* ends this sentence after 'did.'
29. *ILN* omits this and the preceding sentence.
30. *ILN* adds 'It was partly to keep us from getting cold, I believe, too.'
31. **What Katy Did:** an 1872 novel for girls by American author Susan Coolidge (Sarah Chauncey Woolsey). While, characteristically, Daisy remembers the story for its didacticism, Coolidge's work also contains a good deal of humour.
32. **all the perfumes of somewhere or other:** a reference to *Macbeth* V.1, in which the sleepwalking Lady Macbeth laments, 'Here's the smell of the blood still: all the perfumes of Arabia will not sweeten this little hand. Oh, oh, oh!'

Chapter 3   Bill's Tombstone

1. **Bill's Tombstone:** In *Pall Mall*, the title is 'The Soldier's Mother.'
2. **Toady Lion:** The popular novelist Samuel Rutherford Crockett published *The Surprising Adventures of Sir Toady Lion* in 1897. Crockett's other works from this period tend toward the heavily Scottish and romantic; in contrast, *Toady Lion*'s frontispiece is a comic drawing of a slingshot-wielding boy sitting on a sign whose legend begins, 'Too Good Boys Not Allowed to Read This Book.' *Pall Mall* has 'It is the nicest book I have read, written by *Toady Lion's* author' and omits 'the others...them.'
3. **the White Mouse's:** *Pall Mall* has 'my sister Dora's.'
4. *Pall Mall* has '...and Alice and Dora waved the flag, because they are girls, and so politeness makes us let them enjoy the fat of whatever there is going.'
5. **Brooke's soap...Iron Duke:** Brooke's 'Monkey Brand' soap, originating in Philadelphia but subsequently bought by the British firm Lever Brothers, was popular during the late nineteenth century. Wellington Knife Polish was first marketed in the 1860s; Oswald's erroneous belief that it is connected with the Duke of Wellington (1769–1852), hero of the battle of Waterloo, assumes that Wellington's sobriquet 'the Iron Duke' must be connected to cutlery.
6. **the Mouse:** *Pall Mall* prefers 'my brother Noël.'
7. **Trafalgar...the Franco-German War:** The battle of Trafalgar was fought 21 October 1805 between the outnumbered British Navy and the combined French and Spanish fleets. It was a decisive victory for

Britain, despite the loss of British naval commander Horatio, Lord Nelson; Britain lost no ships while the enemy lost twenty-two. The Franco-Prussian War of 1870–71 saw France's defeat by a coalition of German states led by Prussia.

8. *go to South Africa for a bugler: i.e.,* in the Second Boer War (1899–1902), between the British and the Dutch-speaking Boers of South Africa; the victorious British annexed the two Boer republics, which had a substantial British population and controlled desirable mining tracts, as part of the British Empire. For Balliol, see *Treasure Seekers* Chapter 7, note 10. *Pall Mall* has 'father would not let me.'

9. *Fighting Fifth:* Also known as the New Zealand Rough Riders, the regiment distinguished itself in the Second Boer War. *Pall Mall* has '….the grey book father had when he was in the Artists'; the volunteer regiment 'The Artists' Rifles' also saw active service in South Africa.

10. *Pall Mall* adds 'The garden of the house we were staying at joins right on to the churchyard.'

11. *Pall Mall* adds 'and gave an order.'

12. *Mr. Caldecott's pictures:* a reference to Randolph Caldecott (1846–86), pioneering illustrator of children's books. *Pall Mall* has 'We were all standing on the wall that day. Dora had the three-edged rapier to wear […].'

13. *Pall Mall* omits this sentence.

14. *Pall Mall* ends this paragraph 'as they were wearing their busbies.'

15. *Diarmid of the Golden Collar:* Diarmid was an ancient Irish hero. Kipling's comic 'The Taking of Lungtungpen' (*Plain Tales from the Hills*, 1888) similarly compares an intrepid British soldier to this figure.

16. *Stores:* The Army & Navy Stores, formed in 1871 as The Army & Navy Co-operative Society, was a venture originally open only to military officers and their widows. That the Bastables are entitled to shop at the Stores reflects their father's service record.

17. *Pall Mall* assigns this suggestion to Dora.

18. *Pall Mall* gives Denny's remark to Dicky and adds after 'sick,' 'Because he is a poet.'

19. *Pall Mall* ends the paragraph here.

20. *B.B pencil:* a soft lead pencil suitable for shading sketches.

21. *Pall Mall* ends this sentence after 'rakes.'

22. *Pall Mall* has 'where we write down the virtuous actions of each other, when we happen to notice them.'

23. *upas-tree:* a Javanese tree said to kill all in its vicinity.

24. *Pall Mall* has ' "You wicked, God-forsaken children!" she said: "ain't you got enough of your own good ground to muck up and spoil, but you must come bothering into my little lot?"'

25. *Pall Mall* uses 'Dora' instead of 'the other girls.'

26. *Pall Mall* omits 'because we shouldn't be let.'

27. *Pall Mall* uses 'father's box.'

28. *Pall Mall* uses 'Noël' for 'Denny' in this paragraph and omits the final sentence; the next paragraph has 'sanguinaceous' for 'sanguinary.'

29. *Pall Mall* substitutes 'Dicky' for the first 'Denny' and 'we' for the second, omitting 'and he showed us how.'

30. *Pall Mall's* list of flowers is 'white lilac, peonies, white tulips and narcissus, and many other things.'

31. **knew from Kipling:** 'Tommy' or 'Tommy Atkins' has been a generic term for a British common soldier from at least the mid-eighteenth century. Kipling's poem 'Tommy' was published as part of the *Barrack-Room Ballads* in 1892.

32. *Pall Mall* has 'because of a wounded leg he had.'

Chapter 4   The Tower of Mystery

1. **Ministering   Children ... something   or   other   of   Little   Sins:** for *Ministering Children*, see Chapter 2, note 12. Grace Kennedy's *Anna Ross* (1823) describes Anna's movement from a piety motivated from a desire to please her mother to sincere faith. *Ready Work for Willing Hands* (1856), by the American Sunday School writer Lucy Ellen Guernsey, describes a girl's efforts to learn to see and perform the duties close to home. Frances Isabelle Tylcoat's *Elsie, or Like a Little Candle* (1875) was a short religious work for children. 'The something or other of Little Sins' may refer to *The Sinfulness of Little Sins* (1849), a book of Lenten sermons by John Jackson, bishop of London and chaplain to Queen Victoria.

2. **Monte Cristo:** *The Count of Monte Cristo* (1844) is an exciting tale of delayed revenge by Alexandre Dumas *père*.

3. *ILN* adds 'Oswald said.' To 'go to Coventry' is to be expelled, usually temporarily, from group membership – in American parlance, given the silent treatment.

4. **blush to find it shame:** Denny misquotes a line from Alexander Pope, 'Do good by stealth, and blush to find it fame.'

5. *ILN* adds 'and him a white mouse.'

6. *ILN* omits this clause.

7. **like Pharaoh in the Bible afore he was buried:** Presumably the speaker has mummification in mind; he appears to be conflating an awareness of the pharaohs who appear in the Bible with an awareness of the Egyptian archaeological excavations publicized in the late nineteenth-century press, since the Bible does not mention pharaonic burial practices. *ILN* omits this sentence.

8. **Aberdeen graphite:** *ILN* has the more plausible 'Aberdeen granite' and gives Ravenal's date of death as 1769.

9. *ILN* has 'where the man was buried whose beard [...].'

10. *ILN* omits this sentence.

11. **to buy a gun with:** *ILN* instead has 'for Alice's and Noël's birthday, which come on the same day, because they are twins.'

12. *ILN* has 'the most dreadful adventure we ever had' and adds after 'ambush' 'who awaited our sortie.'

13. *'The Battle of the Baltic'...'Nine Gods':* All these poems have some relevance to the children's predicament. 'The Battle of the Baltic' (1801) is a patriotic poem by Thomas Campbell about the battle of Copenhagen, a British naval engagement during the Napoleonic Wars. Thomas Gray's 'Elegy Written in a Country Churchyard' (1751) may strike Denny as appropriate because of its reference to 'yonder ivy-mantled tower' (line 9). For Tennyson's poem on the *Revenge*, see Chapter 2, note 23. Lars Porsena appears in Macaulay's ballad 'Horatius' (1842), in which three Roman soldiers hold a bridge against an army of Etruscan invaders.

14. *ILN* adds 'But we call Daisy Mouse for a pet name.'

15. *ILN* adds in a new paragraph 'We met him at the top door. Alice threw her arms round his neck and cried like anything, and he was so sorry for her he would carry her all the way to the cart – which must have been no joke, for she is not a feather-weight.'

16. *ILN* adds in a new paragraph 'The rest is but a misty picture. Mrs. Pettigrew took us out of the cart and put us to bed, and brought us up hot milk-and-eggs – but we could hardly keep awake to drink them. Albert's uncle, a prey to harrowing anxiety, had gone out to look for us. Dora and Daisy had said their prayers over and over again, and cried all the evening. They had been sure that we had met with a herd of wild bulls, and been hopelessly gored to death.'

17. *ILN* adds 'Indeed, I don't think they need have made it. We had had enough of woods and towers of mystery to last us a good long time.
'They never caught the wayfarer.
'The pig-man turned out to live quite near. He got to be a great friend of ours.'

Chapter 5   The Water-Works

1. *Pall Mall* begins 'This is the story of the most far-reaching and influentially naughty thing...' and concludes 'It happened when we were in the country for our summer holidays.'

2. *Pall Mall* has 'Oswald would rather have his story unremembered [...].'

3. *The Golden Age:* An 1895 novel by Kenneth Grahame narrated by a child, *The Golden Age* shares with the Bastable stories a vision of childhood as separate from and often in opposition to adulthood.

4. *Pall Mall* adds 'And there was a kitten; but it got ill almost at once, and then she would do nothing but nurse it till it died.'

5. *'The Man Who Broke':* 'The Man Who Broke the Bank at Monte Carlo' was a popular music-hall song written by Fred Gilbert in 1892.

6. *Pall Mall* omits this sentence.

7. **rounders:** a sport resembling baseball.

8. ***leave something to the imagination of my young readers:*** As Oswald's next sentence suggests, this phrase is a convention of mid-nineteenth-century romantic novels written in a style that Nesbit enjoys parodying. See, e.g., Mrs E.D.E.N. Southworth's *Vivia; or, The Secret of Power* (Philadelphia: T. B. Peterson & Brothers, 1857), whose narrator remarks, 'I shall pass over the joy of meeting with their friends, and leave to the imagination of my young readers the details of the marriage that took place, as had been arranged, at the little gothic chapel of the Convent of St. Genevieve, in the presence of the pale but tranquil Abbess and her nuns, and of their own family party' (p. 534).
9. *Pall Mall* has 'prices from 21s. to 2s. 6d.' According to the retail price index calculator on measuringworth.com, these sums are equivalent to £88.90 and £10.60 in 2010 currency.
10. ***what the book calls poetic justice:*** The coining of 'poetic justice' is attributed to Thomas Rymer in *The Tragedies of the Last Age Consider'd* (1678). *Pall Mall* has 'books call.'
11. ***to be jawed at:*** *Pall Mall* uses 'to have his conduct misunderstood.'
12. ***'Percy's Anecdotes...the one about lawyers...the cricket ball':*** *The Percy Anecdotes*, a multivolume work compiled by Reuben and Sholto Percy and first published in 1820, contains a section entitled 'Anecdotes of the Bar.' *Pall Mall* has 'his cricket-ball.'
13. ***Stoneham Lock:*** located on the River Medway, in Kent.
14. *Pall Mall* omits this sentence.
15. *Pall Mall* omits 'Dora's foot.... stand it.'
16. ***Falding village:*** *Pall Mall* uses throughout this chapter 'Yalding,' a town on the Medway beloved of Nesbit.
17. *Pall Mall* omits this paragraph.
18. *Pall Mall* omits this sentence.
19. ***By this the storm grew loud apace:*** cf. 'Lord Ullin's Daughter' (1809), Thomas Campbell's ballad about an eloping couple fleeing the wrath of the female partner's father. It includes the lines, 'By this the storm grew loud apace, / The water-wraith was shrieking; / And in the scowl of heaven each face. / Grew dark as they were speaking.'
20. ***But we had to keep on working [...]:*** The racial slur that Oswald uses here would have seemed commonplace to many white readers of the period; as late as 1939, it appeared in the British title of an Agatha Christie mystery later retitled *Ten Little Indians*.
21. ***soothes the savage breast:*** cf. William Congreve, *The Mourning Bride* (1697), I.1, 'Music hath charms to soothe the savage breast, / To soften rocks, or bend a knotted oak.'

Chapter 6   The Circus

1. *Pall Mall* begins the chapter with this sentence.
2. *Pall Mall* adds '(he was writing a novel, and he had come into the country on purpose to do it quietly).'

3. *a story about an animal race:* Daisy may have in mind 'The Menagerie Race,' which appeared in *Punch* on 10 September 1892 and contains the species and event described. *Punch*, a comic magazine aimed primarily at adults, seems unexpected reading for Daisy; possibly Oswald's effort (noted in Chapter 4) to supply her with lighter reading is responsible for her knowledge of this work.

4. See page 218 for short story. [– Nesbit's note]

5. *Pall Mall* has 'Doing *anything* with animals is prime – if they will. Couldn't we have a circus?'

6. *the Vicomte de Bragelonne:* a romantic novel in the d'Artagnan series by Dumas *père*, first translated into English in 1850–51.

7. *real name: Pall Mall* uses 'Christian name'; later in the paragraph it adds '(the Lion)' after 'King of Beasts.'

8. *Haute école:* the most complex branch of dressage, requiring the horse to perform a series of difficult jumps and balances.

9. *Denny and Noël: Pall Mall* has 'Denny and Dicky,' one of several occasions on which a role is assigned differently between the serialized and the volume versions. Instead of 'Mrs Pettigrew,' the *Pall Mall* paragraph uses 'the housekeeper.'

10. *swiftly as the arrow from the bow:* Oswald may have in mind Puck's 'I go, I go; look how I go, / Swifter than arrow from the Tartar's bow,' from Shakespeare's *A Midsummer Night's Dream* III.2.

11. *Pall Mall* omits this sentence.

12. *Pall Mall* has 'Dora's flannel petticoat' and omits the reference to the soldiers.

13. *Pall Mall* has 'The gate of the orchard was open, so was the gate leading to the back door.'

14. *Pall Mall* uses '*Our* words were few. There are times when it is not wise to argue, however little what has occurred is really your fault,' a version of the latter sentence that seems preferable to that of the 1902 edition.

15. *'Rose and Crown': Pall Mall* has instead 'Police Station.'

16. *pursued the pig: Pall Mall* uses 'pursuited' here, one of comparatively few instances where the volume has a standard word and the serial installment a nonstandard one. Two paragraphs below, for instance, where the volume uses 'speedfully,' *Pall Mall* has the more grown-up 'speedily.'

17. *what the village blacksmith's was wet with':* a reference to line 9 of Henry Wadsworth Longfellow's popular 1841 poem 'The Village Blacksmith,' 'His brow is wet with honest sweat.'

18. *Pall Mall* has 'If the learned black pig did not know anything else, it seemed to know its way.'

19. *'black brothers being already white to the harvest':* See John 4:35, 'Behold, I say unto you, Lift up your eyes, and look on the fields; for they are white already to the harvest.' This image, in which Christ refers not to the physical harvest but to the harvest of souls, recurs throughout Christian discourse on missionary work.

20. *Pall Mall* has 'asked pardon very handsomely' and 'his hot blood in check.'
21. **Like the meandering brook:** reference not traced. *Pall Mall* has ' "like a meandering brook," Denny said,' and does not set the line off as a quotation.
22. *Pall Mall* has 'when we had done she said, "Perhaps it was better to hear about than do – especially the goat part; but I do wish auntie had given you tea." '

Chapter 7   Being Beavers; or, The Young Explorers (Arctic or Otherwise)

1. **north pole:** Although their 1909 claim is sometimes disputed, Robert Peary and Matthew Henson have been credited with being the first to reach the North Pole. At the time of *The Wouldbegoods*' publication, the North Pole remained one of the great undiscovered places of the earth. *ILN* ends the sentence after 'times.'
2. *ILN* omits 'and young ladies.' Oswald's style here seems to follow older models than the prose of his own day.
3. **the source of the real live Egyptian Nile:** In 1863, British explorer John Hanning Speke traced the source of the White Nile to the lake now known as Victoria Nyanza. The search for the Nile's source was a particularly dramatic episode in nineteenth-century exploration by Europeans. *ILN* omits the final sentence of this paragraph.
4. *ILN* ends this sentence after 'stable-yard.'
5. *ILN* ends this sentence after 'box-room.'
6. *ILN* uses in place of this clause 'he is very fond of it.'
7. *ILN* omits 'and so are stores of all kinds' and 'but not forever.'
8. **like a picture on a grocer's almanac:** The promotional calendars provided by grocers attracted scorn from the intelligentsia for over-elaborate or sentimental taste. *ILN* omits 'as usual.'
9. **Cleopatra sailed in Shakespeare:** a reference to *Antony and Cleopatra* 2.2; **Mr. Nansen...that big book:** An English translation of Fritjof Nansen's *Farthest North* appeared in 1897. Using the ship *Fram*, the Norwegian explorer led an expedition in 1893–96 that reached a record northerly latitude, 86°14'. *ILN* has 'kind sister' rather than 'gentle sister.'
10. *ILN* omits this sentence and ends the next sentence after 'paddled in it.'
11. **Desert of Sahara:** Deserts were another dramatic focus for European exploration in the nineteenth century. See, for instance, James Richardson's *Travels into the Great Desert of Sahara* (2 vols., 1849) and the accounts by French explorer Henri Duveyrier.
12. *ILN*'s menu is 'Cake, ham, eggs, sausage-rolls, currants, raisins, and cold apple dumplings.'

13. ***Foul Play:*** In Charles Reade's 1869 novel, castaways on a tropical island make pottery and bake turtle-meat in clay. *ILN* omits 'I believe.'
14. *ILN* omits 'unless you keep it much too thick' and 'then.' This paragraph's final clause is another reference to William Congreve's 'Music hath charms to soothe the savage breast'; see Chapter 5, note 21.
15. ***fire-clay…another sort you can eat:*** The term 'fire clay' refers not to combustible but to heat-resistant clay. While cultures around the world engage in eating clay (geophagy), no one variety is involved.
16. *ILN* has 'So we went to the farmer at once.'
17. ***daughters of regiments:*** Beginning with the Napoleonic Wars, vivandières and cantinières, sometimes termed 'daughters of the regiment,' had official standing as women who supplied food and drink to soldiers in camp or on the battlefield. *ILN* has 'you could carry it on your back, like in pictures of the Daughters of Regiments.'
18. ***A Mr Collins wrote an Ode to the Fashions:*** C. H. Waring parodied William Collins's 'The Passions: An Ode for Music' (1750) as 'Ode to the Fashions' in *Comic News* in 1864.
19. ***'Ruin seize thee, ruthless king!':*** a line from Gray's ode *The Bard* (1757).
20. *ILN* omits this sentence.
21. ***Magnet Stories:*** a collection of tales by multiple authors, published annually for some years. Oswald refers to a story in the 1861 volume, Frances M. Wilbraham's 'Not Clever,' in which Theodosia's mother's illness requires treatment by leeches, which only the retiring Elsie is willing to apply. *ILN* omits 'on the piano.'
22. ***'Wounded warriors returning':*** untraced, but presumably a reference to a picture.
23. *ILN* omits this sentence.

Chapter 8   The High-born Babe

1. *ILN* omits this sentence.
2. ***Eiffel Tower lemonade and Marie biscuits:*** Eiffel Tower, headquartered near the Bastables in Maidstone, Kent, sold lemonade concentrate. Another commercial product, the Marie biscuit, was first marketed by Peek Frean & Co. in 1874. *ILN* omits 'Marie' and substitutes 'Tower of Babel' (an imaginary company) for 'Eiffel Tower.'
3. *ILN* omits 'Noël said.'
4. *ILN* uses 'literature' for 'Sunday-school magazines.'
5. ***Or cover it with leaves…like the robins:*** H.O. refers to the traditional story 'The Babes in the Wood,' in which two children abandoned in a wood die of hunger and exposure, and sympathetic robins cover the bodies with leaves.
6. *ILN* ends this sentence after 'church.'
7. ***the kind of enamelling you do at home with Aspinall's:*** The London company Aspinall's Enamel Works manufactured a lead-free paint

designed to be applied to metal, earthenware, wood, glass, and other surfaces in connection with do-it-yourself home-improvement projects.

8. ***just like Betsy Trotwood did in David Copperfield:*** When in Chapter 13 of Dickens's *David Copperfield* David unexpectedly appears at his aunt's house and introduces himself to her, ' "Oh, Lord," said my aunt. And sat flat down in the garden-path.'

9. *ILN* has 'Mrs. Scribaby's at the Lower Farm.'

10. ***Alice in Wonderland nursing the baby that turned into a pig:*** In Chapter 6 of Lewis Carroll's 1865 novel, Alice rescues a baby from the violent Duchess and her cook, feeling that 'If I don't take this child away with me … they're sure to kill it in a day or two.' Caring for the infant does not come naturally, and when Alice begins to worry, 'Now, what am I to do with this creature when I get it home?', it conveniently turns into a pig, whereupon she can release it into the wood. Oswald clearly has in mind the famous Tenniel illustration of Alice with the pig-baby in her arms, but he may also hope for a similarly easy solution to the problem of child care.

Chapter 9   Hunting the Fox

1. ***none of us would have shot a fox on purpose:*** See Chapter 1, note 24. This is the second episode in *The Wouldbegoods* in which the solecism of shooting a fox is raised.

2. **'What dire offence … trefoil things':** a misquotation of the beginning of Canto I of Alexander Pope's *The Rape of the Lock* (1712–17), 'What dire offence from am'rous causes springs, / What mighty contests rise from trivial things.'

3. *ILN* has 'fluttering' rather than 'flattering' and 'Alice' rather than 'Dora.'

4. *ILN* adds after 'came down' the phrase 'to the house where we were staying,' and omits the final clause.

5. ***like snow-wreaths in thaw-jean:*** The reference is to the popular song 'The Land o' the Leal' (words written by Carolina, Lady Nairne between 1797 and 1798), one version of which begins, 'I'm wearin' awa', Jean, / Like snow-wreaths in thaw, Jean.'

6. *ILN* has 'but none of them were important.'

7. ***who it is and his money that are soon parted':*** John Bridges has been credited with originating, in his 1587 *Defence of the Government of the Church of England*, the precise wording of the now proverbial saying 'A foole and his money is soon parted.'

8. *ILN* ends this sentence after 'him.'

9. ***horns … for the huntsmen to wind, like in the song:*** This description fits a number of eighteenth- and nineteenth-century hunting songs, such as one beginning, 'Hark, the Huntsman winds his horn; / See the glow of blushing morn!'

10. *ILN* has 'lunch' rather than 'dinner'; in either case the reference is to the noon meal.

11. **Loretto:** a boarding school near Edinburgh, founded in 1827. Albert's uncle would have been a pupil during the 1862–1903 headmastership of Hely Hutchinson Almond, who emphasized athletics' character-building role.

12. **only with sore throats:** Wrapping red flannel around a sore throat was a popular home remedy.

13. *ILN* ends this sentence after 'ways.'

14. *ILN* omits this sentence and Noël's ode.

15. **'little red rover':** the title of a fox-hunting song by Rowland Eylew Egerton Warburton and included in his 1834 volume *Hunting Songs, Ballads, &c*; in the final verse, the dogs tear the fox to pieces. *ILN* has 'a scratching and whining' and 'the place where we had interred the "little red rover."'

16. *ILN* ends this sentence after 'Pincher' and prefers 'stepped' to 'took a stride' in the following sentence.

17. **'We found his murdered body … mourners stood':** not traced.

18. *ILN* has '… and into the hall, where the floor is black and white marble in squares like a chessboard.'

19. *ILN* has 'looked about him in a comfortable silence – and so did we'; 'comfortable' here is clearly a misprint.

20. *ILN* concludes this sentence after 'thumbscrew.' 'Armada' refers to the Spanish fleet sent by Philip II in an unsuccessful attempt to invade England in 1588; in this context, the rack and thumbscrew probably refer to tortures imposed by the Spanish Inquisition rather than to those associated with the Tudor dynasty.

Chapter 10   The Sale of Antiquities

1. **another very nice writer:** Nesbit was born 15 August 1858.

2. **Maidstone:** a town in Kent. *ILN* substitutes 'Braidstone' throughout this chapter.

3. **you got it out of 'Stalky':** Kipling's *Stalky & Co.* appeared in 1899.

4. **the celebrated Sir Thomas Wyatt:** Both the poet and diplomat Thomas Wyatt the Elder (1503–42) and his son Thomas Wyatt the Younger (1521–54), leader of the unsuccessful Wyatt's Rebellion against Mary I, qualify as 'celebrated' and had associations with Kent. F.R.S. stands for 'Fellow of the Royal Society.'

5. **an amphoræ:** 'Amphoræ' is the plural. *ILN* uses the singular 'amphora,' giving more credence to Oswald's claim of knowledge.

6. *ILN* omits this sentence.

7. **a free wheel:** as opposed to a fixed-wheel bicycle, which cannot coast.

8. *ILN* omits this sentence.

9. **'Hail to thee, blithe spirit – bird thou never wert':** the opening lines of Percy Shelley's 1820 ode 'To a Skylark.'

10. **The Daisy Chain:** Charlotte Yonge, author of the 1856 bestseller mentioned here and of some 160 other novels, blended moral didacticism with lively depictions of family life.

11. **'Come back…O my daughter!':** Nesbit is parodying the penultimate stanza of Campbell's 'Lord Ullin's Daughter.' The original reads, 'Come back! come back!' he cried in grief / 'Across this stormy water; / And I'll forgive your Highland chief, / My daughter! O my daughter!' The poem is evidently a favorite with Denny, who also quotes it in Chapter 5.

12. **Friends, Romans, countrymen, lend me your ears:** This line begins Mark Antony's funeral oration in Shakespeare's *Julius Caesar*, III.2.

13. **You may break…round it still:** Denny is misquoting stanza 3 of Thomas Moore's 'Farewell! But Whenever You Welcome the Hour' (*Irish Melodies*, 1806–07), which runs, 'You may break, you may shatter the vase, if you will, / But the scent of the roses will hang round it still.'

14. **like in Foul Play:** See Chapter 7, note 13. *ILN* omits 'Albert's uncle said.'

15. **true usefulness of scouts…Transvaal War:** Approximately twenty percent of the Afrikaners who fought in the Transvaal (Second Boer) War were 'National Scouts,' Boer auxiliaries fighting on the British side. See also Chapter 3, note 8.

16. **thanking his stars he had been born a happy little Antiquary child:** Albert's uncle refers to 'A Child's Hymn of Praise,' in Ann and Jane Taylor's *Hymns for Infant Minds* (1810), which begins 'I thank the goodness and the grace, / Which on my birth have smil'd, / And made me, in these Christian days, / A happy English child.'

Chapter 11   The Benevolent Bar

1. **where they throw hundreds and thousands…Confetti:** Oswald seems unclear about the distinction between 'comfits' (sweets, as in the 'hundreds and thousands' or candy sprinkles that he mentions) and 'confetti,' the standard missile in the Roman pre-Lenten carnival. In this context confetti included lime dust and heavy pellets, often flung using dippers – hence the need for protective masks.

2. **peppermints…Maidstone:** *ILN* uses 'peanuts' and 'Braidstone.'

3. *ILN* ends this sentence after 'Dicky.'

4. *ILN* omits this sentence.

5. **Sir Philip Sidney and the tramp's need being greater than his:** Many English children were raised on the story of Sidney's gallantry after he sustained a mortal wound during the battle of Zutphen in 1586. When a comrade brought him water, he is said to have relinquished it to another dying soldier with the words, 'Thy necessity is yet greater than mine.'

6. **Eiffel Tower lemonade:** Here as elsewhere, *ILN* uses 'Tower of Babel lemonade.' See Chapter 8, note 2.

7. *All the Year Round Christmas numbers:* Since this magazine ceased publication in 1893, its special Christmas issues would have been more familiar to Nesbit's generation than to Alice's. 'Chink' in the preceding paragraph refers to money.

8. *'Small things...little wings':* The 1856 original, from 'Written in a Little Lady's Little Album,' by F. W. Faber, runs: 'Small things are best. / Care and unrest / To anxious hearts are given; / But little things / On little wings / Bear little souls to heaven.'

9. *'name' and 'game' and things:* ILN has '"flame" and "same" and things.'

10. *e.g., things to drink:* ILN has (correctly) '*i.e.*, things to drink.'

11. *Procrastination is you know what:* possibly a reference to 'Procrastination is the thief of time,' a famous line from Edward Young's poem 'Night Thoughts' (1742).

12. *allieve:* ILN uses 'alleve'; the correct word is 'alleviate.'

13. *bloomin' blue ribbon:* The Gospel Temperance or Blue Ribbon movement promoted total abstinence from alcohol; members wore blue ribbons to signal that they had taken the pledge. By 1890, more than a million Britons, particularly from the lower middle classes, had joined, but the movement also had many detractors.

14. *Dewar's whiskey:* Here and elsewhere, *ILN* omits the brand name.

15. *ILN* has 'The man had a great drink, and then began to swear.'

Chapter 12   The Canterbury Pilgrims

1. *the business of the benevolent bar:* ILN substitutes 'the Dentist had killed the fox we got into such a row about.'

2. *'Canaan's happy shore':* The tune for this American camp-meeting song is shared with 'John Brown's Body' and 'The Battle Hymn of the Republic.' Halma is a board game invented by American surgeon George Howard Monks in 1883; it reappears in Nesbit's *The Magic City* (1910), in which halma pieces come to life.

3. *Let dogs delight:* See *Treasure Seekers* Chapter 13, note 6.

4. *a piece of poetry:* Denny is thinking of 'The Pilgrims and the Pease,' by British satirist John Wolcot (1738–1819).

5. *A Short History of the English People:* published in 1874 by John Richard Green; among many other subjects that this work covers is Geoffrey Chaucer's late fourteenth-century *The Canterbury Tales*, which is built around a colourful group of pilgrims travelling to Canterbury, including the Prioress, the Wife of Bath, the Miller, the Nun's Priest, and other figures mentioned by the children. Alice's 'cockled' hats in the preceding paragraph is her mistake for 'cockle.'

6. *Henry who killed Becket:* Thomas à Becket, Archbishop of Canterbury, was assassinated in 1170 at the behest of his former friend and patron Henry II.

7. *our late general:* See *Treasure Seekers* Chapter 1, note 2.

8. *shines not in undi – what's-its-name? – splendour:* Alice may have in
mind a line from Samuel Saunders's *Discourses on the Lord's Prayer, in a
Series of Lectures* (1825), 'the eternal promise, like the great orb of day,
retains its station, and shines still with undiminished splendour.'

9. *Laura Matildaing:* In Horace and James Smith's *Rejected Addresses*
(1812), a collection of parodies in verse, 'Laura Matilda' is the sig-
nature affixed to the overemotional 'Drury's Dirge,' a reference to
the pseudonym 'Anna Matilda' used by Hannah Cowley in 1787 in
her poetic correspondence with Robert Merry ('Della Crusca'). The
name came to connote what Dorothea Deakin's 1907 story 'Of Laura-
Matilda' defines as 'Early Victorian, lackadaisical, sentimental, useless, fragile, clinging.'

10. *the 'very perfect gentle knight':* Oswald is translating a quotation from
Chaucer's *Canterbury Tales* that Green provides in Middle English.

11. *ILN* has '... reck nought of ports, but Dicky never does play the game
thoroughly.'

12. *'Tramp, tramp, tramp':* Like 'John Brown's Body' (whose tune H.O.'s
'I don't know what to do' borrows at the beginning of the episode),
'Tramp! Tramp! Tramp!' was a popular American song, written by
George F. Root in 1864. Its mournful first verse, which ends 'And the
tears they fill my eyes / Spite of all that I can do, / Tho' I try to cheer
my comrades and be gay,' contrasts with the upbeat chorus beginning
'Tramp, tramp, tramp, the boys are marching, / Cheer up comrades
they will come.' 'The British Grenadiers,' whose words date from the
early eighteenth century, is still a well-known military song.

13. *only about half a mile:* The distance from Eltham to Canterbury is
approximately 50 miles by road. This exchange establishes that for
the purposes of the game, another community will play the part of
Canterbury. Toward the end of the episode, Oswald identifies this
community as Hazelbridge, a fictitious name..

14. *ILN* has 'the church we go to at the Moat House.'

15. *'George and Dragon':* Although there are a number of Kentish pubs
called the George and Dragon, Nesbit may be thinking of one at
Westerham, about 16 miles from Well Hall. A 'footpad' is a thief who
attacks pedestrians.

16. *new bread, which we are not allowed at home:* Freshly baked bread
was thought to be harder to digest than older loaves.

17. *Danejohn ... St. Alphege:* A notable feature of Canterbury is the Dane
John, a pre-Roman burial mound located in the Dane John Gardens.
St. Alphege, Archbishop of Canterbury, was executed by invading
Danes in 1011 when, to spare his flock's pockets, he refused to be
ransomed.

18. *ILN* omits '(*See* Note A.)' and the similar references below.

19. *'The Ballad of Canterbury':* a poem by Nesbit, published in *Lays and
Legends, Second Series* in 1892.

20. *protector of the poor:* a phrase evidently picked up from Kipling, who
uses it in several of his Indian stories. Above, *ILN* has 'As we turned

to go in, Albert's uncle...wind' and omits the paragraph's second sentence.
21. *ILN* omits the sentences between 'his steed' and 'I wonder if he'll catch her.'
22. *ILN* omits all but the first sentence from this paragraph.

Chapter 13   The Dragon's Teeth; or, Army-seed

1. *ILN* begins this sentence 'Jim dug the grave' and uses 'Jim' rather than 'Bill' throughout the chapter.
2. **Ministering Children:** Nesbit's fourth mention of this novel in *The Wouldbegoods*. See Chapter 2, note 12.
3. **when some chap sowed dragon's teeth:** While Jason also sowed dragon's teeth to produce a crop of armed men during his quest for the Golden Fleece, Noël's subsequent reference to Cadmus shows that he has in mind the founding of Thebes. According to legend, Athena instructed Cadmus to sow the teeth of the slain dragon that had guarded a spring sacred to Ares. After causing the resulting warriors to fight among themselves, Cadmus recruited the survivors to establish his city.
4. *ILN* omits 'he is so fat that' and has 'it' for 'this.'
5. *ILN* has 'he said' and omits 'Moat.'
6. *ILN* omits this sentence.
7. *ILN* omits the final clause and uses 'Denny' for 'the Dentist' in the next sentence.
8. *ILN* assigns this speech to Denny and uses 'Braidstone' throughout.
9. *ILN* omits 'by some strange fatalism' and identifies Martha as 'the bull-dog' in the next sentence, using 'the other dogs' for 'Lady and Pincher.'
10. *ILN* omits this sentence.
11. *ILN* omits this sentence's first clause, one of a number in which the soldier describes people in terms commonly applied to horses.
12. **Band of Hope:** a children's temperance organization, founded in 1847 and, by the turn of the century, consisting of over 10,000 local groups that met weekly. While originally the young members pledged merely to abstain from alcohol, the Band of Hope's mission widened to discourage tobacco use and other social problems as well.
13. *ILN* omits this sentence.
14. **Lead on, Macduff!:** a common misquotation of a line in Shakespeare's *Macbeth* 5.8, 'Lay on, Macduff,' meaning 'attack vigorously.'
15. *ILN* has 'He chose Denny and Oswald.'
16. *ILN* ends the paragraph after this sentence.
17. *ILN* omits this sentence and the one beginning 'You would not do this in time of peace.'
18. **Baden-Powell...South Africa:** Robert Baden-Powell (1857–1941), founder of the Boy Scouts, successful spy, and hero of the siege of

Mafeking in the Boer War, first gained renown in the 1880s as a military scout in Natal, among the recently defeated Zulus. *ILN* uses 'Denny' instead of 'Denis Foulkes' in this sentence.

19. *ILN* ends this sentence after 'has.'

20. *Lucky to touch it, a shilling a day:* Alice and Denny are quoting a line from Kipling's poem 'Shillin' a Day,' in *Barrack-Room Ballads* (1892): 'Shillin' a day, / Bloomin' good pay – / Lucky to touch it, a shillin' a day!' *ILN* has 'said altogether' and 'knowing your Kipling.'

21. *ILN* omits this sentence.

22. *Lord Roberts:* Field Marshal Frederick Sleigh Roberts, first Earl Roberts (1832–1914) commanded Britain's forces during the Second Boer War.

Chapter 14   Albert's Uncle's Grandmother; or, the Long-lost

1. *ILN* omits the subtitle.

2. *That sounds like 'consequences':* An ancestor of today's Mad Libs, the parlour game Consequences involves collaboratively inserting words into a template to create coherent nonsense.

3. *The race is run … two and two:* a slight misquotation of a line from Kipling's 1892 poem 'Tomlinson,' 'For the race is run by one and one and never by two and two.' *ILN* has 'on his own hook.'

4. *The Last of the Mohicans:* James Fenimore Cooper's 1826 novel of adventure on the American frontier.

5. *Kentish Mercury:* a local newspaper founded in 1834.

6. *where angels fear to tread:* A famous line from Alexander Pope's *An Essay on Criticism* (1709), 'For Fools rush in where Angels fear to tread.'

7. *The cross of true love never did come smooth:* Denny is misquoting a line from Shakespeare's *A Midsummer Night's Dream* 1.1, 'The course of true love never did run smooth.' The preceding paragraph has 'Dora and Daisy and I don't believe […].'

8. *join the glad throng:* a reference to a popular song of the 1880s by W. Wilson, 'Let us join the glad throng, / That goes laughing along, / And we'll all go a-hunting today.'

9. *ILN* has 'and then he found me – oh, more than ten days ago! – and now I must break it to you.'